Warlords, Artists, & Commoners

Japan in the Sixteenth Century

Edited by
George Elison and Bardwell L. Smith

UNIVERSITY OF HAWAII PRESS
Honolulu

Copyright © 1981
by The University Press of Hawaii
All Rights Reserved
Printed in the United States of America

First edition 1981
Paperback edition 1987

96 97   6 5 4 3

Library of Congress Cataloging in Publication Data

Main entry under title:

Warlords, artists, and commoners.

''The outcome of a seminar on Japan in the
sixteenth century held at Carleton College during
the winter and spring terms of 1974.''
    Includes index.
    1.   Japan—Civilization—1568–1600—Congresses.
2.   Japan—History—Period of civil wars, 1480–1603
—Congresses.   I.   Elison, George.   II.   Smith,
Bardwell L.
DS822.2.W35   952'.02   80–24128
ISBN 0–8248–0692–1

ISBN 0–8248–1109–7 (pbk)

Frontispiece: Detail of HIDEYOSHI VISITING THE
BLOSSOMING CHERRIES AT YOSHINO, c. 1594,
folding screen. Kimiko and John Powers collection.
Photograph by Geoffrey Clements.

Contents

Acknowledgments

This volume of essays is the outcome of a seminar on Japan in the sixteenth century held at Carleton College during the winter and spring terms of 1974 as the second of a series of special seminars on Asia. Selected papers from the first, which dealt with the T'ang period in China, were published in 1976 under the title *Essays on T'ang Society: The Interplay of Social, Political and Economic Forces*. We should like first of all to thank Mr. and Mrs. John M. Musser for their gift to Carleton, which enables the college to hold seminars of this kind.

In addition to Professors Hall, Keene, Malm, and Varley, who contributed chapters to this volume, the scholars who participated in the seminar over its fifteen-week period included Professors Abe Masao, John Rosenfield, and Andrew Tsubaki. To all of them we wish to express our appreciation. The student members, whose free and thoughtful criticism enriched the seminar, have also earned our sincere appreciation. They were David Aki, John Collidge, Elizabeth Gault, Marshall Gittler, Nancy Haven, Katherine Lock, Marianne McIlvain, Gayle Menich, Terry Moss, Kristina Nelson, Cynthia Pietrak, Jay Swanson, Kenneth Titley, James Treece, and David Russell.

Colleagues who shared their time and their wisdom with us in the preparation of this collection include John Curtis Perry, Paul Martin Sacks, and George Macklin Wilson. Their support and suggestions have contributed much to this book's makeup. Julia Meech-Pekarik of The Metropolitan Museum of Art in New York and Satō Jindō of the Shogakukan Publishing Company in Tokyo gave valuable advice and assistance in regard to the book's illustrations, and to them, too, we are most grateful.

We wish to thank those who provided administrative aid at the time of the seminar and since, especially Terry Basquin, then secretary of the History Department at Carleton, and May Okada, administrative assistant to the Dean of the College. Thanks are also due to Barbara Arnn of the Department of East Asian Languages and Cultures, Indiana University, for her help with the index, and to Robin Barnes and William Elison for drawing the map of Japan.

Finally, we should like to acknowledge with gratitude the following institutions for granting us permission to reproduce the works of art which illustrate this volume: Academy for Educational Development, New York; Imperial Household Agency, Tokyo; Jukōin, Daitokuji, Kyoto; Nanzenji, Kyoto; Reiun'in, Myōshinji, Kyoto; and the Tokyo National Museum.

Bloomington, Indiana   GE
Northfield, Minnesota   BLS

Chronology

1467–1477 – Ōnin War: collapse of central authority; beginning of Sengoku period

1471 – *death of the* dōbō *Nōami*

1474 – Shogun Ashikaga Yoshimasa abandons his office (7 January; Bunmei 5/12/19)

1476? – *Sōami completes the compilation of the handbook on Higashiyama aesthetics,* Kundaikan sōchōki, *begun by Nōami*

1479 – Yamashina Honganji founded by Rennyo, the pontiff of the True Pure Land sect

1482 – *Ashikaga Yoshimasa begins building the Higashiyama Villa (site of the Silver Pavilion)*

1484 – by this year, a local autonomous council called the Egōshū is functioning in Sakai

1485 – local leaders of the province of Yamashiro form a league *(ikki)* and take over the administration of the southern part of the province (until 1493)

1488 – adherents of the True Pure Land sect, organized as the *Ikkō ikki,* take over the province of Kaga (until 1580)

1490 – death of Ashikaga Yoshimasa

1496 – Rennyo founds the Ishiyama Dōjō in Osaka: forerunner of the Ishiyama Honganji

1500 – *the Gion Festival, lapsed since the Ōnin War, is revived in Kyoto*

1502 – *death of the tea master Murata Shukō*

1505 – *the great popularity of* Bon odori *in Kyoto causes the shogunate to prohibit the dance*

1506 – *death of the painter Sesshū Tōyō (b. 1420)*

1507 – *Tosa Mitsunobu paints a screen depicting Kyoto for the Asakura daimyo of Echizen: a prototype* Rakuchū-Rakugai-zu byōbu

1513   – *Kano Motonobu and Sōami decorate the Abbot's Quarters of the Daisen'in*

1515   – *Toyohara Sumiaki writes* Taigenshō, *a study of court music*

1517   – *the* renga *master Saiokuken Sōchō records songs heard during a journey in his travel diary,* Utsu no yamaki

1518   – *compilation of the song anthology* Kanginshū

1521   – Miyoshi Motonaga establishes the headquarters of his family, the *Mandokoro,* in Sakai

1522   – *Sen no Rikyū born*

1524   – *Satomura Jōha born*

1525   – *death of Sōami, the last of the "Three Ami"*

1527   – Miyoshi Motonaga, championing the cause of Ashikaga Yoshitsuna, establishes the so-called Sakai Bakufu

1530–   – *Saiokuken Sōchō's diary,* Sōchō shuki, *records songs heard on his*
1531   *travels*

1532   – *Ikkō ikki* attacks the Nichiren sect temple Kenponji in Sakai and forces Miyoshi Motonaga to suicide: end of the "Sakai Bakufu" (July)

        – adherents of the Nichiren sect in Kyoto form the "Lotus Confederation" *(Hokke ikki),* arm themselves, and take over the affairs of the city (August)

        – Yamashina Honganji is destroyed by the forces of the Lotus Confederation (September); Ishiyama Honganji of Osaka becomes the headquarters of the True Pure Land sect

1534   – Oda Nobunaga born

1536   – end of the Lotus Confederation: the main temples of the Nichiren sect are destroyed, and large parts of Kyoto burnt, by armies mobilized by the monks of the Tendai sect on Mount Hiei

        – *from this date onward, the Ishiyama Honganji becomes a major center of Nō, sponsoring performances by the Four Troupes*

1537   – Toyotomi Hideyoshi born probably this year (17 March; Tenbun 6/2/6 [?]); some sources indicate 1536

1539   – Miyoshi Nagayoshi (Chōkei) for the first time occupies Kyoto

        – *Kano Motonobu begins a large interior decoration project at the Ishiyama Honganji*

1542   – discovery of the rich Ikuno silver mine in Tajima province

1543   – Tokugawa Ieyasu born (31 January; Tenbun 11/12/26)

        – *Kano Eitoku born*

        – *Kano Motonobu decorates the Abbot's Quarters of the Reiun'in*

        – Miyoshi Nagayoshi assumes control over Sakai

        – the first Portuguese traders arrive in Japan; introduction of Western firearms

1544   – *the shogunate prohibits* furyū *in Kyoto*

1546   – establishment of the Kanazawa Midō, the True Pure Land sect's governing agency over the province of Kaga and neighboring areas

1547   – the last Japanese mission of the official "tally ship" trade leaves for Ming China

1549   – *the Jesuit Francis Xavier arrives in Japan: beginning of the Christian mission*

1555   – *death of the tea master Takeno Jōō (b. 1502)*

1558   – Kinoshita Tōkichirō, the future Hideyoshi, enters Nobunaga's employ

1559   – *death of Kano Motonobu (b. 1476); birth of Kano Sanraku (d. 1635)*

1560   – Battle of Okehazama: Oda Nobunaga defeats Imagawa Yoshimoto and begins his rise to national prominence

1561   – *Kano Mitsunobu born*

1562   – Nobunaga and Ieyasu form an alliance

1563   – *Satomura Jōha compiles* Hakuhatsu shō, *a book of secret* renga *traditions*
            – *Kano Shōei paints an enormous Nirvana painting for the Daitokuji*

1564   – death of Miyoshi Nagayoshi (b. 1522); his treacherous vassal Matsunaga Hisahide takes over his place in the politics of the Home Provinces

1565   – Matsunaga Hisahide and the Miyoshi Triumvirs destroy Shogun Ashikaga Yoshiteru

1566   – fighting between Hisahide and the Triumvirs threatens Sakai; the Jesuit Luis Frois reports on conditions in the city
            – *Kano Shōei and his son Eitoku decorate the Abbot's Quarters of the Jukōin*

1567   – *Satomura Jōha journeys to Mount Fuji:* Jōha Fujimi michi no ki

1567–   – *Kano Eitoku, with three assistants, does wall paintings for the*
  1568 Kanpaku *Konoe Sakihisa*

1568   – Nobunaga occupies Kyoto and installs Ashikaga Yoshiaki as shogun; Matsunaga Hisahide submits to Nobunaga, sending him a precious tea utensil to seal their alliance

1569   – the Miyoshi Triumvirs, based on Sakai, attack Shogun Yoshiaki but are rebuffed from Kyoto (January); Nobunaga threatens Sakai with destruction until the city submits sometime this summer

1570   – beginning of Nobunaga's "Ten Years' War" against the Honganji and the "religious monarchy" of the True Pure Land sect
            – *about this time, Hasegawa Shinshun (Tōhaku) paints* Rounding Up Horses, *a pair of sixfold screens now in the Tokyo National Museum*

1571 .   – furyū odori *in high vogue during the Bon season in Kyoto; the*

1579 — the donjon of Azuchi Castle becomes Nobunaga's official residence

— Nobunaga orders the Azuchi Disputation between priests of the Pure Land and the Nichiren sects, declares the Nichirenists the losers, and orders three of their principals executed

1580 — the Kyushu daimyo Ōmura Sumitada cedes Nagasaki and vicinity to the Society of Jesus

— Ishiyama Honganji surrenders to Nobunaga (September), and the *Ikkō ikki* of Kaga is conquered by Shibata Katsuie (December): end of the "Ten Years' War" and the "religious monarchy" of the True Pure Land sect

— Nobunaga's regime destroys provincial forts in the Kansai area and conducts land surveys in the provinces of Yamato and Harima

1581 — *Nobunaga presents a screen painting of Azuchi (now lost) by Kano Eitoku to the Jesuit* Visitator *Alexandro Valignano*

— Nobunaga campaigns against the Kongōbuji, the headquarters of the Shingon sect on Mount Kōya

1582 — Nobunaga conquers the Takeda, extending his realm into the Kantō region, his last triumph (April); the imperial court decides to offer him appointment as shogun (May)

— *Akechi Mitsuhide, joined by Satomura Jōha, holds a* renga *session at the Atago Shrine (18 June; Tenshō 10/5/28)*

— Honnōji Affair: Mitsuhide murders Nobunaga (21 June; Tenshō 10/6/2)

— Battle of Yamazaki: Hideyoshi destroys Mitsuhide and begins his rise to hegemony over Japan (2 July; Tenshō 10/6/13)

— Azuchi Castle burnt down (3–4 July)

— Hideyoshi orders a land survey of Yamashiro province (27 July; Tenshō 10/7/8)

1583 — Battle of Shizugatake: Hideyoshi destroys Shibata Katsuie

— Hideyoshi builds Osaka Castle

1584 — *Kano Eitoku and his atelier decorate Osaka Castle*

— *the Yamazato tearoom in Osaka Castle first used by Hideyoshi, with Sen no Rikyū in attendance*

— Hideyoshi and Ieyasu confront each other in the inconclusive Komaki Campaign

— Hideyoshi orders a land survey of Ōmi province on the basis of a new standard square measure: the mature phase of the nationwide *Taikō kenchi* begins

1585 — Hideyoshi concludes peace with Ieyasu (January); he defeats the warrior monks of Negoro and gains the province of Kii (April–May); his armies conquer Shikoku (July–August)

— Hideyoshi is appointed *Kanpaku* (6 August; Tenshō 13/7/11) and *sponsors a program of Nō plays at the imperial palace in celebration; assisted by Sen no Rikyū, he entertains Emperor Ōgimachi at a tea ceremony in the imperial palace (October);* he assumes the family name Toyotomi (October)

- *Satomura Jōha completes* Renga shihōshō, *a work of renga theory*

1586   - *Hideyoshi visits the imperial palace and displays his portable golden tearoom to the emperor (March); he entertains Ōtomo Sōrin in the same tearoom at Osaka Castle (May)*
   - *Kano Eitoku and his atelier decorate Emperor Ōgimachi's retirement palace* (In no Gosho)

1587   - Hideyoshi appointed *Daijō Daijin* (27 January; Tenshō 14/12/19)
   - Hideyoshi conquers Kyushu (April–June)
   - *Hideyoshi orders the practice of Christianity restricted and the Jesuit missionaries expelled from Japan (July), but refrains from enforcing his edicts*
   - *the Grand Kitano Tea Ceremony (November)*
   - *Kano Eitoku and his atelier decorate Hideyoshi's Juraku Palace*

1588   - Ashikaga Yoshiaki renounces the shogunate: legal end of the Muromachi bakufu
   - *Emperor Go-Yōzei visits Hideyoshi at his Juraku Palace: the crowning event of the hegemon's aristocratization*
   - *foundation laid for the Great Buddha Hall ordered built by Hideyoshi in Kyoto; the* machishū *of Kyoto perform a* furyū *spectacle at the ceremony*
   - a nationwide "sword hunt" is decreed by Hideyoshi

1589   - *completion of the* Yamanoue Sōji ki, *a classic text on the tradition of* wabicha

1590   - Hideyoshi defeats the Later Hōjō of Odawara and is supreme in Japan; he transfers Ieyasu from his old domains to the Kantō, with Edo becoming Ieyasu's castle town
   - *death of Kano Eitoku*

1591   - *suicide of Sen no Rikyū*
   - Hideyoshi's edict prohibits the change of status from samurai to farmer or merchant, or from farmer to merchant
   - the last resistance to Hideyoshi is eliminated in northern Honshu: all Japan is reunified under Hideyoshi's hegemony

1592   - Hideyoshi passes on the office of *Kanpaku* to his adopted son Toyotomi Hidetsugi (11 February; Tenshō 19/12/28), himself assuming the title of *Taikō; the Juraku Palace becomes Hidetsugi's official residence; he is visited there by Emperor Go-Yōzei*
   - Hideyoshi's armies invade Korea; *Kano Mitsunobu and members of Hasegawa Tōhaku's atelier go to Hizen in Kyushu to decorate Nagoya Castle, Hideyoshi's headquarters for the invasion*
   - *death of Kano Shōei (b. 1519)*

1593   – cessation of hostilities in Korea
        – Toyotomi Hideyori born
        – *Hideyoshi begins performing publicly in Nō plays*
        – *Hasegawa Tōhaku and members of his school do wall paintings for the Shōunji (now in the Chishakuin)*
        – *versions of the* kouta *collection* Ryūtatsu kouta shū *appear over a twenty-year period from this date*
        – *the Ueyama Sōkyū copy of* mai no hon, *an early collection of Kōwaka texts, is made about this time*

1594   – *Hideyoshi travels to Yoshino to view the cherry blossoms, accompanied by a grand suite which includes Satomura Jōha; the first of Ōmura Yūko's "new Nō plays,"* Yoshino mōde, *commemorates the event, heroizing Hideyoshi*
        – Hideyoshi builds Fushimi Castle; *Kano Mitsunobu and Kano Sanraku are commissioned to decorate it*

1595   – Toyotomi Hidetsugi is disgraced and forced to commit suicide; *the Juraku Palace is dismantled; Satomura Jōha is exiled from Kyoto for his association with Hidetsugi*

1596   – Hideyoshi receives ambassadors from Ming China in Osaka; negotiations fail, and the Korean armistice collapses

1597   – *martyrdom of the Twenty-Six Saints of Japan in Nagasaki on Hideyoshi's orders (5 February; Keichō 1/12/19): first bloody persecution of Christianity*
        – second invasion of Korea

1598   – death of Hideyoshi (18 September; Keichō 3/8/18); the Japanese armies are withdrawn from Korea

1599   – *Kano Sōshū paints panels of the Thirty-Six Poets for the Hōkoku Jinja, the shrine dedicated to the deified Hideyoshi*
        – *a sequence of one hundred Ryūtatsu songs is dedicated to Toyotomi Hideyori*

1600   – the first Dutch ship *(Liefde)* arrives in Japan
        – Battle of Sekigahara: Tokugawa Ieyasu supreme in Japan (21 October; Keichō 5/9/15)
        – Sōan kouta shū, *an anthology of short songs, is probably completed within a few years of this date*

1601   – *death of Kano Sōshū (b. 1551)*

1602   – *death of Satomura Jōha*

1603   – Ieyasu appointed shogun: establishment of the Edo bakufu (24 March; Keichō 8/2/12)
        – *Izumo no Okuni, apparently a priestess of the Izumo Shrine turned wandering entertainer, performs the dance known as* Kabuki odori *in Kyoto*

1604   – *Hōkoku Festival: a seven-day celebration of Hideyoshi's heritage in Kyoto*

1605   – *Kano Mitsunobu paints a great coiled dragon on the ceiling of the Main Hall* (Hattō) *of the Shōkokuji*

1608   – *death of Kano Mitsunobu*

1609?   – Uraminosuke, *a novel* (kana zōshi) *containing short songs popular in the period, is written sometime about this date*

1612   – *the Tokugawa shogunate issues decrees prohibiting Christianity and takes steps against the mission in its immediate domains*

1614   – *Tokugawa Ieyasu orders the expulsion of the Christian missionaries from Japan (1 February; Keichō 18/12/23): the general persecution begins*
        – *the Kojōruri puppet play* Amida no munewari *is being performed by this year*
        – Osaka Winter Campaign (November–January 1615)

1615   – Osaka Summer Campaign; fall of Osaka Castle, death of Toyotomi Hideyori, and the end of Hideyoshi's heritage (4 June; Keichō 20/5/8)

1625   – *publication of the Kojōruri play* Takadachi

1631   – *publication of the Sekkyō Jōruri play* Karukaya

1635   – *compilation of* Kan'ei jūninen odori ki, *an anthology of songs for dance*

1639   – the final Sakoku directive of the shogunate ends the Portuguese trade with Japan and all Japanese traffic with Catholic lands (4 August; Kan'ei 16/7/5)

Map of Japan
in the Sixteenth Century

MAP OF JAPAN
IN THE SIXTEENTH CENTURY

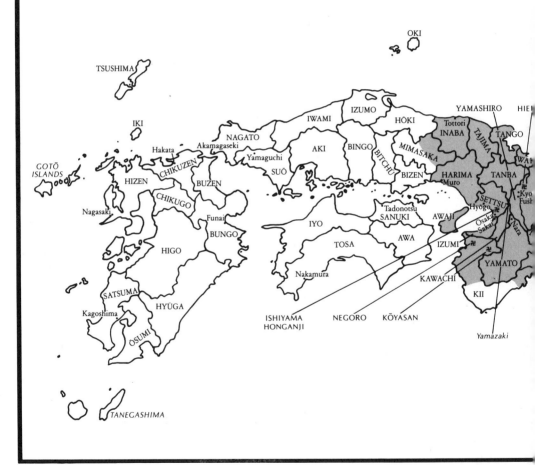

■ *The* Tenka, *Oda Nobunaga's realm, at his
death in 1582*

卍 *Headquarters of major Buddhist organizations*

X *Sites of major battles*

OKI

TSUSHIMA

IKI

NAGATO

IWAMI   IZUMO   HŌKI   YAMASHIRO   HIE

Tottori
INABA   TAJIMA   TANGO

Akamagaseki   AKI   BINGO   MIMASAKA   WA

GOTŌ
ISLANDS   Hakata   Yamaguchi   BITCHŪ   BIZEN   HARIMA   TANBA

HIZEN   CHIKUZEN   SUŌ   Muro   Kyo
Fu

BUZEN

Nagasaki   CHIKUGO   Tadonotsu   SETTSU   Nara
Funai   SANUKI   Hyogo
IYO   AWAJI   Osaka
BUNGO   Sakai

HIGO   TOSA   AWA   IZUMI

Nakamura   KAWACHI   YAMATO

SATSUMA   HYŪGA   KII
Kagoshima   ISHIYAMA   NEGORO   KŌYASAN
HONGANJI
ŌSUMI   Yamazaki

TANEGASHIMA

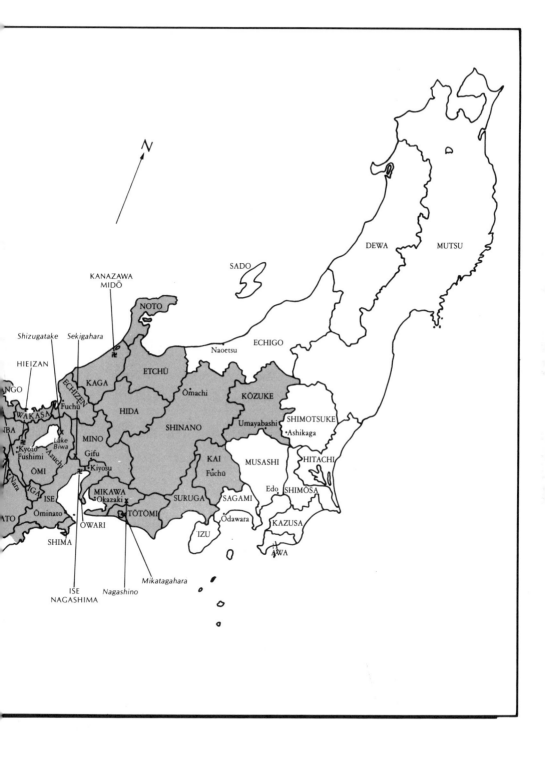

N

DEWA   MUTSU

SADO

KANAZAWA
MIDŌ

NOTO

ECHIGO

Shizugatake   Sekigahara   Naoetsu

HIEIZAN   ETCHŪ   KŌZUKE

KAGA   SHIMOTSUKE

NGO   Ōmachi   •Ashikaga

WAKASA   ECHIZEN   HIDA   Umayabashi

BA   Fuchū   SHINANO

Kyoto   Lake   MINO   MUSASHI   HITACHI
Fushimi   Biwa   Azuchi   Gifu
                    KAI
ŌMI   •Kiyosu   Fuchū

GA   ISE   Edo   SHIMŌSA
    MIKAWA   SURUGA   SAGAMI
TO   Ōminato   •Okazaki ×   KAZUSA
            TŌTŌMI   Ōdawara
OWARI   IZU

SHIMA   AWA

            ISE   Nagashino   Mikatagahara
        NAGASHIMA

Warlords, Artists, and Commoners

GEORGE ELISON

Introduction:
Japan in the Sixteenth Century

A^{S THE} sixteenth century began, the body politic of Japan was
undergoing a collapse. The central organs that had given
validity and vitality to the old governing order—the imperial court
and the shogunate—were exhausted and powerless. Strife among op-
portunist warlords swept the provinces. Commoners banded together
in leagues to maintain security or exercise force amid the ceaseless
struggle which engulfed them. Sengoku, the Country at War, is an
apt name for Japan in this age, and *gekokujō,* the overturn of
authority, appeared to be its incurable condition.

The new emperor, Go-Kashiwabara, forty-five days into his reign
as the century began, was to wait another twenty years and five
months for his formal enthronement.[1] Funds for the ceremony were
lacking, and the agency ordered to provide them, the Ashikaga bakufu, was itself bankrupt in more senses than one. The country had two
shoguns, and neither was his own man. Ashikaga Yoshitaka resided
in Kyoto, where he had been installed by a daimyo's coup d'état,
while his displaced cousin Yoshitada was off in the west of Japan,
seeking another daimyo's support for a return to the capital city. The
latter claimant to a perilous but empty honor was destined to sup-
plant the former, only to be expelled from the shogunate again; both
of them finished in exile.[2] Indeed, not a single one of the Ashikaga
shoguns of this century served out his term without being chased
away at least once. None save one died in his capital, and that one,
Yoshiteru, was murdered.

The high military dignitaries who sought to rule the imperial city
and pretended to make and unmake shoguns were themselves at the
mercy of their treacherous generals, faithless friends, and disloyal relatives. So Hosokawa Masamoto, the constable who had propped up
and manipulated Shogun Yoshitaka, was destroyed by two of his
deputy constables and an adopted son. His other adopted son, Hoso-

kawa Takakuni, was the sponsor and possessor of Ashikaga Yoshitada, and the shogun could at length free himself from the grasp of
this incubus only by becoming a fugitive once again. Takakuni found
himself a new protégé, but was in the end destroyed by yet another
shogunal pretender's backers, namely a nephew, Hosokawa Harumoto, and his majordomo, Miyoshi Motonaga. These two fell out
with each other less than a year after their common enemy's demise,
and Harumoto's allies (the True Pure Land sectarians' league, on
whom he immediately turned with a vengeance) destroyed Motonaga. Motonaga's son, Miyoshi Nagayoshi, would at mid-century
chase Harumoto from Kyoto and assume the dominant influence
over what was left of the Muromachi shogunate; but his fate was to
be dominated in turn by his retainer Matsunaga Hisahide, that paragon among the sixteenth century's many virtuosos of *gekokujō*.

More of the absorbing details of this mêlée of treasons will be
found below in the essay by V. Dixon Morris, who invokes George
Sansom's words—"fantastic, if not farcical"—to describe the state of
affairs which prevailed for much of the sixteenth century in Japan's
heartland. Since the situation in the provinces reflected conditions at
the putative center of authority, it is difficult to disagree when John
Whitney Hall declares in the next chapter that Japan had by 1550
fallen into such a state of instability that order could be restored to
the country only by a "militarily powerful autocrat" relying on
"sheer force" and maintaining an absolute claim to obedience. This
being an excellent description of the likes of Oda Nobunaga and
Toyotomi Hideyoshi, the sixteenth century's new breed of warlord, it
will easily be understood why so much of this collection of essays is
occupied with their deeds and designs.

Military harshness and autocratic rigor were not, however, the sole
attributes of these men of power. They and their congeners avidly
pursued cultural accomplishment, as a means of legitimating their
hegemony if not as an end in itself. This paradox is a recurrent theme
of this book. Sixteenth-century Japan was a country where warlords
affected artistry, artists played a role in politics, and commoners
could achieve distinction by the mastery of noble pastimes.

Although "war" and "culture" seem contradictory terms, Sengoku was far from being a culturally deprived realm. The political
disruption which rent the country over the hundred years from the
beginning of the Ōnin War in 1467 did not mean a break in the development of Japanese civilization. As Donald Keene points out at
the beginning of his essay, the exodus of courtiers and poets from
Kyoto which was caused by that great war served, if anything, to

spread the cultural standards of the capital to the regional hegemonies whose formation had been furthered by the conflict. Lords such as the Imagawa of Suruga, Hatakeyama of Noto, and Ōuchi of Suō sought to reproduce the metropolitan model in their provincial courts, and even the most distant region might prove to be the domain of a Maecenas, the remotest town a "Little Kyoto." Not only did many of the daimyo have cultural pretensions, some of the great names of Sengoku were without doubt accomplished men. "They say Asakura is good at painting," the contemporary report has it of an early sixteenth-century daimyo whose provincial domain of Echizen was also famous as a place where the printer's art was encouraged.[3] Others among the period's worthies who wielded the paintbrush as effectively as the sword include Toki Yoriyoshi of Mino, a liberal host of Kyoto poets and artists; he was chased from his province by the notorious Saitō Dōsan, but the usurper took pains to continue the tradition of cultural patronage. And Miyoshi Nagayoshi, a ruthless warlord who fancied himself a literary man, went so far as to assert—in poetic cadence—that there was an unbreakable link between the art of *renga* and military skill.[4]

Nagayoshi's conviction that it took cultural accomplishment to make a proper military man was shared by many of his class. Indeed, the name of sixteenth-century samurai who were votaries of poetry and the cult of tea no less than of the sterner arts of politics and war was legion. Moreover, courtly aesthetic ideals passed down from the classical age of Heian underlay the Sengoku era's major elegant pursuits. *Gekokujō*, in short, did not imply the inversion of cultural values.

If Sengoku politics were centrifugal, Sengoku culture sought the center. The magnetism of the capital and its cultural traditions affected not only the provincial elite and those interested in polite letters. We learn from Frank Hoff's chapter that it also exerted a powerful attraction on the rural populace and created the central image in a cycle of their folk songs. These songs, called *taue-uta,* accompanied rice transplanting, the climactic event of the farmer's year. In them, the vision of a fecund city appears as the countryman's ideal metaphor for energy and abundance, and its invocation is a kind of magical formula used to secure a bountiful harvest.

A different portrayal of the city and the conditions of the commoner's existence in late medieval Japan will be found in V. Dixon Morris' essay, which explores the nature of urban autonomy in Sakai, next to Kyoto the most important town of that era. Although the notion of the creative force of "the people's energy" is a commonplace in Japanese historiography dealing with this subject, we discover in Sakai little trace of a spirit of ''popular'' resistance against ''feudal'' forces. Instead, collaboration was the citizens' customary mode. The rich merchants who ran the town's affairs avidly cultivated the warlords who were the source of their prosperity. The leading aesthetes of Sakai happily purveyed munitions to the daimyo. Poetry sessions framed prosaic discussions of the problems of war and trade; tea proved a wonderful solvent of antagonisms.

That the symbiotic union between artists and warlords was a key factor in the development of sixteenth-century Japanese culture is a point made in more than one of these essays. The exemplary case of Satomura Jōha, who climbed from humble origins to national celebrity by catering to the poetic conceits of a dizzying series of men of power, is discussed by Donald Keene; the ambivalent mutual dependence of the tea master Sen no Rikyū and the master of Japan, Toyotomi Hideyoshi, is treated by H. Paul Varley and George Elison; and Carolyn Wheelwright shows us how productive such a collaboration could be by permitting us to visualize Kano Eitoku's decorative program for Oda Nobunaga's palatial castle at Azuchi. Here the greatest painter of his age created an aesthetic ensemble with a political message, directing the force of his art to the support of the absolute claims of a new type of rulership over the Japanese realm, Nobunaga's *Tenka*. The castle and the paintings in it did not survive Nobunaga's tragic fall; but the lesson taught there, that art could be made to serve statecraft, was applied by the other lords of the day, most notably by Hideyoshi. This truly voracious patron's unceasing demands for new products may in the end, however, have hastened Eitoku's death.

Art and power in close conjunction are represented perfectly in Eitoku's painting *Chinese Lions*, which graces the cover of this book. The two heroic beasts who stride across a rock-strewn path into golden clouds of glory remind us of the essential double nature of the Machiavellian princes—prepared to be bestial when humane means fail[5] —who reunified Japan after a hundred years of war. The bold concept and novel pictorial elements of this magnificent screen painting show that the institutional changes brought about by the ''Great Unifiers'' were accompanied and aided by an artistic revolution.

In Japanese institutional history, the sixteenth century marked the waning of the Middle Ages and the coming of the new Early Modern order. The diapason of culture also changed. The withered and dreamy ideals of medieval aesthetics gave way to an exuberant and forceful spirit. New forms of expression came to dominate in the pictorial, performing, and musical arts, and were introduced into that peculiarly Japanese ritual, the tea ceremony. European traders and Catholic missionaries contributed further novelty to the varied genre scene of Japan. The century witnessed a dazzling burst of cultural creativity, crowned by the Momoyama epoch, which chroniclers exalted as a golden age.

Bardwell L. Smith's bibliographical essay shows that writers in Western languages can scarcely be accused of neglecting Momoyama, but it also indicates that they have far to go before they fully cover that fascinating era. Some ancillary topics, such as the "Christian Century," have been discussed abundantly by Western authors; apart from textbook treatments, however, there have been few attempts to deal with the dominant patterns and personages of Momoyama Japan. New range and depth are opened up with the appearance of this volume of essays. The chapters by John Whitney Hall, Frank Hoff, and V. Dixon Morris, which take a long and sweeping view at the sixteenth century's institutional and cultural developments, all culminate in discussions of aspects of the Momoyama period. So does the collaborative piece by H. Paul Varley and George Elison, which traces the history of the culture of tea from its origins to its maturation in the age of Momoyama. The other essays in their several ways focus especially on the epoch.

William P. Malm's excursion into the world of Momoyama music lingers with particular affection on street scenes, popular pageants, and plebeian amusements; it makes us believe that in music as well as in other fields Momoyama Japan was the realm of the parvenus, the newly rich, and the commoners who celebrated the coming of a new age of peace with almost frenetic spectacles. Here, too, we observe the grand scale, extravagance, and exotic flavor which were the Momoyama culture's unique characteristics. Japan first entered world history in the sixteenth century, and the expansion of Japan's geographical horizon is as evident in some of the commonplace events in the history of music as it is on the grand stage of politics and military affairs. One might cite the introduction of the shamisen and of Catholic liturgical music into Japan. The former was destined to become the most popular instrument in the country; the latter, however, was doomed to disappear when Japan turned inward and away from the West at the end of the Momoyama period.

In the chapter titled "The Cross and the Sword," I state that the effects of the sixteenth century's encounter between Christianity and

Japan constitute the greatest paradox of Momoyama, and that the "Great Unifiers' " effort to reduce the threat they perceived in all uncompromising religious organizations eventually led to the elimination of the Christian faith from the country. The "Three Heroes" —above all Oda Nobunaga, who repeatedly avowed and implacably pursued the intention to "eradicate" the Buddhist True Pure Land sect, but also Toyotomi Hideyoshi and Tokugawa Ieyasu, both of whom were guilty of religious persecutions—appear at their least heroic and most tyrannical in this aspect of their policy of unification. In viewing the repressive features of their regime, however, we might indeed be wise (as John Hall cautions us) not to lose sight of its creative thrust. The warlords' relentless methods, Hall argues, in the end benefited the commoners. It is true that a new kind of stability and security emerged out of the vortices of Sengoku as a result of the unifiers' actions. If a stable social order is the norm, then Momoyama, an age of novelties, also represents a return to normalcy in Japanese history.

How one of the three great hegemons went about normalizing his political authority and legitimating himself is the topic of my "Hideyoshi, the Bountiful Minister." Hideyoshi, a man of the obscurest origins, strove to make himself into an aristocrat by learning the use of the tools of culture; having subjected Japan by the force of arms, he chose to rule it by assuming the highest offices in the ancient but long powerless civil hierarchy of the imperial court. Having transformed himself into a Chancellor and Imperial Regent, the conqueror also raised his vassal daimyo, the military followers who governed the land in his name, into the ranks of the imperial nobility. We see in Hideyoshi's rule both the palingenesis of antique forms and the climax of an evolutionary process which brought a new body politic into being in Japan. Born a commoner, risen to fame as a warlord, enthusiastic amateur of the arts, Hideyoshi embodies the themes of this book's title and properly occupies its frontispiece. His death came just before the sixteenth century's end, and the collapse of his family's fortunes signaled the end of the Momoyama era.

The sixteenth century brought Japan rout and regeneration. The Country at War was pacified; a fragmented polity was reunited. Medieval tones faded from the culture, and a new opulence blossomed forth. The curtain closed on this dramatic century appropriately, after a last great battle scene. That conclusion, Tokugawa Ieyasu's victory at Sekigahara, was the prelude to more than two centuries of peace.

JOHN WHITNEY HALL

Japan's Sixteenth-Century Revolution

T HE SIXTEENTH CENTURY was one of the most turbulent in Japanese history; it was also one of the most spectacularly eventful. During the first half of the century, the country fell apart into autonomous political fragments, and armed conflict was constant and widespread. During the second half, these fragments were first hammered together into regional alliances by powerful local warrior chieftains, and then methodically forged into a single national political structure by the famous triumvirate of "Great Unifiers": Oda Nobunaga, Toyotomi Hideyoshi, and Tokugawa Ieyasu. If lawlessness and political anarchy were characteristic of the early half of the century, the mailed fist is the principal image we have of the second. The "Three Heroes" of this period stand in history as incarnate symbols of the bloody struggle required to quench the fires of civil war, to restrain the wilful daimyo, and to channel the energies of the Japanese people to constructive ends.

The great castles of the Azuchi-Momoyama epoch, with their massive stone walls and farflung moats, are the monuments of Japan's sixteenth-century military unification. They remind us that Japan was a mighty military power second to none in the Orient of the day. How great this power was may be judged from the fact that Hideyoshi could mobilize a force of 250,000 men for the campaign to subdue the daimyo of Kyushu. Korea was invaded twice as a result of Hideyoshi's grandiose plan to conquer Ming China and divide the East Asian mainland into feudal domains for his vassals. The gold bullion in Nobunaga's and Hideyoshi's vaults began a legend, and art historians still marvel at the grandeur of the gilded decorations of their castle palaces. The Momoyama age has been called Japan's renaissance. Surely, it signaled Japan's emergence as an East Asian power.

Yet within little more than a half century, in fact by 1639, this remarkable age of adventure and expansion had come to an end. Japan's fleet of buccaneering merchants, which had sailed to the faraway Indies and pillaged the China coast, had been called back. Sakoku, seclusion, was the new policy and the national mood. The restless openness of Momoyama had given way to Tokugawa exclusiveness and introversion.

For later viewers, the theme of unification and its symbols, the "Three Heroes," have held an ambiguous place in the historiography of Japan. Was not unity, particularly in the manner it was achieved—through bloodshed, terror, and repression—imposed at the expense of the creative interests of the Japanese nation? The unifiers, for all their heroic proportions, appear as conservative or even reactionary influences: Nobunaga for his brutal destruction of Buddhist communities, Hideyoshi for his restrictive social policies, Ieyasu for placing Japan on the path to national seclusion. Behind all the period's glory, it would appear, lurked despotism, and behind the despotism lay repression and stagnation.

It is clear that by 1550 Japan had reached a state of political and social instability that could only be brought under control by a militarily powerful autocrat. It is the nature of military consolidators that they must rely on sheer force and absolute authority to win their way. It would seem that in that age it was also in the nature of such leaders to use conservative measures in order to consolidate their gains and safeguard their new powers. The "Three Heroes" were no exception to this rule. But is it right to judge their place in history only by looking at the negative, repressive policies they used to impose a new hegemony on the country? Was Sakoku the underlying thrust of their policies? A closer look at this transitional period of Japanese history suggests that the new hegemony created by these men also had its creative aspects.[1]

The movement toward Japan's national unification was not limited to the military dimension. During the sixteenth century, the country underwent a veritable revolution in the institutions through which government touched the people. Nobunaga, Hideyoshi, and Ieyasu adopted fundamental changes in national political organization, local government, and village and town administration as they consolidated their hegemonies. The new institutions devised by them were dynamic and not simply restrictive in their effect. Their historical importance ought to be measured not by reference to the closing of the country in the 1630s but rather by a look at the vigorous manner in which Japan came out of seclusion in the 1850s and 1860s when challenged by the West. They must be judged by the dramatic growth of Japan as a nation, economy, society, and culture during the intervening two centuries.

All major institutional revolutions in Japanese history have been achieved through compromise between rulers and ruled, between the effort to control and the effort to resist control. This was as true of the revolution of the sixteenth century as it had been of the Taika Reform, which in the latter half of the seventh century established the early aristocratic state, and as it was to be of the modern revolution of the Meiji era.[2]

The Meiji example, being more familiar to us, can be used to illustrate this point. Called variously an "absolutist revolution," a "nationalist revolution," or an "aristocratic revolution," it was anything but the kind of violent change through social upheaval that we tend to think of when we use the word revolution. Quite clearly a "revolution from the top," the Meiji Restoration nonetheless brought about fundamental changes in government and society, and in the relationship of both to the sources of power and wealth. The striking feature of all of this was that it was samurai leaders who took the initiative in dismantling the old order and in abolishing their own class privileges. In the case of Meiji, politically conservative leaders adopted revolutionary policies in what they conceived to be the national interest, and incidentally as a prudent compromise between the extreme objectives of those who would maximize central political power and those who would open the way toward popular representation.[3]

The example of Japan's modern revolution is a useful glass through which to view the sixteenth century. For in the Azuchi-Momoyama epoch Japan underwent a revolution which was aristocratic in leadership and autocratic in spirit, yet which took account of a broad spectrum of political and social aspirations within the samurai and non-samurai classes.

At the risk of getting ahead of myself, I should like to explain what I mean by this statement. First, the most obvious result of the unification movement of the sixteenth century was the establishment of a new national power structure in which the national hegemon acquired for himself unassailable, almost monarchial authority. Yet this political authority was won through compromise with the rest of the military aristocracy, and indirectly with the peasantry. Since the daimyo retained their semi-autonomous positions in the countryside, the new hegemon was obliged to share his power with his subordinates. In the new order, moreover, while the national hegemon and his daimyo followers became the unquestioned rulers of the country, they at the same time lifted up into the samurai class a large segment of the rural population, thereby spreading the privilege of aristocratic status many times wider than it had ever been before. The sixteenth-century revolution was to this extent a pro-samurai revolution.

Furthermore, while the unifiers gave to an expanded elite class secure rights and privileges and an assured income, they also obliged samurai government to acknowledge a greater social responsibility. By recognizing certain privileges of popular self-government, they gave to the peasantry and the bourgeoisie new areas of autonomy from the arbitrary exercise of political power. The result was a combination of absolute rule exercised over units of administration within which Japanese of every class—but particularly the peasantry—were given the protection of legally defined spheres of existence. The sixteenth-century revolution was to this extent a pro-peasant revolution.

To understand these assertions we need to go back to the start of the sixteenth century. We begin with a condition of extreme political decentralization and widespread warfare to which the Japanese gave the name Sengoku, the nation at war. The country was divided within itself at every level. There was no national authority which had the power to provide protection and justice. The emperor had long ago become a powerless and shadowy figure. The Ashikaga shogun, lacking significant wealth or armed forces, had by this time lost the capability to act as a balance of power (but not the capacity for intrigue) between the competing factions of the military aristocracy. Without a central power which could be relied upon to maintain a legal process or to guarantee rights over property, the individual proprietor had but three alternatives if he wanted to safeguard his holdings: to become militarily irresistible in his own right, to seek protection by alliance with others like himself, or to subordinate himself to some superior, stronger power.

The warfare of the early sixteenth century gave rise to two distinct types of organization for the purposes of security: those of the daimyo, or domanial lord, and of the *ikki,* or league. The two types were fundamentally different in structure and intent. The daimyo were local warlords who sought to become absolute masters of land and people within their territories, aiming to reduce all samurai to vassalage and all peasants into dues-paying workers of the land. The authority relationship within the domain was basically hierarchal and feudal.[4]

The *ikki* was, on the contrary, collective and in principle egalitarian. Its symbol was the collective oath or compact signed, often in blood, with names written in a circle so that none took precedence over another. Local samurai or small embryonic daimyo made compacts with each other to resist the authority of the shogun, when that was still a factor, or the encroachment of neighboring daimyo. Bands of country samurai and village leaders joined forces to resist taxation or to expel invading military forces.[5]

Ikki tended to be ephemeral. They were effective in resisting authority but had trouble perpetuating a lasting order. In time all such regional confederations either dissolved or moved in one of two directions. They either transformed themselves into daimyo domains, generally as one of their number rose to a position of paramount leadership, or they were converted into religious *ikki*. Of the latter, the most prominent was the organization of the True Pure Land (or Ikkō, "Single-Directed") sect, which held the province of Kaga from 1488 to 1580. Even there, however, with the establishment of the Kanazawa Midō, an ecclesiastical headquarters with extensive political and military power, the *ikki* structure after 1546 became almost indistinguishable from that of the standard daimyo domain.

By the middle of the sixteenth century, there remained only daimyo domains and a few militarized religious communities with sufficient armed force and organizational capacity to hold or safeguard large spheres of local autonomy. Of these two types of political organization, it was the daimyo structure that had the capability of further expansion and ultimately the creation of a national hegemony. Already the daimyo had demonstrated their potential through the formation of large regional coalitions or alliances, based on feudal vassalage. Region by region, the more vigorous of the daimyo secured the submission of weaker neighboring daimyo, and organized them into territorial alliances. By the 1560s such clustering of daimyo into regional leagues had proceeded to the point that national conquest by one of them became a practical possibility.[6]

Although we think of national unification as the work of military giants such as Nobunaga and Hideyoshi, it is more accurate to say that it was achieved by the ascendancy of one daimyo alliance over other such alliances. Within the regional alliance structure there was built in from the outset a compromise between central authority and local autonomy. Nobunaga and Hideyoshi, for all the military resources they could muster, were still first among equals in relation to their most powerful daimyo allies, such as Ieyasu. The wars of unification, except in a few instances (and those largely under Nobunaga), were seldom fought to the finish. Daimyo were often encouraged to surrender their territories by the guarantee of being reinvested in their original holdings or in equivalent territory in exchange for pledges of allegiance. Under Hideyoshi and Ieyasu, even those who resisted, if they capitulated before being totally overpowered, were often reinvested although in suitably reduced circumstances, so long as they swore fealty to the victorious overlord.

In the unification process, the reduction of all daimyo to a condition of vassalage to a national overlord was a comparatively straightforward matter. It involved battle in the traditional manner, leading to an accepted political solution in which the loser acknowledged the overlordship of the victor. Both the battle and the peace agreement were part of the samurai way of doing things. Less easily handled were religious *ikki* and other temple organizations. Such religious communities, since they were bent on preserving their autonomy by military resistance, could not be incorporated into the daimyo system. The only solution was the destruction of the *ikki* nature of these communities and the reduction of all religious institutions to military impotence and political subordination. The ruthless attacks which Nobunaga launched against the warrior monks of Hieizan, the "religious monarchy" of the Ishiyama Honganji, and its subordinate groupings in Ise, Echizen, and Kaga reveal the absolute and uncompromising attitude of opposition which the regime of the unifiers took against these religious-military complexes.

Since the unification process resulted from the ascendancy of one daimyo coalition over the nation and not from the reemergence of a central monarchial authority, the new hegemony, rather than destroying daimyo rule, extended it uniformly upon the people of the entire nation. Daimyo in the first half of the sixteenth century had sought to be both absolute in their control of their domains and autonomous with respect to superior authority. The power of the coalition armies assembled by the "Great Unifiers" reduced the autonomy of the daimyo. And yet, once they had accepted the overlordship of Nobunaga, Hideyoshi, or Ieyasu, they were left to govern their territories with a relatively free hand, even under the more bureaucratically centralized Tokugawa regime.

When we talk of daimyo rule we refer not to a single static system but to an evolving form of government. For all their ambition to achieve total imperative control, daimyo in the early sixteenth century were far from being absolute masters of their localities. Many daimyo domains were only loosely held together, and the daimyo could claim only the weakest powers of overlordship over vassal military families who themselves jealously guarded their local rights. Daimyo struggled constantly to reduce their samurai subordinates to dependent status and to bring the economic resources of their domains under their own direct command.

The critical elements in this struggle were the lowest level of the samurai—namely the *jizamurai* (the terms gentry or yeomanry are perhaps appropriate in this instance)—and the agricultural villages.[7] In the early Middle Ages, the samurai yeomen lived within the agricultural communities which they held in fief, exercising both fiscal (that is to say, tax-collecting) and judicial control over the cultivators. During the fifteenth and sixteenth centuries, farmers organized themselves into *ikki* in an effort to gain freedom from such samurai control.

The *ikki* structure was well suited to mobilize communal action by peasants against village samurai. It was especially effective as village leaders obtained the resources to arm themselves. The *do-ikki* of the fifteenth century, in which peasants from widespread areas banded together into resistance groups, demonstrated the potential of rural leagues. Gradually, village communities won free rights over such aspects of their life as police action, access to water and communal land, and the right to sell property. Most critical was the acquisition of autonomy of tax collection. Villages acting as autonomous units agreed to deliver to the daimyo set quotas of taxes on a contract basis, thus avoiding the interference of samurai tax collectors and the likelihood of rate increases. Such village autonomy tended to be won by villagers at the expense of the local gentry samurai, usually by negotiation with superior daimyo authority. Hence the growth in village autonomy placed the rural samurai in an increasingly precarious position.

The militancy of the peasantry at the village level and the increased demands of military service in the years of the wars of unification brought about fundamental changes in the relationship of samurai to village in the daimyo domains. The daimyo, ever intent on subjecting their vassals to dependent status and direct discipline, took over the dynamism of village autonomy for their own purposes. They did so by acceding to the peasantry's desire to control their own lives, by granting them substantial measures of autonomy so long as taxes were forthcoming, and by enlisting village leaders into their own rural administration.

By thus reaching down directly to the village level, the daimyo forced the local samurai to relinquish their close ties with the land and the peasantry and to move instead to the daimyo's castle headquarters, where they would reside as members of the daimyo's house band and garrison troops. For those among the local samurai whose position had already been threatened by peasant resistance, such a move was undoubtedly welcome. For those local warriors still closely and securely associated with the land, it created a critical dilemma. For them the choice was to give up the sword and become peasants, or abandon the land and become hereditary soldiers of the daimyo. Faced with this unhappy choice, a substantial number of *jizamurai* left the countryside and became castle-town stipendiaries. By the Tokugawa period, the samurai class therefore constituted a remarkably high 7 percent of the population, all living in towns or cities.

At the start of the unification movement, the ideal-typical daimyo domain, one in which the daimyo had become a local autocrat and his vassals a corps of stipended officials, had not yet come into existence. But by the time military unification was completed in 1591, it was well on its way. In the process the daimyo received a major assist from Hideyoshi, who in his later years enforced nationally as a general policy the institutional changes which the more advanced daimyo had been undertaking in their own domains.

A people which had been at war for decades, the Japanese at the end of the sixteenth century held the overriding desire for security, law, and order. Once a certain degree of political stability was attained, it was natural that efforts should be made to reduce the incidence of domestic violence. The most obvious effort in this direction was the series of "sword hunts," begun under Nobunaga, conducted locally by daimyo, and prosecuted on a national scale by Hideyoshi. Hideyoshi's 1588 edict proclaiming this nationwide policy read: "The farmers of all provinces are strictly forbidden to have in their possession swords, short swords, bows, spears, firearms, or other types of weapons. If unnecessary implements of war are kept, the collection of annual taxes becomes difficult and uprisings are encouraged. . . . Thus daimyo using their retainers as agents should collect all such weapons and turn them over to higher authorities."[8] The edict went on to say that this confiscation policy was intended to promote the best interests of the farmers, who would now be able to cultivate their fields in peace, and that moreover the confiscated weapons would not be wasted, since the metal would be used to make nails for the construction of the Great Buddha which Hideyoshi had ordered built in Kyoto.

It has been suggested that the national sword hunt had a social purpose, that of visibly separating warriors from farmers. While this element was probably involved in the decision, it is clear that the measure had a more significant military purpose and was designed to lower the possibility of resistance to tax collection in a countryside from which the samurai had already been largely withdrawn.

How thorough the confiscation was we do not know, nor do we have any idea of the total quantity of confiscated weapons. One document from the province of Kaga records the submission of 1,073 swords, 1,540 short swords, and 160 spears from one county alone. The document is dated just a little more than a month after the issuance of the original decree and is signed by the daimyo of Kaga. Leaving aside the question of whether or not it was to the advantage of the daimyo to relinquish the confiscated weapons to Hideyoshi, it was certainly in their interest to have the rural populace in their domains disarmed. Hideyoshi's edict could provide them with useful backing in their effort to reduce the capacity for violence within their domains. But it is also important to recognize that the sword hunt was to the advantage of the peasantry as well, and to the nation as a whole. The assumption that the sword hunt was simply the device of military conquerors bent on creating a defenseless peasantry is not borne out by the other features of daimyo rule. For once the rural areas were pacified, it became possible to install a system of local administration which permitted the farming population to expand its resources dramatically in the succeeding decades.

Yet although the sword hunt may not have been class legislation in intent, it had the broadest social impact in practice, for it helped to underline the social distinction between samurai, whose profession it was to handle weapons, and farmers, whose job it was to till the soil and cultivate the mulberry. The fact that a functional differentiation between samurai and peasant was being clarified throughout Japan at this time is revealed in Hideyoshi's edict of 1591, which prohibited the change of status from samurai to farmer or merchant, or from farmer to merchant. This edict, coming at the successful conclusion of the campaigns in northern Japan, sought to prevent samurai whose daimyo masters had been defeated in battle from drifting back to the countryside where they might take the lead in stirring up peasant unrest. By that time a clear separation had been achieved between samurai and peasant.

Apart from the battles of unification themselves, the most massive activity begun under Nobunaga and completed by Hideyoshi was the series of land surveys, which by the time of Hideyoshi's death had been pushed across the entire nation to consolidate the practices of land registration, tax assessment, and peasant tenure into a single system. This act, more than anything else, was at the root of Japan's sixteenth-century revolution, laying the base for the new social institutions which brought order and stability to Japan for the next two and a half centuries.[9]

The significance of the new land survey of the late sixteenth century was that it represented the necessary final step in a change in land tenure practices which had been under way for almost four hundred years. Ever since the establishment of the Kamakura shogunate in the twelfth century, there had existed a dual system of legitimation for land ownership at the proprietary level.[10] One system was based upon the imperial court, the other on the military government. During the thirteenth and fourteenth centuries these two systems operated in parallel. With the establishment of the Muromachi bakufu, and particularly after the turn into the fifteenth century, the shogunate provided the only effective machinery for proprietary guarantee and land dispute adjudication. With the decline of the bakufu, the whole area of land right certification was left without superior enforcement authority. Daimyo sought by right of might to become themselves the supreme proprietors within their domains, while religious institutions clung to historical grants of ownership originating in the imperial court. Rural samurai claimed privileges to exploit the peasantry of their fiefs, while village leaders resisted in the name of village autonomy. To resolve the conflicting proprietary claims, the establishment of a new legal authority was clearly necessary.

The more powerful of the daimyo had in fact begun to undertake just that task in their territories, issuing house laws and conducting new cadastral surveys which catalogued all land and recorded its encumbrances. But these attempts were erratic and unsystematic. Moreover, since the problem of land ownership was not purely local, only a truly national effort could resolve the basic issues. The beginnings of a methodical, universal policy to extend the emergent national regime's control over the provinces by means of the land survey can be traced back to Nobunaga's last years, especially after the conclusion of the "Ten Years' War" against the Ishiyama Honganji in 1580; it is, however, Hideyoshi who is properly associated with its successful pursuit on a national scale. Immediately after he succeeded Nobunaga in 1582, Hideyoshi issued orders for a systematic resurvey of the territory under his control, province by province; by the time of his own death in 1598, all provinces had been thoroughly surveyed, in many instances several times over.

The *Taikō kenchi,* as this operation came to be called, proceeded in three steps: measurement of land, assessment of its quality and hence of its capacity to be taxed, and determination of ownership. Quality, depending on whether land was paddy or dry field, was determined on the basis of yield in rice or equivalent product per unit. Yield was measured in units of rice, either actual in the case of paddy or by calculation in the case of dry fields, the unit being a standard *koku* (roughly five bushels). Cadastral registers, *kenchi-chō,* were prepared village by village. On the basis of such registers, superior authorities were provided with precise figures for each village on the total tax base (namely, the sum total of yield figures for all land in the village). These figures, known as *kokudaka,* became the basis of a systematic and uniform tax system. Daimyo could levy at will a tax of 40 percent, 50 percent, or whatever figure they chose upon the assessment base of their domains.

While the cadastral survey achieved its primary purpose of reorganizing the land-tax system of Japan, it had much more far-reaching and deeply significant effects upon the structure of Japanese society. For it became the basis upon which the legal status of both the samurai and the peasant classes rested for the next two and a half centuries.

What did the survey mean for the samurai? Since it was carried out in the name of Hideyoshi as the ultimate feudal overlord of the vassal daimyo, and since the cadastral registers were placed in the possession of Hideyoshi and his daimyo vassals, all superior rights, namely the rights of taxation and governance, were in the hands of the military aristocracy. The power to dispose of these superior rights was Hideyoshi's alone, and he delegated such rights to daimyo, or to religious institutions, over his own vermilion seal. The *Taikō kenchi* swept aside the complicated system of layered estate rights which had persisted under the *shōen* system. Any remaining local authority— whether samurai or religious establishment—which clung to historical claims of proprietorship had those claims nullified and its lands reassigned on the basis of new grants from Hideyoshi or one of his daimyo vassals. In this fashion Japan's military hegemon also became the country's supreme proprietary overlord. There was now but one supreme authority over the land and the people who worked it.

The great land survey also provided the national overlord with new powers of political control. With an accurate chart of the location and productive capacity of the country's land base, Hideyoshi was able to adjust wealth to status in his political hierarchy more precisely. Daimyo were enfeoffed in domains on the basis of so many *koku*, their holdings comprised of a county here or a village there, so as to make up a certain *kokudaka* figure. In the early rounds, the survey was clearly used to ferret out excessive land holdings. The great monastery of Kōyasan was found to have over fifty thousand *koku* in hidden holdings and was cut back to three thousand. Such daimyo as the Gamō of the great Aizu Wakamatsu domain, who tried to falsify their figures, had their lands confiscated. The *kenchi* was a device by which the national hegemon was able to intrude his authority into every corner of the land; it did not, however, work only to Hideyoshi's benefit. It must be admitted that it also gave to every holder of a patent of proprietorship the backing of Hideyoshi's power and authority. And for the daimyo this was all-important.

The use of the *kokudaka* as a basis of calculation for rights of taxation had another subtle but important result. Daimyo were granted their domains from Hideyoshi in terms of *kokudaka*, not land area. It is true that for the larger daimyo the grants usually coincided with whole provinces, and such daimyo remained identified with set locations. But for the vast majority of daimyo, who were enfeoffed at figures of ten or twenty thousand *koku*, the domains—while perhaps centering on a small headquarters castle—had no clearly drawn territorial boundaries, being calculated instead in terms of appropriate numbers of villages whose sum *koku* added up to the requisite figure. Moreover, since the daimyo was allotted his fief in terms of *koku*, not land, it became largely immaterial whether the fief was changed from one location to another as long as the income was not decreased. The daimyo became increasingly dependent upon Hideyoshi's superior power of enfeoffment. Even more important to the nation was the fact that the daimyo held their domains not as private possessions but rather in trust from the national overlord as his delegates. Their rights of exploitation were carefully spelled out by Hideyoshi and later the Tokugawa shoguns. In essence their powers were political rather than proprietary.

The same was even more true of the samurai as a class of former enfeoffed gentry. Although the first round of *kenchi-chō* registered cultivators by plot and indicated the authority to which rents and dues were owed, the direct relationship between samurai and cultivators was soon broken. By the early Tokugawa period, samurai (except in a few scattered and exceptional instances) had been deprived of their direct private rights over the land and its cultivation as a result of the forced move into the daimyo's castle. While in some areas, and for varying lengths of time, former fief holders were permitted to interfere directly in village affairs, setting dues rates and collecting labor service, this practice had disappeared almost totally by the early years of the Tokugawa period.[11]

The warfare of the sixteenth century had forced the samurai to move physically off the land and into the daimyo's headquarters, but it was the *kenchi* that drew a legal line between the samurai and the land. The withdrawal of the entire land-owning aristocracy from the land and its conversion into a military-administrative officer corps attached to national and regional centers of government was perhaps the most fundamental social change of the sixteenth century. Samurai were no longer landowners, and land as taxable property was not transferable by sale among the samurai class. Samurai could not acquire private landed wealth. Their income could be increased only by the acquisition of merit increases of stipend in the service of daimyo or shogun. The *kokudaka* system was unique among East Asian land systems, and it created a ruling class unlike any other in East Asia.[12]

The *kenchi* also had a revolutionary impact upon the cultivator class. By registering land in village units and imposing taxes village by village, the survey first of all acknowledged the autonomy of the village communities over broad areas of communal life. While villages were held strictly accountable for exact and timely payment of taxes, the villagers themselves were given the right to determine how the village put together its quota. Within the village, the headman was the prime authority; and although he was accountable to daimyo law, he was at least a member of the village, and often the chosen representative of the villagers.

Perhaps the most important feature of the cadastral survey from the cultivator's point of view was the factor of registration itself. Registration worked in two ways. It identified the villager with a certain plot of land, making him responsible for tax payment on the plot. It also confirmed the villager's right to cultivate that land or to have it cultivated. While the first condition placed a number of restraints on alienation, the second provided security of tenure which had not existed in the past.

The *kenchi* affected conditions within the village only incidentally. It did not reduce all villagers to the status of paddy-land cultivators, and it did not necessarily break up landholding farm families whose patriarchal organizations contained unfree dependent households. What the survey did accomplish was to give new legal status to an entire class of land-cultivating farmers, the *hyakushō,* who by being entered in the cadastral registers became what might be called copyholders, secure in their occupancy and free under certain conditions to alienate their property. Above all, the *hyakushō* class as a whole was cut away from the private interference of a military gentry and placed under the uniform laws of the realm or of the domain. But the converse was also true. No *hyakushō* could make his way into the samurai class by virtue of landed property. The farmer, by definition, owned only the cultivator's rights to his land. The samurai class, in the name of the national hegemon, exercised political rights which were forever out of the farmers' reach.

Domestically, the sword hunt and the cadastral survey marked a major turning point in Japanese social history. The *kenchi,* by systematically and legally defining the relationship of the two major classes (the samurai and the *hyakushō*) to the land, brought into being the Early Modern Japanese state, which vested political authority in the samurai class but placed the samurai under the absolute constraints of their leaders and of the strict laws of the land. The sword hunt, while its immediate objective was to suppress rural unrest, had a deeper political meaning. For it is significant that the confiscation order had to be couched in terms which emphasized the benefit it would bring to the people and the nation. This is the beginning of the use of moral justification for public policy, a practice which was to become increasingly common in the next decades, particularly as Japan's rulers absorbed the vocabulary of Neo-Confucian political theory. It is the beginning, in other words, of the acknowledgment of responsibility on the part of samurai government toward the rest of the population.[13]

It is natural that we, as later observers of the sixteenth-century scene, should think of the main characteristics of the age in terms of the military exploits of the great unifiers and the overseas adventures of the era's armies and merchant fleets. Hence we are apt to overemphasize Nobunaga's ruthlessness and to adjudge Hideyoshi's social policies repressive; to us, the foreign policies of the early Tokugawa shoguns appear to mark the end of a glorious age of adventure and expansion. Yet the true measure of Japan's greatness during the sixteenth century was to be found in the social and political institutions which, though less dramatically apparent, transformed Japan into a nation capable of stability and future growth. In the next two and a half centuries Japan was to grow in population and wealth, in political sophistication, in social organization, and in cultural achievement. This was a growth which rested on the social and political institutions created by Nobunaga and Hideyoshi in the sixteenth century.

V. DIXON MORRIS

The City of Sakai and Urban Autonomy

A SIDE FROM the capital city of Kyoto itself, perhaps the most important urban area of sixteenth-century Japan was Sakai. Although today it is dwarfed by Osaka, its giant neighbor to the north, four hundred years ago Sakai was a prosperous port city which had gained its prominence as a center for the transshipment of estate rents to the Home Provinces and as the outfitter for official embassies to Ming China. For historians, however, Sakai has signified much more—they have also called it Japan's "free city," the one town so wealthy that it could challenge the arrogant warrior class and defend itself from the turmoil of the age. Its citizens, it is pointed out, even dared resist the conquering Oda Nobunaga.

Sakai's singular position among Japanese cities gave it a significance that extended to the understanding of Japanese history in general. Its "freedom" called to mind the free cities of Europe, the urban phenomenon which grew up outside the feudal order to become one of the principal agents in the collapse of the medieval world and the rise of the modern West. Historians therefore looked to Sakai for similar clues to the problem of historical change in Japan. For some, the existence of this one city spelled the end of feudalism and the beginning of modern Japan, and the implications of this attitude for their approach to the remainder of Japanese history were profound. There were, for example, scholars who insisted that in the sixteenth and seventeenth centuries, Japan, like Europe, entered a period of absolutism and that the Edo bakufu was an absolute monarchy. Greater numbers maintained that, although feudalism was collapsing before the advent of the "Great Unifiers"—Oda Nobunaga, Toyotomi Hideyoshi, and Tokugawa Ieyasu—these three were able to revitalize feudal institutions, but only after they had destroyed Sakai. Still others saw Japan as entering feudalism for the first time with the emergence of the samurai regime of Nobunaga and his successors. For them, too, the reduction of Sakai was an integral part of the process of feudalization. In all of these cases, Sakai was viewed as a mighty and independent city capable of defying the petty barons who ruled Japan in the sixteenth century.

One of the earliest learned articles on Sakai described it as a "free city" and said that neither the Ashikaga shogunate nor its regional constables had any means of controlling its residents. The article then proceeded to quote at length from the letters of Jesuit missionaries, such as Gaspar Vilela, to the effect that Sakai was exceedingly rich and powerful and was governed by its own laws, as Venice was.[1] The same analysis persists in the postwar era. Takao Kazuhiko, writing in one of the most respected symposia on Japanese history, repeated Vilela's statement comparing Sakai to Venice and asked rhetorically, "How can we of the twentieth century deny the views of these foreigners who knew the free cities of Europe and who lived in sixteenth-century Sakai?"[2]

Indeed, the Jesuits were keen observers, and we rely on their reports for much of what we know of sixteenth-century Japanese conditions, for they often described matters of genuine interest that native writers regarded as commonplace and therefore unworthy of comment. Unfortunately, Vilela did not elaborate on his remarks about the autonomy of Sakai, so we cannot be entirely sure what he meant. Moreover, Japanese accounts of the city's government provide no further aid. There is, nevertheless, enough information from various sources to suggest that Sakai was, in fact, self-governing and that its institutions of autonomy began in the fifteenth century. Sakai's independence from the warrior class that ruled the countryside, however, is not nearly so well portrayed.

The distinction between autonomy and independence is an important one, but it has tended to become blurred in common usage. For the sake of clarity, this essay employs the former term to refer to self-government without implying freedom from outside control by others. Thus, both Sakai and Venice may have had city governments that were in the hands of local residents, while yet being quite dissimilar in the degree of freedom that each enjoyed. The term autonomy as employed here, moreover, carries no connotation of democracy. The vast majority of the residents of Sakai had little opportunity to participate in municipal administration but were directed by a council whose members were wealthy merchants. The concept of popular rule was lacking.

What, then, was the nature of Sakai's autonomous institutions? What is the meaning of urban autonomy in the context of sixteenth-century Japan? These are the questions we shall explore, while inquiring also into this city's relationship with the military class through the period when Oda Nobunaga brought Sakai under his direct control.

Sakai's First Autonomous Institution

In searching for the origins of Sakai's autonomy, one must go back to the period before the Ōnin War of 1467–1477. During that era the city still relied on the estate proprietors who used it as an entrepôt in shipping their rents from the outlying provinces to Nara and Kōyasan. The competition of Hyōgo (modern Kobe), which was the most convenient link between Kyoto and the Inland Sea area, limited economic contacts with the capital and the warrior society there, but political ties were more direct, for the Muromachi bakufu took an early interest in the control of the city. In the beginning of the fifteenth century shogunal authorities gave the residents their first, brief opportunity for self-government by permitting them to collect their own estate rents without direct interference from the outside.

The particular administrative arrangements under which Sakai first gained autonomy were complex. Local areas everywhere in the country before the creation of the unified domains of the Early Modern period were subject to multiple levels of government and overlapping jurisdictions; administrative responsibility was simultaneously in the hands both of military officials and of civilian proprietors. Sakai's position was even more complex than that of most other areas, for it had grown up at the provincial boundary between Settsu and Izumi, so that administratively Sakai was divided into Settsu Sakai (called Sakai Kita no Shō) in the north and the larger, more populous Sakai Minami no Shō in Izumi to the south. This meant that the authorities treated the two parts of the city quite separately. One result was that Settsu Sakai earned special privileges much later than the southern estate.

In general, the bakufu attempted to keep Izumi Sakai, the more prosperous part of the city, under the jurisdiction of its closest allies. Following the battle of Sakai in January 1400, at which the bakufu crushed the rebellion of Ōuchi Yoshihiro, the shogun Ashikaga Yoshimitsu named the Hosokawa as military constables of the area. As the holder of the civilian proprietary rights to the southern estate he selected the Shōkokuji. The shogun enjoyed a special relationship with each of them. The Hosokawa were his closest retainers, while the Shōkokuji was a Zen temple that Yoshimitsu himself had founded.

The source which tells us of the proprietorship of the Shōkokuji over Izumi Sakai is a particularly significant one, for it contains information about the management of the estate as well. It is a decision of the bakufu on an appeal from the residents of Sakai in 1431, and is based on an earlier document dated 1419. It ruled that the residents of the city were jointly responsible for a rent to the temple of 730 *kanmon,* and stated that there was no "estate master" *(shōshu)* in residence there.[3] This is the first indication of autonomy in Sakai. As early as 1419 the people of the city had no estate official directly over them but collected their rents themselves. This form of rent payment was called *jigeuke,* literally "receipt by commoners," and was analogous to a contract in which the leading residents guaranteed to meet the annual dues for the whole city. In turn, they determined the specific sums that the other family heads would have to pay.

Sakai's administration of its own rents appears not to have lasted long, however. Sometime before 1441 the shogunate claimed Izumi Sakai as its own holding. Then in that year it returned the estate to the constable who was to govern Sakai himself and pay a fixed rent to the Shōkokuji.[4] Thus, the temple had rights only to income, while the constable had the administrative rights as its deputy. The residents of Sakai were left without any of their former privileges. Thereafter, until the Ōnin War, the southern estate of Sakai was held by the bakufu either in its own right or indirectly through the Shōkokuji or the Hosokawa, and was administered by deputies.[5]

During this same period the proprietorship of Settsu Sakai, the northern estate in Sumiyoshi-gun, is in doubt. During the fourteenth century it had been in the hands of the Sumiyoshi Taisha, and it may have remained under that prominent Shinto shrine's control.[6] Since the shrine was in the immediate vicinity of its Sakai holding, it would have had no need for deputies or for a system of rent collection by commoners. The priests were close enough for direct supervision. Later, as the distinctions marked by estate boundaries lost their significance, the bakufu took over both North and South Sakai and controlled them as direct holdings *(chokkatsuchi),* thereby recognizing the essential unity of the two parts of the city.

The actual operation of the estates and the part the residents played are unclear. In the Edo period, when villages were responsible for meeting collective tax assessments, councils of elders assigned certain quotas to each of the families under them. Moreover, the councils also undertook projects that were of local concern, such as irrigation or joint use of village lands. This experience may lead one to believe that a similar system was employed in the fifteenth century as well. Contemporary documents, however, say nothing about a local assemblage in Sakai before the Ōnin War, although the brief existence of joint responsibility for rent payment suggests it.

There was one other brief instance immediately before the Ōnin War in which one might expect to find the city managing its own taxes. That was in 1465, when the shogun Yoshimasa authorized the constable to collect a so-called *utokusen* from Izumi Sakai. *Utokusen* literally means "money from those with virtue," but virtue was a euphemism for wealth, since this special tax was levied only on those identified as being rich. Contemporary records make it plain that the Shōkokuji as proprietor protested the tax vigorously, citing previous exemptions as precedents.[7] The bakufu, however, sent a representative to the temple to explain the necessity of cooperation with the constable, and so refused to grant the exemption. Since the city's residents, not the temple, bore the ultimate tax burden, it is reasonable to assume that a representative council, had it existed, would have been mentioned in connection with the negotiations. The temple's concern, moreover, must have been the difficulty of administering the tax. Negative evidence can scarcely be conclusive, but it does suggest that Sakai did not have an autonomous council on the eve of the Ōnin War, and that the Shōkokuji still had an active interest in Izumi Sakai. In this particular case, the residents' only role seems to have been tax payment. The bakufu made the assessment; the temple collected it; and the proceeds went to the constable.

Local Autonomy in Medieval Japan

Although the negotiations over the tax imposed on Sakai in 1465 contained no mention of autonomous institutions, there is direct evidence that self-government began shortly thereafter. The first extended eyewitness account of Sakai, the *Shoken nichiroku* written two decades later, contains notices which indicate that the city at that time had a local governmental council. If Sakai did, indeed, begin to enjoy permanent autonomy during the turmoil of the Ōnin and Bunmei periods, then it is typical in that respect of numerous villages and cities, in its own area as well as in other parts of Japan.

Throughout the country, and especially in the advanced Kinki district, the residents of local areas formed into bodies to manage their own affairs. The customary unit of government was a hereditary council, though later some small villages included all adult males. The responsibilities of the local governments normally included tax collection, peace preservation, and the sponsorship of festivals for the patron deity of the neighborhood. These basic attributes of local autonomy late in the fifteenth century were the same in all areas and in both cities and villages. One can hardly claim that Sakai's council was in any sense unique.

Local autonomy was, in fact, an integral part of the creation of the villages themselves. The Muromachi era witnessed the transformation of estates from below into village units and from above into military domains. This process brought about the village system as the fundamental administrative arrangement in the countryside. The old estates had been characterized by complex rights that had required the constant attention of officials resident on the land. By contrast, the new domains involved the rationalization or simplification of rights into relationships that were based on vassalage. For practical purposes this meant that the village as a whole could be made responsible for a fixed amount of taxes and labor services that could be apportioned locally, thus easing the burdens of the barons who were anxious to devote their energies to affairs in the capital or, later, to territorial expansion. Indeed, as John Whitney Hall points out earlier in this volume, the barons by the end of the sixteenth century encouraged local autonomy as a means of facilitating the removal of the samurai gentry or yeomanry (*jizamurai*) from the village to their own garrisons. In a sense, self-government was therefore thrust upon the village by the upper classes. This village system evolved earliest in the Kinki area, but ultimately it spread all over Japan and provided the precedent for autonomy that was applied to cities.[8]

Although the original and most important justification for autonomy was collection of taxes and labor services, the activities of the village units soon spread to other functions as well. The villages did not have boundaries coterminous with the estates but formed naturally around sources of water for irrigation in order to take advantage of improved agricultural techniques. This entailed a considerable realignment of local administrative units and caused numerous disputes over use of resources. Before the emergence of *sengoku daimyō* who adjudicated such disputes, villagers themselves had to represent their own interests when conflicts with other groups occurred. Within the village, moreover, the residents had to have some means of assigning shares of common land and water, and these responsibilities also came into the hands of the self-governing bodies. The phenomena of *sō-okite* and *sō no okibumi* appeared in order to meet such needs. These were, in effect, laws passed and enforced by the people of the village. Most of them were designed to solve the problems of agriculture, but in times of emergency they were extended to cover criminal matters for the sake of preserving public order; even the death penalty was not uncommon.[9]

The union of villagers that undertook the demands of self-government was known as the *sō,* a word that signifies "all" or "entirety." It comprised the whole population of the village, but the actual operation of government was often confined to a few elders who sat in council over the rest of the people. Since the groups were not created by any national body but originated naturally in response to conditions within the village, a variety of terms grew up to describe them. The most common were *otona, toshiyori,* and *nengyōji,* words that remained in frequent use throughout the Edo period.[10]

The social composition of the councils is the subject of heated debate and speculation among students of the medieval village, for there is no documentary evidence to prove precisely which class supplied its membership. In many villages an organization called the shrine guild *(miyaza)* became the nucleus of the new councils. These bodies had arisen in the Heian period to lead celebrations for the local patron deities. Their members were drawn from the *myōshu* class on the estates, and it was probably this stratum of society that became the leaders of the villages and organized the first councils.[11] Not all villages had shrine guilds. Where they did exist, age, residence, and ability as well as status may have been among the initial criteria for selecting the elders; official standing as a *myōshu,* however, was probably the first consideration in all villages.

Later, as the system became more formal during the latter half of the fifteenth century, positions became hereditary in the same families. Many of the local leaders abandoned the village to join the armies of the warring barons as they erected their domains after the Ōnin War, while others stayed behind to attend to local government. Although the antecedents of both these types were aristocratic and military, those who were left in the village gradually lost their former prestige. They were separated from the warriors physically; more important, their life-style came to resemble that of the peasantry. All members of the village shared common anxieties over meeting the joint tax responsibility and defending themselves from bandits. All knew the joy of festivals for the patron deity and profited together from bountiful harvests. By the end of the sixteenth century, particularly after Hideyoshi's cadastral survey, the headmen became merely a village elite.[12]

References to councils of elders first began to appear before the Muromachi period and became more frequent toward the middle of the fifteenth century. Permanent bodies had been formed in most areas of the country by the Ōnin War and were an integral part of the village system. Most such groups paid their taxes and met their labor obligations, but a few, especially those that had come under the influence of the militant sects of Buddhism, displayed a remarkable degree of independence from the military class. In some instances, they created leagues *(ikki)* and took up arms against the bakufu, the constables, and their deputies.

The first major rising of this type occurred in 1428 in the province of Ōmi to the east of Kyoto, and the disturbances that it caused spread as far as Sakai. Sporadic outbreaks followed elsewhere and increased in numbers. In 1485 the local leaders of Yamashiro, the capital province, organized into an independent self-defense force, ejected the constable's deputy, and demanded that the Hatakeyama armies leave the area.[13] For almost a decade they controlled the government of the very heart of Japan. At the same time, adherents of the Buddhist True Pure Land sect in Echizen also created free communities that served the cause of their church with such fanatical devotion that they were known as the *Ikkō Ikki* (Single-Directed League). In 1488 they killed the lord of Kaga and set up a government of their own that exercised jurisdiction over the provinces of Kaga, Noto, and Echizen for nearly a century. Among the other prominent Ikkō groupings were those of Saiga in Kii province, to the south of Sakai, and of Nagashima in maritime Ise province. Their chief temple was the Ishiyama Honganji, established in 1496, the headquarters of the True Pure Land sect's farflung "religious monarchy" from 1532 until its fall to Oda Nobunaga in 1580. The site of this temple-fortress was immediately to the north of Sakai, in present-day Osaka, and Sakai made substantial profits by handling contributions from the various Ikkō Ikki to Ishiyama. These revolts are merely the leading examples of a type that was often seen during the Sengoku period.

City Administration

The development of the institutions of autonomy in villages throughout Japan in the late medieval period helps to provide some perspective to the growth of similar structures in cities. The self-governing bodies in both had the same basic characteristics and responsibilities. Councils collected rents, kept order, and sponsored local festivals in cities just as in villages.

In fact, contemporary observers made little distinction of any kind between the two types of communities. Both formed during the same era and, despite the differences in their economic origins, the proprietors must have regarded them in much the same way at the outset.[14] The initial disparity in size was not great, and people were unaccustomed to thinking in terms of cities as opposed to villages. It is natural, therefore, that the administrative techniques applied to one should be applied to the other as well. The lack of distinction in nomenclature is an indication of this. Both were treated as estates and had the same kind of names, such as Sakai Minami no Shō or Hirota no Shō, although the former was emerging as a city while the latter remained isolated on the island of Awaji. Each paid rents that might be collected either by the residents themselves or under the supervision of an official representative of the proprietor. The councils of elders, too, had the same sorts of names whether they controlled villages or cities. In fact, it is only in retrospect that one can see differentiating factors at all. The estates that ultimately developed into cities had relatively larger populations engaged in commerce and industry, while the villages were tied to a largely self-sufficient agricultural economy.

It was hardly necessary for townsmen in Japan to demand autonomy from the ruling classes. They required no special economic advantage or power to secure what was being freely granted as one part of the nationwide streamlining of administration which accompanied the dissolution of the estate system. Indeed, the first instances of self-government in the fourteenth and early fifteenth centuries preceded the full development of the economic strength of cities. The prime reason for giving town dwellers a hand in their own affairs was rent collection, just as it was in the village.

Urban growth, however, introduced certain innovations. Despite the continued presence of farmlands in cities well into the Sengoku period, it became impractical to limit rent assessments to agriculture alone. Accordingly, various new types of rents and taxes appeared to take advantage of the economic base that cities presented. Special levies were applied to lands with numerous houses and to the buildings and residences themselves.[15] These new categories reflected the adjustment of the proprietors to the changed realities of Japanese life brought about by urban development. Moreover, such levies made cities especially profitable to the rulers, because the merchants there were able to pay their rents in money more easily than villages could. The ruling classes, therefore, made positive efforts to extend their protection to towns and to bring them under control.

The mutual desire of townsmen and rulers for the prosperity of trade led to further advances in autonomy. Both wanted to preserve the orderly operation of the markets. The merchant wanted safety for himself and his property, while the ruler knew that his tax collection could only be hindered by criminal disruptions. With the formation of the military domains in the sixteenth century, cooperation became especially pronounced as merchants came to play a leading role in the barons' economic policies, which were designed to increase their capacities for aggressive warfare. Under that arrangement the successful trader was one who could serve the warriors as an effective quartermaster.[16] In the beginning the baron protected commerce himself by issuing regulations prohibiting the carrying of weapons and outlawing forced sales or purchases in the markets, and these were soon extended to apply to the whole town and not simply to the business area. As the commercial class grew, however, the barons found it expedient to relinquish a portion of their legal jurisdiction to the townsmen, who could maintain order for themselves under the supervision of the warriors. One of the earliest of these provisions came late in the fifteenth century, when the Ōuchi allowed the merchants of Akamagaseki to exclude from the town those persons who would not pay their share of a tax. Similar instances appeared in increased numbers through the sixteenth century until the phenomenon of judgment by townsmen (chōnin sabaki) developed.[17]

In addition to assuming these responsibilities in rent collection and the keeping of order, town and village governments customarily undertook to sponsor festivals of the locality's patron shrine or temple. Although this was actually a minor function in comparison with the other two, it was considered one of their more important obligations. The influence of the shrine guilds in the estates was apparent in this religious responsibility.

Self-government in cities was invariably entrusted to councils of elders. Descendants of estate officials, who comprised the councils of the villages, did not emerge into prominence in medieval towns, but an equivalent class did. Those who formed the town councils can be spoken of as a single class only in the most general sense, however, for their origins were somewhat different in each of the several kinds of cities. Servants attached to shrines and temples as handicraft workers became merchants and artisans by the fifteenth century, and those who supervised them, initially as officials, became the foremost residents of the temple towns. The *egō* council of Uji and Yamada outside the Ise Shrines was typical in that it was formed of such functionaries shortly after the Ōnin War. By the middle of the sixteenth century, the leadership can be identified as merchants; they managed the market as a group, independently of the shrines, and were charged with paying fees called *reisen* (literally, "gratitude money") on behalf of the residents.[18] The local magnates of the post towns were much more closely related to village elders as officers of estates. In that position they acted as hosts to travelers, and so gradually transformed themselves into innkeepers, the chief citizens of their towns.

Finally, in port cities such as Sakai the leading citizens were *toimaru*, officials who were originally placed at ports to supervise rent shipments for the estate proprietors.[19] By the fifteenth century, they handled the affairs of more than one patron and accordingly were in fact in business on their own account; to that extent, they were independent of their former connections. As councils of elders organized, the *toimaru* joined them, for they had the prestige that was requisite for membership. In Hakata, Hyōgo, Sakai, and the other ports that engaged in the official missions to Ming China, some of the *toimaru* were able to become foreign traders, and their names are often linked to the councils of their respective cities.

Both in towns and in villages, therefore, it was a generally similar class of the estate system that provided the elders. Although the experience of temple towns did not conform in detail to this pattern, the members of their councils were from the same general level of the officialdom. In the estate system all had served in the lowest ranks of the central institutions as a bridge to the common people. After the old regime collapsed, they continued to act as intermediaries, but were identified as the highest members of the local society .

A basic form characterized all of local self-government. Each area had its own council whose members were from a similar social stratum, and all communities undertook such functions as joint tax collection and the maintenance of public order. Within this general framework, however, there was considerable local variety. The names given to the councils of elders in different cities were quite distinct, and the numbers of the council membership were far from uniform.[20] There also were more significant differences between them than those of names and numbers.

Historians have maintained that a few of the autonomous bodies had a potential for independence from the military class that might have provided an alternative to the "feudalism" of the Edo period. The leagues *(ikki)* seem to have been especially free of outside control, and their expulsion of the bakufu's agents from the territory under the influence of their councils illustrates their capabilities. In general, however, cities were less able to oppose the warriors, for they were more dependent on them for their livelihood. The evolution in the economy that Japan witnessed during the fourteenth and fifteenth centuries brought a measure of geographical specialization and urban-rural differentiation, but the process was far from complete by the Sengoku period. The leagues were still largely self-sufficient and could subsist on the goods they produced on their own lands. By contrast, cities, the chief beneficiaries of commercialization and the growth of the money economy, relied heavily on the custom of the warriors who were the only group that could effectively demand their services. The peasantry who made up the bulk of the population would be drawn into the urban orbit only in the Edo period.

Among cities themselves, however, certain types had greater restrictions than others. The smaller towns that lay clearly within the domain of a single regional hegemon came to assume the functions of his commissariat, and the merchants there became officially sponsored quartermasters. Post towns and periodic markets that had grown up under the supervision of estate officials were completely in the hands of the warriors who succeeded to local power. This was even more characteristic of the castle towns, which owed their very existence to the barons who created them after the middle of the sixteenth century.

Some scholars assert that port cities and temple towns were less obviously under the direct authority of the military class.[21] Temples and shrines as estate proprietors held out against the incursions of the constables longer and more successfully than did their secular counterparts because of their greater manpower and military strength. The cities at their gates borrowed a portion of their might and received their protection. This freed the townsmen from the military class, but it did not confer independence from the religious institutions themselves.

The ports were even less restricted, for they did not have to depend on any single baron or temple to secure their economic base. When they were engaged primarily in the movement of estate rents, both the source and the destination of any given shipment were under the control of one proprietor, but *toimaru* subsequently grew into merchants who would handle freight for any client and between any points. Foreign commerce also became a significant economic factor with the reopening of the Ming tribute missions, placing at least one end of the trade completely outside Japanese jurisdiction.

This should have brought a degree of freedom to the residents of port cities, but Sakai's experience indicates that even foreign trade needed official sponsorship, for the most lucrative source of foreign commerce was that connected with the embassies to Ming China. It is well known that private traders accompanied these missions, but the "official" character of the trade was nevertheless important, since no one could accompany the ambassador without the permission of the bakufu or its representatives. Cities and their residents therefore had to have patrons highly placed in the bakufu. It is noteworthy, for example, that when the Hosokawa family controlled Sakai and also controlled the embassies, Sakai was the site chosen to equip the ships. Hakata, controlled by the Ōuchi, was the site when the latter were dominant.[22] Domestic interdomanial trade might have provided a measure of independence, but it was still too small to support a city of great size.[23] The independence of port and temple towns, therefore, was only relative.

The contention that merchants might have supplied a viable alternative to Tokugawa feudalism or absolutism is further weakened by the nature of their affiliation with the military class. They sought to cultivate no sources of legitimacy other than those available to them through the warriors and the shogunate. Conditions in Europe often made it possible for townsmen to ally themselves with their kings against the local nobility, but Japanese merchants correctly identified the barons as the fountainhead of their prosperity and acted to cement their bonds with them. The relationship was rarely one of confrontation, and more often one which both sides viewed as mutually beneficial. In any case, it would not have been one of contractual obligations, for there was no abstract concept of rights to which the townsmen could have appealed. When Japanese translators of Western works in the Meiji period first faced the ideas expressed in such words as *droit civil* and "rights," they had to create new words as their equivalents, for there were none to be found in the native tradition.[24]

Nobunaga and Hideyoshi are said to have crushed the rights of cities. In fact, their connections with merchants were unusually close, and cities prospered under their rule. Indeed, townsmen adapted to unification with far greater ease than did the Buddhist sects, the peasantry, and many members of the warrior class.

The Egōshū

Sakai has so often been called unique that its representative facets tend to be obscured. The city's population was exceptionally large and affluent in comparison to most of the other towns of sixteenth-century Japan, but through much of its history it developed in a way that was typical of port towns elsewhere. Like Ōtsu or Ōminato, Sakai grew up around *toimaru* and their trade, and like Hakata or Hyōgo, it reached its peak of prosperity by equipping the Ming missions. Its institutions of autonomy, too, had parallels in virtually every town and village of the Sengoku era. An examination of Sakai's council of elders reveals that its membership and functions were far from unusual, and that even in its relationship to the warrior class Sakai did not stand alone.

Several different terms were used in contemporary documents to refer to the council at Sakai, but the earliest and most common was *Egōshū*, literally, "the group that meets together," or simply *Egō*, "meeting together." The origins of the name were probably Buddhist, for the *Tamon'in nikki*, a journal kept by Eishun and other priests of the Kōfukuji in Nara, mentioned on many occasions a group of fifteen clergymen there whose meetings were designated *egō*.[25] The practice as well as the name spread from the temples to the newly arisen cities.

The first specific reference to the council of Sakai was in 1484 in a brief passage of the *Shoken nichiroku*, the diary of the Zen priest Kikō Daishuku.[26] Though it mentioned the Egōshū by name, the note was only tangential, so one cannot know how long the group had been in existence before the entry was made. Nevertheless, Kikō wrote of the Egōshū several other times during his stay in Sakai, and despite the lack of detail in the diary, a reasonably clear picture of the broad outlines emerges. The Egōshū was a local autonomous body that ruled over the residents of the entire city. Though Sakai was still nominally divided into northern and southern estates, the residents regarded the city as a single entity and had only a single council with representatives from both areas. The town hall was probably the Kyōdō in the northern estate, which the diary identified as the meeting place of the commoners *(jige)*.[27] This may have been the council headquarters, though Kikō did not say so specifically. There is some confusion about the exact number of members that were on Sakai's council, because later records referred to the sixteenth-century council as a body of thirty-six. When this journal was written, however, it is clear that there were ten. On three separate dates Kikō noted that figure.[28] This is borne out also by an Edo-period history which mentions a group that leased warehouses by the waterfront and was led by ten men who heard and decided appeals.[29]

One can also infer from the *Shoken nichiroku* that the Egōshū performed some of the same functions that councils undertook elsewhere in Japan. Most immediately apparent was its responsibility for conducting shrine festivals. In fact, the first reference to the council occurs in the account of a celebration for the Mimuragū, the shrine of Sakai's patron deity.[30] The leaders of the festivities were two members of the council. One may imagine from this that Sakai's Egōshū, like other town councils, originated as a shrine guild that directed the worship of the local deity.

City elders customarily carried out the important duty of preserving public order, in addition to honoring the local shrine. The *Shoken nichiroku* portrayed this in Sakai in entries during 1485. In the eighth month the ten members of the Egōshū called on Kikō to report that a disturbance was about to arise in Izumi, and they requested that he use his good offices to have the retainer of the constable put it down. Though he did as he was asked, his efforts were in vain, for during the next three days the vagabonds came and stirred up trouble anyway. Kikō said that at night he was uneasy and had entrusted his personal effects to someone for safekeeping.[31] On this occasion the council did not employ a police force of its own but satisfied its obligations for defense by representing the residents in their approach to the constable for protection by his troops.

Tax collection, another of the primary functions of councils, did not appear in Kikō's diary, but Sakai's experience early in the fifteenth century of assuming a joint obligation for estate rents suggests that the council may have taken on fiscal responsibilities at various times. As a matter of fact, the residents probably did not collect their own rents while Kikō was in residence, for in 1487, a few months after his diary ended, the *Onryōken nichiroku*, an account kept at the Shōkokuji which contains records of Sakai's estate rents, noted that the people of Sakai had expressed a willingness to collect the estate rents, with the implication that they had not been doing so in the immediate past.[32] It is only in the Edo period that one finds unmistakable evidence of this function. It probably began, therefore, at some later, uncertain date.

In terms of economic and social position, the members of the Egōshū were wealthy merchants of high standing in the community.[33] Most of them belonged to families which entered foreign commerce when Sakai first began to equip Ming missions, and so were dependent for their great wealth on their all-important connections with the Hosokawa. These people, who held the administration of the city in their hands, would not be inclined to oppose the military class per se, for the source of their livelihood was a trade which was an integral part of the traditional tribute diplomacy of East Asia. For Japanese to engage in the Ming embassies it was essential, as noted above, to bear the symbols of legitimacy that only the bakufu or its chief retainers could provide. As members of a former official class—even though they had become merchants—they moreover enjoyed a social position which was basically equivalent to that of the warriors who were establishing the military domains of the Sengoku period. Foreign traders from the port cities were able to associate freely with the most powerful warriors as late as Ieyasu's time.

The daily activities of the Egōshū in their operation of the government of Sakai remain a cipher. The details of the installation of new members of the council, their exact powers, the apportionment and collection of taxes, as well as other matters of interest to the historian can only be imagined. Kikō was merely a temporary resident at the Kaieji, and though he came to know a number of the townsmen, he did not become intimately involved in the life of the city. The *Shoken nichiroku* is basically the diary of an outsider. Unfortunately, no other source provides more information about the Egōshū itself until the decade of the 1560s, when Nobunaga rose to power. The supplement to the *Kenmu shikimoku* indicated in 1508 that there was a *myōshu* judicial officer *(satanin)* in Sakai, and this may be interpreted to mean that townsmen sat in judgment over their fellow residents.[34] In 1535 the Nenbutsuji collected one *kanmon* each from several townsmen and listed the donors according to place of residence.[35] The names of the various parts of Sakai suggest that the city was partitioned into administrative subsections, though these may have been only popular designations that had nothing to do with government at all. These two references support the supposition that there was continuity in autonomy during this rather poorly documented period. Moreover, the *Shiranki,* an Edo-period history, also spoke of the Council of Ten as if it had existed throughout the sixteenth century. There may have been changes in it, however, for the later records mentioned a council of thirty-six members.

In any case, there were strong similarities between the Egōshū in Sakai and councils in other cities and villages. In terms of the date of its founding, the number of members and their social backgrounds, and the functions that it carried out, the Egōshū was a typical institution for local self-government in the late medieval period.

Sakai in the Sengoku Wars

Sakai had its full complement of autonomous institutions, and on the basis of the experience of other local areas during the sixteenth century, as well as of scattered references later, one can imagine that self-government continued. Autonomy did not bring independence, however. The military families that exercised control over the general area also made their authority felt in the city itself. Sakai was constantly occupied by a succession of armies until the 1560s, and as the train of military competitors vied for supremacy, the city was embroiled in warfare and made to contribute from its rich coffers to the expenses of the campaigns. The citizens paid military taxes; they knew bloodshed and the sound of troops marching in the streets. Indeed, because of Sakai's importance as a port, it was even more closely governed than most other cities.

During the Sengoku period, local power in Settsu, Kawachi, and Izumi—as in most of the rest of the country—was subject to violent upheavals. The bakufu existed as a shadow government until 1573 and ruled Sakai in name as a direct holding during most of this period, but the shogun was manipulated by powerful official families, including the Hosokawa who controlled the Sakai area until their demise in 1558. By the early sixteenth century, the Hosokawa themselves had become the puppets of their retainers, the Miyoshi, who were in turn ultimately threatened by their own inferior, Matsunaga Hisahide. This situation, described by George Sansom as "fantastic, if not farcical," was characteristic of the age, and produced for Sakai a political scene that was bewildering in its complexity.[36] Sons betrayed fathers, retainers changed sides, and brothers fought in order to gain the legitimacy that rested in the hands of powerless office holders. How did this situation affect Sakai? Let us take a brief look at the changes in the control exercised over the city in the late fifteenth and early sixteenth centuries, when the Hosokawa supplanted the estate proprietors and were themselves in turn replaced by the Miyoshi.[37]

During the Ōnin War Sakai remained securely under the control of the Hosokawa of the Eastern Army and their allies in the Hatakeyama family. In 1477, however, when the fighting moved out of the capital city of Kyoto into the countryside, there began a contest of power that represented, in a sense, the death of the old estate proprietors' ownership of Sakai. Within a dozen years military power completely erased civilian interests there.

After the war was over, Hatakeyama Yoshinari, a former adherent of the Western Army, attacked his brother, the Hosokawa deputy at Sakai, and expelled him from the city. Yoshinari placed his own candidates in each of the Sakai estates, and for five years ruled them in defiance of the bakufu and the Hosokawa, the powers that had legitimate interests there. During that time he had the rents paid directly to him and forwarded only a portion to the Sūjuin, the civilian proprietor.[38] By 1482, however, pressure was evidently mounting against Yoshinari and his position in the city: Abbot Jinson of the Daijōin in Nara noted in his diary the rumors of battles impending over Sakai, and reported that Yoshinari had announced his intention of burning the place to the ground if his brother's troops attempted to recover it.[39] Fortunately, the residents of Sakai were spared that disaster, for a truce and an exchange of lands averted the battle. The result for the city was that it passed once again under Hosokawa control.[40]

Although the late fifteenth century was generally a period of growing prosperity for Sakai, the effect of Yoshinari's illegal occupation of the city and the fighting that accompanied it was to reduce the population by half as the residents took refuge in Hosokawa holdings in Settsu. Yoshinari's deputies used this as an excuse to pay only 400 *kanmon* to the Sūjuin instead of the customary 730, and the Hosokawa continued to pay the lesser amount when they regained Sakai after 1482.[41] But the city had recovered by the latter half of the 1480s, and there was a scramble among the powers of the capital to seize control of the valuable southern estate for the funds that they could obtain from it.

The subsequent maneuvers took the form of political negotiations within the bakufu. By the end of 1486, the Sūjuin, the Hosokawa, and even members of the Hatakeyama family had all entered claims for the proprietorship.[42] The shogunate, in confusion, acted indecisively, so that for some months the issue remained in doubt. Ultimately it decided the matter of proprietorship in its own favor, and made Sakai a direct holding with the shogunal officer for finances as the deputy.[43]

After 1487 Sakai continued to be directly under the shogunate, but it was apparent that the estate system no longer provided a viable means of control. Military power was the key. Within three years the Hosokawa as the warrior masters of Izumi effectively extended their influence over the city even while it remained in name under the bakufu. In 1490 the Hosokawa had one of their retainers appointed deputy of Sakai in place of the shogun's own officer, and he extinguished all claims of the Sūjuin by exchanging another holding for Sakai.[44] As officers of the bakufu, the Hosokawa accomplished this within the legitimate framework of the estate system and did not find it necessary to resort to armed force, but it was significant that the competitors who had no local base of power lost out even as they made plaintive appeals to precedent. The Sūjuin in particular was most reluctant to abandon its rights in Sakai and continued to protest the Hosokawa action, but it steadily fell into decay without regaining its former prestige. The premature death in 1489 of Ashikaga Yoshihisa, the last shogun to attempt to exercise authority on his own, was undoubtedly one of the factors that enabled the Hosokawa to place their own retainers in Sakai, for Yoshihisa's heirs presented no obstacles.

The success of the Hosokawa in gaining undisputed control over Sakai marked the end of centuries of civilian interest in the city through the estate system. For all practical purposes, Sakai remained under the military class from 1490 until the Meiji Restoration of the nineteenth century. The Hosokawa themselves lost out to their retainers, the Miyoshi, within a few years, so it is difficult to ascertain how they administered the city. It is clear, however, that they enjoyed a good relationship with the residents. This aided them in maintaining their position over the city.

The Hosokawa made every effort to cultivate Sakai. Most readily apparent was the action they took to promote the Ming trade and to use Sakai as the port of departure. Other examples that provide some insight into the family's rule there might also be cited. While the Hosokawa were still engaged in maneuvering in the capital to secure rights to the Sakai estates, the shogun authorized them to collect a special tax of two thousand *kanmon* from the city to cover the expenses of a planned military campaign in Ōmi. The residents, however, paid only four hundred. Rather than try to extort the balance from the city, the Hosokawa apparently dropped the matter.[45] The reason may have been that lines of authority in the capital were confused, but it is more likely that the Hosokawa were reluctant to drain the city of so large a sum and wanted to avoid damaging their relations with the inhabitants.

This episode stands in marked contrast with another that occurred a few years later, in 1495. At that time Hatakeyama forces in the Kii Peninsula to the south of Sakai, hostile to the Hosokawa, were sending repeated forays north in a campaign of attrition. On one of these they emerged from their southern lair, burning as they went, and proceeded to Sakai. They demanded from the residents ten thousand *kanmon,* a staggering sum by the standards of the day.[46] Since the alternative was fire, the city paid. The residents had no opportunity to bargain or to reduce the amount as they had done earlier. The Hatakeyama army, in fact, treated them as enemies. If Sakai were ruined, the economic base of the Hosokawa would be weakened to that extent, and the Kii forces would be that much closer to success.

The latter incident also shows the city's inability to defend itself during this period. Sakai stood helpless before the Hatakeyama army. Responsibility for protection against such incursions lay with the Hosokawa and their military allies. At times individual townsmen would take up arms and become warriors, but the city as a whole did not take collective measures for its own defense during the battles of the late fifteenth century.[47]

Despite the Hatakeyama invasion, one may conclude that the Hosokawa were largely successful in developing good relations with Sakai during the years of their ascendancy and thereby helped to assure their control. The head of the family occupied the most influential post in the bakufu and was normally able to extend the benefits of trade and protection to the city. The townsmen, moreover, appeared to reciprocate his efforts. When he visited Sakai in 1506, they presented him with a huge gift of six thousand *kanmon* and gave various smaller amounts to his retainers.[48]

Hosokawa popularity in Sakai, however, did not mean that the family was equally well liked in other parts of its domain. Its principal holdings were in Shikoku, but the head of the family could rarely visit them because of his responsibilities in the capital as *kanrei,* the chief shogunal officer. He was, therefore, unable to maintain the intimate personal contact with his deputies that was necessary for effective control. Like other constables before him, he was destined to fall to his own inferiors. The first overt sign of trouble came in 1504 when a revolt in the family ranks, ostensibly over succession to the family headship, caused the retainers to divide into opposing factions. That event was especially significant for Sakai, because it brought the Miyoshi into the city for the first time.

In 1504 the Miyoshi were the principal Hosokawa retainers in Shikoku. They came to Sakai in support of the head of the house, but they were destined ultimately to wrest the city from their masters and to destroy the Hosokawa line. One of the long-range strategic elements in the Miyoshi drive to power was to secure the port of Sakai for their own use. The harbor facilities in the city were in constant demand by all the armies active in the Home Provinces, but for the Miyoshi they were vital. Since the source of their strength lay in their holdings in Shikoku, maritime communications were not merely a convenience but a necessity, if the Miyoshi were to be able to assert themselves in the military arena on the main island. One of their earliest acts, therefore, was to erect a fortress in Sakai. It was an imposing structure with watchtowers manned by guards on monthly rotation and a full arsenal of weapons. It became the headquarters for smaller forts in the surrounding provinces and protected the Miyoshi supply lines.[49] At first their foothold in Kinki was tenuous, and they had to flee back to Shikoku, but in 1521 Miyoshi Motonaga, the son of the builder of the fortress, returned and ordered the defenses completed. He called it "Mandokoro," a name that indicated its importance as the headquarters of his family.[50]

The fortifications were only one aspect of the establishment of Miyoshi power in Sakai. In general, they tried to exercise much closer control than the Hosokawa had. For one thing, they actually resided there, unlike their predecessors. Though they constantly left to fight battles in various places around the Kinki area, they returned at frequent intervals and were therefore able to maintain their contacts with the residents. While in the city, too, the Miyoshi directed administration more carefully. In 1527, for example, they issued duplicate commands to both Sakai estates setting forth guidelines that they probably intended the Egōshū to carry out. The orders stated that only commoners would be permitted to lodge in Sakai. Disputes were to be avoided, but if they should occur, neighbors and relatives of the participants must report them. Punishments were to be meted out to both sides, regardless of right or wrong. Further provisions warned against forced sales, ordered the death penalty for thieves, and prohibited vagrants and gamblers from operating in the city.[51] Laws such as these and the ability to see that they were enforced were as important as the fortifications in securing Sakai for the Miyoshi.

Indeed, Miyoshi Motonaga must have believed himself secure in Sakai, for the immediate motive for the issuance of his order to the citizens of Sakai was that he had just landed in the city the day before to establish what one scholar has called the "Sakai bakufu."[52] Motonaga was the foremost military power in a coalition that espoused the cause of Ashikaga Yoshitsuna as shogun and Hosokawa Harumoto as *kanrei*. He brought the two and their entourage to Sakai, installed them in the Kenponji, one of the city's temples, and from that site issued orders to the powerful temples of the capital. In point of fact, the "bakufu" changed Sakai hardly at all, since both shogun and *kanrei* were mere puppets of the Miyoshi and powerless to act on their own. Moreover, it soon ended when the coalition which had given it its ephemeral existence fell apart. Harumoto, having fallen out with Motonaga, secured the backing of the Ikkō adherents of the Ishiyama Honganji, and in 1532 they fell on the Kenponji, forcing Motonaga to suicide. For some weeks the sectarians occupied Sakai, until the Miyoshi forces regrouped under new leadership and succeeded in driving them out of the city.[53]

Short as it was, Sakai's experience with its "bakufu" does suggest some significant aspects of the city's relations with the military class during this period. For example, after the advent of the Miyoshi, Sakai was more likely to have its rulers physically present in the city. Previously, they had been aristocrats who lived in the capital, whereas later they did not have such a lofty status. They were more nearly on a social level with the members of the Egōshū. Because they lived in Sakai, they were able to give closer scrutiny to affairs there, and they could have a cordial and mutually beneficial relationship with the leading citizens. The increasing military effectiveness of the Miyoshi, too, meant that the city was better protected. Despite the Ikkō invasion that cost Motonaga his life, the number of such incursions seems to have declined, perhaps because of the availability of protection from the Miyoshi. One incident from the year 1531 is illustrative. In that year word reached the city that an enemy general was approaching with twenty thousand troops. Since many of the Miyoshi forces were temporarily absent from the city, the residents were terrified and shut their gates to await the worst. Within days, however, reinforcements arrived from Shikoku to turn the balance, and the city was saved.[54] In fact, the Ikkō invasion was the only successful one during the early period of Miyoshi ascendancy. These trends toward closer contact between citizens and military—and toward better protection—became even more pronounced in subsequent years under Miyoshi Nagayoshi (popularly known as Chōkei) and Matsunaga Hisahide.

Nagayoshi, Hisahide, and Sakai

The three decades that span the middle of the sixteenth century were a seemingly endless kaleidoscope of battles, suicides, and shifting alliances in the Kinki area. Historians have maintained that the disorder prevented the effective operation of any authority, so that cities during this era achieved their greatest freedom from the interference of the warriors.[55] But in retrospect we can see that this was also a time when certain institutional innovations within the military domains were producing a new order.[56] While the highest classes of warriors were at the mercy of their retainers, strengthened bonds of command undercut the independence of potentially insubordinate inferiors at the lowest ranks, thus making possible the creation of ever larger unified territorial hegemonies. During this period the Miyoshi consolidated their position to such an extent that they were able to oust Hosokawa Harumoto, while Matsunaga Hisahide, the very type of the treacherous retainer who makes his way to the top through the process of *gekokujō*, was preparing to assert himself over the Miyoshi.

Since the men who emerged as leaders of the growing domains were no longer members of the uppermost stratum of warrior society, they had antecedents more nearly like those of the merchants in the cities, and there was increasing evidence of association between the two groups on a footing that approached equality (although complete parity was by no means attained).

In Sakai the chronicles depict members of the Egōshū as mediators between opposing armies and give the merchants credit for fending off hostilities. The townsmen were in constant contact with the warriors not only as their quartermasters but also as their companions in the tea ceremony. A mastery of ceremonial tea was an essential accomplishment of the chief Sakai merchants, and they shared their knowledge with military men, often of several different clans. Hence they were in a position to respond to requests that they serve as go-betweens for hostile armies. The next few decades, then, show the townsmen taking a more active role than what they had played previously.

The principal figure whom the Sakai merchants served during this period was Miyoshi Nagayoshi (Chōkei), who carried the ambitions of his family to the pinnacle of their success. As the eldest of Miyoshi Motonaga's six children, Nagayoshi followed his father in the position of head of the clan. At the time of Motonaga's early death, however, Chōkei was still a child, and as a result he had to spend most of his early life trying to secure his birthright from the threats of his uncle, Masanaga.[57] On coming of age he raised troops in his stronghold in Shikoku in preparation for his emergence into Kyoto politics, and in 1539 he marched there at the head of an army. He did not have the strength to confront his enemies immediately, however, so he quickly accepted the good offices of the Rokkaku family of Ōmi province and placed his arms at the disposal of Hosokawa Harumoto and Masanaga, the very persons who had been responsible for his father's death. His first duty in their service was to give battle to Hosokawa Ujitsuna, a rival claimant for Harumoto's post in the bakufu. By 1543 the campaign led him into Sakai. In a battle there he expelled Ujitsuna from the city and placed his own retainers over it.

The venture brought Nagayoshi into personal contact with the city that his forebears had made their home on the main island, and it was to become one of the keystones of the power structure that he was attempting to erect. He was less successful than many of his contemporaries in recruiting local warriors into his army. He tried to coerce them into his service as retainers to form subordinate units for local rule, but that method meant that disaffection was a constant threat.[58] This necessitated his employing a variety of other means to compensate for the weakness. His original base in Awa on Shikoku remained important to him, and the legitimacy that he derived from the bakufu through Hosokawa Harumoto was a second element in the early years, for he remained nominally a Hosokawa retainer and acted in their name. The addition of Sakai to his sphere proved to be equally valuable. Any deficiencies in his financial arrangements could be covered easily by recourse to impositions on the merchants. He could acquire military supplies there as well. Although Nagayoshi did not take up permanent residence in the city, he left a younger brother, Sogō Kazunari, in charge. Since Kazunari and two other brothers were his most trusted retainers, this action is a clear sign of Chōkei's desire to ensure that the city would not be lost to him.

If Sakai was a treasure chest for the Miyoshi, the Miyoshi also promised to be profitable to the merchants, and each of the two groups sought to cultivate the other. Their mutual involvement is best revealed in their practice of the arts. Modern students of Japan tend to think of the aesthetic values of townsmen as being quite different from those of the military class, on account of the distinctive cultural milieu that developed in the cities of the Edo period. In the sixteenth century, however, *renga* (linked verse), the tea ceremony, and the other arts that were held in highest esteem were enjoyed by both townsmen and military men alike. Indeed, the warriors often accepted the invitations of townsmen and in turn invited them as guests to poetry meetings and tea ceremonies. The latter in particular were most intimately associated with Sakai.

During the ascendancy of Miyoshi Nagayoshi, the foremost tea master in Japan was Takeno Jōō. He is best known today as the teacher of Sen no Rikyū, the greatest of all masters and founder of the modern schools of the tea ceremony. Jōō, like his more famous student, was a native of Sakai, and he epitomized the merchants' relationship with the Miyoshi. He earned his living directly from the warrior class, for he was a supplier of armor.[59] It was to his advantage, therefore, to be on the best of terms with the Miyoshi. Nagayoshi himself preferred poetry to tea as a pastime; as Donald Keene shows elsewhere in this volume, he was one of the patrons of Satomura Jōha, the leading *renga* master of the day. His younger brothers, however, sat at Jōō's feet on numerous occasions. Through him they formed an acquaintance with other Sakai merchants, including those who were members of the Egōshū. Tsuda Sōtatsu and his son Sōgyū, who belonged to Sakai's wealthy Tennōjiya family, and Imai Sōkyū were all participants at these sessions; while Jōō was the leading light, these were the subordinate luminaries of the tea world. Their several roles as tea masters, as merchants, and as Egōshū members were in fact inseparable, for after they had taken tea they commonly discussed matters of business and cemented their ties to the Miyoshi. Tennōjiya and Imai even traveled to the Miyoshi stronghold in Awa on Shikoku.[60]

Such connections were sufficiently strong to encourage the townsmen to take extraordinary measures when necessary in defense of the Miyoshi interests. In 1546 Hosokawa Ujitsuna conspired once again to oust Harumoto. The latter learned of his plans and dispatched Nagayoshi to Sakai to counter him. As Ujitsuna's army approached the city, however, it became apparent that he had overwhelming numerical superiority and would surely defeat Miyoshi. The Egōshū took the initiative and negotiated with Ujitsuna's generals so that Nagayoshi would have a chance to escape. He withdrew and almost immediately received reinforcements from his brothers in Shikoku, so that he was able to continue the fight.[61] One of the reasons for the success of the negotiations was that advantages were offered to Uji-tsuna's forces beyond the consideration that troops' lives would be saved. A bloodless invasion meant that the city would be preserved intact and protected from rapine, so that the new rulers could begin immediately to requisition funds from it for their own purposes. Right after arrival, the invading army issued an order prohibiting its soldiery from unruly behavior and exempting at least one of the city's major temples from the need to quarter troops within its precincts. A second edict the following month outlawed the importation of saké into either North or South Sakai.[62] These measures give us a glimpse of some of the standard tactics of the generals of the day, all of whom actively pursued the economic side of warfare as well as the military. In this instance the policies were abortive, for with his reinforcements Nagayoshi was able to recover the city within a few short weeks. Except for one brief incursion into the northern estate in 1549, he held Sakai and made it safe from attack until his death in 1564.

Nagayoshi's subsequent career made him the most powerful man in the bakufu. In 1548 he turned against his uncle and rival, Masa-naga, and destroyed him, relying in the process on an alliance with Hosokawa Ujitsuna. This in turn alienated Harumoto, but by 1558 Chōkei made him his prisoner and tied his own strings to the puppet shogun, Yoshiteru. Unfortunately for Chōkei, position in the bakufu had only ornamental value by the time he attained it. Worse, Naga-yoshi had neglected more meaningful institutions, such as a strong warrior band, and had depended too heavily on the aid of his brothers. He was, therefore, exceedingly vulnerable to treachery by ambitious subordinates. One such retainer was Matsunaga Hisahide, and it is he to whom we must turn in order to discover the nature of Sakai's further relations with the warriors of the Kinki area in the last years before Nobunaga come to power.

Hisahide was the very model of the *gekokujō* period's warrior, in the sense that he rose to high rank from obscure origins and usurped the powers of his lord. His name was mentioned for the first time among Miyoshi retainers in 1541, and by the 1550s Nagayoshi was entrusting him with such key responsibilities as the governance of Kyoto. Since Nagayoshi exercised his authority over the Kinki area al-most exclusively through his three brothers, he stood to become com-pletely isolated should he lose their support. This did in fact begin to happen with the death of his brothers Kazunari in 1561 and Jikkyū in 1562. The process was concluded with the murder of the third brother, Atagi Fuyuyasu, in the fifth month of 1564, eight months after the mysterious demise of Nagayoshi's son and heir Yoshioki. It was rumored that Hisahide had arranged both deaths: that he had administered poison to Yoshioki and further looked after his welfare by insinuating that Fuyuyasu had treasonous intentions and thus inciting Chōkei to have his own brother killed. In any event, it is clear that by the time Nagayoshi himself died in the seventh month of 1564, Hisahide had already arranged to deprive him of the substance of his control and to take over, virtually without change in the administrative structure.[63]

Although he had made himself master of Nagayoshi's domains in most respects, Hisahide was unable to secure exclusive powers in Sakai. He did not take up residence in the city as the Miyoshi had done, but habitually lived instead in Shigisanjō or Tamonjō, his two castles in Yamato province. From these bastions he led his armies in campaigns all over the Home Provinces. He had, moreover, to share Sakai with the Miyoshi Triumvirs (Sanninshū), namely Iwanari Tomomichi, Miyoshi Nagayuki, and Miyoshi Masayasu. The Triumvirs constituted a regency for Miyoshi Yoshitsugu, whom Nagayoshi had adopted as his heir after the death of his son Yoshioki. Hence they could claim that by acting in the name of Yoshitsugu they were the legitimate executors of the Miyoshi estate and as such had powers in Sakai.

Hisahide and the Triumvirs did not immediately fall upon one another as one might have expected but worked together for a time, for Hisahide also held Yoshitsugu as his lord. Their most notable cooperative venture came in the fifth month of 1565, when they attacked Shogun Yoshiteru and drove him to suicide so that they could set up Ashikaga Yoshihide in his place. By the eleventh month of that same year, however, the Triumvirs had taken Yoshitsugu under their own control and declared war on Hisahide.

The ensuing conflict centered in its early stages on Sakai, for it lay in the path of the contending forces. They met in their first great battle in 1566 in Kawachi, just outside the city. The Miyoshi were victorious and took the heads of 463 of Hisahide's allies, as the survivors among the vanquished fled to Sakai for refuge.[64] Three months later Hisahide himself left Tamonjō and tried to capture Triumvir castles in Kawachi; but he, too, encountered defeat and had to seek safety in the city. The forces of the Triumvirs pressed their advantage and pursued him there. They had fifteen thousand troops, while Hisahide's army numbered no more than six thousand. Moreover, they blocked all routes of egress, so that victory seemed within their grasp. The price of the destruction of Hisahide, however, was the leveling of Sakai, for the city would surely be burned in the event of fighting in its streets. For that reason the Egōshū once again stepped in to act as mediators. The agreement that resulted made the Miyoshi Triumvirs the victors and allowed them to enter the city after Hisahide's men had returned to their forts.[65]

If one ignores the embellishments of subsequent chroniclers, the records of these two encounters are brief in the extreme, but they do allude to the nature of Sakai's relationship with Hisahide and the Triumvirs. The Egōshū had free access to both sides in the dispute and could serve as negotiators, as they had done in 1546. As before, the tea ceremony gave them an important entrée. Hisahide was an even more ardent devotee of tea than the Miyoshi, and his collection of tea implements was widely known. One of his utensils, named Tsukumogami, even attracted the attention of the Europeans of the day.[66] Moreover, Hisahide and the Miyoshi Triumvirs as well were frequently mentioned as hosts and guests in the tea diaries of Sakai merchants; both sides must have had partisans whose livelihood depended on their custom.[67]

Despite their close relations with individual citizens, neither side had a permanent establishment in the city. During most of the century, the Miyoshi family head had either lived there or had had his deputies in residence; but in the 1560s the role of the council in keeping order must have become especially important. Conditions in the city in this decade are somewhat better documented than any since the days when Kikō wrote his *Shoken nichiroku*, because several European Jesuits visited Sakai and wrote accounts of it.[68] One of them, Luis Frois, was present during the conflicts of 1566. He wrote that the battles took place outside the city. Although he made them appear more bloody than the Japanese sources did, he reported that the city itself was completely undisturbed and that victor and vanquished could walk the streets together in peace. According to this observer, five paces outside the walls enemies would fall upon one another in mortal combat, but inside they carefully observed the proprieties of polite conduct.[69]

Frois did not mention the Egōshū in this connection, nor did he speak of any general mobilization of the populace for their own defense. Elsewhere, however, he and his confreres did describe how the city maintained public order. For example, Gaspar Vilela explained that, with war preventing him from returning to Kyoto, he remained in Sakai because it was safe even while the provinces were embroiled in fighting. The city, Vilela felt, was unassailable because it was washed on the west by the sea and girded on the other sides by deep moats that were always kept full of water. Internal tumults and quarrels were likewise unheard of, for the streets had gates with guards who would close them at once in case of need. Offenders, therefore, had no avenue of escape, for local officials would apprehend them immediately and bring them to trial.[70]

The organ responsible for the routine policing of the city was undoubtedly the Egōshū. The custom of placing residents of cities and villages in charge of their own administration of daily affairs was well established by that time. Hisahide and the Triumvirs, each claiming jurisdiction over Sakai, could confidently expect such matters to be handled efficiently by the residents themselves.[71] What seemed more remarkable to the Jesuits than internal order, however, was Sakai's apparent immunity from external attack. They noted on several occasions how much more peaceful it was than the surrounding countryside, and at one time Vilela even reported that it had never been destroyed.[72] In seeing the physical defenses as the chief factor in the city's security they were wide of the mark. They failed to understand the community of interest that had grown up between Sakai and those members of the warrior class who were attempting to control the Kinki area. The warriors continued to provide defense from outside aggression; the council had an opportunity to act only when they could offer their good offices. They might have been able to marshal some effective means of physical defense against massive attack apart from that provided by the Miyoshi and Hisahide, but such means were hardly necessary. What is perhaps most significant about the Jesuit letters in this connection is that they fail to report any defensive preparations, even when great armies were drawn up about the gates.

Sakai did not, however, have an understanding with all the barons who were carving out domains in the outlying areas. The city's immunity was valid only so long as the Miyoshi and Hisahide were prepared to guarantee it. When an outside power that had little stake in the city's prosperity threatened to invade it, Sakai stood as defenseless as any other town. Indeed, only two years later, in 1568, the city was unable to stand alone against the demands of Oda Nobunaga.

Oda Nobunaga

While Hisahide and the Miyoshi Triumvirs were maneuvering for position against each other in the Kinki area, a small territorial chieftain named Oda Nobunaga was forging through luck and skill what was to become the most powerful domain in Japan. Although still a relatively obscure figure away from the capital in the province of Owari, he had by the end of 1565 attracted the attention of Emperor Ōgimachi and the shogunal pretender Ashikaga Yoshiaki, the murdered Yoshiteru's brother. Each for his own reasons desired Nobunaga's support—the one to secure the return of some imperial property, the other to prosecute his case for the shogunal title. Receiving repeated imperial approbation and acting in the cause of Yoshiaki, Nobunaga entered Kyoto and the national political arena for the first time in the ninth month of 1568.[73]

Nobunaga was a mere upstart to Hisahide and the Miyoshi, who had served in the highest positions in the capital; but his army, drawn from four provinces, was sufficiently large to command their respect. Accordingly, Hisahide promptly submitted and sent his famed Tsukumogami as a token of his good faith.[74] In return he was confirmed in his holding of Yamato province. The Miyoshi Triumvirs, by contrast, simply withdrew. They had supported Yoshihide as shogun in opposition to Nobunaga's candidate Yoshiaki, and though Yoshihide had just died, they were not yet on good terms with his competitor. Neither side offered resistance to Nobunaga's entry into Kyoto.

As soon as he had ensconced himself there, Nobunaga began to take advantage of his new social prestige and strategic position in the capital by demanding contributions to his war chest from the cities and temples of the Home Provinces. He levied a tax of one hundred and fifty pieces of silver on the Hōryūji and five thousand on the Ishiyama Honganji, and from Sakai he called for twenty thousand *kan*. The others paid, but the residents of Sakai regarded the exorbitant sum as ruinous and refused. For the first time the city was forced to take steps to defend itself. According to the *Nisen bunryū ki*, the townsmen raised towers, deepened moats, and planted obstacles at the northern entrances of the city.[75] At the same time the Egōshū sent a messenger to the elders of the town of Hirano, north of Sakai, and urged them to join in an alliance against Nobunaga.[76]

Although the townsmen did not know it yet, Nobunaga was more than a marauder bent on booty and destruction. As George Elison shows in the next chapter, he had the ambition to create his own new order, the *Tenka*—a realm designed to spread over all Japan. For this reason he probably would not have burned Sakai. Like the Miyoshi before him, he wanted to avail himself of the city's riches. He did not take any immediate action to punish the residents for their failure to cooperate but withdrew his troops from Kyoto and returned to his base at Gifu.

Just at this same time the Miyoshi were regrouping their forces for another attempt on the capital, and they chose Sakai as their marshaling center on the main island. Soon after New Year's day of Eiroku 12 (1569), the Triumvirs invaded Kyoto and surrounded the new shogun Yoshiaki in his quarters at the Honkokuji. Nobunaga's allies rebuffed the Triumvirs, who fled to Awa, but when word of their incursion reached Nobunaga, he was enraged.[77]

A share of culpability in the incident was imputed to Sakai. Nobunaga sent emissaries to the city to accuse the townsmen of abetting the Awa army's invasion: they were to be punished for their part in the affair. The citizens trembled before this warlord's wrath and moved their goods to neighboring towns.[78] The tea master Tsuda Sōgyū noted that Sakai had been in turmoil since the Triumvirs had lost their battle with the shogun's troops; the residents had deepened the moats, erected towers, and moved their belongings and their women and children to Osaka and Hirano.[79]

In effect, the residents of Sakai were the victims of their own miscalculation. Having had every reason to expect that the Miyoshi would be able to deal with Nobunaga handily, they refused to accede to his demands for funds and supported the Triumvirs, who—they hoped—would soon put the upstart in his place. At first they were contemptuous; now, unhappily, they were naked before him.

It is probable that the council of Sakai was not unanimous in its decision to resist. There is not enough evidence to discover the existence of factions among the townsmen, but there is reason to suppose that one man, at least, took it upon himself to cultivate Nobunaga. Perhaps he had been a partisan of Hisahide's against the Triumvirs and merely followed Hisahide's example when he surrendered to Nobunaga. That man was Imai Sōkyū, a wealthy merchant and tea master identified in Edo-period records as a member of the council. At the same time that Hisahide submitted to Nobunaga, Sōkyū called on the latter and presented him with two famous tea treasures, Matsushima no Tsubo and Jōō no Nasu.[80] Even as the other residents of Sakai were deepening their moats, Sōkyū was ingratiating himself with Nobunaga.

The tea master may have persuaded his fellow council members that Nobunaga was the future ruler of Japan and that resistance would be both unwise and futile. If so, his argument was surely made convincing by the fact that the Miyoshi Triumvirs had failed to provide any protection. In any event, the determination of the Egōshū collapsed. They agreed to meet the imposition of twenty thousand *kan* and apologized for their recalcitrance. Further, they swore not to employ *rōnin* (masterless samurai) or to ally with the Miyoshi again.[81] The city's connection with the Miyoshi effectively ended, and it became a direct holding, first of Nobunaga, and then of the other central military figures until the Meiji Restoration.

For historians who view the capitulation as the death knell of a free city, the event is a tragedy. In Sakai itself, the episode soon passed, and new ties formed with Nobunaga. Not surprisingly, Imai Sōkyū fared well. Nobunaga ensconced him on the outskirts of Sakai, where he manufactured arms for his patron's troops, and from which he served as deputy in the northern part of the city. In the southern part, Matsui Yūkan, an Oda retainer of merchant background, was installed in the old Miyoshi Mandokoro.[82] Under this new regime the previous pattern of threats by hostile armies and their abrupt demands for cash stopped. Equally important for the city's prosperity, the merchants forged new links upward to Nobunaga through commerce and the tea ceremony and became active participants in the wars of unification.

GEORGE ELISON

The Cross and the Sword:
Patterns of Momoyama History

Ever since the advent of the Taikō Hideyoshi, gold and silver have gushed forth from the mountains and from the plains in the lands of Japan. Moreover, silks and damasks, crapes and golden brocades, from Korea, from Ryūkyū, and from South Barbary, as well as all the famous products that there are in China and India [have come to abound here]; men vie with each other in presenting ever new and rarer things to His Highness, so that it has been like piling up mountains of treasure. In the old days, no one as much as laid an eye on gold. But in this age, there are none even among peasants and rustics, no matter how humble, who have not handled gold and silver aplenty. Our Empire enjoys peace and prosperity; on the roads not one beggar nor outcast is to be seen, all on account of the Taikō Hideyoshi's devotion to acts of compassion and mercy. By his deeds you shall know the quality of a prince! His power and glory made his a blessed reign.

This vision of a golden age invokes the opulent spirit of Momoyama Japan with an enthusiasm akin to wonder.[1] Its author, Ōta Gyūichi, was the era's foremost chronicler; but his radiant imagery was surpassed by at least one of his contemporaries. Writing under the date 1614, Miura Jōshin proclaimed that it was the "Age of Maitreya" in which he lived. "What a marvelous age! Even peasants like me enjoy tranquillity and happiness, and there are wonderful things to be heard and seen. . . . In this age, humans have escaped from that Burning House, life in the Three Realms Without Peace; they dwell in the land of bliss. If this is not a Buddha-World, then how is it that I and other men could meet with such great fortune?"[2]

It would be intemperate to suggest that Momoyama Japan was populated exclusively by optimists or that Gyūichi's and Jōshin's exclamations of joy represent the spontaneous consensus of the age. Moreover, these statements emanate from a material sense of relief;

they contain none of that proud delight in a new life of the mind which motivated European humanists such as Ulrich von Hutten when he declared, "What a century! What studies! It is a joy to be alive!" Yet there is present in these Japanese authors that same essential consciousness of a process of renewal which informed so many of the European writers of the Renaissance.[3] Gyūichi's and Jōshin's phrases are both hyperbolic and naive, but we may trust their general perception. The Momoyama period meant a type of renascence for Japan; it marked the departure from the perturbed state of the Middle Ages. In order to appreciate more fully their images of regeneration—for we must remember that Maitreya is the Savior Buddha who appears in this world after a long period of decline—and in order to understand their slogans of revival, we ought to take at least a brief look at the epoch which preceded Momoyama: Sengoku, when Japan was a Country at War.

After the middle of the fifteenth century, when the Ashikaga shogunate began slipping into a long and unstoppable debility, Japan entered a period of political fragmentation, and was transformed into a congeries of contenders for power. The downfall of the legitimate order was signaled by the immensely destructive Ōnin War, which broke out in 1467 and continued for a decade, embroiling the paladins of the shogunate in savage struggle and devastating the capital city of Kyoto. The shogun Yoshimasa abandoned his office in the middle of the great war, choosing instead the life of an aesthete. "I have grown weary," he said, "because the state of the world is total lawlessness."[4] The abdicated ruler's words are echoed by those historians who characterize the century after the Ōnin War as the age of gekokujō, a topsyturvy in which even the base servant could "through his talents, industry, or fortune" come out on top by ruining his master.[5] Such descriptions may be misleading, because the colorful phrases obscure the fact that solid new structures were developing in the midst of seeming chaos. Moreover, the disarray of the body politic did not mean the disruption of lines of cultural continuity. Nevertheless, the paramount significance of Sengoku is that it was an age of change: in all of Japanese history, it is rivaled as such only by the Bakumatsu-Meiji "Restoration" period. Sengoku was an immense release of energy, a vortex (as one distinguished commentator puts it) of "raging storms and angry billows."[6] The breakdown of the political and the social order—indeed, of the heretofore accepted norms of life—was so severe and appeared so complete that contemporary accounts are full of images of anarchy.

The famous Sengoku general Asakura Sōteki Norikage observed that ruthlessness dominated over his era: "The warrior doesn't care if he's called a dog or a beast; the main thing is winning." The great Jesuit missionary João Rodrigues Tçuzzu found his apt phrase in Juvenal: "Let wilfulness take the place of reason."[7] Other Jesuits of the Japan mission, such as Luis Frois and Alexandro Valignano, painted one scene of horror after another. To be sure, their intention was to curse (or to redeem) the sins of a people who were "pulled asunder by wars," who tormented each other "with continuous carnage" and butchered each other "with total impunity" *because* they were not governed by the restraints of Christian morality; hence rhetoric runs rampant over analysis in much of what they have to say. But when Valignano, for instance, speaks of a country whose princes "promiscuously defraud and deceive each other in turn, with artifice, fraud, and stratagem everywhere dominant," the force of his message is inescapable: it gives us the image of a Machiavellian world.[8] So let us for a moment refer to the words of the Master himself; for in his "Exhortation to liberate Italy from the barbarians" he utters the same sort of wishful prophecy that Ōta Gyūichi and Miura Jōshin thought they had seen fulfilled in their own day in Japan.

In the final passage of *The Prince,* Machiavelli calls upon a savior to arise and restore his country to its former unity and glory. "And I cannot express," he says, "with what love he would be welcomed in all those provinces which have suffered from these . . . inundations, with what thirst for vengeance, with what resolute loyalty, with what devotion and tears. What doors would be closed to him? What people would deny him their obedience? What envy would stand in his way? What Italian would refuse him allegiance?"[9] Or, to transpose this vision into Japanese terms: Who can resist the saving power of Maitreya?

Although in Italy Machiavelli's exhortation went unheeded, it was Japan's fate to be delivered by Machiavellian princes. And those who rejoiced over the unifier's coming never dreamt to what sort of regime they would be subjected.

What sort of man is the Machiavellian prince? In a truly striking word-picture, Federico Chabod describes him as "the new man" who steps onto the stage of history as

a solitary figure, ruthless, thoughtful, inscrutable, epitomizing in himself the life of the whole State. For now all other voices are silent. The people have become a scattered mob. . . . The nobility . . . is no longer united as

a class. . . . . It is a heterogeneous amalgam of individuals who wish to op-
press the people (yet are incapable of doing so) in a way in which the people
are unwilling to be oppressed, though they lack the energy to defend themselves unaided. Plebs and *Grandi* alike dissipate their energies in petty, cal-
culating trickery, in desultory strife devoid of any serious plan or purpose, or
even of the individual grandeur of personal heroism. The material is there,
waiting supinely for the advent of the "virtuous" prince. . . . The manna is
about to fall from heaven; and men await it with open beaks.[10]

The manna, however, falls in unforeseen ways. The prince is
meant to establish a new order in his society: although he must not
neglect ancestral institutions, he must "adapt policy to events"[11] and
be relentlessly pragmatic; if he does not obtain the goodwill of a conquered territory's inhabitants, he must extirpate discontents by terror.[12] "Indeed, there is no surer way of keeping possession than by
devastation."[13] For, in the final analysis, the destruction of traditional social modes is the new prince's only surety.

To grasp the opportunity when it appears—that is greatness. The
princes who founded new orders "do not seem to have had from fortune anything other than opportunity. Fortune, as it were, provided
the matter but they gave it its form; without opportunity their prowess would have been extinguished, and without such prowess the opportunity would have come in vain."[14] The prince's ultimate reliance
is his own prowess—that energetic and decisive concentration of
human powers which Machiavelli calls *virtù*—and the means he
chooses to attain his purpose are governed solely by the consideration
of what is politic and effective.

Early Modern Japan was not built by individual prowess alone; but
its historical substance for better or for worse bears the stamp imposed on it by resolute hegemons. The men who presided over
Japan's reconstitution in those few exciting decades, the Momoyama
era, met the standards which Machiavelli set for the ideal unifier. The
"Three Heroes" who occupied the center stage of Momoyama were
possessed of the kind of virtue which Machiavelli valued above all;
and it may be ironical to note that two of them in the end were vic-
timized by *virtù*'s antithesis, mysterious *fortuna*, or—as their Japanese contemporaries put it—*Tentō*, the Way of Heaven.

When treason put an end to his life, Oda Nobunaga was well on
his way to accomplishing for Japan the role which Machiavelli would
so dearly have reserved in Italy for his model Cesare Borgia, that perfect *chevalier sans peur et sans remords* whose ruin he attributed to

fortune. Toyotomi Hideyoshi incarnated Machiavelli's ideal of a prince combining the qualities of the fox and the lion, but he was not fated to safeguard his heritage for posterity. Those qualities were also abundantly present in Tokugawa Ieyasu, the legendary "Old Badger" *(tanuki oyaji)*, whose "great campaigns and striking demonstrations of his personal abilities"[15] surely made him the equal of another of Machiavelli's models, Ferdinand of Aragon, the founder of the modern Spanish state—especially if we view Ieyasu as the spiritual father of a Japanese Inquisition, in which the objects of scrutiny were, however, Christians.

That most perceptive of all the contemporary Western observers of Momoyama Japan, the Jesuit João Rodrigues Tçuzzu, in reviewing the deeds of the "Three Heroes" lists as the first of their accomplishments the fact that the country "was completely united under one sole leader and was peaceful and quiet; until then it had been completely divided." To him, the Momoyama period represents a *return to normalcy* in Japanese history, and that indeed is the period's prime and determinant characteristic. Rodrigues does not fail to list the epoch's *novelties,* however; indeed, the fifteenth and last item in his summary estimate of the era reads in part: "Japan has been completely renovated and is almost a different nation from of old, even as regards ceremonies and customs."[16] That, too, is a salient characteristic of the period. The return to political normalcy (or, to be more precise, the restitution of a stable political order) combined with the introduction of cultural novelty makes up the essential Momoyama ambivalence. We are presented with a dazzling kaleidoscope: for the brief period of forty years, a series of entirely new cultural elements, some of them never again to be repeated, fell into place, composing the Momoyama spectacle. Let us refer once more to Miura Jōshin's vision of Maitreya. It is an apocalyptic notion. For once, history is seen not as decline but as revival; it is the realization of popular hopes; and in that vision, novelties are within the realm of the expected. For when Maitreya signals his appearance, then naturally prodigies and wonderful signs and marvels are to be seen.[17]

What were some of these novelties? The unique characteristics of the Momoyama culture were, first and foremost, its incomparable grand scale; its luxury if not extravagance; and the presence of an overtly exotic element in Japan. These characteristics reflect the following historical conditions of the age: (1) the reunification of Japan by three heroic and grandiose hegemons; (2) the development of a mining technology which made precious metals "gush forth from the mountains and from the plains throughout the lands of Japan,'' the boom in the commercial economy, and the development of rich urban centers, in particular the revival of the ancient city of Kyoto; (3) the vast expansion of Japan's geographical horizon.

In many ways, the last of these three factors is the most fascinating. For once, there is a genuine international dimension in a period of Japanese history. This cosmopolitan aspect is caused by the presence of Portuguese traders and by the activity of Catholic missionaries. The merchants were drawn by Japan's abundance of silver and fueled the period's luxurious tastes by the importation of ''all the famous products that there are in China and India.'' The priests were attracted by the talents of a people they considered in most respects equal or even superior to Europeans; they were driven by the ambition to make this people Christian. It is therefore possible to say that the Momoyama period coincided with the presence of the ''Southern Barbarians'' and the growth of a Japanese Christianity. The definitive full stop was set to this epoch when the international dimension was destroyed—when the missionaries were eliminated, the Portuguese expelled, and the Christians exterminated by the policy of Sakoku, which made of Japan a Closed Country.

As we consider this set of historical circumstances, we detect yet another series of ambivalences. The reunification was accomplished by raw power, but there were careful and conscious attempts to dress its process in the legality of precedent, most notably on the part of Hideyoshi—a parvenu if there ever was one—who tried to mask his dubious ancestry by legends of a provenance from the loftiest of lineages and by the actual assimilation of his style of government into the hallowed traditional modes of the imperial court.[18] The commercial boom was not accompanied by the development of free cities of the European type, as indeed Dixon Morris has just told us. Finally—and most important to us—the international aspect of Momoyama history contains an interesting paradox or two. Japanese policy made a full circle during the century after 1543, the birthyear of Ieyasu, the last of the ''Three Heroes'':[19]

a. Receptivity to contacts with Europeans after the first appearance of the Portuguese traders that year
b. Seeming encouragement of the Jesuit missionaries in the time of Nobunaga
c. Continuation of the Portuguese trade, but also the issuance of

decrees banning the missionaries, and the first bloody martyrdom of Christians in the time of Hideyoshi

d. Far-flung overseas trade by Japanese in officially sanctioned "vermilion-seal ships" *(shuinsen),* beginning under Hideyoshi

e. Invasion of the mainland of Asia in 1592, followed by withdrawal after Hideyoshi's death in 1598

f. General persecution of Christianity from 1614, in the time of Ieyasu

g. Total prohibition of Japanese travel abroad in the 1630s, and finally the expulsion of the Portuguese and the coming of Sakoku, national isolation, in 1639

In viewing the Momoyama scene, we may admire its cosmopolitan appearance, its expansive nature, and its grand scale; but we must not fail to note that these are transient elements. The seemingly wide open doors toward the outside in fact are on the verge of closing. For a historical moment they stay ajar, only to slam shut on account of internal pressures. Social and ideological structures arise within Japan which cannot tolerate free intercourse with foreign nations.

What years determine the limits of the Momoyama era?[20] If we take the strict nominalist point of view—that is, if we specify the period when the Japanese cultural scene had its focus in Hideyoshi's palatial castle at Momoyama in Fushimi—we come up with the remarkably short time span of 1594 to 1598. (Strictly speaking, the name itself is a misnomer, for the site of that castle was not called Momoyama until after the period had passed.) We obviously must expand our scope; and, indeed, the period is more properly called Azuchi-Momoyama, to encompass the epoch not only of Hideyoshi but also of Nobunaga, the prime mover of the reunification of Japan. To be sure, we ought to avoid what may be called the Procrustean fallacy: trying to make a complex of cultural history coincide with a schema of political history. Nevertheless, it is true that the great castles built by these two hegemons in their ascent to power and glory—Nobunaga's Azuchi Castle, and Hideyoshi's pleasure domes of Osaka, Juraku in Kyoto, and Momoyama—are at the same time representative of their cultural aspirations and their patronage of the arts. These men of power were also ravenous connoisseurs of artistry. In their residential castles we therefore find the best symbols of the period's tastes. Hence it is appropriate to set the period's dates between 1576, when Nobunaga built the castle of Azuchi, and 1615, when

Osaka Castle (and with it Hideyoshi's heritage) was destroyed. Tokugawa Ieyasu's Edo Castle is the visible sign of another era.

What we call the Momoyama culture—that is to say, the formal artistic developments of the period—was an elitist culture. It was centered in western Japan, particularly in the Kyoto-Osaka-Sakai triangle. It continued at least as long as there existed a political center to support it, and that was present in Osaka until Ieyasu liquidated the last vestiges of the Toyotomi regime in 1615. It is true that the afterglow of Momoyama continued into the 1630s, but the fall of Osaka truly signalled the end of the epoch. The focus of artistic creativity gradually shifted eastward to Edo, and the subsequent cultural flowering was largely the product of the townsman class.

One of the special characteristics of Momoyama was the use of art as a cachet of power. Although luxury was not the sole, nor even the most important, feature of the period's taste—for we must remember that another ambivalent aspect of Momoyama was the coexistence of ostentation with restraint, of golden dazzle with studied rusticity—and although we therefore must not concentrate exclusively on the factor of gaudy display as the hallmark of the epoch, we cannot deny that it was there. What was the seedbed of this opulence? Some commentators have sought it among rich merchants and enterprising bourgeois (upper-level *machishū*);[21] but it would be more accurate to say that the period's artistic abundance was called into being by the ardent desire for distinction on the part of autocrats, parvenus, and the newly rich. It was a novel sort of aristocracy that sought to bolster their acquired status with artistic glitter; hence the most striking aspect of the era's artistic product is the elaborate ornamentation of the lords' residences and of the religious shrines they patronized. And, above all, the splendor of their castles.

In contrast with the unprepossessing forts of the previous age, the Momoyama period's castles soar to the heavens.[22] One of the obvious reasons for their grand scale was the introduction of firearms,[23] which made necessary more extensive fortifications than had been needed in the past. Another reason was the consolidation of daimyo authority and the rationalization of its economic base, which made the colossal architecture possible in the first place. The third and overwhelming reason was the lords' ambition to impress all with their wealth and power.

The donjon of Nobunaga's Azuchi Castle may be the perfect symbol of the age: it was a grandiose but not an enduring edifice, begun in 1576, inaugurated in 1579, and burnt down in the aftermath of

Nobunaga's own terrible end in 1582.[24] In short, its term of existence was but three brief years. The visible sign of Nobunaga's accomplishment and ambition was consigned to doom together with its maker.

No contemporary pictorial representation was passed down to the present day, and we have had to make do with the scattered but admiring reports of Jesuit missionaries, such as Stephanoni, who spoke of the donjon's graceful walls as a vision golden at the top and pure white in the sweep downward. When the sun struck the tower, he says, the effect was dazzling.[25] A detailed description of the interior decorations could be found in Ōta Gyūichi's "Account of the Donjon of Azuchiyama" (cited below), but this was scarcely an adequate source for attempts to reconstruct its overall appearance. Beyond the bare foundation stones themselves, there was no solid basis for such a reconstruction.

Recently, however, there was announced what surely ranks as a major discovery. The architectural historian Naitō Akira of Nagoya Kōgyō Daigaku, having found a copy of the builder's plans, has projected a new and surprising picture of the edifice. The tower was a colossal structure which soared some 138 feet into the air from the top of a hill rising 360 feet above the waters of an inlet of Lake Biwa.[26] It had seven internal levels, although from the outside only five were apparent. The interior had some unsuspected, unprecedented, and unimitated features. The center of the structure was unceiled up to the level of the fifth floor, almost 62 feet from the ground. A stage for theatrical performances thrust out into this empty space from the third floor; a bridge crossed it at the fourth level, which was also provided with spectators' galleries. The novelty of this design has caused Professor Naitō to speculate on some possible European influence, derived from the Jesuits (whose churches, such as the exact contemporary, the Gesù in Rome, are noted for their spectacular vaults). If so, then Nobunaga was unusually eclectic. Confucian, Taoist, and Buddhist themes abound in the donjon's decorations; and its most remarkable conceit is a Buddhist stupa set squarely over center bottom. It is easy to visualize it as a representation of Mount Sumeru, the center of the Buddhist universe. Not for nothing did the monk Nange Genkō compare Azuchi with the residence of the lord of that mountain, Indra the conquering deity.[27]

Nobunaga was indeed lord of all he surveyed; he could afford to consider himself master of a world which he had created. In 1575, the year immediately prior to the castle's foundation, he had fought and won two crucial campaigns, defeating his principal enemy among the daimyo, the house of Takeda, at the battle of Nagashino, and destroying the secular power of the Ikkō sect, his most tenacious adversary, in the province of Echizen. He had thereby achieved dominion over central Japan. The measure of his continuing ambition may be gauged by the slogan he flaunted on his seal: *Tenka fubu,* "the realm subjected to the military."[28] What he meant by *Tenka* was a universal public order under his own aegis, replacing the dilapidated system of the Ashikaga shogunate and transcending the particular and private organisms of Sengoku.[29] Nobunaga's realm was built by military might and functioned through the reorganized allegiances of the military class; but it was the compelling power of his will which breathed life into it, and his prowess that held it together. This was a prince who identified the realm with himself and ordered his vassals to revere (if not to adore) him. His castle's magnificence had its purpose: it served the cult of his personality.

The architectural bravura must have impressed anyone who approached Azuchi. But the tower's internal decoration is perhaps even more illustrative of Momoyama tastes than the brilliant external display, especially since Nobunaga commissioned Kano Eitoku, the greatest painter of the age, to execute it. Ōta Gyūichi has left us a record of the pictorial profusion which resulted. It is a fascinating account which deserves quotation *in extenso.* We begin with the second story.[30]

In a twelve-mat room on the west side, Kano Eitoku was commissioned to paint pictures of plums in *sumie.* From top to bottom, everything in these chambers, wherever there are pictures, all is gold. This same room also contains a studio space *(shoin).* Here is depicted the scene of the evening bell at a distant temple; in front of it is a miniature landscape *(bonsan).* Next, in a four-mat room, there are shelves *(tana)* decorated with pictures of doves. Wild geese are depicted in another twelve-mat room, so that it is called the Wild Goose Room *(ga no ma).* There follows an eight-mat room. In the back room, of four mats, there are representations of pheasants nourishing their young. In yet another twelve-mat room, on the south side, are pictures of Chinese scholars. . . .[31]

The third story. Here is a twelve-mat room with paintings of birds and flowers, namely the *kachō no ma,* and a separate, raised four-mat chamber for the lord's use *(goza no ma),* also with paintings of birds and flowers. Next, on the south side, there is an eight-mat room, called the Room of the Wise Men *(kenjin no ma);* here may be seen the picture of a steed emerging from a gourd. On the east side is the Civet Room *(jakō no ma)* of eight mats, and one of twelve mats above the tower gate. Next, in an eight-mat room, are to be found portraits of the Taoist Immortal named Lü Tung-pin and of Fu Yüeh. In a twenty-four-mat room on the north side are paintings of a roundup of horses. Next, in a twelve-mat room, is depicted the Queen Mother of the West. . . [32]

The fourth story. In a twelve-[mat] room on the west side are paintings of all sorts of trees among cliffs, so that this is called the Cliff Room *(iwa no ma)*. Next, on the west, is an eight-[mat] room with the scene of dragons and tigers in combat. In a twelve-[mat] room on the south side are painted all sorts of bamboos, and this is called the Bamboo Room *(take no ma)*. There follows a twelve-[mat] room with nothing but pine trees depicted in various ways, called the Pine Tree Room *(matsu no ma)*. On the east is an eight-mat room with the painting of a phoenix on a paulownia tree. In the eight-mat room which follows are representations of Hsü Yu washing out his ears and Ch'ao Fu thereupon returning home with his ox, as well as the sight of their native village. Adjoining it is a tea room *(onkozashiki)*, of seven mats, which is done in gold dust only and has no pictures. The twelve-mat room on the north is also without pictures. The next twelve-mat room has a [fourteen-foot] space on the west where hydrangea bushes are depicted. The eight-mat room which follows contains the scene of falcon young in a bamboo coop, so that this is called the Falcon Room *(ontaka no ma)*. . . .[33]

The fifth story has no paintings. . . .

The sixth story. . . . The outside pillars are vermilion, the inside pillars all gold. Here may be seen paintings of the Ten Great Disciples of Buddha, as well as depictions of the Buddha Establishing the Way and Preaching the Law. In the surrounding gallery are pictures of hungry ghosts and demons, and on its shutters are painted dolphins *(shachihoko)* and flying dragons. The balustrades are adorned with spherical bosses *(giboshi)* and with carvings.

The seventh story, [seven yards] square. Inside the room all is gold. The outside also is gold. On the internal pillars to the four sides are dragons ascending and descending; on the ceiling may be seen angels in their earthly manifestation. Inside the room are portrayed the Three Emperors and the Five Sovereigns, the Ten Accomplished Disciples of Confucius, the Four Wise Men of Shang Shan, and the Seven Sages of the Bamboo Grove. . . .[34]

Pictorial profusion is not the word for it; this was extravagance. Surely the surfeit of decorative splendor sated even Nobunaga, who was not a man of simple tastes. We note that only one or two of the paintings were in ink wash; the rest were done in polychrome, a riper medium for ostentation. The modern observer laments the loss of this riot of color and gold to the fire; some contemporaries implied that it was fated, or sneered at the hegemons' vain pretensions. The irreverent Kyoto townsman's lampoon, posted in the streets of the capital in 1591, perhaps is the best summary of the view from below:[35]

ishibushin	So what's the use
shirogoshirae mo	Of hauling rocks
iranu mono	And building castles? —
Azuchi Odawara	Just look at
miru ni tsuketemo	Azuchi or at Odawara!

Little or nothing remains of these two, reputedly the period's stoutest castles; and little remains of the fortresses and pleasure domes which symbolized Hideyoshi's power and glory in the same way that Azuchi stood for Nobunaga and Odawara for the Later Hō-jō. Of Osaka Castle there are left only the colossal embankments of the inner moat; of Juraku, Hideyoshi's Assembly of Delights in Kyoto, and of his nonsuch Fushimi Castle there survive only a few buildings transported elsewhere. We can only guess at the sumptuous artistry of the grandees' residential interiors from scattered ensembles. But this does not mean that the "heroes' " efforts were futile. What was the nature of their careers?

Among all the contemporary accounts of Oda Nobunaga, none is sharper than the following sketch, which was composed in 1569:

A tall man, thin, scantly bearded, with a very clear voice, much given to the practice of arms, hardy, fond of the exercise of justice, & of mercy, proud, a lover of honor to the uttermost, very secretive in what he determines, extremely shrewd in the stratagems of war, little if at all subject to the reproof, & counsel of his subordinates, feared, & revered by all to an extreme degree. Does not drink wine. He is a severe master: treats all the Kings and Princes of Iapan with scorn, & speaks to them over his shoulder as though to inferiors, & is completely obeyed by all as their absolute lord. He is a man of good understanding, & clear judgment, despising the *Câmis*, & *Fotoquès*, & all the rest of that breed of idols, & all the heathen superstitions.[36]

This is a superb portrait, informed with that trait established by Renaissance historiography which Federico Chabod calls a "conceptual" realism, where the quick impressionistic touch of outward physical detail perfectly sets off the image of an inner puissance.[37] The pen is that of the Jesuit historian Luis Frois, whose depictions of Momoyama personages are the most imaginative that we possess. No Japanese chronicler of the age had his energetic style and expansive vision or treated personality with his dramatic intensity. To be sure, there is a severe bias in Frois' reportorial technique: his subjects tend to appear either as glorious heroes or as spectacular villains, and his entire concept is governed by the urge to exalt virtue and excoriate vice. This priest's judgment of Nobunaga was undoubtedly swayed by the conceit that he could and must convert the most powerful figure in the land, and then all of Japan would turn Christian. Nobunaga inspired him with hope: for this was a pagan potentate who nevertheless had "good understanding" *because* he despised the Shinto gods, and Buddhas, and "all the rest of that breed of idols." Ultimately—insofar as our dramatist was concerned—the failure to bring to fruition that grace of "good understanding" proved to be Nobunaga's tragic flaw. Hence his composite view of Nobunaga is mixed: first he praises this Caesar, but in the end he buries him in hell.[38]

Subsequent Western authors have had less ambivalent feelings about this man. James Murdoch—scarcely a Jesuit, but no less censorious, and moreover imbued with the certitude of the Victorian—concludes that Nobunaga "favoured the Christian priests, and . . . as a consequence reaped his reward in being committed by them to the pages of history as 'this great prince,' [but he] was at bottom and essentially merely a magnificent savage."[39] And Sir George Sansom elaborates, also with moral certainty: "If his virtues are open to doubt, his vices are unquestionable. He never showed a sign of compassion. His vindictive ruthlessness is apparent from the beginning of his career, when he killed his brother, to his last years, which were filled with wanton slaughter. He became the master of twenty provinces at terrible cost. He was a cruel and callous brute."[40]

The major value of such characterizations is that they make Nobunaga all too human a hero, a man exemplifying grimly the corrupt stain inborn in all mankind. This type deflects the neutral view, and that is what makes Nobunaga such a fascinating figure. Does it, however, put his significance into a true perspective?

By and large, Japanese historiography has not served its personages well: altogether often, major actors of rich historical spectacles have been made to posture on a two-dimensional stage. But Nobunaga, dauntless across the measures of time, resists relegation to the realm of the abstract. The attempts to transform him into a mere reference point in the periodization of historical processes are doomed to failure, for he is fated to survive as something more: a daemon and a whirlwind incarnate. One must, of course, beware of too personal a fixation; else the image becomes a grotesque, and the historian is reduced to the level of a historical novelist. Perhaps Nobunaga ought indeed to be represented dispassionately as the embodiment of a force which had its moment when the curves of the old order's decline and the modern daimyo institution's rise coincided. But is that enough for one who has been called Luciferian, a "Japanese Attila," another King Ahasver, and "the veritable *Übermensch*"?[41]

Erasmus, they say, laid the egg which Luther hatched. Similarly, one might say that Nobunaga broke the eggs for that famous omelette which Hideyoshi made and Ieyasu then devoured. If it is possible to maintain that any single man set in motion the process of Japan's reunification, then that man was Nobunaga. The regime founded by him reconstituted Japan's body politic and brought it out of the Middle Ages. That suffices. There should be no need for moral judgments. Historical importance is not measured by the standard of gentility.

Above all, it is important to realize how much Hideyoshi and Ieyasu owed to Nobunaga. The facile contrast which deprecates Nobunaga as a destructive—even if a magnificent—savage while attributing constructive genius to his successors is false. The basic outline of the pattern which emerged under the other two unifiers was imbedded within the Japanese polity in Nobunaga's day. His actions clearly prefigured those of Hideyoshi and Ieyasu.

Nobunaga's regime initiated the policy of disarming the rural population and separating the peasant from the samurai status;[42] Hideyoshi, who had acted under Nobunaga's direction in pursuing these ends, expanded the scope of these measures when he succeeded to the hegemony; the final result was the rigidly defined class structure of the Tokugawa realm. The policy of cadastral surveys, which was such an important tool of his successors' efforts to subject the land to a nationwide system of controls, began under Nobunaga.[43] When he parceled out domains to his subordinate generals, transferring them to another province if it suited him, and when he suddenly dispossessed even his closest vassals, castigating them for failure to "meet the standards of the Way of Arms," he started a sequence which was to make of daimyo the famous "potted plants" of the Tokugawa era.[44] Only in the sphere of foreign policy do we fail, initially, to see any obvious preconditioning moves. Nobunaga indeed "favoured the Christian priests," and his attitude toward overseas contacts at least seemed open. But even in this area he prefigured subsequent developments.

Hideyoshi's most notorious exploit is his invasion of Korea; the bombastic manner in which he detailed his plans for the subjugation of China is familiar; it is common to attribute his vision of a conquest of the Asian mainland to megalomania. But was there no precedent and no rationality at all to his devices? We must not forget that the Spanish-Portuguese worldwide empire had supplied the Japanese with a nearby model for overseas expansion (as other imperialist powers would do again three centuries later, with the most unfortunate results for that same China and Korea). Moreover, the geographical meaning of *Tenka*—"the realm," but literally "all under heaven"—was ambiguous and flexible. It could transcend the borders of Japan; for Hideyoshi, it clearly did. But for Nobunaga as well, the term came to encompass more and more as his career advanced. As we have seen, at the outset he used it as a slogan which symbolized his design to assume imperative control over Japan. But in the last year of his life (if Frois' report can be trusted), the "realm" within the span of Nobunaga's ambition had grown to extend as far as China, which he intended to conquer and partition among his sons.[45]

Overseas designs were entirely abandoned under the Tokugawa regime in the interests of internal stability. The determination to shut off all contact with Christianity, which was deemed a subversive social force, was the cardinal element of Japan's seclusion policy. In the emergence of this policy, Nobunaga played a role which is not obvious but was nonetheless direct.

Long before the final solution of the Christian problem was proposed by the Tokugawa, Oda Nobunaga was engaged in a merciless campaign against Buddhists of the True Pure Land (or Ikkō, "Single-Directed") sect, its widespread "religious monarchy," and its headquarters, the temple-citadel Ishiyama Honganji in Osaka. The eradication of the followers of the Honganji and the persecution of the Christians were part of the same design, meant to eliminate the threat which organized religion's competing cadres of loyalty posed to the regime of the unifiers. Hideyoshi based his initial decision to ban the Catholic mission on a historical analogy which made True Pure Land Buddhism and Christianity into converging parallels: one sect (he stated) had brought great harm to the realm until Nobunaga crushed it; the other was, if anything, even more subversive, and its spread had to be stopped before it was too late.[46] As they rejoiced over the ruin which Nobunaga visited upon Buddhist institutions, his Jesuit friends surely did not suspect that he was laying open the road which led to Sakoku and to their own martyrdom.

In viewing the development of Nobunaga's regime, it is impossible to overlook the fact that the major part of his career as a national figure was spent in struggle against the Honganji and its adherents. Indeed, at least one recent commentator, Fujiki Hisashi, has argued that the clash between the unifying power and the Ikkō sect was the fundamental axis around which turned the entire social conflict of the age.[47] The growth of this sect's organizational structure continued into the 1570s, enveloping entire provinces and making a major daimyo of its pontiff, the Honganji *monshu*. This structure constituted a powerful base of resistance not only against Nobunaga but other daimyo as well, most notably Ieyasu.[48] When need be, the Ikkō confederations *(ikki)* could muster impressive forces of men under arms, but they also engaged in subtler forms of recalcitrance, such as the refusal to pay rents and dues; this problem was endemic and antedated Nobunaga himself. For us, however, it is of utmost importance to note that this widespread organization's major areas of strength coincided precisely with Nobunaga's primary sphere of interest: the sect was particularly well entrenched in Owari, Mino, and Ise, the place where his regime was born and the platform of its early development; in Ōmi, athwart his vital route to the capital; in the Home Provinces and their immediate periphery; and in Echizen, Noto, and Kaga, on the flank of his core domain. It was practically inevitable that, as the regime grew and the area within its grasp expanded, a military conflict between it and the Honganji would follow. The Ishiyama War, which lasted for ten years between 1570 and 1580, was in more than one sense a clash between two irreconcilable forces.

As we inspect the geographic setting of Nobunaga's rise, we can easily see why the "Single-Directed" sect was an unremitting political and military threat to him. From a certain standpoint—if we grant that the sect's ideology did in fact undercut the policies of unification and acted as an organizational binding force for the emerging samurai regime's opponents—it is also easy to view it as a powerful social obstacle to Nobunaga's aims. To this formula, Professor Fujiki adds a heretofore neglected factor. He maintains that the conventional thesis of the Ikkō sect's rural, peasant-based character is incorrect, and that its so-called temple precincts *(jinai)*, aside from being fortresses, were in effect "independent provincial towns possessing extraterritorial rights" and a well-developed commercial nature.[49] According to Fujiki, Nobunaga's well-known free-market and trust-busting policies *(rakuichi rakuza)* were not merely intended to prosper his own castle town but were consciously directed at the Ikkō sect's *jinai* and aimed at destroying these urban centers' financial position. The suggestion is that, on top of everything else, the sect was also Oda's economic rival.

Professor Fujiki's argument is overdrawn; it is too single-directed. His novel thesis is nevertheless quite useful. Without a comprehensive view of the Ikkō problem and an appreciation of its deep and widespread roots, Nobunaga's actions cannot be explained and it is difficult indeed to attribute anything more than "vindictive ruthlessness" to this scourge of the Buddhists.

The Ikkō sect was far from being Nobunaga's sole concern; but it was certainly his principal concern. The enemy was in the Honganji. When all is said and done, the Pure Land was the only true competitor of his *Tenka*.

Sengoku seems such a confused topsyturvy because prior to Nobunaga's advent the contention was limited in scope; only Nobunaga had the vision to aim for national hegemony. The strategically advantageous position from which he launched his career may have been an accident of fortune; but he alone of all the daimyo of his day truly knew what to do with the opportunities presented to him. For all their bluster and their reputations, the other "contenders for power" were incapable of originating a far-reaching plan; in the main, the initiative was Nobunaga's, and the others could at best react to his moves in futile stop-Nobunaga coalitions.[50] And the key factor of these coalitions was the Honganji. It was the omnipresence and the deep-rooted nature of its organization that made Nobunaga shuttle from western to eastern and from northern to southern front, like a man possessed. To quench this ever-smoldering resistance totally appeared to him the only remedy. The Honganji had "concocted a foul plot against the realm"; no matter how its adherents pleaded pardon, they could not be granted mercy but must be "finished off in a flash"; they were a "plague upon the realm," one which had to be stamped out or the damage would be boundless.[51] He would "eradicate" *(negiri)*, "wipe out" *(nadegiri)*, "mow down" *(tategiri)* these insurgents. In short, he would search them out and destroy them all.

Nobunaga's utterances on this topic have not lost their power to shock even today. When he boasted to the daimyo Date Terumune in November 1575 that he had "wiped out several tens of thousands of the villainous rabble in Echizen and Kaga" two months previously, he was not exaggerating. From the scene of the carnage and at the time of the event, he had written two immensely expressive letters to his governor of Kyoto, Murai Sadakatsu.[52] The first remarks that the scene was worth showing. The second itemizes why: it is a body count with the grisly refrain, "X-number were taken alive, so their heads were cut off" *(ikedori X-yonin, sunawachi kubi o kiri sōrō).* To be sure, this sort of savagery is not peculiar to a "Japanese Attila," nor even to a premodern age. It may instead be the law of the peasant war; we have witnessed it in our own, presumably more civilized century.

Those followers *(monto)* of the Honganji whom he did not kill, Nobunaga made sure he converted. More precisely put, he applied the splitting technique to the True Pure Land sect, acknowledging that adherents of the sect's other branches were "different from Osaka" and promising them protection in exchange for "loyal service."[53] This policy was successful. For instance, followers of the sect's Takada branch not only captured and killed Shimotsuma Chikugo Hokkyō, one of the Honganji's principal deputies in Echizen, but also cooperated actively in the regime's effort to secure the hearts and minds of the populace. In recognition of this "incomparable loyalty," their temples were given authority over the remaining *monto* of Echizen. Village headmen were made to send in pledges such as this: "Although this village should be punished for being Honganji sectarians, we have instead been ordered to become affiliates of the Three Takada Temples, and we are grateful for this favor." In the spring of 1576, the villagers themselves, "man or woman regardless," were forced to put their signs to oaths abjuring allegiance to Osaka. Professor Fujiki comments that these measures "bring to mind the subsequent inquisition of Christians"; he states correctly that "the Oda regime began the [policy of] *shūmon aratame.*"[54] The analogy becomes complete when we note that the recusants who then banded together (forming an *ikki*) and rose against the regime were burnt at the stake, boiled alive, or crucified.[55]

This is the true face of the conflict between the sect and the unifiers' regime. It is the dark side of the glittering Momoyama era. It is necessary to expose it to view because the nature of that regime is a highly controversial problem. Western historiography tends to ascribe a generally positive effect to Japan's sixteenth-century reunification.[56] This is not the opinion held by many recent Japanese historians, who tend to emphasize the brutal and (dare we say it?) reactionary aspects of that process and of the authoritarian system which was its result. They fervently wish that something else had emerged.

What that "something else" might have been is, however, an unanswerable question. Perhaps the rejoinder should be that, given the historical conditions, nothing else could have been expected; for the unifier had to "know how to act according to the nature of both" the beast and the man, being aware "that he cannot survive otherwise."[57]

Echizen is an excellent illustrative case because Nobunaga was well aware that he had conquered the province once before when he defeated Asakura Yoshikage in 1573, only to see it slip from his grasp and into the hands of the Ikkō sectarians. In 1575 he was determined to make the dispositions which would ensure that, once and for all, the enemy would stay prostrate.[58] He himself remained in the province for a good month after he had initially reported his victory to Kyoto, supervising the mopping-up operations and setting down the law for the vassal he installed as the military governor of the province, Shibata Katsuie. In the Regulations for the Province of Echizen we have a good summary of the feudal despot's modus operandi.[59] The nine articles of the main text are a fascinating mix of the public and the private aspects of Nobunaga's concept of government; in the end the two merge into one.

Nobunaga begins by cautioning Shibata not to levy inappropriate imposts on the province, not to treat the provincial samurai wilfully, and not to play favorites when he sits in judgment. He continues by ordering the return of Kyoto court aristocrats' estates "insofar as they actually exercised authority over them before the disturbances," but reserves for himself the right of refusal; he reminds Shibata that barriers where merchants are forced to pay dues have been abolished in all his provinces, and that the same shall obtain in Echizen. There follows the compendious article 6:

A large province is being left in your hands. Guard it carefully: negligence will be considered criminal. Take care of Arms above all. Stockpile weapons and supplies, so that you are certain the province can be held against attack for five or even ten years. In any event, do not be greedy: determine what is due, ascertain that it is paid. Stay away from young boys; abstain from amateur theatricals, parties and promenades, and other such diversions.

After instructions that Shibata also do without falconry ("for it profits you nothing"—an oddly unsympathetic or perhaps merely a jealous interdict on the part of the premier falconry enthusiast of his age), and that he always keep estates available for the purpose of rewarding "those who are exemplary in their dedication to Arms," the main text of the document concludes. But then there follows a post-script addressed to Fuwa Mitsuharu, Sassa Narimasa, and Maeda Toshiie:

The province of Echizen is for the most part left at Shibata's disposal. You three, however, shall act as Shibata's overseers and are assigned two districts. Hence you shall report without duplicity on the good and bad points of his conduct, and Shibata shall report on the good and bad points of yours. Above all, act with due care that you sharpen each other's efficiency. If you are negligent, you will be held in contumely.

This is the extent to which Nobunaga subscribed to the principle of collegiality.

Nobunaga's solipsism and his imperious presumption are, however, illustrated best of all in the remarkable article 9 of the Regulations:

At the risk of repeating myself: You must resolve to do everything as I say. For all that, do not flatter me when you feel that I am unreasonable or un-just. If anything should trouble you in this regard, tell me, and I may comply with your request.

In any event, you shall revere me *(wareware o sōkyō shite)* and shall bear me no evil thought behind my back. Your feelings toward me must be such that you do not even point your feet in the direction where I am. If you act that way, then you will be blessed with good fortune forevermore, as befits the proper samurai. . . .

How are we to interpret the meaning of *sōkyō?* To be sure, we have it on the best of authority—the *VOCABVLARIO DA LINGOA DE IAPAM* published by the Jesuit mission press in Nagasaki in 1603–1604—that the term may properly be applied to human beings.[60] But there does exist one source which alleges that the reverence Nobunaga wanted was greater than that which is due the ruler of all the realm under heaven. In a letter written in November 1582, the Jesuit Luis Frois asserts that just before he went to his doom Nobu-naga proved himself to be beyond even "Nebuchadnezzar in temeri-ty, & insolence, endeavoring to be adored by all, not as a human be-ing of this earth, & a mortal, but as if he were divine, or the lord of immortality."[61] According to Frois, Nobunaga installed the emblem of his divinity *(Xintáy,* sc., *shintai)* in the Sōkenji, his temple on Azuchi Hill—"someone having brought him a stone suitable for the purpose, called *Bonçāo''*[62]—and guaranteed prosperity and a long life to all who came to venerate it; for he maintained that he was a living god and Buddha *(Câmi, & Fotoquè viuo)*, "in his desire to be adored on earth" impressing on all "that there was no other lord of the Universe, & author of nature."

Frois no doubt exaggerates the measure of Nobunaga's claims. Rather than report Nobunaga's death, he strives to represent the tragedy of the tyrant's demise. His account's tone and content are determined by his sense of tragedy; hence we need not wonder at the prodigies he makes appear, including "something like a comet [that] fell on Anzuchíyama" to announce the impending disaster; his tale progresses relentlessly toward a direful moral. This is highly effective drama, less creditable history. In the absence of corroborative evidence, it is difficult to believe Frois' detail.[63] Nobunaga's notion of divinity could not have been the biblical conception reflected by the missionary. Moreover, he knew that he had conquered as the prophet of Arms, not as a mystagogue, and he was politic enough to realize that he did not have the power of "forcing the incredulous to believe."[64] What Frois presents as a demented insistence "that there was no other who should be adored outside of Nobunánga himself" may be nothing more than the distorted form of the hegemon's repeated appeal to an exclusive loyalty, a hyperbolic interpretation of *wareware o sōkyō shite.* If Nobunaga indeed persuaded his vassals to accept such a commandment, then this phrase expresses singularity of purpose even better than Borgia's famous *aut Caesar aut nihil.*

In Nobunaga's *Tenka,* Nobunaga himself was the supreme ultimate of allegiances. He countenanced other hierarchies of authority only insofar as they conformed with his needs. Although he became a national figure by playing the role of Ashikaga Yoshiaki's champion, he was intent on maintaining an independent posture from the very start of their association. Having installed Yoshiaki as shogun in Kyoto in 1568, he refused his protégé's offer to make him vice-shogun or *kanrei,* the bakufu's executive officer.[65] Instead, he dictated to Yoshiaki how to behave in his office;[66] the nominal head of the military hierarchy was forced to acknowledge that "since the affairs of the realm have been left entirely in Nobunaga's hands, he may take measures against anyone whatsoever as he pleases, without first consulting the shogun."[67] In 1573, no longer willing to tolerate the hapless Yoshiaki's intrigues, he chased the shogun out of Kyoto —but not before he had recited to him a litany of outrage at his high crimes and misdemeanors, concluding with the scornful charge, "Even the peasants call you a bad shogun."[68]

A similar if less extreme independence characterizes Nobunaga's relations with the imperial court. On the surface, these appear to have been cordial. Nobunaga acted as the court's benefactor, and was in recognition of that generosity (no less than of his actual power) appointed to a series of high aristocratic posts.[69] On 15 May 1578, however, the Minister of the Right, General of the Right, and courtier of the Second Rank proper, Taira no Nobunaga, resigned his imperial offices. His letter of resignation attributes the decision to the fact that not all of the "Four Barbarians" had yet been subdued; he will be ready to resume his loyal service as the pillar of the throne, he says, "when all within the Four Seas is pacified."[70] But this cannot be the full explanation of his withdrawal from the court. In striking contrast with Hideyoshi, Nobunaga refused to identify himself with the imperial hierarchy; he held back from being enmeshed in the traditional system of court ranks. Indeed, he presumed to dictate terms to the sovereign himself, stating that he would accept a court appointment again once Emperor Ōgimachi abdicated in favor of Nobunaga's own choice, Prince Sanehito.[71] After Nobunaga's last triumph, the total destruction of the Takeda—or subjugation of the "Eastern Barbarians"—in 1582, the court offered "to make him shogun" or even appoint him "to any rank at all." He refused to give a direct answer to the imperial emissaries, and was killed before the matter could be raised again.[72] He sought to demonstrate that even the most hallowed symbols of authority bent to his fiat; in that sense perhaps it may be said that Nobunaga wanted no other gods before him. He was the complete autocrat.

At the time of Nobunaga's violent death in June 1582, the realm under the control of his regime comprised twenty-nine of Japan's sixty-six provinces and substantial portions of two others. It occupied a continuous area stretching from Kōzuke in the east to Harima in the west and from the Sea of Japan to the Pacific Ocean, almost a third of the land mass of the sixteenth-century Japanese empire. In addition, his forces were poised to conquer Shikoku; he had already issued preliminary orders on how to divide and rule that island.[73] Most of these provinces were in the hands of Nobunaga's own men, vassals whom he himself had installed as military governors and who remained subordinated to him in a command relationship. Their conduct of affairs within their domains was autonomous but subject to the guidelines imposed by the overlord Nobunaga.

Fissures became apparent in this structure after its builder's demise. Nobunaga's assassin Akechi Mitsuhide was eliminated by Hideyoshi a scant eleven days after his treacherous deed, but the spoils did not automatically belong to the victor; there were competing interests and ambitions in the *Tenka*. Hideyoshi had to destroy Shibata Katsuie (1583) and reach an accommodation with Oda Nobukatsu and Tokugawa Ieyasu (peace in January 1585) before he could assume the mantle of a national hegemon. In April and May 1585, Hideyoshi defeated the warrior monks of Negoro and completed the conquest of the province of Kii; in July and August, his army of eighty thousand swept over Shikoku. The realm under the control of the central regime now exceeded the boundaries of Nobunaga's day. In the next six years it underwent a spectacularly rapid expansion. When the rebellion of Kunoe Masazane in the extreme northern province of Mutsu was crushed in the summer of 1591, all of Japan was reunified under Hideyoshi's hegemony. This rapid process involved obvious organizational problems, and as a result the regime acquired a greater willingness to compromise than had been the case in Nobunaga's day. In the end, Hideyoshi figured as the leader of a grand coalition of daimyo; indeed, John Whitney Hall argues in this volume that he was as national hegemon a *primus inter pares*. Needless to say, this notion does not imply that he lacked coercive powers. On the contrary, he could uproot even the greatest of daimyo. This dominant fact was demonstrated in 1590, when Hideyoshi transplanted Tokugawa Ieyasu from one region into another, ostensibly in reward for loyal service; Oda Nobukatsu, who expressed a preference for staying in his home terrain, was stripped of his possessions.

Other chapters of this collection amply discuss the characteristics of Hideyoshi's rule, so there is no need to go into detail here. We shall content ourselves with the inspection of a contemporary summary of the means by which Hideyoshi governed the realm, agreeing with the author—the Jesuit Padre Organtino Gnecchi-Soldo—that these are "verie woorthie to be well considered and marked."[74] It is particularly interesting to note how nicely this sixteenth-century writer's list matches and complements the major items selected for discussion in Professor Hall's modern study of Hideyoshi's policies.

ffirst, if he geve his woorde of securitie to any, after he hath conquered a Cuntrye, theie shall have no harme, which was not observed by *Nobunanga*, who neuer conquered any towne or Cuntrie, but that he putt all the Gouernoures therof to the sworde. But this kinge doth not onlie not kill them that he conquereth, but also assigneth them sufficient mayntenance for theire estate, for the whiche theie live vnder him quietlie, and doe obeie him trulie.

Secondlie, he hath so impouerished all the rude and rusticall multitude, (which were theie, that cheiflie caused and procured ye tumultes and hurle-burlie of all theise Kingdomes) that theie have scarslie enoughe wheron to live, takinge from them beside, all theire Armor, & weapons.

Thirdlie, he hath taken awaie, all the privatt quarrels, and questions, whiche gave alwaies occasions of theire farther risinges, and tumultes. Whosoeuer is nowe founde in any of theise risinges & tumults, he is sure to die therefore, and if any of the parties culpable Doe flie, and escape awaie, theire frindes & kinsfolkes, that tarrie behinde, doe suffer for theire offences. . . . By whiche seueritie it is broughte to passe, that yo^w shall seldom heare of any of those former sturres or broiles in all *Japonia.*

ffourthelye, he vseth indifferencie and equallitie withe all men, in ministringe iustice, not sparinge his owne kinsfolkes and cheifest captaines althoughe theie be of the bloode imperiall. . . .

ffiftlie he will not suffer any of his souldiers or gentlemen to live in Idlenes, settinge them a woorke wth buildinges and repairinge of his foartes . . . so as theie have no tyme, nor leasure to procure or practise any treasons or rebellions.

Sixthlie, he vseth to change the people and Potentates of one cuntrie, and place them in another far off.

Seventhlie, he hathe greate regarde, that all his souldiers, be well and trulie paide theire wages, and all other thinges that theie have neede of sufficientlie yeilded them, by whiche meanes, he so winneth the souldiers good will, that he bringeth to good effecte all y^t ever he hath gon aboute hetherto, savinge onlie the enterprise of *China,* whiche farre exceeded his pow^r to compasse, yet keepeth he still his forces in *Caraya,* to the ende he maie make an honorable composition withe the *Chinèès.*

Eighthlie, he is well advised, for givinge favoure or countenance to any, that is of any highe and aspiringe mynde, and thereby were likelie to trouble the state after his Deathe, withe makinge revolts and tumultes in the Cuntrye.

Nynthlie, he will never admitt any Captaine of valoure or power to be resident within 4 or 5 daies iorney aboute *Meaco.*

Lastlie, he hath broughte his revinewe vnto the summe of two millons of golde by the yeare.

Organtino concludes with the hope that by Hideyoshi's "good endeuoures, & diligent observations" peace will prevail in Japan, "and so consequentlie, a firme disposition growe by the grace of god, whereby theis cheif states of theise cuntries, maie become Christians."

In September 1594, when he wrote this letter to the General of the Society of Jesus, Organtino had reason to be optimistic. Although

Hideyoshi had proscribed the spread of Christianity in 1587, he had chosen not to enforce his edicts. The Jesuits had continued their work discreetly, and with a good measure of success. Organtino could report with satisfaction that in the previous two years more than six hundred persons—for the most part gentlemen, including some "men of greate accoumpte"—had been converted in the capital city of Kyoto, notwithstanding Hideyoshi's "hard prohibition." This "Kinge of *Japonia*" and his retinue actually fancied, if not the Christian religion, then at least the apparel and the demeanor of Christians. The result was a surface enthusiasm for Western things which would not be equalled in Japan until the Rokumeikan era almost three centuries later. The fashionable of the day affected rosaries and reliquaries about their necks; one was not *au courant* unless he wore a cross or an Agnus Dei on his costume.[75] There is ample evidence of this fashion in the period's paintings. Hideyoshi himself set the example, and "the whole Nobilitie" took up the fad. "Theie goe nowe also apparailed after the *Portingall* manner, so as yow shall scarse take them for any other then *Portingals* indeede, and some of them the more to resemble them doe learne the *Pater noster,* and the *Aue Maria. . . .*"

Little more than two years later, that same Organtino witnessed quite a different scene in Kyoto, Hideyoshi having ordered the arrest and mutilation of a group of Christian missionaries and their converts. After being paraded in ignominy through the streets of the capital, they were to be executed upon the cross in Nagasaki. *"This I command to be donne and farther I will that there be no more preaching of this law hereafter."*[76] Hideyoshi reiterated his prohibition of the alien faith in word and in deed. With this martyrdom of the Twenty-Six Saints, who were crucified on 5 February 1597, there occurred the first bloody persecution of Christianity in Japan, and the stage was set for the final act of our drama.

Hideyoshi had also decreed that all the Christian Fathers with the "rest of theyre companye (except *Fa: Rodrigues* [Tçuzzu] and some fewe withe him for the trafficke of the Portingall shippes) should departe" the country.[77] Death prevented him from carrying out this harsh measure, and after he passed from the scene in 1598 there followed a temporary reprieve for Japanese Christianity. Tokugawa Ieyasu, who gained the hegemony over the realm in 1600, at first showed himself well disposed toward the missionaries; in the first decade of the seventeenth century, the number of their converts reached its peak of some three hundred thousand. In 1612, however, the Tokugawa shogunate issued its first anti-Christian decrees. On 1 February 1614, Ieyasu ordered the expulsion of the priests, and the general persecution of Christianity began. The traffic of the Portuguese ships was permitted for another twenty-five years; but with the issuance of the final Sakoku directive in 1639 even that contact was terminated. What is the significance of these events?

Japan first confronted the West in the sixteenth century. It did not prove a harmonious encounter. In the minds of the Japanese, the West was almost entirely identified with Christianity. The propaganda of the Christian faith, which in certain instances was supported by the secular power of regional lords, involved assaults upon the native tradition.[78] The Japanese response, which at first produced a sizable number of converts, in the end was redirected inward. In the seventeenth century, a consciously adopted policy of seclusion cordoned off a country within which all effort was made to control heterodox religious strains. But Christianity was found to be the quintessential heresy, and was persecuted by a merciless inquisition. To the extent that the West was identified with Christianity—and, to reiterate, it was almost entirely so—the West was rejected.

The policy of national isolation, which was inspired by the fear of what we shall call the Christian Peril, was to remain in effect until the middle of the nineteenth century. In time, it advanced to the hallowed status of the Tokugawa regime's ancestral law. Indeed, the vehement debate over this law's implications was one of the prime motive factors of the Meiji "Restoration," which in the nineteenth century thrust Japan once again into the West's civilizing embrace. In the final event, the Tokugawa shogunate was skewered by the necessity to abandon its own sacred dogma. If for no other reason, then on account of this paradox the Early Modern rejection of the West's Christian ideology is an important question of Japanese history.

The anti-Christian propaganda mills ground on throughout the Tokugawa era, producing a slew of malefactory images. The slinkily elegant Christian Padres of Momoyama picture screens turned into owl-screeching apparitions more frightful than any goblin ever seen, the Kirishitan Bateren. They haunt the pages of the Edo period's popular literature with a fluttering of blackrobes, of batlike wings; on the Kabuki stage, their magical formulas are muttered by would-be usurpers of the realm. The populace was reminded that only the valor and vigilance of the Tokugawa had kept Japan from being ensnared in the web of a sinister imperial conspiracy which emanated out of the Land of Yaso (Jesus).

This theme was pursued also on a higher intellectual level. The continuing reference to the Christian Peril is a dark stain which blotted the minds of Tokugawa thinkers from Hayashi Razan, the chief Confucianist behind the throne of several seventeenth-century shoguns, on down to Fujita Tōko and Aizawa Seishisai, the leading activists of the Meiji "Restoration's" prime intellectual source, the Late Mito school; in short, it spans the history of Japanese political thought from Momoyama to Meiji.[79]

What was it that made them hate and fear Christianity so? It was the conviction that the Christian ideology perverted society. By the use of a dialectic built upon basic East Asian cultural premises, it could be demonstrated that Christianity was an outrage against the most sacred norms of the moral order. Did not the Christians' First Commandment demand exclusive loyalty to a jealous God? Did it not urge disobedience to the sovereign's or the parent's orders if compliance would counter God's will? The conflict between the Christian West and the reunified Japan of Hideyoshi and the Tokugawa was the product of such fundamental issues. At the root of the Sakoku—"Closed Country"—decision was the problem of the Christian ideology.

If the anti-Christian element is taken out of the Closed-Country consciousness, then all its constituents collapse, and we can say along with Professor Hayashiya Tatsusaburō that there was, in effect, no Sakoku.[80] For, needless to say, the Tokugawa throughout the centuries of "isolation" tolerated what they deemed a benign Western growth in their body politic. To be sure, the Dutch were confined to Nagasaki; but their presence provided not only a means of foreign trade but also a funnel for the introduction of Western scientific knowledge into Japan. Generations of *Rangakusha* availed themselves of the opportunity to seek this knowledge. There is no parallel in the Momoyama era. To search for one in the intellectual climate established by the Jesuit missionaries would be unreasonable and anachronistic. No Riccis and no Verbiests came to Japan in all the years of relatively free activity that the mission was vouchsafed from 1549 to 1614. To point this out is not to blame the Jesuits for negligence or to imply that the Japanese soil would have turned fertile had the Christian seed been implanted scientifically. It is merely to say that in Japan the missionaries did their best according to their lights but their method was foreclosed from succeeding by forces beyond their control.

In a superb essay on the Counter Reformation, A. G. Dickens observes: "The craving of a troubled but order-seeking world was a craving for precise guidance, and this [the Jesuits] offered. . . . Within the ordered security of their system, the whole potential of a man's will could now be developed, harnessed, and projected outward."[81] Dickens speaks in the European context, but the standards he cites can also be applied to the Sengoku and Momoyama realm. Sixteenth-century Japan also was a disturbed world; it also craved salvation and submitted to guidance; under the Tokugawa, it would be reintegrated in a system of ordered security. There was a great potential for Christianity in this dimension, and the missionaries recognized it. Their fatal flaw, however, was that outward projection of their system. The trouble was that "outward" in the ultimate sense was "upward," onward to God. This thrust the unifiers could not tolerate because to them it meant away from secular loyalty.

The sixteenth century's Jesuit mission to Japan represents a heroic effort to westernize that country. The missionaries made an attempt to introduce a Western culture in its pure form. This form would be assimilated first by the ruling elite, whom the missionaries systematically sought to influence, and then would be imposed upon the populace. In short, the missionaries tried to capture Japan through the force of ideas. Although in certain instances they used the lure of the Portuguese trade in order to obtain entry into a daimyo's favor, and although there were a few military adventurists among them, we cannot question the sincerity of their dedication to this goal.

It was assumed that the sheer force of rhetoric would persuade the Japanese. They were to be overwhelmed by the weight of the Christian message, ensnared in the tight meshes of Christian logic, and argued into submitting to eminent Christian truths. So that the ideology could be effectively presented, there was prepared a tight regimen of authorized instruction. An impressive body of devotional literature was created. The arts were utilized to bring the message closer to the populace.

But that was the totality of the Christian arsenal. No further weapons could be expected from Portugal or from Spain. The foreign missionaries were defeated by the *force majeure* of a native regime which was buttressed by a different sort of universal ideology. This was a hollow victory for the regime of the unifiers; for it created a problem which lasted well past the conclusion of Japan's Early Modern age.

Although the Japanese response to the West in the nineteenth century is almost universally praised as positive, forceful, and successful, it contained dilatory, negative, and confused factors because the reactive processes of ideologues and policy makers were in part paralyzed by the impulsive need to cleave to Sakoku in order to preserve the Land of the Gods from the Christian Peril. In the end, Sakoku could not be maintained, and anti-Christian attitudes by and large faded away. But traces of the Closed-Country consciousness remained in Japan beyond the Meiji "Restoration."

It may be true that the views of those exuberant Meiji "modernizers" of the Japanese spirit—men who actively sought the westernization of Japanese society as a positive goal—have at length prevailed over the sensibilities of the nationalists who saw in westernization the destruction of the Japanese identity.[82] But it is also true that in the intervening century large numbers of Japanese intellectuals have been vociferous in expressing their discontent with the West and their country's approaches to it. In a study of the Meiji "Restoration's" heritage, Kawano Kenji has commented that the essential quandary of modern Japan is the antinomy of two opposing forces, the need to assimilate and the latent tendency to reject the West. "The Meiji Restoration," Kawano states, "was a revolution intended to westernize Japan in order to resist 'the West.' Resistance did not mean that 'the West' could be obliterated; assimilation did not mean that Japan, which was essentially an Asian nation, would westernize anything and everything. This was Japan's agony. Unable to rest content in its Asian identity, Japan nevertheless could not recognize itself as part of 'the West.' " He goes on to say that this paradox is at the heart of modern Japan's being.[83] If so, then is it not possible to trace that paradox back to its Momoyama antecedents?

There may not be much real value in such impressionistic conceits as those of the contemporary writer Endō Shūsaku, who in his immensely popular works *Chinmoku* (Dead silence) and *Ōgon no kuni* (El Dorado) depicts Japan as a vast swamp which sucks in, drowns, and transforms within itself all foreign influences, so that even the most stalwart of missionaries apostatize and become the tools of their own destroyers—for no divine help can save them, nor any divine voice respond to them *ex nihilo*. This sort of orientation to the problem of the "Christian Century" has, however, occupied the thoughts of some eminent Japanese men of letters. Akutagawa Ryūnosuke, for instance, anticipated Endō by a half century in pointing to the fatal tenacity of the Japanese spirit. In one of his series of "Kirishitan Stories," this master of elegant ironies confronts Padre Organtino with a Japanese deity who has come to interview him in order to make it quite clear that the soil of Japan is absorptive enough to swallow up even the most confident and powerful of intruders. Confucius was transformed in the Japanese climate (the deity points out); Lao Tzu and the Buddha were transformed. Why should the Christian God alone be impervious to the native tradition?[84] The supreme irony of the "Christian Century" may be that the only trace of Christianity which could survive the Tokugawa era's persecution was the hermetic cult of a Deus whom peasants had transfigured into a Japanese *kami*.

In the third year of the new Meiji era and in the new international port of Yokohama, John Reddie Black, the Scottish publisher of *The Far East* (An Illustrated Fortnightly Newspaper), wrote with all the assurance appropriate to his age:

But two invasions of a different character have been made upon [Japan]. First, that of the Portuguese missionaries in the 16th century—which was eminently successful, so long as they adhered strictly to their Christian teaching and forebore from civil intrigue. Then retribution came upon them and upon all who named the name of Christ, and their invasion was upset.

And now comes Commerce. . . . It has been amply proved that such commerce is the primary civilizing agent. . . . That which has turned the world upside down has come hither also; and Japan will soon rejoice in this new invasion.[85]

Black's estimate of the reasons for the failure of the first attempt to westernize Japan is not entirely correct. But he did not miss the mark in his prediction on the results of the second.

In the Meiji period, the Japanese had to absorb foreign Western techniques in order to compete. Some of them, in order to discover the full dimension of the Westerners' success, chose also to adopt the internal aspect and the spiritual message of the West because they thought that ideology was the secret. Indeed, some of them on that account adopted Christianity. But in the sixteenth century, the Japanese confronted a different sort of West. The challenge of the West did not come in the form of a massive assault of new technologies or even of a fleet of Black Ships descending upon the shores. It came rather as the sharply pointed effort to insert a specific message, the gospel of Christianity. As has already been stated, religious ideology was the only Western weapon. To the extent that it could be brought to bear on the historical situation, that weapon might be successful. Indeed, during the Sengoku period it was. But once the "Three

Heroes'' completed their work and the country was reunified, it no longer could be.

Upon the Momoyama renascence there followed what might be called the Tokugawa Restoration. In the Tokugawa era, a classical East Asian culture blossomed forth in Japan. Moreover, this culture was in a true sense cosmopolitan: some of its major aspects were founded on an integral application of the Chinese Confucian system, whose standards were ancient and had spread over a vast sphere of civilization. That sphere did not include the West, and the West of the Christian missionaries did not offer many attractions for the reintegrated Japanese realm. This West could be—and was—obliterated. Viewed in this context, the "Christian Century" becomes an accident of Sengoku. It is the exotic side of Momoyama, a fascinating period's greatest paradox.

CAROLYN WHEELWRIGHT

A Visualization of Eitoku's
Lost Paintings at Azuchi Castle

KANO EITOKU (1543–1590) transformed Japanese painting style,
redirecting the spatial perceptions of his generation toward a
new world of abstraction in pictorial elements. His innovative vision
responded to the artistic and social requirements of the second half of
the sixteenth century, when the most important commissions were
large-scale *shōhekiga* (wall paintings) for palatial residences. Society's insistence on ceremony and the patron's demand for self-
glorification obliged the artist to work with a painting format having
functional and symbolic dimensions above and beyond the spatial
prescriptions of the architecture itself.

Conditions for a creative surge coalesced when the hegemon Oda
Nobunaga commissioned Eitoku to decorate Azuchi Castle in 1576.
An audacious patron and an energetic artist joined in a project to re-
cast existing conventions into a new environment which would serve
the purposes of political manipulation and social control. Departing
from the prevalent model of a castle as a fort built for military defense, Nobunaga conceived his residence as an impressive symbol of
his authority and a visible sign of his self-confidence in ruling the
Japanese realm, his *Tenka*. Nobunaga's castle was the first major
citadel to give priority to a grand display of personal power and glory.
It announced a new era in which the lord's physical surroundings
would become an integral part of his rulership, and interior decoration would reinforce statecraft.

Although nothing remains of the paintings at Azuchi Castle, they
were a landmark in Eitoku's career and probably a significant stage in
the development of his painting style. Had they remained in existence, they would provide a better understanding of the spatial revolution that occurred in pictorial expression around this time. Perhaps

a mental image of the *shōhekiga* at Azuchi Castle can be formed by considering large-scale paintings associated with Eitoku, and discussing their relevance to the architectural program of Nobunaga's castle. Wall paintings and folding-screen paintings produced within a forty-year period beginning in 1566 are available for illustration. They provide a visual survey of the evolution of Eitoku's style during the latter sixteenth century and aid in the effort to supply the missing link at Azuchi Castle.

First it is necessary to be aware of the specifications Eitoku was asked to meet in creating his paintings, for *shōhekiga* are always done in the context of a larger architectural plan. Just three months after the first foundation stone was laid and a year and a half before the roof was put in place, Eitoku was summoned with other artisans and workmen to reside at the Azuchi building site.[1] While the walls were being erected, Eitoku learned the structure of the building. He was told the function of the rooms, the size and arrangement of the walls, the decorative context to be provided by carpenters, artisans in lacquerwork, metal craftsmen. He was directed by Kimura Jirozaemon, the construction commissioner,[2] who communicated Nobunaga's desires and added ideas of his own, probably prescribing subjects and styles to be used in certain areas. Not until he had absorbed this background did Eitoku create designs to be submitted for approval.

The structure Eitoku was asked to embellish with paintings has recently been exhaustively studied and reconstructed in drawings and floor plans by the architectural historian Naitō Akira.[3] The decorative program of the Azuchi Castle donjon has been known through Ōta Gyūichi's account in the *Shinchō kōki*,[4] cited in George Elison's preceding essay, "The Cross and the Sword." But Naitō's discovery of a reliable copy of the builder's plans (the *Tenshu sashizu* or "Specifications of the Donjon") makes a more complete visualization possible.

Naitō emphasizes that Azuchi Castle should not be considered as a military fortification but rather as the influential predecessor of early seventeenth-century warrior residences built for political purposes. It was a significant stage in the development of *shoin-zukuri*, the style of residential architecture that provided a structured environment for social contacts between lords and vassals in the Early Modern period. The first four of the donjon's seven stories contained a vertical distribution of the three major divisions of *shoin-zukuri*: the *omote* suites for public audiences and entertainments, the *nakaoku* areas for daily activities, and the *oku* apartments for wife and concubines. These rooms surrounded a central open vault, which functioned vertically

much as the main garden does on a plane surface in fully developed
shoin-zukuri, associating the individual sections into a unified complex.[5] In very general terms, the first four stories could be divided diagonally, from northeast corner to southwest corner, into rooms with
a formal and public function on the south and east, and rooms with
an informal and private character on the north and west.[6]

The public *omote* area began at the main gate on the southeast
corner of the ground floor. From here, the main staircase led to the
initial reception room *(tōzamurai)* on the second story directly above
the entrance. The south side of the second floor was occupied by the
taimensho suites used for holding audiences with chief vassals. In a
row on the extreme south were two large *zashiki* (formal *tatami*-
matted sitting rooms) and a small *shoin,* which by the 1570s had developed into a nonfunctional desk alcove used as a decorative focus.
Along the north side of these three rooms another series bordered the
central vault: a small room fitted with shelves for the artistic display
of prized objects *(tana)*, a large *zashiki,* and a small elevated room for
persons of highest status *(jōdan)* provided with decorative wooden
doors leading to an adjoining room where guards were stationed. On
the southeast corner of the central vault were two service rooms *(nando)*[7]—probably *tatami*-matted waiting rooms for retainers, for they
were directly across the corridor from the initial reception room.

The third-floor rooms with a public function bordered the south
and east sides of the central vault, while on the north side a stage projected into the open space. The unit of a Nō stage facing formal reception rooms across a garden space corresponds precisely to the plan
of warrior residences in developed *shoin-zukuri.* Directly opposite
the stage was the *hiroma* suite of highest status rooms for formal entertaining, consisting of a four-mat[8] elevated room *(jōdan)*, a twelve-
mat *zashiki,* and a two-mat room with shelves *(tana)*. Along the east
were the *zashiki* where the guests' more important retainers viewed
the entertainment from a slight angle. The final room of the public
omote unit was the tearoom *(cha-zashiki)*, located in the northeast
corner of the fourth floor.

The food-service function of the *nakaoku* began on the east side of
the second floor with the kitchen area, continuing via staircases and
corridors to the food supply center intermediary between kitchens
and other rooms *(irori no ma)* in the southeast corner of the third
floor. The *nakaoku* areas serving as entrances and guest areas began
across the corridor from the second-floor kitchen, with several splendid service rooms *(nando)* bordering the east and north sides of the

central vault,[9] and continued on the north side of the third floor with two very large *zashiki* and a twelve-mat elevated room on the extreme north.

A relatively isolated series of *zashiki* on the west side of the second floor appears to have functioned as the *kuroshoin*, in other words, as an inner sequence of rooms where the master conducted his daily business.[10] Staircases connected this complex with the master's room *(goza no ma)* on the west side of the third floor, which was adjacent to the formal reception rooms on the south and, via a long service room, the large *zashiki* on the north.

Judging from the painting subjects on the fourth floor, all *zashiki* on the east, south, and west were *nakaoku* living rooms, with the two on the south that are identified as having *toko* (here, probably a decorative alcove) and *tana* (decorative shelves) being the most formal. These rooms, and the two on the east, quite likely served honored guests rather than permanent residents. The northeast corner room was the *omote* tearoom, while the *zashiki* on the north side probably functioned as the private apartments of the *oku*. All rooms faced a corridor that encircled the central vault with a bridge running from north to south across the open space. Thus, occupants could amuse themselves by observing the activities taking place in the rooms below.

The central vault ended here, and a ceiling enclosed the four levels of space for public ceremony and private living. The fifth floor provided service areas for the rooms below, as well as two *tatami*-matted rooms that may have been observation posts. A sumptuous Buddhist chapel occupied the sixth level, and a square *zashiki* decorated with Chinese Confucian themes capped the seven-story castle.

The *Shinchō kōki* identifies painting subjects in the *taimensho* audience suites on the second floor, in the *hiroma* and other public reception rooms bordering the central vault on the third floor, and in all *zashiki* except the tearoom (which is specified as having no painting) on the fourth floor. Some of the other rooms surely contained *shōhekiga*, and the sources give occasional hints that certain rooms were painted in gold or with ink painting *(sumie)*, or imply that painted walls were the norm by commenting that specific areas had no paintings at all. The sixth-story chapel had its walls, its ceilings, its surrounding gallery, and even its columns covered with Buddhist paintings, and the seventh-story black lacquer-and-gold room featured didactic Confucian subjects on its walls and floral motifs on its ceiling. This pictorial abundance with its variety of subject matter confronted the man commissioned to bring it into being with an immense challenge. Nobunaga was an exacting patron, Azuchi Castle an enormous project.

Eitoku's success in handling his task at Azuchi may be gauged by the great demand for similar luxuriance in the decoration of subsequent residential castles. Made aware of the overriding importance of environment in influencing the behavior of groups, the lords required that their mansions project an aura of their prestige. The subject matter, design concept, and pictorial technique employed in the wall paintings had to relate to the desired ambience of each room. In castles of the Momoyama period, *shōhekiga* were intended to control the psychological receptivity of guests as well as their physical assembly. Each unit of interior space was conceived to have a distinct character consistent with its social function.

Azuchi Castle's *taimensho* audience suite, in accord with typical warrior residences at the end of the sixteenth century, was designed with formal simplicity in mind.[11] Its paintings were executed in monochrome. The four-mat raised *jōdan* on the northwest of the six-room sequence displayed a picture of pheasants nourishing their young. In the adjoining twelve-mat *zashiki* on the east, wild geese were painted. The two-mat room beside it featured a *tana* with doves. These could have been small paintings on the sliding panels across the top of the built-in shelves, or larger works on the wall behind the shelves. South of these three rooms were two more large *zashiki* and a decorative desk alcove *(shoin)*. The western twelve-mat room was separated from the northwest *jōdan* by a stationary wall, but communicated with the Wild Goose Room through two sets of sliding-door panels *(fusuma)*, and contained ink paintings of plum trees. The northern half of its west wall opened to the desk alcove, where a painting of *Evening Bell from a Distant Temple* could be viewed. This is one of the famous Chinese scenic spots, the *Eight Views of Hsiao and Hsiang,* favored by Japanese landscape painters from the fifteenth century onward, and it provided an appropriate complement to the miniature landscape *(bonsan)* set in front of it. Somewhat dissociated from the other two large *zashiki* by its theme was the eight-mat southeast room furnished with ink paintings of Chinese Confucian scholars. This room was also mentioned last in Ōta Gyūichi's account, even though it joins the room with the plum painting, which Gyūichi described first.

The distribution of subjects in this suite of rooms differs markedly from the arrangements established in the earlier Muromachi period.

Although the residences of Ashikaga shoguns are known only from scattered and insufficient references in historical records, the arrangements of *shōhekiga* in the Abbot's Quarters *(Hōjō)* of several important Zen institutions are fairly well understood. In the three major rooms of these buildings—the Central Room *(Shitchū)* of highest status, the Upper Room *(Jōdan)* of second importance, and the Lower Room *(Gedan)* of third rank—there was a conscious attempt to combine flower and bird, figure, and landscape subjects in contrasting styles associated with major Chinese artists, especially the thirteenth-century painters Mu-ch'i, Hsia Kuei, and Liang K'ai. In general, flowers and birds were depicted in the Central Room, figure subjects in the Upper Room, and landscapes in the Lower Room.[12] At Azuchi Castle, a profusion of flower and bird themes replaced this balanced distribution. With their immediately grasped appeal to the senses, flowers and birds were better suited to large-scale architectural surfaces, and were favored by artists and patrons during the second half of the sixteenth century. Second in popularity were figure subjects. When landscapes appeared, they were usually located in private rooms or at focal points to allow for longer reflection.

Evening Bell from a Distant Temple is the only landscape Gyūichi mentions in his account of the Azuchi Castle donjon. The isolation of a single scene from the *Eight Views of Hsiao and Hsiang* is a new occurrence in *shōhekiga*. It is difficult to find for illustration comparable paintings that are reliable enough as indicators of Eitoku's style.[13] It is possible, however, to speculate about the Chinese model that Nobunaga asked Eitoku to follow in painting *Evening Bell*. Of the four Chinese sets of the *Eight Views of Hsiao and Hsiang* known in Japan by the late fifteenth century,[14] the most likely prototype for Eitoku's Azuchi Castle painting was the one associated with the fourteenth-century Chinese monk-painter Yü-chien. Sometime after being recorded in the Ashikaga Shogunal Collection in the third quarter of the fifteenth century, the eight segments of Yü-chien's original handscroll were dispersed into private collections. These small paintings harmonized with the aesthetics of the tea ceremony *(cha-no-yu)*, and were revered by sixteenth-century connoisseurs of tea. Nobunaga, a notorious collector of tea treasures *(meibutsu)*, owned at least three of Yü-chien's *Eight Views*. One of these was *Evening Bell from a Distant Temple*, acquired about 1570 and used in a number of important tea ceremonies sponsored by Nobunaga throughout the succeeding decade.[15]

Evening Bell was the most prized of Yü-chien's *Eight Views*.[16]

Therefore, a wall painting based on this celebrated tea treasure would create a contemplative focus in Nobunaga's Azuchi Castle audience suite. It would remind visitors of Nobunaga's prestige as a collector of valuable objects, and of his liaison with the powerful merchants involved in Sakai tea society. Unfortunately, *Evening Bell from a Distant Temple* is not one of the three fragments from Yü-chien's Hsiao-Hsiang scroll that has survived,[17] so conjecture must be limited to a general visualization of a landscape with a multistoried temple, rendered in strongly contrasting ink tonalities applied spontaneously with effortless brushwork.

For the paintings of Confucian scholars and the flower and bird themes in Nobunaga's audience suite, better comparative material exists. Eitoku's paintings in the Abbot's Quarters of the Jukōin in the Daitokuji provide excellent illustrations of how he might have approached these subjects. Executed in 1566, when Eitoku was just twenty-three years old, they indicate the direction he was taking ten years before he began the Azuchi Castle project. Like the *taimensho* audience suite works, they are basically ink paintings, with the figure subject (the *Four Accomplishments*) in an important secondary room and the flower and bird theme *(Flowers and Birds of the Four Seasons)* in the principal room.

The Four Accomplishments of the cultivated Chinese gentleman are playing the lute *(ch'in)*, the game of *go*, calligraphy, and painting. As was the usual practice, in the Jukōin Eitoku rendered the theme in the formal academic style of the Chinese Southern Sung painters Ma Yüan and Hsia Kuei. Both subject and style acknowledge Eitoku's training in the shop of his grandfather, Kano Motonobu (1476–1559).[18] On eight sliding-door panels composed sequentially across the east and north walls of the Upper Room *(Jōdan)*, these paintings show Confucian scholars in a landscape setting (pl. 1). This is probably Eitoku's most conservative work. Not only does it incorporate subject, type-style, and motifs from Motonobu's shop, but it also retains the Muromachi-period compositional method of framing open areas with concentrations of forms at the outer edges. Where the east wall joins the north wall, opposing forces pull away from the corner axis to provide a caesura while still allowing continuous movement from one wall to the next. Triangular rocks thrust up from the bottom edge to furnish a foreground bridge between actual room space and the middle-ground picture stage where the flow of activity occurs. Distant views emerge across lake expanses, giving the horizontal flow a rhythm of alternating mass and void.

Yet hints of Eitoku's new direction already are evident in the Ju-kōin *Four Accomplishments*. His foreground rocks are less three-dimensional than are comparable works from Motonobu's shop,[19] so there is less distance between room space and the picture's main scenes. His middle-ground stage plateau tilts up a little more, giving a closer view of larger figures acting out their roles. The southeast thrust of the foreground rock in the corner seems to pass in front of the vertical axis of the pine tree sending its sharp branches both south and west. And the movement from middle ground tends more often to be up the picture plane rather than back into distant landscape. In general, Eitoku seems to be more aware of the two-dimensional wall surface and the possibility of bringing the picture up to the edge of the room space rather than pulling the viewer into the picture.

In the *Four Accomplishments,* Eitoku's individual interpretation of motifs is already perceptible: he is enlarging and simplifying, stressing outlines, reducing tonal gradations. Allowing his powerful brush to dominate, he is reinterpreting natural forms with the abstract language of art. And yet, it is the *Flowers and Birds of the Four Seasons* in the adjoining Central Room *(Shitchū)* of the Jukōin (pls. 2 and 3) that declares the new vision of the Momoyama period and indicates the direction Eitoku must have pursued in his paintings of plums and wild geese at Azuchi Castle.

The differences in Eitoku's two series of paintings at the Jukōin are striking. Most obvious, of course, is the dissimilarity in subject matter and type-style. The *Four Accomplishments* depicts figures in a landscape with the angular forms and sharp lines of the Ma Yüan–Hsia Kuei tradition. *Flowers and Birds* presents birds among trees and flowering plants using the stringy texture strokes and rounder forms associated with the style of Mu-ch'i. The *Four Accomplishments* is done in ink with light color, *Flowers and Birds* in ink only, but with gold mists suspended in the atmosphere. This kind of contrast was sought in *shōhekiga* in the interest of variety and distinction between rooms. Already by the late fifteenth century, Eitoku's great-grandfather and founder of the Kano line of artists, Kano Masanobu (1434–1530), was being supplied with Chinese model paintings of different styles to be followed in his decoration of Ashikaga Yoshimasa's Higashiyama Villa.[20]

More remarkable is the difference in composition. The *Four Accomplishments* is a panoramic landscape scene of forms completed within the picture frame. Groups of logically small figures drawn in careful detail occupy cells of space somewhat removed from the viewer. *Flowers and Birds of the Four Seasons* is a close-up view of middle-ground motifs, too large to be completely contained within the vertical dimensions of the wall surface. This too is a conscious choice of pictorial mode. Perhaps this contrast illustrates what Kano Einō was referring to in the *Honchō gashi* (1678) when he said of Eitoku:

He did landscapes, figures, flowers and birds, all in *saiga* [small or elaborate paintings]. Frequently he did *taiga* [large or expansive paintings]. When he chose to do *taiga,* his brushwork had the vigor of leaping cranes and fleeing snakes.[21]

As Eitoku's large commissions increased, Einō says:

Eitoku had no time to do *saiga,* but did *taiga* completely. Some of his pine and plum trees extended one hundred or two hundred feet and some of his figures were three or four feet tall. His brushwork became rugged and tempestuous. No one compares his quality with Motonobu's, though. In ink painting, he used a straw brush and, for the most part, had his grandfather's style, yet he produced a strikingly new conception. It was extraordinary, having a unique fascination not present in the art of his predecessors.[22]

It is precisely by comparing Eitoku's painting with the art of his great predecessor, Motonobu, that this new conception, present in the Jukōin and surely developed at Azuchi Castle, can be understood.

The prototype for Eitoku's *Flowers and Birds of the Four Seasons* is Motonobu's *Flowers and Birds of the Four Seasons* in the Central Room *(Shitchū)* of Myōshinji's Reiun'in (pl. 4) done twenty-three years earlier, in 1543. Both paintings present a seasonal sequence of birds and flowers in a continuous horizontal surface of three walls. The composition begins at the south end of the east wall, announcing spring with misty bamboo and flowering plum branches, moving northward past summer waterfalls, turning the corner into autumn, while representing winter with snowy mountains in the background. But as Einō suggested, Eitoku adopted Motonobu's ink painting vocabulary to express a new relationship between the abstract world of art and the real world of interior space. Eitoku used Motonobu's S-shaped pine trees, his oversized cranes, his coveys of wild ducks and clusters of hibiscus, but he exaggerated the size of these motifs. The trunks of Eitoku's trees, for example, have twice the girth of Motonobu's, and their powerful roots grip the earth at the very base of the wall surface, almost seeming to grow from the floor of the room itself rather than being set back on an earthen bank.

Eitoku's enlargement of motifs is but one factor indicating a basic structural change that establishes a new interaction between the wall surface and room space. To appreciate the innovation, it is necessary to understand the prototype.

Motonobu's painting is a continuous wall surface in three subsections. On the east wall, a watery area in the center of the spring scene is bracketed by the curve of a bamboo grove and lake shore on the right, and the reverse curve of a gnarled plum tree dipping into the water below an overhanging pine branch on the left. This large, slowly sweeping curve encloses a spatial volume further defined by the sloping hillocks in the foreground and their echo in the stepped recession of earthen banks in the middle ground. The focus of the composition is the northeast corner, where the greatest concentration of motifs is found. Counterbalancing the southward pull of the pine on the east wall, the rocks on the north wall incline to the west, marking the start of a second sequence. In front of a torrential waterfall, a crane perches on a gnarled horizontal pine branch that carries the movement to the left. A brief foray into depth via wintery mountains and a distant grove of trees is possible below three flying geese that swoop diagonally toward the flock huddled in the northwest corner inlet. A spit of land and blowing reeds enclose the second scene for another pause before the southward-bending growth of hibiscus pulls the viewer to consider the autumn setting of the west wall. From the rather small mass of luxuriant blossoms in the northwest corner, the angle of vision expands to enclose another sphere of middle-ground space and end with a large crane shrieking in a willow grove that overhangs marshy banks.

The rhythmic movement across the three walls undulates from top to bottom of the picture surface, and concurrently circulates from back to front of middle-ground space. It requires time to move in and out as well as up and down, so the tempo is slow and stately. There are pauses at corners and occasional suggestions of a space that contains more than is shown. At these places, the viewer can reflect for a moment before being caught again by an overhanging branch or a flying bird and returned to the motifs that are explicitly delineated.

In Eitoku's painting, there is no pause for reflection, nothing that would require the viewer to contemplate what he cannot see. Eitoku conceived of the three walls as a single unit. His enormous forms sweep across the surface, jumping over room space in the corners to continue on the next wall without being slowed by codas of framing elements. The sequence begins with a few bamboo stalks, but this motif does not act as a bracket for a void area, as does the bamboo with its earthen bank in Motonobu's Reiun'in *Flowers and Birds*. Instead, muscular tree roots immediately capture the eye, compelling movement through the exaggerated S-curve of the oversized plum tree. A shooting branch whips over the springtime violets and swimming mandarin ducks to the gushing rapids in the northeast corner. Its momentum jumps the corner to the cascades on the north wall, sweeps back with the torrent splashing to the east wall, then rushes westward again on the waves to the night heron. This movement passes a background wall of distant snowy mountains, arches over the top branches of two huge pine trees that shelter large cranes, is caught by a swooping goose, and ends with the responding geese on the ground.

In the northwest corner, Eitoku appears to retain Motonobu's centrifugal separation technique, for the giant pine trees swing away from each other in the direction of their respective walls. But these trees are not frames for subunits of the total composition. Their movement tends to be outward into room space, once again spanning the corner. A large root of the tree on the north wall hooks over to fasten on the ground of the west wall; the inner branches of the two trees pull in countermovements to intertwine across the top of the angle. The repetition of the giant crane motif under the arching pine branch on each wall requires that the entire corner be seen as one unified grove of trees providing refuge for a pair of large birds.

Eitoku accomplishes this compelling lateral movement by confining foreground motifs to the minimum of a few triangular rocks, bringing a very narrow middle ground forward, and eliminating background altogether. He reduces the number of motifs in this middle ground and greatly enlarges what he retains, using the entire height of the wall for his forms and suggesting further size by radically truncating the tops of trees. He blocks possible recession by suspending streaks of gold-dust clouds across the surface. These clouds are not vaporous suggestions of atmosphere, but are positive objects with physical substance. Thus, another key to Eitoku's commanding movement is his denial of void space and his assertion of positive form. Whereas Motonobu's motifs surround pockets of space, in Eitoku's painting the motif dominates. Eitoku's subject is the awesome energy of nature as it flows through natural bodies. The plum tree relays its force into the rushing water, which carries it to the lusty cranes and vigorous pine trees, and they transmit it to the stalwart geese.

There is no room for the viewer to enter the painting and find his place in this world of form. Instead, the painted objects are brought to the surface of the wall, to the very edge of living space. At the corners, they even audaciously span that space. Eitoku's powerful brush lines and strong tonal contrasts contribute to immediate understanding of explicit forms. It is an artistic conception ideally suited to environments of social interaction.

Surviving works show that Eitoku's style developed rapidly and displayed a remarkable sensitivity to architectural context. The ink paintings done for Azuchi Castle's *taimensho* ten years later than the works at the Jukōin must have been far more aggressive. It is unusual at this time, although not without precedent, to find "plums" mentioned as the painting subject for an entire room.[23] The dominating plum tree that Eitoku painted in the Central Room of the Jukōin Abbot's Quarters was not considered the subject of the sequence, which was referred to as *Flowers and Birds of the Four Seasons*. Therefore, Ōta Gyūichi's description of the Azuchi room as containing "pictures of plums" suggests even greater magnification of the tree motif, perhaps approaching the commanding form of a late composition such as the Tokyo National Museum's *Cypress* (pl. 9).

In addition to this predictable increase in visual dynamism, Eitoku may have made a significant innovation in his paintings for Nobunaga's audience rooms: he may have incorporated gold leaf into monochrome painting. While the *Tenshu sashizu* specifies that these were all ink paintings *(sumie)*,[24] the *Shinchō kōki* notes that "from top to bottom, everything in these chambers, wherever there are pictures, all is gold."[25] This is not necessarily a contradiction. However, although gold dust and gold paint had been used with ink paintings throughout the sixteenth century, judging from existing large works, gold leaf was not combined with ink monochrome before the 1590s. Yet, such a union would have been a logical next step for Eitoku in the 1570s. The gold-dust clouds of his Jukōin *Flowers and Birds of the Four Seasons* present solid forms that defy allusion to depth. It is reasonable to suppose that he did make a conceptual leap by substituting abstract gold-leaf clouds in Azuchi Castle, in order to create dramatic contrasts of black and gold; for he had already used them in works of a different genre.[26]

The aesthetic effect of such a combination can be seen in a set of wall paintings attributed to Hasegawa Tōhaku (1539–1610) and probably executed near the end of the sixteenth century, the *Rocks and Waves* owned by Zenrinji in Kyoto.[27] Unlike gold paint, which has the character of a pigment, gold leaf is a flat, denaturalized surface. Wherever it is applied, it creates an impenetrable, reflective plane, affirming the two-dimensional nature of the wall and establishing a disengaged context for depicted motifs. Its unreality reinforces the assertive substance of painted objects. It immediately informs the viewer that he is looking at a newly created reality, and not at an image of his own world.

The resplendence of Momoyama gold-ground and strong-color *(kinpeki)* painting burst forth in the third-floor *omote* rooms for public entertainment. This is the style that made Eitoku famous. His *kinpeki shōhekiga* at Azuchi were an instant success, and Eitoku was much in demand for the remainder of his short life. Kano Einō says in the *Honchō gashi:* "Lord Toyotomi Hideyoshi built two great castles, Juraku and Osaka. He had Eitoku paint them in *kinpeki.* Whenever the lords of the day built grand residences to be furnished with gold walls, they always wanted [Eitoku] to paint them."[28]

Many of these great lords were received by Nobunaga at Azuchi Castle in the brief period of its existence from 1579 to 1582. There they saw the flowers and birds painted by Eitoku in brilliant colors and gold in the twelve-mat *zashiki* and its adjoining four-mat *jōdan* that formed Nobunaga's *hiroma.* They surely relished the exotic flavor of the eight-mat Civet Room *(jakō no ma)* on the east side, or the popular themes of Chinese hermits and sages in the two *zashiki* flanking the Civet Room. Here was a painting style that could exploit a wealth of sensual elements: the luxury of shining gold, the brilliance of saturated colors, the rhythmic affirmation of strong line. Unfortunately, no technique could ensure permanence for this magnificent art. Most *kinpeki shōhekiga* from the era of Nobunaga and Hideyoshi perished with the castles they decorated. Very little survives, and those paintings that are extant have suffered with time, retaining only a shadowy hint of their original splendor.

The best remaining examples of *kinpeki shōhekiga* associated with Eitoku from the Tenshō years (1573–1593) now adorn the rooms of the Dai Hōjō (Large Abbot's Quarters) at the great Zen monastery Nanzenji in Kyoto. These paintings were originally created by Eitoku's shop for a building of the Imperial Palace, which was given to the Nanzenji in 1611.[29] Scholarly opinion is divided concerning whether they were done for Emperor Ōgimachi's In no Gosho (Retirement Palace) in 1586, or for Emperor Go-Yōzei's Seiryōden

(Ceremonial Residence) in 1591, and whether or not Eitoku's own painting can be found in the series. There are problems in terms of style, since few of these paintings possess the striking grandeur of conception of the Jukōin cycle of *Flowers and Birds of the Four Seasons* (pls. 2 and 3) or the boldness of later large *kinpeki* works attributed to Eitoku (pls. 7 and 8). Although none of the Nanzenji paintings can be accepted as works by Eitoku himself, they do reflect contemporary currents within his Kano school. They also illustrate a development of wall-painting style in response to the unique character of gold leaf.

The flower and bird paintings in Nobunaga's *hiroma* may have given an effect similar to that of the Nanzenji *Willow and Camellias* (pl. 5). On a grassy bank among colorful flowers, the branches of a willow tree are caught by spring breezes, and swing over a brook toward a large shrub of blossoming camellias. Clouds of gold leaf serve both as background to silhouette vividly colored shapes and as positive forms to structure the composition. Of the Nanzenji *kinpeki* paintings,[30] these are among the most conservative group.

In his perceptive analysis of *kinpeki shōhekiga,* Takeda Tsuneo identifies three developmental stages based on a distinction between gold clouds and gold ground.[31] Gold clouds generally occupy the front of a picture plane, taking a positive role in composition by isolating important motifs and by suggesting passage of time or space. Gold ground is a background of gold leaf, establishing the back plane against which painted objects are suspended. The first stage in Takeda's schema of evolution is the use of gold clouds only, developed from the cloud forms *(kumogata)* in the *Yamato-e* tradition of narrative illustration of Japanese classics. Since no background plane is fixed, recession into depth is possible. The second stage is concurrent use of gold clouds and gold ground, and is the mode prevalent in the last quarter of the sixteenth century. Generally the gold clouds and gold ground define a narrow space where objects exist between the foreground plane and the background plane. The tendency is toward loss of this distinction. In some earlier instances, segments of plain ground remain to allow glimpses into depth, and in some later instances, the gold leaf acts as foreground cloud in one section but unaccountably becomes background in another. Finally, the third stage is gold ground only. It is not seen in its pure form before the second quarter of the seventeenth century.[32]

In the Nanzenji *Willow and Camellias,* the gold clouds are always distinct cloud forms, although they slide in front of some motifs to isolate the forms of others. Occasionally the clouds break to uncover a suggestion of depth, as in the upper part of the left panel, where a few misty trees appear. Thus the wall presents a successive layering of planes, with a reminder that depth is still possible.

Both gold clouds and gold ground are present in the painting of *Civets in Pine* (pl. 6). The nine panels of this sequence, as reconstructed by Kobayashi Chū, form the most substantial overall composition that remains at Nanzenji.[33] Both in its subject matter and in its organization of motifs under the spreading branches of a large S-shaped pine tree, this painting serves as a useful means to visualize the effect of Azuchi Castle's Civet Room. If the original ultramarine were still on the water and the brilliant greens and reds remained on the flowers and grasses, it would be an even better illustration. As is the case with the *Flowers and Birds of the Four Seasons* in the Jukōin, a few rocks at the bottom of the wall suggest a foreground between room space and a close-up middle ground of enlarged motifs. But at Nanzenji, the civets and rocks and peonies interact across a lateral passage that has nothing behind it except two layers of gold: gold clouds floating across a gold ground. To distinguish the two, greenish-white gesso was used to build up the scalloped edges of the clouds before the gold leaf was applied; then the contours were outlined with gold paint. Since gold paint has a different nature and less luster than gold leaf, it provided a subtle contrast. Today, however, this gold has flaked off, exposing the gesso and the ink outline of the clouds.

On both sides of the Civet Room at Azuchi Castle were rooms painted with famous Chinese sages and Taoist immortals.[34] Figure subjects in *kinpeki* are rare among surviving works attributed to Eitoku, and the only large-scale paintings with serious claims to his authorship are the *Twenty-four Examples of Filial Piety (Nijūshikō)* and *Chinese Hermits (Sennin)* (pl. 7) from Nanzenji. Of these two, the sequence of seventeen panels illustrating stories of Chinese hermits is thought to be closer to Eitoku's accepted works, although Japanese scholars have many doubts that Eitoku actually painted it. The style, with its strong *Yamato-e* character, is closer to the manner of Eitoku's son, Mitsunobu (1561–1608), who is known to have completed his father's unfinished work after Eitoku's sudden death in 1590.[35] In terms of motif, the group of gentlemen playing *go* in plate 7 closely resembles the arrangement in the *go* scene (the third panel from the right in pl. 1) of Eitoku's Jukōin *Four Accomplishments,* and the tree in the second panel of the illustrated *Chinese Hermits* has the same configuration as the tree in the hanging scroll of *Ch'ao Fu* by Eitoku in the Tokyo National Museum.[36] This certainly does not mean the same artist painted all three works, but it suggests that the painting of Chinese hermits came from Eitoku's shop.

The techniques of figure depiction in Nanzenji's *Chinese Hermits* are derived from Chinese painting as interpreted by sixteenth-century Kano artists, but the coloring and compositional techniques come from the *Yamato-e* tradition. Instead of the predominance of the strong mineral pigments generally favored by Kano artists, we find gentle pinks and lavenders and milky greys.[37] The scenes are arranged on a ground of gold, with a strong reliance on gold clouds to structure the composition and to provide spatial transitions from one scene to the next. Although this is a technique that originated with *Yamato-e* artists, by the second half of the sixteenth century it could be employed at will by artists of all schools, and in this case it gives a distinctive *Yamato-e* flavor. A century later, in 1678, Eitoku's descendant, Kano Einō, gave Kano artists specific instructions on how to paint *Yamato-e* compositions.

The *Yamato-e* manner is an expression of human sensibilities, so it is gentle. . . . Clouds are placed above and below the scenes to differentiate space and to emphasize what is important by covering the trivial. There are many pine trees in the design. These are done by arranging a series of similar branches one above the other and painting them in dark green.[38]

The pine in *Chinese Hermits,* while having the trunk configuration of the tree in Eitoku's *Ch'ao Fu,* has the stylized layering of scalloped green clusters in the *Yamato-e* manner, rather than the individually separated wheels of needles seen in the Chinese-derived style of *Civets in Pine.*

Aside from matters of stylistic derivation of motifs, the structure of the painting moves a step further away from the realistic stage space of the magnified middle ground in *Civets in Pine.* In *Chinese Hermits,* the layering of planes by gold clouds begins on the very bottom edge of the wall. Behind the gold clouds, multifaceted rocks crop up, emphasized by a background of gold. Against this metallic gold ground, groups of Chinese hermits act out their stories. These forms are not bound to a specific locale defined by green grass and earthen banks. Their environment is neutralized by a denaturalized, inorganic expanse of gold. Figures, rocks, trees, even a running brook, are disengaged from the tangible world and rearranged on an abstract plane. Actors cannot penetrate their metallic background, but they can be imagined to move left or right along the lateral avenues organized by the stratification of clouds. Thus the use of gold ground and gold clouds in *Chinese Hermits* affirms the planar character of the wall and emphasizes the horizontal movement of the composition around the room.

The two north *zashiki* on Azuchi Castle's third floor also contained *kinpeki shōhekiga.* The larger, twenty-mat room was painted with *Horses in Pasture,* a popular theme in the warrior society of the late sixteenth century. No comparable paintings by Eitoku's school have survived, but some idea of possible treatments of the subject can be gained from two sets of folding screens that were shown in the 1975 Momoyama exhibition at the Metropolitan Museum of Art in New York. *Horses in a Landscape* by Unkoku Tōgan (1547–1618) depicts the same subject, but is an ink painting produced by an artist of a different stylistic lineage about twenty-five years after Azuchi Castle was decorated.[39] *Rounding Up Horses* by Hasegawa Tōhaku was executed closer to the time the Azuchi *shōhekiga* were done and is in color, although there is no gold.[40] Tōhaku is said to have begun his artistic career in the Kano style, only later establishing his own school,[41] but these screens are very early works and may have been painted before Tōhaku arrived in Kyoto in the 1570s. Therefore, *Rounding Up Horses* may not be at all comparable to Kano shop productions of the late 1570s.

Hsi Wang-mu was depicted in the twelve-mat *zashiki,* as in all likelihood was her consort Tung Wang-kung.[42] Again, contemporary Kano examples are lacking, but the subject was treated throughout the sixteenth century. An early example formed part of the commission executed by Motonobu and his shop for the Daisen'in during the first quarter of the century.[43] A late example exists in splendid *kinpeki* in Nishi Honganji's *taimensho* suite, painted in the early seventeenth century.[44]

The painting topics of all the *zashiki* on the fourth floor of the Azuchi donjon are given in the *Shinchō kōki:* craggy rocks, dragons and tigers, bamboo, pine, phoenix, hydrangeas, falcon breeding, and Chinese examples of model conduct.[45] The range of subject matter and the fact that Gyūichi specifically names them illustrates another function of *shōhekiga:* to clarify room divisions. The sliding-door panels on which these themes were painted served as partitions between one area of living space and another, and the paintings supplemented the architectural scheme. They not only decorated the walls, but also created an aesthetic environment sufficiently different from surrounding space to identify each room. As the *Kaoku zakkō*, an Edo-period encyclopaedic manual on residential architecture, points out: "It is a great inconvenience when it is difficult to distinguish between rooms in many-chambered buildings. Accordingly, the walls and sliding doors are painted so that names can be given the various rooms, and not necessarily just to create splendid interiors."[46] The Jesuit Luis Frois compared the interior of Nobunaga's Gifu Castle to the Labyrinth of Crete,[47] and his fellow missionary João Rodrigues Tçuzzu commented on Japanese palaces of the 1590s by saying that "it is necessary to have competent guides in such houses."[48] A great deal of ingenuity was required of the artist who worked on this kind of residence. He had to design a series of different environments, each conveying the distinctive character that was appropriate to the function of the room being decorated.

The *zashiki* on the west side of the donjon's fourth floor are mentioned first in the *Shinchō kōki*. Since Gyūichi consistently begins with the most important rooms on each level, these probably formed Nobunaga's apartments. Aggressive subjects—trees on rugged cliffs, and dragons and tigers—conveyed a forceful image of natural power. An analogous work is the oversized folding screen of *Chinese Lions (Karajishi)* in the Imperial Household Collection (pl. 8).[49] This screen of two imperious beasts stalking through a rocky passage was supposedly presented by Hideyoshi to Mōri Terumoto as a peace offering at the time of the siege of Takamatsu Castle in 1582. It bears the authentication of Kano Tan'yū (1602–1674) in the lower right corner and is universally accepted as an Eitoku painting, although some scholars consider it closer to 1587 in date.[50] It fairly throbs with the audacity which those two lions, Nobunaga and Hideyoshi, applied to establish their control over a warlike society.

In *Chinese Lions*, the direction Eitoku was taking in the Jukōin *Flowers and Birds of the Four Seasons* toward simplification and exaggeration of forms has proceeded to a stage of terrific dynamism. Motifs have been reduced to three: a pair of enormous animals, an adamantine rock, and a twig bearing a few desiccated leaves. Or perhaps the motifs should number four, since the gold ground itself is a material substance, transforming at will to gold cloud with no change of inherent nature. The distinction between gold ground and gold cloud has nearly vanished, and with its dissolution the stratification of foreground plane and background plane disappears. Only in the upper-left section, where the gold surface unaccountably forms scalloped edges of gold clouds, does a layering of planes occur. The change in effect is dramatic: like apparitions, the lions emerge from the visionary gold surface on the right to approach a fixed narrow passageway between a foreground rock in lower left and a rock cliff locked in position by gold clouds. The gold ground on the right ejects these phantasms from its surface, and the beasts magnify its force by virtue of their own bold contours and clear-cut patterns of line and color. Only the vestige of layered space on the left ties them to the picture surface.

Dynamic pictorial elements make a positive statement. Foremost is the gold surface, catching and reflecting light, animating the space it confronts. Against this vibrant, impenetrable base, Eitoku's decisive lines reiterate the density of the gold and affirm the substantial bulk of the Chinese lions. Gold spirals are captured in the whorls of the lions' manes and tails, linking them with the unreal world of their mineral environment. The vivid green of the crystalline rocks is consistent with this inorganic context. Exaggerations of size, of precision, of color intensity: these are the aesthetic carriers of an incisive message.

Such paintings create environments expedient to the purposes of social control. They are meant to overwhelm. By their very presence, they establish the dominating tone which a feudal ruler adopts toward his vassals: they aggressively confront the lord's subordinates. They defy reflection on selfhood and force individuals to respond submissively to the power they represent. Surrounded by this kind of imperative atmosphere, Nobunaga's vassals were all the more aware that they must heed his paramount decree. This environment constrained them by the artistic force of its message.

Continuing the theme of assurance but neutralizing motifs of confrontation, the two south-side *zashiki* contain paintings of bamboo and of pine. These probably were the most public of the fourth-floor rooms. The Pine Room *(matsu no ma)* may have looked something like the large entrance hall of Kyoto's Myōhōin, where enormous pine trees extend their branches across a gold ground above rocks and a few clumps of bamboo.[51] This painting, however, although based on Eitoku's style, probably was executed several decades after his death and displays a delicate grace characteristic of the early seventeenth century. Another giant tree painting with a better claim to Eitoku's authorship might provide a more reliable image of the Azuchi Castle Pine Room. This is the eight-fold screen of *Cypress* in the Tokyo National Museum (pl. 9).

ILLUSTRATIONS

PLATE 1. *Four Accomplishments (Kinki Shoga).* Kano Eitoku. Sliding-door panels, ink and color on paper; four east panels, each 175 × 143 cm; two of four north panels, each 175 × 95 cm. Upper Room *(Jōdan),* Jukōin, Daitokuji, Kyoto.

PLATE 2. *Flowers and Birds of the Four Seasons (Shiki Kachō).* Kano Eitoku. *In situ.* Central Room *(Shitchū),* Jukōin, Daitokuji, Kyoto.

PLATE 3. *Flowers and Birds of the Four Seasons (Shiki Kachō).* Kano Eitoku. Sliding-door panels, ink and gold dust on paper; four east panels, each 177 × 143 cm; four outer north panels, each 177 × 92 cm; four inner north panels, each 177 × 74 cm; four west panels, each 177 × 143 cm. Central Room *(Shitchū),* Jukōin, Daitokuji, Kyoto.

PLATE 4. *Flowers and Birds of the Four Seasons (Shiki Kachō).* Kano Motonobu. Sliding-door panels, ink and light color on paper; four east panels, each 178 × 143 cm; four north panels, each 178 × 118 cm; four west panels, each 178 × 143 cm. Central Room *(Shitchū),* Reiun'in, Myōshinji, Kyoto.

PLATE 5. *Willow and Camellias (Yanagi ni Tsubaki).* Kano school. Four sliding-door panels, color and gold leaf on paper, each 184 × 98 cm. Yanagi no ma, Dai Hōjō, Nanzenji, Kyoto.

PLATE 6. *Civets in Pine (Matsu ni Jakō).* Kano school. Nine sliding-door panels, color and gold leaf on paper; four right-hand panels, each 185 × 72 cm; middle panel 178 × 86 cm; four left-hand panels, each 184 × 98 cm. Jakō no ma and Nishi no ma, Dai Hōjō, Nanzenji, Kyoto.

PLATE 7. *Chinese Hermits (Sennin).* Attributed to Kano Eitoku. Four of twelve sliding-door panels, color and gold leaf on paper, each 184 × 98 cm. Ohiru no ma, Dai Hōjō, Nanzenji, Kyoto.

PLATE 8. *Chinese Lions (Karajishi).* Kano Eitoku. Six-fold screen, color and gold leaf on paper, 225 × 460 cm. Imperial Household Collection, Tokyo.

PLATE 9. *Cypress (Hinoki).* Attributed to Kano Eitoku. Eight-fold screen, color and gold leaf on paper, 170 × 460 cm. Tokyo National Museum.

Although it is now mounted as a folding screen, traces of sliding-door handles reveal that *Cypress* was originally a *fusuma* painting. Many Japanese scholars consider that it formed part of the large commission that Eitoku, assisted by his younger brother Sōshū (1551–1601) and his son Mitsunobu, was painting for the palace of Prince Tomohito at the time of his death in 1590.[52] If so, then whether actually executed by Eitoku or by an important assistant, the *Cypress* screen provides an example of Eitoku's late style.

Since *Cypress* does not retain its original format, conclusions about total composition can only be tentative. However, judging from the size of the paper sections in terms of its total height, only a few inches were lost from the top and bottom edges when *Cypress* was re-mounted as a folding screen.[53] Therefore, the radical truncation of the top and bottom of the commanding tree was present from the beginning. Foreground rocks have vanished; the burly cypress occupies the very front plane of the wall. Its rich reddish-brown trunk is shaded with black and highlighted with gold, then adorned with whitish-green lichen clusters. Gold ground silhouettes its muscular limbs, with a gold cloud particularly accenting the branch extending to the left, paralleling the deep ultramarine water below. A great hulking rock rises behind the cloud. Once again, there is a layering of horizontal planes, directing attention laterally across the wall surface.

The compact gold sheet and the equally uniform ultramarine water surface behind the husky tree and stalwart rock create tensions that frustrate naturalistic illusion. The inorganic surface denies space, but it affirms the material nature of objects. Motifs are reduced to their most legible components and rendered so large that they give a heightened perception of reality, appealing directly to the senses. Thus the tree and the rock have substantial bulk, but they do not displace space, for in this painting there is no space to displace. The only direction in which the forms can expand is horizontally, around the border of the room. They are locked within the homogeneous planar surface of the wall.

The themes of the two east-side *zashiki* are proselytizing, suggesting that these rooms were intended for guests. In one, a phoenix in paulownia was painted; in the other, Hsü Yu and Ch'ao Fu were depicted. The phoenix has a long history in China as a symbol for the reign of a virtuous king, while the Chinese hermits Hsü Yu and Ch'ao Fu had become a favored illustration of military comradeship in sixteenth-century Japan.[54] No contemporary examples of these themes provide comparable illustrations for what Eitoku might have designed at Azuchi Castle.[55]

The three *zashiki* north of the central vault probably made up the *oku* apartments for the women of the household, since the subjects named by Gyūichi are quieter than the themes in the other suites. The northeast corner room had a *toko* (decorative alcove) and *tana* (shelves) and was painted in *kinpeki* with scenes of nurturing falcons. This became a popular subject for genre painting in the seventeenth century, but comparable contemporary examples are rare.

The adjoining twelve-mat *zashiki* had hydrangea depicted on its west wall. A hydrangea bush is painted in the right two panels of *Civets in Pine* from Nanzenji (pl. 6), but the effect of the Azuchi wall might have been more similar to the elegance of the *Cherry and Willow* panels at Nanzenji.[56] Sinuous slender trees with a decidedly *Yamato-e* flavor bear delicate white blossoms against a background with gold clouds. The gold predominates, presenting an ethereal world quite distinct from the images of dynamism and aggression in other rooms.

No paintings were found on the fifth level, but the sixth-story Buddhist chapel and the seventh-story Confucian room were sumptuously decorated.

The octagonal sixth floor was totally Buddhist in theme. A gallery about seven feet wide surrounded an eight-sided room that was about twenty-one feet in diameter. Arched windows in the outer wall of the gallery were decorated with ornate railings, and images of fantastic dolphins *(shachihoko)* and flying dragons on the window shutters produced an encircling rhythm like ocean waves. On the ceiling of the gallery, between each intercolumnation, were a pair of dragons. Hungry ghosts *(gaki)* and demons *(oni)* were painted on the walls opposite the windows. The columns and rafters were vermilion, and ascending and descending dragons emblazoned the inner columns. Inside the octagonal hall, all columns were gold and all paintings were *kinpeki*. On the walls were depictions of the *Ten Great Disciples of Buddha* and *Buddha Establishing the Way and Preaching the Law*, and on the coffered ceiling were Buddhist angels.[57] The chapel presented a radiant microcosm of the Buddhist universe, from dragons in the depths of the earth to divine spirits in the heavens.

This kind of Buddhist decoration certainly formed part of the professional activity of sixteenth-century Kano artists, but it tended to be conservative in nature, and would not have been the vehicle for stylistic innovation. The Buddhist paintings probably were relegated to an assistant in a commission as large as Azuchi Castle—especially since Nobunaga had little use for Buddhist traditions.

In fact, surmounting this spiritual realm, another world occupied a position even higher and more exalted than that of the celestial Buddhist angels. The square room on the top story symbolized Nobunaga's aspirations to rule all of Japan, and must have been the most important decorative project at Azuchi Castle. It was painted with Chinese culture-heroes, political models, and sages, its theme being good government as sanctioned by the Chinese concept of the Mandate of Heaven.[58] About twenty-one feet square, the room had an entrance in the middle of each of its four sides communicating with an outer gallery. Such dignified symmetry would reinforce the aura of moral rectitude. The pillars, the beams of the coffered ceiling, the windows lining the encircling gallery, even the floor gleamed with lustrous black lacquer, setting off the brilliant *kinpeki* paintings on the wall panels and ceiling coffers, and creating a stunning contrast to the gold of the castle's exterior at this level. The room must have given an effect very similar to the Tsukubu Suma Jinja Honden, painted in 1602 by Eitoku's son Mitsunobu, who had assisted his father at Azuchi Castle.

But Mitsunobu's paintings at Tsukubu Suma Jinja are graceful flowers and grasses. The subject matter of Eitoku's work at Azuchi, combined with the greater forcefulness of his style, would have given the seventh-story room a much stronger impact. The *Tenshu sashizu* identifies the subject of each wall. On the southeast walls were Fu Hsi and Shen Nung, the Chinese culture-heroes who are credited with developing such arts of civilization as writing, fishing and trapping, agriculture and commerce. In the southwest corner was Huang Ti on the south wall and Lao Tzu on the west. Huang Ti (the Yellow Emperor) is the mythical sage-king associated with the inception of Taoism, who is cited in the *Tao-te ching* and frequently linked with its legendary author, Lao Tzu. The association of the two here would have evoked the Taoist conception of the ideal ruler as a sage who governs on the basis of his comprehension of the mystic principle of Tao.

In the northwest corner was King Wen in his carriage, about to meet the wise hermit T'ai Kung-wang on the adjoining wall. King Wen received Heaven's Mandate to overthrow the decadent Shang rule and found the Chou dynasty, and was one of Confucius' models of benevolence and virtue. T'ai Kung-wang ended his voluntary exile to serve King Wen as chief counsellor. On the east end of the north wall was the Duke of Chou, another model of virtue extolled by Confucius. As regent to King Wen's grandson, King Ch'eng, he devoted himself so conscientiously to the tasks of government that he would interrupt his bath, holding his wet hair to one side, in order to deal with affairs of state. On the east wall were the Ten Disciples of Confucius on the north, and Confucius himself on the south.

The wall paintings follow a chronological progression from the sage-kings of the mythical past through historical paragons of virtue to Confucius, the codifier of a political system based on the integrity of a wise ruler. The subjects of the *Seven Sages of the Bamboo Grove* and the *Four Wise Men of Shang Shan,* paintings that are mentioned in the *Shinchō kōki,* are not indicated on the *Tenshu sashizu.* Naitō speculates that these were located on the wooden panels above the doors in the center of each side wall,[59] where Mitsunobu painted wisteria in the Tsukubu Suma Jinja. Since both of these themes deal with gentlemen who shunned government service in times of political degeneracy, they would underline the need for the good rulers depicted on the major walls.

There is no precedent in Japanese architectural decoration for such a room: the seventh story of Azuchi Castle heralds the new age. Documentary materials referring to fifteenth-century shogunal residences do not mention comparable Chinese political subjects, but after the collaboration of Eitoku and Nobunaga at Azuchi in the 1570s, and in accord with the increasing emphasis on Confucianism as a model for social conduct, Chinese historical subjects became prominent themes for *shōhekiga.* Among the earliest examples still in existence are the Nanzenji wall paintings of *Twenty-four Examples of Filial Piety* and *Chinese Hermits* (pl. 7), painted by Eitoku's shop for rooms in the Imperial Palace at least a decade after Nobunaga's castle was designed.

Such a room presented demands which must have intensely stimulated Eitoku's accomplishment of a spatial transformation. The theme of a Utopia decreed by a prince sublimely confident of his mission to reunite and revivify the Japanese realm—that is to say, establish his own new order, the *Tenka*—required an environment displaying symbols of authority beyond those found in the common surroundings of daily life. The architect provided a square with axial openings to reinforce that environment's stability, recalling similar arrangements in Buddhist architecture, such as the early eighth-century Kondō of the Hōryūji. Lacquer craftsmen furnished a shimmer of reflective black on all structural members, an effect not achieved to the same degree in the Tsukubu Suma Jinja Honden, since this later interior lacks the rarefied luminosity of the Azuchi donjon's lacquered floor. An equivalent image is created by the dazzling floor of the third-story room in the Kinkaku, or Golden Pavilion, of the Rokuonji,[60] an important architectural prototype for Nobunaga's residence, which was built nearly two centuries earlier by that other great political visionary, Ashikaga Yoshimitsu, as a symbol of his earthly paradise.

In this room of denaturalized veneers, Eitoku would have fused amplified motifs into the front plane of an impenetrable gold surface. By asserting the physical existence of his materials, he would have refuted any expectation of illusionist space within the picture. Rather than being a mirror image of reality, Eitoku's new spatial world was a restructured abstraction of physical forces. His sensory elements of rhythmic line, commanding shape, saturated color, and brilliant gold leaf communicate on an essentially intuitive level. They appeal not so much to the mind as to the body.

Eitoku's message on the seventh story of Azuchi Castle was explicit. It confronted visitors with an aesthetic vision of Nobunaga's ideal realm and compelled them to respect it, for Eitoku's sense of pictorial space was perfectly attuned to the commanding spirit of the age of Nobunaga.

DONALD KEENE

Jōha, a Sixteenth-Century Poet
of Linked Verse

THE SIXTEENTH CENTURY, as far as literature was concerned, was a period of beginnings and ends, rather than of fruition. The incessant warfare, starting with the Ōnin War in 1467, had driven the writers of the traditional court literature from the capital to the countryside, to seek refuge with local potentates, spreading the court culture to many distant regions. This effect was in itself desirable, but there was no longer any one center where men could meet to create the typical literary products of the first half of the fifteenth century—the *waka*, linked verse *(renga)*, the Nō plays, or poetry in Chinese. Eventually, as order was temporarily restored, poets drifted back to the capital, but by this time the great figures of the past were dead. Perhaps that is why so many new literary arts germinated in this period, notably the *haikai*, or comic, style of linked verse.

The arts that originated at this time included Kabuki and Jōruri, both created towards the close of the sixteenth century and destined to evolve into the most popular forms of drama during the following century. Even the Nō, which had fallen into a decline in the sixteenth century because of the breakup of the aristocratic society in Kyoto that had long been its patrons, showed signs of developing in new directions, but the unconventional plays with large casts, openly dramatic action, but little ghostly beauty, led the way not to a revival of Nō as a living theatrical art but to an enhancement of Kabuki. This was not the only instance of promising beginnings not culminating in major artistic results. The literature written under the inspiration of the European works introduced to Japan by the Portuguese and Spanish missionaries was killed off in embryo by the prohibition of Christianity in the seventeenth century.

Among the genres which met their end during the sixteenth century none was more conspicuous than renga. It was the chief poetic art of the period, and surely none of its practitioners dreamt that their art was dying; but rare is the scholar today who can name even one poet of serious renga from the seventeenth century or later. I emphasize the word "serious," for the comic variety of renga was still being composed well into the nineteenth century, and had much earlier given rise to the independent haiku in seventeen syllables, the most famous of Japanese verse forms. But the serious renga, which had emerged into prominence in the fourteenth century and reached its apogee in the fifteenth century with the great Sōgi, ended with Jōha, the last of the masters.

Jōha is little known today except to scholars of renga, but he was no doubt the outstanding figure of all sixteenth-century Japanese literature. His poetry is no longer quoted, and exceedingly few people can still compose linked verse in his traditions, but his career remains of special interest, both because of what Jōha stood for in his day and because of the light it sheds on the fate of artists living in violently changing times.

Jōha was born in 1524 in Nara, the son of a temple servant at the Ichijōin. This was a humble occupation, but probably not without influence within the temple, perhaps the most richly endowed abbacy of the great Kōfukuji monastery, and as such one of the most important of the Hossō sect. A not always reliable account of Jōha's life written many years after his death states that his father ran a public bath.[1] This small fact—if indeed it is one—has confirmed the tendency among certain Japanese scholars to insist on Jōha's humble origins, as if his rise to celebrity was more important than his poetry itself.

Even if his family background was humble, Jōha received a good education. He began from an early age to study renga with a wealthy townsman, a silk dealer who was also an amateur poet.[2] Jōha was only twelve when his father died, but this misfortune apparently did not cause him undue hardship. However, he knew that as a younger son he would have to make his own career, and as a first step he became a *kasshiki* at a Hossō temple.[3] A *kasshiki* was a young man who studied at a Buddhist temple, but did not necessarily intend to become a priest; for this reason he did not shave his head like the other acolytes. Jōha was taught not only the Buddhist scriptures but also works of classical literature. He maintained his interest in renga and presumably received guidance from the various renga masters who visited the Kōfukuji, the main temple of the Hossō sect. Perhaps that is how he met Shūkei, a leading renga poet of the day, in 1542. The young Jōha, eighteen that year, had finally shaved his head and been formally ordained as a priest, but he seems not to have been satisfied with his prospects. Even within the Buddhist temples, despite the possibilities they offered for talented men of humble birth to rise to high position, family background was never ignored, and it was unlikely that the second son of a temple servant would achieve eminence. Jōha decided to become a renga master instead, and when Shūkei returned to Kyoto, Jōha went with him.

In later years Jōha told his disciple Matsunaga Teitoku what had prompted him to make this decision. He said, "A man who fails to make a name for himself before he is thirty will never succeed in life. I examined my prospects carefully, and it seemed to me that becoming a renga master would be an easy way to get ahead. After all, at renga gatherings even artisans and townsmen sit side-by-side with members of the nobility. And, I thought, if I didn't succeed in this career, I would ask for a letter of recommendation from the abbot of the Hyakumanben Temple, go down to the East, and learn how to deliver popular sermons as a way of making a living."[4]

Jōha remained a Buddhist priest even after choosing his new career, perhaps because he thought it would be something to fall back on if he failed as a poet. In any case, renga masters normally shaved their heads and wore the habit of Buddhist priests, in part because this was the custom among learned men, even doctors and Confucian scholars, in part because priestly garments were helpful in passing through the barriers along the highways.

Jōha was fortunate in having had Shūkei accept him as a pupil. Although Shūkei died in 1544, only two years later, he had provided Jōha with the foundations for a career as a renga poet. Jōha learned not only the rules of composing linked verse, an extremely demanding art, but the formalities of conducting a renga meeting, including the placing of the desks, the proper manner of grinding the ink from the stick, the prescribed intonation when reading completed verses aloud, and many other technicalities. The earliest mention of Jōha at a renga composition states that he was the scribe of a session held in 1545, the year after Shūkei's death, indicating that he had learned the formalities well.

Jōha chose as his next teacher Satomura Shōkyū (1510–1552). The leading figure in renga after Shūkei's death was Tani Sōboku (d. 1545), but Jōha for some reason chose to study under Shōkyū instead.[5] This proved to be another stroke of good fortune, for Sōboku died the year after Shūkei, leaving Shōkyū as the leading renga poet. Jōha remained a pupil of Shōkyū for seven or eight years, until Shō-kyū's death, gradually acquiring the expertise needed to participate in renga sessions with the experts. By now he was well on his way to-ward becoming a professional. The competition was severe, and Jōha was ambitious. He knew that to get ahead he would have to remain in the good graces of his teacher, who alone could provide him with opportunities to join with first-rate poets in making renga. In 1545 he travelled with Shōkyū to Nara, where they and the local poets composed a renga sequence in one hundred links, the oldest exam-ples of Jōha's poetry. Not until 1550 did Jōha take part in a renga se-quence with poets in the capital.[6] It was a slow business gaining rec-ognition, and Jōha sometimes considered giving up renga altogether. Teitoku recorded, "Time and again he became disgusted with his studies and announced his intention of leaving for the East; but the renga masters stopped him."[7] No doubt the strain of "concentrating all day long and then all night long"[8] on his poetry at times did not seem worth the effort, but he had admirers even among the estab-lished poets.

Gradually Jōha had built up a reputation as a promising young poet, but he had a rival in Tani Sōyō (1526–1563), the son of Sōbo-ku. Sōyō, though two years younger than Jōha, not only enjoyed the advantage of having been born into a celebrated family of renga poets, but had greater talent. The presence of this rival undoubtedly made it more difficult for Jōha to gain wide recognition. At the renga session in one hundred links of 1550, he contributed only six links to eleven by Sōyō, a clear indication of their relative standing.

In 1552 Shōkyū died at the early age of forty-two. No doubt Jōha was grieved by the loss, but at the same time he must have realized that he was now within an ace of being the leading renga poet. Only Sōyō still ranked higher. Shōkyū left behind a son, later known as Shōshitsu, a boy of eleven, and asked Jōha to serve as the boy's guar-dian, leaving Jōha his entire estate in return. It is strange that Shōkyū should have asked a man of twenty-eight to assume this serious re-sponsibility, but it seems likely that Jōha had by this time married a sister or niece of Shōkyū. It is hard to understand otherwise why Jōha should have used Shōkyū's surname, Satomura, from this time on, instead of Matsui, his own surname.[9]

After Shōkyū's death Jōha became the head of the Satomura school of renga, and in this capacity he was honored with the Bud-dhist title *hokkyō*.[10] Now he could participate in poetry gatherings of the nobility; his dream of sitting beside men of high birth had indeed been realized. He made his living by teaching renga composition, chiefly to members of the military class who were eager to acquire culture. He also pursued his studies of the waka, no doubt in emulation of the court poets.

The nobles at this time were hard-pressed financially because of the loss of their country estates, and they had almost no political power, but they were still respected for their lineage and because they were the repositories of the old traditions. Jōha became intimate especially with members of the Konoe and Sanjōnishi families, both of impeccable descent. He first attended a waka session at the Konoe household in 1553, the beginning of a long relationship. In the seventh month of that year, an army led by Hosokawa Harumoto (1514–1563) broke into Kyoto and burnt down much of the city. A few days later Harumoto's deadly enemy Miyoshi Nagayoshi (Chōkei; 1522–1564) entered the city with twenty thousand men, and the shogun fled for his life. Konoe Taneie joined the shogun in temporary exile; after his return, his relations with Jōha became closer than before. When Taneie died in 1566, Jōha composed a solo renga *(dokugin)* which he offered to his friend's memory. The postscript stated that Konoe Taneie had given Jōha instruction in the Konoe traditions of the secret transmission of the *Kokinshū,* the most jealously guarded bits of abstruse poetic lore. Apparently this took place after Sanjōnishi Kin'eda (1487–1563) had refused Jōha similar instruction on the grounds that Jōha's interest in the secret traditions was commercial.[11]

Despite this rebuff, Jōha became a frequent visitor at the Sanjōnishi mansion. In the spring of 1553, when Sanjōnishi Kin'eda journeyed to Yoshino to admire the cherry blossoms, he took Jōha along. The country was in disorder and Kin'eda was suffering real financial hardships, but he was a pillar of whatever was left of the old court culture, and Jōha was delighted to travel in such distinguished company. At the outset of the journal *Yoshino mōde no ki* (Record of a pilgrimage to Yoshino) Kin'eda described his companion in these terms: "Jōha is deeply committed to the art of renga. Lately he has been living in the capital, where he has visited me day and night. He is moreover by no means incompetent even at composing waka."[12] Kin'eda quoted in his account thirteen waka by Jōha in addition to sections of the two sets of renga they composed together. They travelled first to Nara, where they visited the Kasuga Shrine, the Hall of the Great Buddha, and various other tourist sites. On the twenty-fifth of the second month, a day sacred to Sugawara no Michizane, they worshipped at a temple dedicated to his memory. Kin'eda wrote this opening verse *(hokku)*:

ume ni mazu	Double-petalled cherries!
nioi wo kose yo	First send us the fragrance
yaezakura	Of plum blossoms.

Jōha responded in the second verse *(wakiku):*[13]

kasumi ni fukaki	A spring breeze in a garden
niwa no harukaze	Buried deep beneath the mists.

The mention of plum blossoms was dictated by their association with Michizane and other scholars; the second verse referred to the conventionally noted spring mist hanging over the blossoms. The two men continued in this vein, adding two at a time, until they reached a full hundred a week or so later.

Kin'eda and Jōha had planned to arrive at Yoshino on the second day of the third month, but when they learned that the cherry blossoms there were still not fully opened, they journeyed instead to Mount Kōya. The ascent had to be on foot, a difficult climb for Kin'eda, sixty-six that year, but he apparently enjoyed his exertions. Two days later they left for Yoshino, where the cherry blossoms impressed them as being even more magnificent than they had imagined.[14] They happily drank saké, and Jōha wrote a comic verse commemorating the day. This labored, untranslatable verse was unfortunately typical of both men when in their cups. The modern reader will regret that they did not have a more compelling sense of humor.

The most interesting feature of this travel account, which consists mainly of descriptions of temples, places mentioned in poetry, and the blossoms at well-known spots, is the unspoken fact that the son of a temple servant was associating familiarly with a great noble, despite the differences in their social position and age. Jōha was certainly astute in his choice of profession: in an era when birth still counted for much, only the mastery of an artistic skill could have enabled him to rise so conspicuously. Perhaps Kin'eda thought of Jōha, who had grown up in Nara, as a guide rather than as a companion, but there is no trace of condescension in his remarks.

Jōha as yet was not an especially accomplished renga poet, but now that he was established as the head of the Satomura school, he attracted important patrons. Their support not only enabled him to live comfortably but assured the continuance of his school. Jōha had patrons among the military lords even while he was still Shōkyū's disciple. The two most important were Matsunaga Hisahide (1510–1577), who entered Kyoto with Miyoshi Nagayoshi's army in 1549, and soon afterwards Nagayoshi himself. Nagayoshi (popularly known as Chōkei) was one of the most powerful warlords of the day, but despite his sometimes ferocious behavior, he was devoted to literature, especially renga. At one time he even planned the compilation of a sequel to *Shinsen Tsukuba shū* (1495), the finest collection of renga.[15] It was in order to advance Jōha's career that Chōkei about 1550 personally arranged for a two-man renga *(ryōgin)* to be composed by Jōha and Tani Sōyō, the one poet who still ranked higher. In 1554 Nagayoshi himself, along with Sōyō and Jōha, composed one hundred verses in memory of the aged master Shūkei, who had died not long before.[16] As the military strength of Nagayoshi and Hisahide grew, Jōha's prestige as a poet was enhanced by association. By 1555 he had more or less achieved equal footing with Sōyō, despite the latter's advantages. Moreover, with the death of Shūkei there were no longer any senior poets to dispute with their gray hair the supremacy of these two young men.

Jōha was thirty-one in 1555, unusually young for one occupying so exalted a position in a traditional art. He participated in the "One Thousand Links on Plum Blossoms" sequence in the first month of that year along with high Buddhist dignitaries, the Imperial Regent *(Kanpaku)*, and other nobles. Obviously he was much in demand on such occasions. Despite the uncertainties of life in the capital and the chaos elsewhere, renga was flourishing. A particularly interesting session was held in the eighth month. The names of chapters in *The Tale of Genji* were used as the themes of a one-thousand-link sequence composed at the Ishiyama Temple, traditionally the site where Murasaki Shikibu began writing her masterpiece. No doubt this session was a product of the special lectures on *The Tale of Genji* delivered by Sanjōnishi Kin'eda to the abbot of the Daikaku Temple. Instruction of this nature was normally secret, and given only as a special privilege. It was therefore usual to celebrate afterwards by holding a renga or waka session followed by a drinking party. Sōyō and Jōha, who had been permitted to audit the lectures, took part, and the scribe was Shōshitsu, the son of Shōkyū being educated by Jōha. Clearly Jōha had taken his responsibility as a foster parent seriously.[17]

In 1556 Jōha and Sōyō composed another *ryōgin*. They also participated in a *wakan* session in one thousand links at the Daikaku Temple. A *wakan* was a mixture of alternating verses in Japanese and Chinese, and naturally required a knowledge of the poetic conventions of both languages in order to keep the chain of verses from breaking. The Chinese links were normally composed by Buddhist monks and the Japanese links by renga masters. Jōha was friendly with a number of poet-monks, especially Sakugen Shūryō (1501–1579), with whom he frequently composed *wakan*.[18] At another session of 1556 Jōha first joined in composing renga with Hosokawa Yūsai (Fujitaka; 1534–1610), a military aristocrat who later gained recognition as the outstanding authority on waka. Jōha and Yūsai became close literary acquaintances.

The records of renga sessions of the following years indicate that Jōha continued to add to his stature as a renga master, but most of the poetry he composed has been lost. In 1560 he took part in a one-hundred-verse sequence with Sōyō, Yūsai, and Shōshitsu (his debut as a full-fledged poet). On that occasion Ōmura Yūko (d. 1596) also joined in the composition. Yūko later gained fame as the official chronicler of Toyotomi Hideyoshi's exploits. It is easy to obtain the impression that Jōha knew everyone worth knowing not only in the literary but also in the political world.

In 1563 Jōha compiled a book of secret renga traditions called *Hakuhatsu shō* (Essays by a white-haired old man). It is typical of his critical writings: he describes the special uses of particles and similar points in accordance with oral traditions handed down for years among professional poets, but provides nothing of a more theoretical or personal significance. Such works were generally written at the request of a patron who desired special guidance in composing technically accurate poetry and was willing to pay for the privilege. In some of the earlier renga criticism, notably that by Shinkei (1406–1473), there are breathtaking insights into the nature of poetic expression that still compel admiration, but Jōha's criticism died with renga. Nobody is interested in his secrets anymore.

Toward the end of that year, Sanjōnishi Kin'eda died at the age of seventy-six. The grief-stricken Jōha composed a solo one-thousand-link sequence in eighteen days in honor of his late mentor and friend. It begins:[19]

toshigoto no	How bitter to think
hana naranu yo no	The world is without him; yet flowers
urami kana	Bloom year after year.

furinishi ato mo	Even amidst the old remains
niwa no harukusa	Spring grasses in the garden.
yama no ha no	I can see the dew—
usuyuki nokoru	All that lingers of the thin snow
tsuyu miete	That lay on the mountain edge.

The elegiac tone conveys feelings deeper than usual in Jōha's poetry, and the sequence as a whole has been rated as his finest work.[20] Aware of its importance, he himself provided it with two separate commentaries.

Another event of this fateful year, 1563, was the death of Miyoshi Nagayoshi's son Yoshioki. It was widely rumored that he had been poisoned by agents of Matsunaga Hisahide, Jōha's erstwhile patron. Jōha had been the young man's teacher, and this tragedy no doubt stirred thoughts on the uncertainty and danger of life in so turbulent a society. But the most important event of the year for him was unquestionably the death of Tani Sōyō at thirty-seven. Jōha had never quite displaced Sōyō as the leading renga poet, but death, once again, removed a rival. The lucky Jōha was now the single figure at the apex of the hierarchy of renga poets.

Jōha's patron Miyoshi Nagayoshi died the next year, 1564, but nothing indicates that this event caused unusual grief. As Odaka Toshio, who wrote the most extensive study of Jōha, put it, patrons were an expendable commodity in an era of warfare, and a renga master was unlikely to mourn one very long.[21] Jōha, even after he reached the top, remembered Sanjōnishi Kin'eda and his other teachers with affection and piety, but his financial backers were hardly more than rungs on the ladder of success. Now when he attended a renga session he took it for granted that he would compose more links than anyone else. Although this eminence made him less dependent than before on patrons, he maintained his relations with the military lords, and even became involved in their disputes.

In 1565 Miyoshi Yoshitsugu and Matsunaga Hisahide murdered the shogun Yoshiteru. The scarcity of literary compositions by Jōha at this time suggests that he may have been busy with behind-the-scenes activities. His special influence with the military and court leaders also resulted in his being approached by dignitaries from the provinces who wished to be invited to poetry gatherings attended by the great men of the day, and no doubt the visitors paid Jōha liberally for his intercession. He was not the only one to trade his literary influence for financial rewards. The nobles, fallen on hard days, gratefully accepted gifts even from the most boorish warlords, and the emperor himself was not above taking presents, showing his appreciation by giving the donors samples of his calligraphy.[22] The nobles not only invited rank upstarts to their homes for renga sessions but copied out classical texts like *The Tale of Genji* for the visitors to take home to their wives and daughters as souvenirs of the capital. Renga poets served the function of intermediaries between these country visitors and the nobles, who were above seeking financial support directly even though they desperately needed it.[23] Jōha apparently felt no hesitation about serving as a kind of pander to the nobles who longed to sell the aura of their names to rich bumpkins attracted by the old culture.

In 1566 the younger brother of the assassinated shogun Yoshiteru, Ashikaga Yoshiaki, returned to the laity from the Buddhist priesthood and attempted to restore the shogunate, but the warfare continued. Jōha, unaffected by the vicissitudes of the society, enjoyed greater prosperity than ever, leading a life of refined pleasures more luxurious than the emperor's, and proudly inviting noblemen to his spacious residence.[24] A party he gave in the fourth month of 1566 was attended by literary men of the highest ranks. On this occasion Jōha displayed to the guests his collection of rare manuscripts and entertained them with music and an elaborate feast. No wonder the hard-pressed nobles were willing to attend parties offered by this son of a servant! Nevertheless, it must have been galling for some to associate with a man who conspicuously betrayed his origins. Here is the description of Jōha written by Matsunaga Teitoku some years later: "His face was large and without eyebrows. His eyes were sharply cut, and his large, prominent nose had dark spots here and there. His ear lobes were thick. He had a loud voice with such a fierce ring that he sounded angry even when he made a joke."[25]

Jōha's income was derived chiefly from the correction fees he charged amateurs who sought his guidance. A wealthy amateur would submit samples of his renga to the master who, with professional authority, changed a word here and there, imparting artistic grace to the composition. Jōha's fees were apparently high, but Teitoku recalled that he was accepted as a pupil even though he could not pay the usual fees. He wrote, "People are wrong to accuse Jōha of having been miserly. If he had been miserly, why should he have invited a poor boy like myself to his house and treated him with such kindness?"[26] Jōha, no doubt recognizing Teitoku's precocious talents, made an exception in his case; his fees were probably scaled to the pockets of his pupils. He also held regular monthly poetry gatherings at which he charged a flat fee for all participants; one man noted having paid a sack of rice for this privilege.[27] Jōha not only guided students in renga composition, but frequently delivered private lectures on classical texts. Undoubtedly his highest fees were for his manuals of the secret principles of renga composition, written to special order. As a result of these literary activities, he was able to lead a life in no way resembling the austere existence of the hermit-priests of the Middle Ages. Far from taking refuge from the turmoil of the world in a hut in the mountains, Jōha lived in the city, surrounded by admirers. He married twice, even though he had taken orders as a Buddhist priest. By his first wife he had a daughter who eventually married Shōshitsu, and his second wife bore him three sons. There is also evidence in his diaries that he had relations with young men.[28]

The year 1567 was one of desperate fighting. The country was torn by warfare and in the capital there was no central authority. This was the year Jōha chose to fulfill his cherished dream of viewing Mount Fuji. He set out in the second month and was on the road for over six months. Before leaving Kyoto he stopped at the Gion Shrine to pray for safety on his journey. The prayers were apparently efficacious: though he came within sight of the fighting, he himself was unscathed, and his journal rarely indicates that he was traveling through a war-torn country.[29] The high points of the journey for Jōha were the *utamakura*, the sites celebrated in the poetry of the past, and he stopped again and again to immerse himself in the surroundings which had moved his predecessors to compose poetry. One especially moving passage describes his visit to the lonely hut on Utsuyama where the renga master Sōchō had lived forty or fifty years earlier.[30] Wherever he went Jōha was royally entertained, and he engaged in many renga sessions with local dignitaries. He was accompanied not only by his own servants but by escorts provided by his hosts at dangerous places on the way.

On the thirteenth day of the fifth month Jōha worshipped at the Sengen Shrine at the foot of Mount Fuji. It is curious that, despite his announced purpose of going to see Fuji, and the space he devoted to descriptions of less important places, he failed to mention his impressions of the mountain.[31]

The atmosphere of the journal is prevailingly cheerful, and there are the usual accounts of drinking parties and of the comic verse composed on these occasions. Jōha also mentioned, however, that he was forced to turn back at one point because Oda Nobunaga's army was attacking the nearby castle of Nagashima, held by the fanatical Ikkō sect. Jōha himself experienced little discomfort, but was lavishly entertained at a nearby town. Even while the most desperate fighting was in progress at Nagashima, Jōha and his hosts enjoyed their feasting and poetry. But he also wrote, "Some time after midnight I happened to look to the west, and I saw that the castle at Nagashima had been taken and many fires set. The light was bright as day, so I got up out of bed." He thereupon composed this waka:[32]

tabi makura	A traveller's pillow—
yumeji tanomu ni	I had set forth on a path of dreams,
aki no yo no	But now I shall spend
tsuki ni akasan	This night of autumn moonlight
matsukaze no sato	In a village of pine winds.

This conventional poem is surely inadequate; one would hardly guess the circumstances!

A few days later Jōha passed through a village where some houses were still smouldering after Nobunaga's army passed through, but he was met by a gentleman, an amateur renga poet, who escorted him to his palatial home. In another few days, Jōha was back in Kyoto, and he celebrated his safe return by getting drunk, in his accustomed manner. The journey had been happy, despite the unpropitious times. Jōha concluded his account with a remark expressing his uncertainty (real or conventional) over the life ahead of him.

In the following year, 1568, Oda Nobunaga entered Kyoto with Ashikaga Yoshiaki, his choice as shogun. The next fourteen years, until he was assassinated by Akechi Mitsuhide, are known as the age of Nobunaga. During the fighting that accompanied Nobunaga's entry into the city, Jōha took refuge at the Daitoku Temple, where he drank saké, wrote poetry, and joined with a Zen priest from the Shōkoku Temple in composing *wakan*.[33] When the fighting died down and it became apparent that Nobunaga was the new master of the capital, Jōha was among the first to offer his congratulations. He could not have looked forward to this meeting. Sir George Sansom, the mildest of scholars, described Nobunaga as a "cruel and callous brute."[34] Reports had spread through the capital that Nobunaga was a monster "more terrifying than any demon," and people trembled at the horrid fate awaiting them.[35] Nonetheless, the prudent Jōha, always eager to be on the winning side, hurried to the Tōfuku Temple, Nobunaga's headquarters, and offered him a pair of fans, reciting these verses:

| *nihon te ni iru* | Oh, the joy I feel today |
| *kyō no yorokobi* | You take these two fans in hand. |

The point of these lines is the pun on *nihon,* meaning "two fans," but also "Japan." Jōha was no doubt seeking to ingratiate himself with the conqueror in this manner. Nobunaga, though not known for his literary talent, replied at once with:

maiasobu	These are fans
chiyo yorozuyo no	For joyous dance of a thousand,
ōgi ni te	Ten thousand ages.

His unexpected skill at renga was quickly reported throughout the capital. Oze Hoan's *Shinchōki* (The life of Nobunaga), published in 1622 and thus, to be sure, not a contemporary source, follows the account of the presentation of the fans and the exchange of renga with this passage: "Throughout the capital, old and young were speechless with astonishment when they learnt this. People had supposed that because this man was a fierce warrior he would be just as violent as Kiso no Yoshinaka when he burst into the capital many years ago, in 1183; but Nobunaga seemed to be gentle and refined. They were relieved to think that things were likely to go easily, and everyone breathed a sigh of relief."[36]

Surely the political and social functions of renga had never been more conspicuously displayed. Some scholars have suggested that the opening link of renga was delivered by Nobunaga followed by Jōha, Nobunaga expressing his delight at taking the two fans (and Japan) in hand, and Jōha assuring him that the fans (and Nobunaga's rule) would last a thousand ages. This seems plausible, but it is hard to imagine Jōha offering the fans without a salutation, or of his testing the poetic abilities of the conqueror by waiting for the first verse.[37] In any case, it is apparent from this incident that Jōha was the spokesman for the traditional culture of the capital.

Jōha also began about this time to cultivate relations with other military leaders, notably Hosokawa Yūsai, the literary daimyo, and Akechi Mitsuhide, Nobunaga's lieutenant who was a devoted amateur of renga. In 1574 Mitsuhide, by command of Nobunaga, took the castle in Yamato held by Matsunaga Hisahide, Jōha's old patron, and soon afterwards invited Jōha to the castle for a renga session of celebration. Old loyalties did not inhibit Jōha, who eagerly accepted. In 1578 another renga session was held under Mitsuhide's auspices, and this time Jōha and Yūsai both participated. Mitsuhide, unlike

Nobunaga, had wide cultural interests, and was especially devoted to the tea ceremony, but he was something of a brute himself. In 1582 he assassinated his master Nobunaga at the Honnōji in Kyoto. A few days earlier he had joined in a one-hundred-link renga sequence with Jōha, Shōshitsu, and other poets, ostensibly by way of prayer for victory in an attack over the Mōri family. Renga was attributed with the power to move the gods to grant victory in warfare and similar benefits, and Mitsuhide no doubt desired such assistance in the assassination he was contemplating. He opened the session with the lines:[38]

toki wa ima	Now is the time
ame ga shita shiru	To rule all under heaven—
satsuki ka na	It's the fifth month!

The point of the verse was the pun on *toki,* meaning "time," but also Toki, the clan-name of Mitsuhide's family; one meaning of the words was, therefore, "The Toki are about to take control of the country." The verse all too plainly revealed Mitsuhide's designs, and Jōha was supposedly so alarmed that he modified the second line to make the meaning less explicit. The fact remained that, only a few days before Mitsuhide killed Nobunaga, he and Jōha had composed renga together.

After the assassination Jōha was interrogated by Toyotomi Hideyoshi about his role. He admitted that he had suspected Mitsuhide might be planning something of the sort, but felt it would have been improper to discuss a mere intuition. He managed to convince Hideyoshi, but his actions may have spoken louder than his words: a lucky incident saved Jōha's skin. Mitsuhide's troops, as part of the coup, attacked the Nijō Palace in order to kill Nobunaga's son who was there. The crown prince happened to be in the castle. He attempted to make his way back to the imperial palace, but his terrified escort deserted him. Jōha was also in the Nijō Castle. Sizing up the situation, he bundled the prince into his own palanquin and sent him to safety. This action, more than his explanations, probably enabled Jōha to remain in Hideyoshi's good graces; in fact, he rose under Hideyoshi from the status of a renga master to that of an adviser on all cultural matters.

Hideyoshi was no less a military man than Nobunaga, but he seems genuinely to have enjoyed such aristocratic pastimes as the tea ceremony, renga, and Nō. As early as 1578 he had joined with Jōha in composing a one-thousand-link sequence to pray for victory over the Mōri family. Jōha, nothing if not impartial in his choice of renga partners, a few months later composed renga with a direct vassal of the Mōri, and in 1580 presented Mōri Motoyasu with with a manual of renga composition.[39] He saw nothing strange about participating in renga sessions of enemies, not even when the purpose of these compositions was to secure victory in war. He began his most important work of renga theory, *Renga shihōshō* (Book of the supreme treasure of renga), at the request of Akechi Mitsuhide, but presented it on completion to Mitsuhide's archenemy Hideyoshi, along with a fulsome preface acclaiming the new master of Japan.[40]

Jōha enjoyed friendly relations not only with Hideyoshi, but with his nephew Hidetsugi, a man who (in Sansom's words) "lived a vicious life, performed no useful function, and was so brutal that he was known as Sesshō Kampaku, the Murdering Regent."[41] Indeed, Jōha's presence was so much in demand at renga sessions of the great that the quality of his poetry deteriorated, even in his own opinion. When Matsunaga Teitoku suggested compiling a collection of Jōha's renga, he replied: "That would be pointless. I can no longer write decent poetry. When I was young I used to give deep thought to every line I composed, but of late, when I attend gatherings every day, my only thought has been to keep the sequence going, and I never give deep thought to anything. If you are determined to make a selection of my poetry, I suggest you start with the *uchikoshi*."[42] The *uchikoshi* was the third verse in a sequence and was prized not so much for its content or expression as for the skill it showed in shifting the subject away from the themes treated in the first two verses. Jōha evidently still felt confident of his techniques, but he realized that overactivity had diluted his expression.

Jōha, for all his fame and skill, was never an especially appealing poet. He is praised for the lack of faults in his renga more often than for positive qualities. The one-thousand-link solo sequence composed after the death of Sanjōnishi Kin'eda is more moving than most of his poetry, perhaps because it reveals genuine grief. One *hokku* (opening verse), written after the death of Shōshitsu's small son Kiku, was acclaimed in his day as his supreme masterpiece:[43]

ne sae karete	Even the roots have withered—
haru ni wakaba no	In the spring there are no young leaves
kiku mo nashi	On the chrysanthemums.

This poem, echoing the imagery of a waka by Ariwara no Narihira found in the *Kokinshū*,[44] is ingenious in its use of the name of the boy Kiku and the chrysanthemum *(kiku);* but modern scholars tend to be less impressed by this virtuosity than by the feeling the poem expresses.

Jōha was skilled at every aspect of renga composition and had mastered the traditions of the past. Although he contributed little that was new or distinctive, in the opinion of many scholars he was one of the most important poets in the entire history of renga. It was not so much his inadequacies when compared to the great masters of renga —Shinkei, Sōgi, Sōchō and the rest—as his lack of poetic vision and his pragmatic approach to life that kept disciples at arm's length. Perhaps that is why renga, to all intents, died with Jōha.

Jōha took an increasingly active part in politics under Hideyoshi, and was himself surrounded by sycophantic admirers. In 1593 a party was held to celebrate Jōha's sixtieth birthday (by Japanese reckoning), and all the most prominent men of culture attended, including members of the high nobility. Hideyoshi employed Jōha at times as his intermediary in dealing with such troublesome dignitaries as the abbots of monasteries, and he even consulted Jōha in 1591 when his advisers were debating what response to make to a letter received from the Philippines.[45] Jōha visited Hideyoshi's palace almost every day, and Hideyoshi sometimes returned the visits and composed renga at Jōha's house. On one occasion Hideyoshi composed this *hokku:*

okuyama ni	Open a path deep
momiji fumiwake	Through red leaves in the mountains—
naku hotaru	A firefly is singing.

Hosokawa Yūsai at once added a second verse, but someone in the gathering murmured that fireflies do not sing. Jōha agreed, much to Hideyoshi's annoyance, but Yūsai insisted that there was textual evidence that fireflies sang, quoting an ancient poem which ended *hotaru yori hoka naku mushi wa nashi* (apart from the fireflies, not an insect sings). Hideyoshi's good humor was restored, and he praised Yūsai's profound understanding of renga. Some days later, when Jōha visited Yūsai, the latter expressed his surprise that a master of renga should have exhibited such a lack of understanding of people. Yūsai admitted that he had himself made up the "ancient poem" on the spot, in order to ease the tense situation.[46] This was a rare occasion when Jōha, always an exponent of discretion, erred for once in the cause of truth!

In 1591 Sen no Rikyū, the great master of the tea ceremony (under whom Jōha studied), committed suicide by order of Hideyoshi. Jōha naturally did not protest. He continued to serve Hideyoshi assiduously, as if nothing had happened. In that year he took part in twenty-three renga sessions, the largest number for any year in his career.

At the beginning of 1592 Hideyoshi's nephew Hidetsugi was appointed *Kanpaku* (Imperial Regent). For all his terrible faults, he was most enthusiastic about literature, and delighted especially in composing Chinese poetry and prose. At one time he considered reviving the literary traditions of the Five Zen Monasteries of Kyoto. He was also fond of renga. In 1594, when Hideyoshi went to see the cherry blossoms at Yoshino, Hidetsugi, Jōha, and other renga masters went along so that the occasion could be properly celebrated. In 1595 Hidetsugi ordered the preparation of the first commentaries on the texts of the Nō dramas, no doubt to please Hideyoshi, who was passionately interested in Nō.[47] Jōha assisted in making the annotations, well equipped for the task thanks to his knowledge of the old poetry. Jōha worked closely with Hidetsugi. This proved to be a costly mistake: later in 1595, Hidetsugi fell from Hideyoshi's favor and was ordered to commit suicide. Hideyoshi's wrath extended to Hidetsugi's wife, two small children, and thirty-five concubines, all of whom were put to death. Jōha, as an associate of Hidetsugi's, was sentenced to banishment. This was a severe punishment, but it should be noted that Jōha was one of only three men associated with Hidetsugi who were not obliged to commit seppuku.

Jōha was exiled to the Miidera, a temple west of Lake Biwa, his stipend of one hundred *koku* was terminated, and his house and property were confiscated. This first piece of bad luck in Jōha's life must have surprised him. His disciples thought that he had been the victim of rivals who had slandered him to Hideyoshi.[48] But there was no way to resist punishment, and Jōha apparently did not consider suicide. After all, the Miidera was not very far from Kyoto; this was no case of distant banishment. Before long, friends and admirers were going to visit Jōha. Matsunaga Teitoku, well aware of Jōha's love of saké, took him a cask, to Jōha's great delight. He felt bitter only about the attitude taken by Shōshitsu, Shōkyū's son. He told Teitoku: "When Hideyoshi bestowed my possessions on Shōshitsu, rather than on a stranger, people supposed that this was an indication of compassion for me. I reared this Shōshitsu from the time he was a small boy, and showed him even greater affection than I did to my own son. I taught him everything I knew. But he has been merciless toward me. He even took away my desk of mulberry, the one you remember."[49]

An interesting account of Jōha in exile is found in the diary of Gen'yo, a priest who accompanied the nobleman Konoe Nobutada (1565–1614) back to Kyoto from exile in Kagoshima, where he had been sent by Hideyoshi in 1594 because of his overeagerness to accompany the Korea expedition. (Hideyoshi did not approve of high-ranking nobles serving in the military forces.) In 1596 Hideyoshi permitted Nobutada to return to the capital. He and Gen'yo (the priestly name of Aso Koretada) arrived in Kyoto toward the end of the ninth month of 1596. A few days later they participated in a renga session with Hosokawa Yūsai, and on the next day visited Shōshitsu, the reigning authority in renga circles, now that Jōha was out of the way. On the thirteenth day of the tenth month Gen'yo went with Yūsai to the Miidera. He recorded in his diary: "The halls at the Miidera are all in a state of disrepair. Jōha's quarters are next to an old temple. We spent the day in quiet conversation and left as it grew dark. The bell of the Miidera tolled faintly. It is a lonely place."[50]

Gen'yo left some renga with Jōha, and after his return to the capital received the corrections. Several exchanges of gifts took place. Gen'yo visited Jōha for the second time in the second month of 1597, shortly before he returned to Kyushu. The two men spent the night talking. Gen'yo wrote, "When I left Jōha's lodgings he presented me with a fan and other gifts and saw me off a great distance."[51] No doubt it was comforting and even flattering to Jōha to think that he had not been forgotten, and that his reputation extended as far as distant Kagoshima. Jōha was pardoned in the autumn of 1597 and went back to the capital. Soon he was again actively taking part in renga sessions; he had regained his old supremacy. In the third month of 1598 he accompanied Hideyoshi on an excursion to Daigo to see the cherry blossoms. He had been forgiven.

Jōha, the master of survival, outlived Hideyoshi by four years, dying in 1602. I should like to think of him serving Tokugawa Ieyasu during his last years, thus completing the cycle of all the important military figures of the period; but although some commentators state that he did so, I have seen no firm evidence to this effect. In any case, there cannot have been many men who served Nobunaga, Mitsuhide, Hideyoshi, and Hidetsugi in that era of sudden deaths.

In the years after Jōha's death his works of renga criticism continued to circulate in manuscript, and he was widely esteemed as an expert on ancient lore. He figures in this capacity in *Ugetsu monogatari* (Tales of wind and rain) by Ueda Akinari.[52] He was more sardonically treated by Masamune Hakuchō in his play *Mitsuhide and Jōha*

(1926).[53] But, on the whole, the man and his poetry have grown steadily more remote from the Japanese, and his works of renga criticism are no longer of much interest.[54] No doubt Jōha, for all his worldliness, genuinely loved renga and thought of it not merely as a way to make a living but as a noble calling. A waka poet could live in solitude; but renga by its very nature required the poet to share the company of others and join in mutual efforts. It is unfortunate for Jōha's later reputation that he tended to choose his companions for their rank rather than for their poetic ability.

Jōha died in 1602 in Nara, at the house of his brother. For a time his death went unnoticed in the capital, but when Hosokawa Yūsai learned of it from Teitoku, a look of grief passed over his face. He said, "We'll never see his likes again."[55]

FRANK HOFF

City and Country:
Song and the Performing Arts
in Sixteenth-Century Japan

CITY AND COUNTRY—this polarity continues to be a familiar element of Western culture. One outlook might stress the harmonization of these opposites, but more prevalent is the view implied in pastoralism that the city is a corrupt and negative force while the countryside is a healing and wholesome environment for man to live in. The city was regarded differently by farmers in sixteenth-century Japan, who sang a long sequence of song as part of their annual ritual and work of transplanting rice. In this sequence we glimpse the mirror image of Western pastoralism, for the city is an energizing force in these songs from the Japanese countryside. As we shall see, the city was one of several metaphors which seemed to open up channels for a flow of vitality between the singers and the earth.

The *Tauezōshi,* as the written version of these songs is called, was not poetry to be read but part of a performance which had a social and religious function within the agricultural community where it originated. However, songs in this setting shared qualities with those popular elsewhere in Japan, which were sung under quite different circumstances. For that reason, we begin with a discussion of representative aspects of *kouta,* the short song, as the prevailing genre of song in the sixteenth century was called. The coordinates of city and countryside will form our initial frame of reference, both because of the associations which this approach may provide for the subsequent treatment of the city as a theme in the *Tauezōshi* and because of a predisposition, born out of Western pastoralism, to regard the city-country dialectic as a universal.

There is something akin to what we in the West think of as pastoralism in the Kyōgen play *Wakana* (Early green in spring fields).[1] A group from the city sets off in spring to enjoy the countryside on the outskirts of Kyoto. After a while, several young women arrive to pick green shoots; they are singing. The men from the city invite them to join their party. An initial refusal is overcome; drinks are passed around, songs and dances exchanged; the two groups enjoy themselves together until late in the afternoon. Love is mentioned in the songs that are sung, but although the men's insistence that the girls join their group may suggest amorous intentions, the erotic element which is prominent in Western pastoralism is explored no further. What we have instead is a quiet nostalgia. Strangers meet, enjoy one another's company on a perfect spring day, and then part, the light fading—this is the mood left behind at the end of the play. *Wakana* depends upon song for much of its effect; we shall take it as a first example of the interrelation of song and the performing arts in sixteenth-century Japan.

Along with Nō drama, the Kyōgen comedy was one of the principal dramatic forms of medieval Japan. By the middle of the sixteenth century, it was evolving from an extemporaneous theater toward what we know today, a theater which uses a fixed text. One of the most important landmarks along this road is seen in the manuscript known as the *Tenshō kyōgenbon,* which is our earliest record of songs, repartee, and plot outlines used in Kyōgen. The subscript, dated Tenshō 6 (1578), is by a different scribal hand from that in which the main body of the manuscript is written, and is not usually accepted as genuine. Opinion does agree, however, that the work as a whole dates to the latter part of the Tenshō period (1573–1593). Some 104 plays are described in the sketchy way characteristic of this work.[2] The nature of the entries is itself indicative of the process of Kyōgen's evolution. Some are brief plot outlines. But the entry for a play like *Wakana,* which throughout its development toward a fixed form has relied heavily upon song, merely gives a simple record of the songs which were included. Entries indicating what happens on the stage are brief, although, to be sure, there is more detailed description for plays with a larger plot element.

Wakana is the eighty-second play included in the *Tenshō kyōgenbon.* Three of the short songs *(kouta)* recorded under the entry for this play are also included in the *Kanginshū,* an anthology of 311 songs compiled in 1518. One scholar, Araki Yoshio, argues that these three *kouta* were in fact selected from the *Kanginshū.*[3] This observation provides him with the first of two points within which to date the formation of the play *Wakana*. The second is the record of a four-day subscription performance of Nō and Kyōgen held in Kyoto in 1564, which lists *Wakana* in the repertory of the first day's performances.[4] Accordingly, Araki attributes the play's emergence to the half century between 1518 and 1564.

"Many women come out" is the way the entry for *Wakana* in the *Tenshōbon* starts. The opening of the play as seen today—preparations for the group of men to leave the city and a brief scene upon their arrival in the spring fields—is omitted; in the period whose performance conventions the *Tenshōbon* records, the play's beginning may still have been extemporaneous, differing from one occasion to another. What follows the brief opening stage direction in the *Tenshōbon* is a listing of songs, with occasional and fragmentary stage directions by way of transition to subsequent songs. A single song is generally set off by a special typographic indicator, but the first song of *Wakana* is not treated in this way. This piece—*harugoto ni kimi o iwaite wakana*—is also known by the name *Yukiyama,* and may be seen performed by today's Kyōgen actors as an independent song for dance *(komai).*[5] Then there follows, without any stage directions, a song which is made up of two *kouta* from the *Kanginshū* anthology, no. 3, *na o tsumaba:*[6]

> If you gather young shoots, then
> Parsley and its root in wet fields,
> The *itadori* on peaks,
> Deer hiding in the grass.

and no. 72, *koi kaze ga:*[7]

> The love wind blows,
> Twisting back my sleeve,
> Oh the weight of my sleeve—
> Yes, the love wind is heavy.

Next we find that *Wakana* has incorporated *obana no shimo ya,* song no. 98 of the *Kanginshū*, again without stage directions:[8]

> Frost is on the pampas grass tonight, but it is not cold—
> An autumn night is full of regrets:
> I do not like hearing the insects, either;
> I sleep on my own arm for a pillow. The moon dips low.

"At this time the travelers speak to them; there are greetings," is the transition to the song *tabibito no michisamatage*, "Delay the traveler on his path," which is a section from the Nō play *Motome-zuka* (The sought-for grave).[9] A single bit of dialogue follows, taken in today's Izumi version by the group of women: "What foolish thing are you asking us to do?" The next direction establishes the central scene of the play: "Everyone takes up his place in the group. They have a drinking party." The single word "daimyo" which follows has been interpreted as meaning that someone in the group of men performs a song or a dance. The play continues with the long song *Oharagi*, which today falls to the women's part but is not so attributed in the *Tenshōbon*. *Oharagi* was also popular off the stage, as pure song, in the sixteenth century; at a later date it became a standard number in the repertories of early Kabuki, and today it is still performed by groups in the countryside whose traditions very likely continue those of the late sixteenth century and early seventeenth.[10] After *Oharagi* and dances by the women, the play draws toward its conclusion. The single word "song" introduces *ariake no tsuki oba nan to matō zo*, "Are we to wait, then, till the moon fades at dawn?" Through this song the women convey the message which terminates the party: it is growing dark, and it is time for us to leave. Short exclamations of mutual regret at parting are noted before the song *yuku mo yukarezu*. The final indication in the *Tenshōbon* is brief: "Ends with flute."

Today's Izumi performance version contains even more songs than were attributed to *Wakana* in the *Tenshōbon*. Adding songs was one way for plays in which this element predominates to grow. Such plays as *Naruko, Hanago,* and *Mizukumi,* for example, are sometimes even referred to as *kouta-mono* because they contain so many songs. *Kouta* used in today's performances of all these plays are also found in the *Kanginshū,* although for the most part in related, not identical versions. This anthology collected songs from various contemporary performance types, as well as what was sung in drinking parties or for private enjoyment; an identification of each song's provenance was made at a date slightly later than 1518, the year of the original compilation. Despite the general assumption that popular songs were widely used in Kyōgen, only two of the 311 songs in the *Kanginshū* (nos. 152 and 171) are specifically identified as *Kyōgen kouta*. Early in the sixteenth century there evidently was a large common stock of popular song which could be drawn upon at will, perhaps even extemporaneously, by Kyōgen actors. It was only at a later date that certain songs tended to be identified with a particular play.

In *Wakana*, a group from the city visits the countryside. In other Kyōgen plays, farmers from the countryside visit the capital. Plot summaries of two such plays, *Mochisake* and *Suehirogari*, are given in the *Tenshōbon*.[11] *Mochisake* is typical of plays depicting the annual New Year's visit of country folk to the tax man in the city. There is a brief formulaic scene in which these rustic visitors express their reactions to the city; afterwards they set about finding the home of the official in order to present the gifts they bring from their respective provinces. Here is their introduction to the sights of the big city, taken from the Ōkura Azuma text of the play:

(They walk about the stage, then go to the *hashigakari,* where they stop at the first pine.) "We have already arrived at the capital." "Yes, arrived." "It is not like the country. Even the way they build houses is different. From over there in the distance to as far as you can see in the other direction," (he looks as if into the distance) "houses are snugly arranged side by side, set very close to one another." "Yes, indeed. Fit right up next to one another. . . ."[12]

The situation is standard. Very likely it was filled out extensively and extemporaneously in performance. *Suehirogari,* considered to be a model play in many respects, contains a similar scene: a countryman on an errand for his master arrives in the capital. He is stunned by its size and the activity along its streets.

Thus we learn from the *Tenshō kyōgenbon* that the city dweller's visit to the countryside and the arrival of country folk in the capital were among the themes of Kyōgen plays in the last quarter of the sixteenth century. Of country life itself, we have *Taue* (Rice transplanting; now also known as *Onda*), the fifteenth entry in the *Tenshōbon*.[13] This play treats a theme which has been basic to the life of the Japanese farmer ever since wet rice cultivation was introduced into the island country, an event of protohistory.

As it is staged in today's Ōkura School performances, the play opens with the priest of the Kamo Shrine coming out to identify himself. This, he says, is the day for performing at his shrine the annual festival of transplanting in the god's field; only after the work has been completed here can it begin in other fields. The women parishioners are to act as transplanting women *(saotome)*—their labor promotes the general well-being and prosperity of all aspects of the community's life. It is time to begin; he calls the women out and starts the planting. The women appear. They sing two songs, *kami-yama no* and *nawashiro o;* it is with these that the entry for *Taue* in the *Tenshōbon* begins. The priest initiates a brief dialogue by remarking how splendidly dressed the women are. After the ceremony of blessing the water at the place where it comes into the field, they begin in earnest with their transplanting work, which is accompanied by song. A long sequence of songs is traded between the priest and the women, composing the main body of the play.

It is possible to cite other works from the late sixteenth century and the early seventeenth which contain scenes of transplanting or incorporate songs used on that occasion. Our examples are from oral traditions which were a part of the performing arts of the period. As time passes, works in an oral tradition are likely to be supplemented by the addition of more current material from age to age; hence their dating presents a problem. Printed texts of *Kōwaka-mai, Kojōruri,* and *Sek-kyō,* for example, may not have appeared until the first half of the seventeenth century or even later; what we know of their development and initial popularity, however, places them among the performing arts of the previous century.

This is quite clear in the case of Kōwaka-mai, an art with a long history of development, which had by the early part of the sixteenth century evolved into its mature form as dance to the melodic recitation of lengthy narratives. Diary entries from the years between 1545 and 1567, conveniently set out by James Araki in *The Ballad-Drama of Medieval Japan,* record the popularity of this performance type during that period.[14] Kōwaka enjoyed particularly high esteem among members of the military class. Perhaps its best-known aficionado was Oda Nobunaga, often pictured as a rough warrior, who was in actuality a skilled amateur of several arts, including *kouta.*[15] Nobunaga is identified in particular with the Kōwaka *Atsumori:* the story of his dancing a passage from this piece before his retainers on the eve of the battle of Okehazama in 1560 is the very paradigm of a samurai preparing himself spiritually for a critical encounter.[16] Almost as noteworthy is the account of an entertainment Nobunaga gave for Tokugawa Ieyasu at Azuchi Castle just before his own death in June 1582, at which Kōwaka Hachirō-Kurō and the head of the Tanba troupe of Nō were asked to perform. The Kōwaka master was declared the winner of the contest, with a program which prominently included the piece *Tauta* (The transplanting song).[17] *Tauta* is the name of an independent performance number taken from the longer Kōwaka play *Fushimi Tokiwa,* in which transplanting songs are a prominent feature.

Fushimi Tokiwa, one of the "Yoshitsune" pieces in the Kōwaka repertory, treats an episode in the flight of that popular hero's mother Tokiwa from Kyoto after her husband's defeat and death in the Heiji Disturbance of 1160. A snowstorm detains her on the outskirts of Fushimi, and she is given shelter by an elderly couple. Five servant women of the neighborhood, the natives of five regions of Japan, "entertain Tokiwa by singing and dancing the folk dances of their home provinces."[18] The close relationship between the transplanting songs performed here (especially by the first woman, from Izumo), those included in the Kyōgen *Taue,* and those actually sung by workers in the fields at the time of transplanting, has been noted by Asano Kenji, who quotes from a printed text of this Kōwaka piece dated 1618.[19] In a more general discussion of the circumstances under which song is used in the oral narrative of the Early Modern period, Manabe Masahiro refers to the Kojōruri version of *Fushimi Tokiwa* printed in 1661.[20] Kojōruri (early Jōruri) is another of the many narrative arts which were popular in the sixteenth and seventeenth centuries. In its developed stage, it is distinguished from Kōwaka by its use of puppets manipulated to the accompaniment of a recited narrative. We know that materials involving Tokiwa and drawn from the same "Yoshitsune" cycle of the Kōwaka repertory had been adopted by Kojōruri as the seventeenth century began. Visual evidence is provided by the so-called Funaki Screen, which may be dated c. 1615–1617, that is to say the end of the Azuchi-Momoyama epoch as George Elison defines it in this volume.[21]

The Funaki Screen, actually a set of two six-panel screens kept in the Tokyo National Museum, is of great value to the student of the performing arts of Japan in that period because of its many views of actual performance. It belongs to the general type known as *Rakuchū-Rakugai-zu,* depicting the capital and its surroundings. Of particular interest to us is the fifth panel of the right screen, which shows commercial theaters where Kabuki and puppet performances are in progress.[22] The two puppet plays illustrated here are identified on the painted surface as *Munewari* (The chest-splitting of Amida) and *Yamanaka Tokiwa.*[23] The latter play, familiar from the Kōwaka version, deals with the (purely fictitious) episode of Tokiwa's murder at Yamanaka in Mino province and Yoshitsune's ensuing revenge of his mother's death.[24] Unfortunately we do not have a text of a Kojō-

Theaters at the Shijō Riverbank in Kyoto. Detail from one of a pair of six-fold screens depicting *Activities In and Around the Capital (Rakuchū-Rakugai)* and known as the "Funaki Screen." Tokyo National Museum.

ruri version dating from the time of the Funaki Screen; there does exist, however, an illustrated handscroll of *Yamanaka Tokiwa* dating to the Kan'ei period (1624–1645), with a text whose language is believed to be that of a Kojōruri version.[25] At the very least it is interesting to note the confluence of several artistic genres on an obviously popular theme.

We have seen that transplanting song accompanies labor in the field in the Kyōgen play *Taue;* it is the title of a Kōwaka piece performed before Oda Nobunaga, Tokugawa Ieyasu, and assorted other dignitaries in 1582; it is a requirement of the plot in another Kōwaka-mai, *Fushimi Tokiwa,* for which we have a text printed in 1618 but which dates without a doubt to an earlier time. In the Kyōgen play *Wakana,* other types of *kouta* are sung at a drinking party. In each case, song is a part of the text of a performing art, and is motivated by its plot. Later we will turn to examples of song as a functional part of real life, outside the theater. But first let us examine a more difficult case: the fragmentary adaptation of portions of the lyrics of song and of its melodies into a recited narrative.

Sekkyō or *Sekkyō Jōruri* is an oral narrative tradition related to storytelling used as a means of Buddhist preaching. Like Kōwaka, it has a long history of development. Recent scholarly opinion holds that it came of age as a distinct genre toward the end of the sixteenth century, although documentation is sparse.[26] At first Sekkyō was an art performed alfresco by individual reciters to the accompaniment of the *sasara,* a simple percussive instrument, one form of which consists of bamboo rubbed against a serrated stick. In the early seventeenth century, it advanced into the commercial theaters and adopted the use of puppets in competition with Kojōruri; its characteristic story types were shared by Kojōruri performers.

The version of the Sekkyō play *Oguri Hangan* which was published in 1675 is of special interest to us because the text of one of its sections has incorporated fragments of transplanting songs.[27] This section (the fifth *dan*) is the famous travel scene *(michiyuki)* in which Terute draws the cart containing the corpse of her lover Oguri toward Kumano, where he is eventually revivified by the power of the Kumano deity in the hotspring waters.[28] In the 1675 text there are indications of how the passage was sung in performance. This is its introduction:

Ta-fushi [field melody; term probably equivalent to *tauta-bushi,* melody for the field song]. Looking down from Yamada, [she saw] very lovely planting girls *(saotome).* They had rice seedlings in their hands and they were singing. *Sansa-bushi,* "The battered plaited hats of. . . ." *Honta-fushi* [the main *fushi* for the field song], "Plant the field, *saotome.* Plant, plant, *saotome.* . . ."

In live performance, the reciter seems to have incorporated (probably in an adapted version) the melodies sung during the actual transplanting in the fields: this is implied by the notations, *ta-fushi* and *honta-fushi.* The interpretation of the third sort of melody mentioned in the text, *sansa-bushi,* is more complex. This melodic pattern's appearance here may be the "signature tune" of the reciter whose special text was printed in this particular edition of the work.[29]

A splendid handscroll version of the Oguri story, kept in the Imperial Household collection, has been identified by recent scholarship as a copy made during the time span of the Kan'ei (1624–1645) and Meireki (1655–1658) periods.[30] Its language is closer to that associated with Sekkyō as an oral narrative tradition. The passage which uses planting songs is not found in this version of Terute's *michiyuki.* However, it shares many place names and related descriptive fragments with the text printed in 1675. Since the order of the places visited by Terute along her way to Kumano is similar, it is clear that the transplanting scene viewed from Yamada has simply been inserted in the printed version. We do not know when the addition was made, but it is tempting to imagine that adding the description of a transplanting scene, complete with melodies actually sung during work in the fields in real life, evoked appropriate associations in the hearer's mind: the image of the growth of rice from seedlings to maturity may well have foreshadowed the revivification in which the journey with Oguri's putrescent corpse is to culminate.

The description of transplanting women seen from Yamada during a *michiyuki,* recited with melodies suitable to the scraps of transplanting songs included, follows upon what is identified in the printed version as a scene of "traveling along the highway by the sea," *Kaidō kudari. Kaidō kudari* is a well-known theme found in the repertories of various performance types at the end of the Middle Ages.[31] By that time it had a long history of development: there are Kamakura-period examples of the travel song type to which *Kaidō kudari* is related thematically and stylistically. Among forms which it took in the Muromachi period may be mentioned *Kaidō,* the three-part recited narrative *(katarimono)* or song *(utaimono)* incorporated in the *Enkyokushū.*[32] There is also the *kusemai* or *rankyoku* version, *Tōgoku kudari.*[33] The use of the theme in a *kouta* of the Kyōgen play *Kumo nusubito*[34] and as an independent dance *(komai)* for Kyōgen[35] mark stages in its transition into the Early Modern period, culminating in the seventeenth century with a dance number in Kabuki.

This type of use of Kyōgen material was a major factor in the development of Kabuki repertories and techniques. We note in particular that *Kaidō kudari* was to become the special dance number of the celebrated Kabuki actor Ukon Genzaemon. The account of his performance with the Hikosaku Kabuki troupe in Edo in 1650 shows how a dialogue context was framed in order to culminate in dance, as one of several experiments undertaken in the period in search of new forms of dance-drama. Of special interest to us, however, is the linkage Genzaemon made between the plot of the Kyōgen *Wakana* and the *komai* dance version of *Kaidō kudari.* Much as the meeting of the city strangers and the country women in the original Kyōgen play led into an exchange of songs, a similar encounter in the Kabuki version culminated in Genzaemon's performance of the dance *Kaidō kudari.* To be sure, an openly sensual element, whose absence was noted in the Kyōgen original, apparently was a part of the novelty of this play from the *Wakashū* (Young Men's) period of Kabuki.[36]

This is the version of the *Kaidō kudari* theme which is found in song no. 216—*omoshiro no Kaidō kudari ya*—of the *Kanginshū:*[37]

It is beautiful to travel the road along the sea—
Whatever you say about it comes short of the truth.
First, you cross the Kamo river, then Shirakawa—
And here is Awataguchi where you meet the one you love.
At Shinomiya-gawara is the temple Jūzenji—
Next you go through a barrier set up along the mountain road
To arrive at Matsumoto where someone is waiting. . . .
Looking off into the distance you notice
The long bridge of Seta,
And that Noji and Shinohara
Seem to be covered in mist—
Though no rain falls, Moriyama is full to overflowing,
And you pass through.
Here is the inn at Ono—
A narrow road runs up to the pass of Surihari.
It is evening, so we will rest here in the open. . . .
We wake from a brief sleep under the stars and go beyond Samegai.
At the village Banba there is a strong wind and we are cold;
Fierce gusts whistle down from Ibuki mountain—
But the barrier guards at Fuwa do not bother to close the gate
Because the age we live in is a happy and a prosperous one.

In the *Kanginshū*, this song is identified as part of the repertory of the Hōka performers. A Nō play by the name of *Hōkazō*, which portrays two of these itinerant entertainers and includes *kusemai, kouta,* and a dance performed to a *kakko* drum, gives us a sense of what their public appearances were like.[38] An interesting feature of this play is the incorporation of another song identified in the *Kanginshū* as part of the Hōka's stock in trade: no. 19, *omoshiro no hana no Miyako ya.* Our own special perspective upon city and country allows us to contrast it with the *Kaidō kudari* song, where place names met with on a journey away from the capital are given. Instead, what we have here is a romantic description of the city in the older *zukushi* form, which first lists familiar city sights before turning to items which bump, scrape, or jostle one another as a preparation for the concluding lines:[39]

The capital. Brilliant. Splendid—
What you write can never really match it.

To the east is Gion
Kiyomizu. Water coursing down the falls of Otowa,
And in the storm there,
Petals of the famous cherry tree that scatter, *chirijiri.*
To the west, the temple Hōrin and the temple at Saga.
Go round. Go round. Water-wheel—
And come out at the dam before the Risen temple. Water in the river,
Branches of willow trailing in the stream, churned by the waves.
Fat swallows, buffeted by bamboo;
Oxen in the capital, bumped by wheels;
Susuki grasses in the fields, swept by the wind;
The tea mill, shaken by the pestle—
Oh yes, I have forgotten something, haven't I?
These two sticks which the Hōka beats together—
Two bamboo sticks called *kokiriko.*
Age after age. Pile up. Double the space between the joints.
Blessed is the peaceful and wondrous age we live in.

A number of performing types contemporary with the editing of the *Kanginshū* are depicted on a hand scroll in the collection of the Imperial Household. This volume, *Shichijūichiban shokunin uta-awase* (Poem competition: seventy-one professions), includes the picture of a Hōka performer manipulating the "two bamboo sticks called *kokiriko.*"[40] This visual evidence elucidates the conclusion of song no. 19, and suggests that the numerous references to sounds in the text had a concrete performance analogue, since the sticks are actually struck together. A similar punning relationship between text and performance can also be seen in the concluding lines. The bamboo sticks have nodes *(yo),* of course; but the word *yo* also stands for the "age" in which the performer and his audience are living. This age is honored at the conclusion of a series of vignettes showing the city at peace and terminating with a mention of the pair of sticks which the Hōka beats together as he sings.

The songs of the Hōka are of particular importance in tracing the early development of the *kouta,* the most representative song category of the period we are treating. Yet another song identified with these performers is no. 254—*Ōtonoe no Magosaburō ga*—in the *Kanginshū:*[41]

Magosaburō of the Guard Room wove
Cloth with consummate skill—
Peonies and tangled vines. Lions and elephants.

Snow falling on the bamboo or a rustic fence with broad bell flowers.
One after another, designs change. White chrysanthemum alters
Under a bamboo tree beside the guardmen's post;
A wind blows the leaves. They sound like someone approaching . . .
Thinking about it makes me sad—
Though I meant to close the wooden gate, I didn't:
I wait for him. He does not come. Why?

Only recently has it been noticed that a portion of this song—the last
two lines in the translation—has been scribbled down among the
fragments of what may be other popular songs, comic poems, and
random conversations beside the figure of a performer on a raised
platform depicted in a hand scroll of *Mabutsu ichinyo ekotoba* (Demons and Buddhas are as one: an illustrated tale), a variant of the
story known as *Tengu no sōshi*.[42] This scroll is considered to date
from the early Muromachi period. The performer is identified in the
body of the text as a Zen monk—recalcitrant, it appears, since he has
refused to shave his hair—who is a Hōka performer. Just above his
picture are the words "Jinen Koji."

The name given the performer is of extreme interest, for it reminds
us of *Jinen Koji*, the Nō play by Kan'ami.[43] In the play, Jinen Koji
describes himself as a *sekkyōja*, which is a familiar medieval type
bridging the borders between Buddhist preacher and entertainer; he
dances a *kusemai*, improvises the bamboo whisk and serrated stick of
a *sasara* from his rosary and a fan, and plays the *kakko* drum. The
play gives us an insight into the nature of a type of public performance popular in the Middle Ages; the scroll's identification of
Jinen Koji as a Hōka suggests the close affinity of the performance
types.

Shown just below Jinen Koji in the scroll is a group of three other
performers. They are proceeding on a journey, presumably from one
engagement to the next. The appearance of the fragment from *Ōtonoe no Magosaburō ga* in this context indicates that at least by the
early Muromachi period Hōka were publicly performing songs like
those later included and identified as part of their repertory in the
Kanginshū, which collected songs considered by the anthologist to
belong to the *kouta* song type.[44]

We have seen that the theme of one Hōka song, no. 216 of the
Kanginshū, is travel along the highway which links the capital city of
Kyoto with the provinces, and that another, no. 19, deals with the
capital itself. The roots of Sekkyō recitation were in the countryside:

our model tale, *Oguri,* is closely linked with the Shōjōkōji, a temple in Fujisawa (present Kanagawa prefecture), once a way station along the Tōkaidō, the "highway by the sea."[45] The most characteristic story in the early formation of what is now called Kojōruri, the *Jūnidan-zōshi,* is also closely associated with an area outside the capital, Yahagi in Mikawa. But by the early seventeenth century, when the Funaki Screen shows us thriving performances of Jōruri recitation with puppets, the city is the main stage of the action. The transition from performance by transient groups outside the city to entertainment at commercial theaters in Kyoto is beyond the range of this discussion. The implication of the linkage between the two is, however, worth the passing notice we have given it: the treatment of themes from the countryside in city performance will serve to introduce a discussion of the *Tauezōshi,* to which we now turn.

In the tradition of Western pastoralism, city poets have chosen the countryside as a way to speak of the limitations of a life led in a complex urban setting and of their aspirations for the imagined simplicity of country life. The mirror image of this situation would be farmers finding a place to sing of the attraction which the city exerted over them in a form of literature nurtured in the soil of their own lives. We find this, and more, in the sets of transplanting songs *(taue-uta)* sung in late May or early June at the time when rice seedlings, which have grown to a certain height in protected nursery-fields, are replanted into the larger fields where they are to grow to maturity. This is the annual event which gave its name to the Kyōgen play *Taue.*

Religious and practical considerations limited the work to a single day. In order to speed it, labor was communal. Women did the actual transplanting of the seedlings, apparently also for religious reasons. Songs sung by the planting women from morning to evening could be grouped together to make up a daylong structure for large-scale transplanting events in fields dedicated to the deity of a local shrine or in the paddies of a major landowner. This special transplanting custom is known as *hana-daue* or *ō-taue.* The leader of the day's work and of the singing was called *sanbai,* a name which associated him with the field god. The singing was supported by instrumental music performed by young men; various drums, flutes, and cymbals were used. Song and music helped to regulate the rhythm of the day's work as well as provide an ambience of excitement which was deemed necessary to forward the whole undertaking to a felicitous conclusion.

The chief representative of one major variant of such a sequence has been translated into English as *The Genial Seed*.[46] I refer to this particular sequence as "the" *Tauezōshi* and to others (some of which are closely related to it) simply as transplanting sequences. The *Tauezōshi* contains in all some 134 songs. Each is made up of the following components: one line, called *oya-uta* (parent song), sung by *sanbai*, the leader of the work; a second, called *ko-uta* (child song), sung by the transplanting women; and from two to four lines or more each, called *oroshi,* sung by both *sanbai* and the women. In its original form, the sequence is thought to have begun with four sets sung in the morning, but only the last three are extant today. In its present form, these are followed by two noon sets, a short set sung after saké is drunk, and two more noon sets. The sequence draws toward a conclusion with four sets for the evening, and the whole is finally rounded off by what is called the *agari-uta,* concluding song. There is a measure of agreement that the original manuscript took the shape it has today toward the end of the Japanese Middle Ages or at the beginning of the Early Modern period. Dating an oral work is a task beset with difficulties, but recent scholarly opinion favors the view that the *Tauezōshi* can be ascribed to the Azuchi-Momoyama period.[47]

It is of considerable interest that this period produced, on the one hand, a large-scale verbal structure of song to be sung from morning to evening in the fields of the countryside, and on the other, the comprehensive view of the capital city seen in all its manifold activities, the visual panorama of the *Rakuchū-Rakugai-zu*. Perhaps not only because of my own concern in this essay with the polarity of city and country, it seems to me that the importance of each of these works of art becomes the clearer in comparison with the other. Though each encompasses considerable variety and detail, the basic principles and means of organization are simple ones which arise from central issues—in fact, from *the* central issues for the survival of the society mirrored in each: the power relationship which supports city life and man's ecological position in the natural world.

From the early sixteenth century, when a prototype of the *Rakuchū-Rakugai-zu* is recorded as having been painted, this pictorial map, plan, or panorama of the capital and its surroundings had been a means of attesting to the powers—military, social, and economic— whose balance made possible the existence of the city as a political unit.[48] In a very real sense, the changing visual perspectives upon Kyoto afforded by examples of the genre reaching from the sixteenth century well into the seventeenth lead us into the very heart of the accomplishments and the aspirations of the classes which supported and maintained the city. If not a *politeia, urbs dei,* or secular mandala, these diagrams are certainly eloquent statements about man and his city.

Taken together, the songs of the *Tauezōshi,* sung from morning to evening throughout the planting day, are another statement about man: they locate him in an ecological balance with nature. The sequence places the farmer of the period in his universe, for the songs are an array of representative aspects of the entire range of his cultural experience, making sense of them by fitting them into a larger and overarching pattern. The pattern was actualized in performance each year at the time of the most central and crucial moment of the farmer's religious and social being—the day of transplanting.

There may be a further significance to the fact that both forms reached their fullest and finest statement in the sixteenth and early seventeenth centuries—the Sengoku and Azuchi-Momoyama age— even though the basic elements of each, rice transplanting and city life, had certainly been present for a long time before. Although this remains a contentious problem among historians (as indeed is indicated by other essays in this volume), it appears that elements of political and social freedom and mobility came together in this period just before the class system was effectively frozen and fixed by the social and political experiences to come. A suggestion of this can be seen, for example, in the relation of field laborer to landowner reflected in the songs of this period when compared to those used for the same work later in the Tokugawa period.[49]

The tranquillity and serenity of the countryside is often idealized in Western pastoralism. In contrast, it was the vitality and variety of the city that fascinated the Japanese farmers who sang transplanting songs in the Azuchi-Momoyama period. Some actually had an opportunity—once in a lifetime, perhaps—to visit Kyoto. If they had not seen the city themselves, its merchants often visited the countryside; they may even have chosen for their visits the favorable marketing conditions of the festive transplanting day itself. These market, fair, or festival days constituted a sort of temporary urban experience transferred to the countryside. The city was a theme for song in part because of the fascination its material products exerted over country people: the wares of its merchants excited the imagination; mention of its legendary sights kindled the anticipation of prospective travelers and revived memories long afterward. This is but one example of a *Tauezōshi* song where various city themes merge:[50]

[oya-uta]	Look at the streets in the capital. Broad avenues.
[ko-uta]	Seven lined up, broad avenues.
[oroshi]	Marketing has begun. Let us sell the set of seven fitted bowls.
[oroshi]	Taking the stranger along, setting out for the Gion quarter,
[oroshi]	Taking the stranger along, let's be on our way. . . .
[oroshi]	Dressed in our best, at the town Saijō let us sell. . . .

Another way to view the importance of the city as a poetic image in transplanting sequences is to note that the city dynamic, the general pulse of teeming life, and the variety of experiences found in the metropolis gave it a unique and commanding place in poetry where verbal imagery was at the same time an expression of the singers' hopes and prayers. Farmers wished for an abundant crop, so they sang of a dense, a teeming and thriving city. Song about the city also had a place in a second image group or pattern. This was the sequence of the journey. The transplanting women sang of a journey to the city; then followed songs about enjoying the sights of the city; and then there was song about the return from the city.

The importance of the city as an image is clear from the way in which it serves to focus and supplement the fundamental journey imagery which underscores the basic concerns of an agricultural society in touch with the cyclic rhythm of the year. The image of a journey to an imagined city is integrated into the actual circumstances of the day's activities in the fields. These circumstances conditioned the order of the songs, as we shall note later; they provided the real conditions for a poetics of the sequence. The journey doubles up with the disappearance of the lover in the morning and his return at dusk; and with the journey and the appearance in the local area of the god of the field *(ta no kami),* his residence there during growth, and his eventual withdrawal after the harvest. Of course, it implies man's own life energies, first waxing toward noon, then diminishing to a quiet evening, but kindled finally with the ultimate sexual encounter which promises rebirth and a continuation of the cycle. In fact, the poetry itself is circular: much of what comes in the last set for the evening picks up (or perhaps we should say forecasts) the imagery of the second set for the morning and what we assume to have been the content of the first set of the *Tauezōshi,* which is now lost. It is difficult, for me at least, not to associate the blinding light of daybreak —"brighter than gold," *kogane ni mashitaru asahi*—in the first stanza of the *Tauezōshi* with this simple line coming at the end of the day: "Dark. So a carpenter lights his shavings."[51]

What finally elucidates the key position of the city in the sequence is the ultimate function of the large-scale transplanting event itself—song, music, and spectacle.

Transplanting can be referred to as *hayashi-da*. *Hayasu* means to provide excitement through music and rhythm; hence *hayashi-da* means the field excited in this way. In Asa-gun of Hiroshima prefecture, transplanting is referred to as *isami-da:* the excited field, or perhaps the field of excitement. The procession of bulls, richly adorned, coming into the field to plow it up in advance of transplanting is only the first of various devices which promote a flow of vitality.[52] *Isamu*—to start energy flowing—is a significant term in the sequence. A song found in the *Riyōshū*, a collection of folk songs from the same area of Japan made early in our own century, expresses the idea:[53]

Everyone together, come, *yare,* stir it up. Plant it *(isande uete ino yo).*
Stir it up, *yare.* Stir it up. Plant it.

A song from another area speaks directly of the role of song in similar language: "Sing. . . . Sing and make this place jump."[54] This may be slightly too colloquial a version of *utōte kono ba no isamu yō ni,* but the spirit is right. What is suggested by Manabe Masahiro as a possible version of the missing first sequence of song for the morning in the *Tauezōshi* includes this verse: "On a white horse, let's get the field god going *(sanbai nosete isamashō).*"[55] A closely related song in which the landowner is doubled up with the god of the field, and both are seen through the image of a warrior on horseback, also mentions exciting a horse so that it starts to run:[56]

The lord's horse, the lord's horse, where is it tied?
        Beyond the ridge, beyond the valley, tied to a bending pine.
    Beyond the ridge, tied to a pine at the edge of the field,
    Tied in the moor. Let us get it going *(koma o isamashō).*

Several songs of a related type—prayers supplicating the field god to make his appearance during the transplanting ritual—are found in valuable documents which date to 1578.[57] One song is about the place where *sanbai,* the field god, grew up; another mentions the decorations strewed over the road he is to travel; the third is the well-known song about his arrival on horseback, "From the shrine, *yare,* on a white horse with the reins in his hands. . . .'' These songs in a sense outline the journey which the field god makes on this crucial day. But what is noteworthy is the term *nigiwai* used in the title given to these songs in the early documents: songs "to manifest *sanbai;* songs to make plentiful [*nigiwai,* which can mean teeming, crowded, abundant]."

A related key expression in songs of this sequence is *shigeshi.* Of trees and foliage, it means thickly verdant. This word appears in several songs in the *Tauezōshi,* and it has to be translated in each according to the context. Thus we have:

Song 17. "Serving at court keeps you busy" *(miyazukai wa shigeimono)*

Song 34. "Flowers on the chestnut tree bloomed thick" *(shigyō saitari)*

Song 102. "Fast pony there. Look at the frantic baton" *(shigyō sai o mite na)*

Song 111. "Falling fast now" *(shigyō otsuru wa):* "That's the way with early-ripening chestnuts"

Song 134 [to mark the close]. "Let water run full in the river for our washing" *(miaraikawa ga shigyō nagarekashi)*[58]

A rapid flow of water suggests plenitude also in this song from a different source:[59]

[Water in the] kitchen and the rapids of the stream. Always fast-flowing. The sound of this flow is a good sound to hear.

Plenitude and variety of subject matter imply a vitality which has its own role to play in transplanting songs. Singing of the city, however, seems to me to have been a quite specific way of incorporating the city's vitality into the act of transplanting. Mentioning the city is magic in a sense. Without having to say, "May our fields be thick with nodding heads of rice," the farmers simply sang about an abundant city.

There was another way of energizing the field. This was to discover the proper magic paradigm, one might say, for the farmers' labors and enunciate it in their song. There is a shrewd economy about the activity of transplanting which underlies these sequences. It provides an effective commitment of the total labor force of the community over a single area and within a single day. It is a mechanism of great concentration. The commitment is not only of physical labor, however. The greater wisdom of the community has discovered in the songs a means of committing also the large range of its cultural, psychic, and erotic energy to the engagement. The field is energized, in one way, by a poetic association with the massed deployment of military forces, and this image was in the minds of those who sang the *Tauezōshi* and related sequences. A concrete expression of the concept is *omoshiroi wa Fuji no makigari na,* song no. 26 from the *Tauezōshi:*[60]

> A fine sight. The grand hunt at Fuji.
>   All in order—bows, falcons—the grand hunt at Fuji.
>   Beaters at the grand hunt at Fuji—horsemen, fifty thousand strong;
>   I myself took part . . . straw apron for Daisen Fuji.
>   Won't you lend it to me? I'm on my way to the shogun's hunting ground.
>   Shaggy apron. What they wear at the hunt is splendid.

In the background of this song is the famous hunting scene which is a central event in the *Soga monogatari.*[61] A great deal could be said about the importance of this (at one time oral) epic to the general culture of the period under discussion, in particular to its performing arts and to those which were to develop in the Early Modern period. In a larger discussion of the issue, a place would be found to explain how aspects of countryside religion and folk belief nurtured the development of this epic of the Kantō region, thus guaranteeing its continued relevance to the folk imagination. But more important here is to note that, just as the hunt relates especially to the men's roles in the field, so a song such as *Ōiso no Tora Gozen,* no. 119 in the *Tauezōshi,* contains a useful paradigm for the planting women because of their familiarity with another incident in this epic, the details of the tragic tale of the parting of Soga Jūrō and his beloved. The episode was particularly popular in the repertories of the blind women reciters known as *goze* and other itinerant performers:[62]

> Lady Tora of Ōiso is drowning in love;
>   Lord Soga Jūrō comes along to ease his passion—
>   Lady Tora, enough lovemaking for now;
>   In love you make up songs—
>   Come tell me, Lady Tora, when did you see me and fall in love?

There was a special immediacy in this story to the late May or early June planting scene: Jūrō is said to have died—his life "fading away with the dew of the fields at the foot of Mount Fuji''—on the twenty-eighth day of the fifth month of 1193, according to the popular version of the story.[63] Rain during the transplanting season is sometimes referred to as *Soga no ame,* "rain of the Soga." Some local traditions have an interdiction against planting on the fifth day of the fifth month. At other places, rain on the twenty-eighth day of the fifth month is considered lucky. A sudden fall of rain during transplanting could be associated by the singers with the well-known tale of the Soga. In this way singers made meaningful and sometimes extemporaneous connections—though the patterns themselves were traditional ones—between the sights and sounds of the hours of their work in the fields and the more romantic imagery used in songs (such as this one, which alludes to an incident from the *Soga monogatari*), as well as the quite homely and realistic images of an animal or a bird that happened to cross their line of vision as they worked in the fields.

In song no. 26—*omoshiroi wa Fuji no makigari na*—the story situation in the myth has been superimposed on the transplanting activity. It fits neatly: the group spectacle of transplanting seems like serried ranks deployed for the fabled hunt. Planting women, musicians, teams of oxen, and other workers as well are arrayed on the field; the efforts of the entire company are focused upon a single end. The second *oroshi* shows clearly how the farming activity could be associated on quite a personal level with a mythic theme: "I myself took part . . . straw apron for Daisen Fuji." The men in the field are warriors, if not at the legendary hunt below Mount Fuji then at least by implication, since they stand in the shadow of their own local mountains in this peacetime array. The last *oroshi* is an irony admitting to the fact that, after all, one does make but a poor show as a member of the fabled shogunal hunt when one is only a farmer in a shaggy apron working in wet fields.

Documents known as *Tauta yuraisho* or *yuraiki* (which date, to be sure, from a period considerably later than Momoyama) throw an interesting sidelight upon the question of how the farmers interpreted what they sang in transplanting sequences. These documents include instructions as to what type of song should be sung during what sequence at what time of day; taken together, they constitute a body of poetics for the *Tauezōshi*. This is a portion of such a *yuraisho:*

During the songs in the second set for noon, sing of fans. Make songs about going up to the capital. The reason for this is that from morning the sun itself sends out its bright beams like a fan. . . . And [the reason for singing] songs about going up [to the capital] is that the sun is now progressing onward from the eastern hills. And as for plants and trees, they wax till midsummer. While men, too, gradually come to maturity.[64]

In the same *yuraisho* we find this entry under the first set for the evening:

The reason to sing songs about returning [from the capital] in this set is that the sun is declining toward the west, and the fruit of trees and plants is full, hanging heavily down.[65]

This type of prescription has contributed much to modern scholars' understanding of the *Tauezōshi,* and has led an eminent critic to observe that "it is the continuing growth and abundant fruitfulness of plants, especially of the rice crop, that is symbolized within the structure of songs about going up to and coming down from the capital."[66] In other words, going up to the capital *(Kyō-nobori)* is related to the waxing of sun, plant life, and man's own growth; coming down or returning from the capital *(Kyō-kudari)* is equated with the late afternoon sun, with the fullness and fruitfulness of plant life, and with man's declining years.

Shida Engi has made a useful listing of references to Kyoto found in songs of the *Tauezōshi.* He adds a tentative distinction between those related to the theme of coming down from Kyoto and those alluding to the subject of going up to Kyoto. The list is as follows, citing the line where the reference to the capital city is found:

Kyō-kudari
Song 15.   "Buy me a Kyoto comb. A Kyoto comb's the thing"
Song 20.   "At the dyer's in Kyoto I learned about dyeing—patterns and how to attach the collar"
Song 42   [not included by Shida]. "I'll give it to the girl. The fan with Kyoto pictures"
Song 55.   "Yesterday it came down from the capital, the white field hat"
Song 64.   "Yesterday from the capital came rice called *mekuro*"
Song 72.   "The officer on his way from the capital. How has he covered the pack on his back?"
Song 73.   "Down from the capital. A carpenter from the capital with tie-dye patterns next to his flesh"
Song 74.   "My lover left the capital yesterday"

Song 75. "Women from the capital. What is on their skirts?"
Song 78. "What a sight! Merchants from the capital"
Song 79. "Do I love the merchant? Do I love his wares?"
Song 87. "On his way back from the capital he brought me an *obi* I hadn't expected"
Song 89. "Wings are white. Isn't that the way with birds in the capital?"
Song 96. "The bamboo sticks from Kyoto, girls. Without breeding you can't play them"
Song 109. "I learned the trick of dyeing by patterns at a dyer's in Kyoto"
Song 133 [to mark the close]. "A real Kyoto locksmith is making the lock for the storehouse"

Kyō-nobori

Song 39. "When you go to the capital, in the forest near Muronotsu"
Song 41. "When you go to the capital, first of all, in the lodging house at the port of Muro"
Song 50. "Tarō-Tarō wanted to see the capital"
Song 61. "Look at the streets in the capital. Broad avenues"
Song 76. "My lover serves in the capital cutting grass, they say"[67]

As noted by Shida, there are earlier references to Kyoto than song no. 39, *Kyō e noboreba Muro no hayashi ni na*. But according to the *yuraisho* cited above, it is the second set of noon songs where song about going to the capital should begin. This set starts with no. 36 and includes nos. 39 and 41, both of which refer to the way station of Muronotsu:[68]

When you go to the capital, in the forest near Muronotsu,
    Crying bulbul, for whose love do you cry?
      The bulbul is the bird that cries: *hiyo-hiyo*. The mandarin duck is the bird living by the pond.
      Mandarin ducks on the pond never taking flight with the one they love.
      Tail feather. I have one from the mandarin duck—something to rely on.

When you go to the capital, first of all, in the lodging house at the port of Muro,
        Shooting at the target, aiming at the stuffed bull's eye, he hit the mark.
      The arrow he used for target practice had feathers of a white heron from the capital;
      In the feathered quiver thrust thirty-five arrows for target practice.
      Buy. Try your luck. One try—thirty-five *mon*.

Muronotsu in Harima province (present Hyōgo prefecture) was a major harbor for waterway traffic leading along the Inland Sea to or from Kyoto. Although its fame as a port of call dates from a much earlier period than Azuchi-Momoyama, it reached the height of its prosperity in the sixteenth century. The place was especially well known for its women entertainers and prostitutes. There is even a Nō play, *Murogimi*, about them.[69]

These two songs form one example of the underlying narrative element which is traceable in several sequences of the *Tauezōshi*.[70] Read together, they suggest a picture of travel in the period. A group of three or four farmers or samurai journeying to Kyoto stop on the way at a lodging in Muronotsu. They pass through its crowded marketplace; perhaps it is New Year's or some other festive occasion. Their eyes are distracted by the many shops and they listen to the calls of the vendors. They spend some time shooting arrows, a popular form of diversion at fairs, although at the same time the activity *(hama-yumi)* had not lost its older religious significance. Especially in agricultural communities, shooting was a way of forecasting the events of the New Year. In a sense, the travelers purify themselves through this quasi-religious sport before resuming their journey to the capital. To be sure, Muronotsu had other sports and diversions to offer as well.

There are many versions of sequences of transplanting songs related to the *Tauezōshi*, some written down only recently. A comparative study of the available versions yields a great many insights into the underlying tradition which they all share, and amplifies the meaning of the *Tauezōshi* itself. Song no. 41, for instance, is elucidated by a text from a related sequence, the *On'utazōshi*, which depicts the lover who has arrived at Muronotsu as shooting arrows at a target.[71] The traveler on his way to Kyoto who is touted into trying his luck for thirty-five coppers was perhaps at one time imagined to be the lover who often came to mind, it appears, when the planting women sang, for love and the anticipated aftermath of the day's work were a theme consciously employed to distract them from their toil. A comparison of songs in some nine versions of sequences closely related to the *Tauezōshi* provides evidence that at one time song no. 41 had a fourth *oroshi*, continuing the image of a target used in the shooting contest. The target is made of a strong-fibered vine called *katsura* and is seen in the song as gently swaying, perhaps under the impact of a lover's arrow sped straight to the mark: "The *katsura* target turned gently around."

Shida Engi notes that a number of *kouta* are related to the first

oroshi of song no. 39, "The bulbul is the bird that cries: *hiyo-hiyo.*"
A variant is included in the *Sanga chōchūka* (also known as *Shokoku Bon-odori uta;* 1772), a collection of folk songs from throughout Japan; another is found among songs sung as part of the *Ta-asobi* agricultural ritual at the village of Niino in Nagano prefecture; yet others are to be seen among transplanting songs from Kumano in Wakayama prefecture and Kamiukena in Ehime.[72] Manabe Masahiro extends the list and suggests that an earlier *kouta* of this sort, popular in the capital at the end of the Middle Ages, was incorporated into sequences for transplanting.[73] On the other hand, it was also taken up into the art songs *(geiyō)* of a later period, sung as private music at homes or in the theaters, and it appears, for example, as *Hiyodori* in the *Matsunoha,* a collection of *kouta* published in 1703.[74] Related songs used elsewhere at the time of transplanting are noted by Manabe; since their dates, however, are later than the *Tauezōshi,* they may have derived directly from it. The *Kanginshū* of 1518, however, contains a song related to the second *oroshi* of the one we are discussing; and this fact supports the view that *kouta* such as these existed earlier than the *Tauezōshi* and independently of it. This is the *Kanginshū* song, no. 229:[75]

> My sleeve shows how sad it is to part. . . .
> Oh to fly off, a pair of birds
> Together.

The expresssion "sad it is to part" contains a pun, not translated here, on the name of the pair of birds, *oshidori* or Mandarin ducks. These same *oshidori* occur also in the second *oroshi* of *Tauezōshi,* no. 39: "Mandarin ducks on the pond never taking flight with the one they love."

Manabe also draws attention to how the implied contrast between the bulbul and the Mandarin ducks in *oroshi* two and three was later to become a set pattern in folk song of the Early Modern period; the topos is a preference for the bird who is silent when in love to the one who noisily calls aloud his passion.[76] The final *oroshi* is about a feather kept as a talisman in love, a real-life custom as well. It is clear that the general drift of the shorter individual songs which together make up no. 39 is toward love; this would be in keeping with the reputation mentioned earlier which this particular port of call, Muronotsu, had for its famous "Murogimi," and would support the equation of the bowman of song no. 41 with the archetypal lover.

One local tradition says that songs about *Kyō-nobori* and *Kyō-kudari* are somehow related to the annual journey which the god of the field takes from the mountains or other distant place—beyond the sea, perhaps—to the fields where he resides during the growth cycle of rice. Though not widely accepted, this notion does put into an interesting light an aspect of travel found in this group of transplanting songs. Evidently singing about travel contributed to the energizing process discussed earlier. The relation of *isami-da* with travel by boat is seen quite clearly in this song from a manuscript of a transplanting sequence similar to the *Tauezōshi:*[77]

> I would like to go up to the capital, so let's board a boat.
> Boarding a fast boat gets me so excited *(kokoro isamu)*. Yes, indeed,
> Boarding a fast small boat is fun. . . .

Aspects of travel, the *michiyuki,* have been a feature of Japanese poetry, song, and prose for a very long time. Quite developed travel songs listing points on a journey to Kyoto from the Saikoku area, Kyushu, and the region of southern Honshu known as the Chūgoku are found in a branch of transplanting songs collateral to the *Tauezōshi.* A narrative element is strong in these pieces, called *nagare,* which are found in the Bingo region, the eastern area of Hiroshima prefecture, and therefore known as the Bingo style of transplanting songs. There is an association between sequences of songs descriptive of travel to the capital in this tradition and that of the *jinku,* a ballad-like song type sung during the Bon Festival.[78] The latter developed in the Early Modern period, so the *Tauezōshi,* in this regard as well, may have provided a formative element to the large body of folk song popular throughout Japan in the later period.

Song no. 50 of the *Tauezōshi* represents a type which comes between *Kyō-nobori* and *Kyō-kudari,* that of songs which tell of sightseeing in the capital and are called *Kyō-asobi* or *Kyō-nagusami,* enjoyment of the capital:[79]

> "Ready your bow. Ready your arrows." We did get them ready, still. . . .
>> Tarō-Tarō wanted to see the capital—
>> Let's take him with us and worship at the Kiyomizu Temple in the capital.
>> I'll sit down to rest beside the pine called Sango and compose a poem.
>> Larch at the capital were very much like cedar in the country.

Kyō-asobi were traditionally sung when saké was brought out to be drunk or as part of the third set of noon songs, which follows closely upon the break for food and drink. Slightly drunk after their noon meal, the farmers imagine the pleasures of seeing the famous landmarks of the capital. Perhaps they see themselves as the Tarō of the song; they are taken off by the landowner—himself slightly drunk, no doubt—to enjoy a rest from the field work. Here, too, a comparison of related variants suggests that at one time in the *Tauezōshi* another *oroshi* came between the first and the second of the present version. This song depicted a sightseer resting on the veranda of the main building of the Kiyomizu Temple after a long and arduous climb up the slope to it; even today this is a customary place to stop for a while and look out over the city. A song about resting on this platform would have provided a smooth transition between *oroshi* one and two. A song in still another sequence mentions the Otowa waterfall at Kiyomizu; yet another speaks of the Yoshida Shrine and Mount Atago. Thus many of the customary landmarks on the Kyoto sightseeing course of the day were included in songs which served to educate the farmers about what to expect on a visit to Kyoto, as well as to free their minds from the present toil. *Oroshi* two, about resting beside the pine called Sango to compose a poem, is a topic which was very popular from an earlier period in both poetry and prose; it is related to what was sung when farmers were tired out and wanted to rest from their real work in the fields, not just from the imagined exhaustion of sightseeing along the streets of the capital city.

With song no. 72 we enter the area of *Kyō-kudari*. This theme becomes prominent in the first set of evening songs (which begins with no. 70), in accord with the specifications of the *yuraisho:* "Make songs about coming down [from the capital] in the first set for the evening because the sun is now moving westward. The fruitfulness of trees and plants is plentiful. Men have but fifty years to live, and day by day they grow older."[80]

The officer's journey from the capital in song no. 72, the carpenter's in no. 73, and later the merchants' in no. 78 in a sense prepare for the return of the lover, which is prominent toward the end of the fourth set of evening songs. Mentioning patterns dyed on the carpenter's dress picks up the reference to clothing in song no. 72. Close descriptions of patterns on cloth or dress is a topos of widespread popularity in the literature of the Japanese Middle Ages. For instance, *Bunshō zōshi,* a tale *(otogi-zōshi)* dating from the middle Muromachi period, has a long section where a merchant describes in poetic language the designs of the material he has for sale.[81] This is a curious mixture of the sales pitch as a real-life situation and the poetic rhetoric of a former time. The Hōka song quoted earlier, no. 254 in the *Kanginshū*, is another example of the use of this motif. And probably there was a specific group describing the summer dress of a carpenter, for this is what we have in song no. 73 of the *Tauezōshi*.

The same topos occurs also in *Banjōya* (The carpenter), a song used for dance *(komai)* in Kyōgen.[82] Where *Banjōya* has carpenter's tools making up the design of the garment, however, song no. 73 of the *Tauezōshi* substitutes bows, arrows, and a quiver. This substitution of weapons from the armory of the samurai may reflect the special appeal of the warrior class to the farmer, which we have already observed behind the imagery of song no. 26 about "the grand hunt at Fuji." In the sense that *Banjōya* also draws upon the everyday life of the commoner class, its poetry is similar to what we have been examining in the transplanting sequence. Let us have a look at this fetching song:

> The carpenter's daughter wears a summer kimono:
> At her shoulder is a picture of the carpenter's tool box,
> At her waist his small chisel, small hand axe, wooden hammer, a saw, and
> An awl.
> Oh. I forgot: a bamboo brush with ink to mark the wood.
> On the skirt, wood shavings from the plane flutter and scatter,
> Flutter and scatter—
> I don't like leaving you, my darling.
>
> While beside the shore and through the rapids hurries a fishing boat
>   pulled reeling along the floating lines:
> Ahoy, there!
> Let's go back soon.

I personally am fond of a poetry which can draw upon the simple elements of everyday life, leaving them more or less as they would be found there. In *Banjōya*, however, we have a slight dislocation of sense after "Flutter and scatter." The lines which follow seem to belong to a separate song, as they may very well have done originally. An unexpected dislocation of this sort is a device used with effect in Kyōgen *kouta*. The prosaic quality of a list of carpenter's tools—in reality patterns on a girl's dress—suddenly opens out when followed by the emotional statement, "I don't like leaving you, my darling." Then we see a boat moving along the sea, then two boats are within hailing distance, and then simply, ''Let's go back soon.'' All quite rapidly and puzzlingly, these separate modes of diction succeed one another.

Whenever it was that a song such as this began to be used in dance, the transition surely opened up the words to a new frame of interpretation when the movement of fan, sleeve, and the dancer's body added a physical and dynamic gloss of their own. Quite simple and (expectedly) realistic touches are of course also included, such as the movement ''beckons'' *(maneku)* specified in a recent annotation for *hōi,* ''ahoy!''[83] What one would most like to see, however, is how the catalogue of tools and the beautiful culminating shower of shavings are translated into fan and sleeve gesture.

The growing interest in the adaptation of song to dance, as well as the arrival of the samisen in Japan, were features of the cultural life of the Azuchi-Momoyama period which prepared the way for major developments in the commercial theater of the cities and for other advances in the performing arts in the seventeenth century. The middle of the Eiroku period (1558–1570) has been a widely accepted date for the introduction of the samisen from Okinawa.[84] It took a while for the presence of this instrument to be widely felt, however. In fact, it is generally believed that even the *kouta* in the collection made by Takasabu Ryūtatsu (1527–1611) of Sakai, versions of which appeared over about a twenty-year period beginning in 1593, were not meant to be sung to the samisen.[85] However, the samisen was a prominent instrument in the early seventeenth century's Women's Kabuki, as we see from the visual evidence of the Funaki Screen. Songs for dance in this repertory, such as those collected in the Tenri Library volume *Odori,* were no doubt sung to the accompaniment of this instrument.

The type of dance to song which culminated in the repertories of Women's Kabuki early in the seventeenth century can be traced to a dance phenomenon of the sixteenth, *furyū odori.* A large-scale performance of these, held in 1574 under the auspices of Ōtomo Sōrin, the celebrated ''Christian daimyo'' of Bungo in Kyushu, is fairly well documented.[86] The costumes of the dancers and the opening verses of many of the songs are recorded. We know, for instance, that the repertory included the dance *Oharagi,* the pure song version of which has already been mentioned as part of the Kyōgen play *Wakana.* Dance no. 20 of the Tenri collection *Odori* is this same dance.

It is not clear exactly when sequences of *kouta* began to be grouped together to serve as accompaniment to dance for *furyū.* It appears that *kouta* collected in the *Kanginshū* were sung individually and were meant for a performance which, when not purely vocal, was accompanied by the *hitoyogiri shakuhachi*. However, entries from the year 1571 in the diary of the courtier Yamashina Tokitsugu imply that he had been asked by members of the prosperous townsman class *(machishū)* of Kyoto to write out a sequence of songs to be used in dances.[87] In other words, at least by 1571 songs like those found in the *Kanginshū* were linked to one another for use as an accompaniment for dance. A text containing songs for *Bon no odori*—if the dating, 1538–1539, is authentic—would take even further back this type of experimentation in linking popular song together for dance.[88]

Of greater interest, perhaps, are portions of what appear to be song sequences jotted down on the reverse side of entries from Tokitsugu's diary.[89] Though these sequences may not have been intended as song for dance, they certainly are sets of song and not the individual *kouta* we find collected in the *Kanginshū*. One set appears on the reverse of an entry falling in the year 1527, the other on the reverse of one for a date in 1566. It is not absolutely clear that the songs were actually written down in those years; but if they were, then the first set was recorded less than ten years after the compilation of the *Kanginshū*. Evidence such as this, fragmentary as it is, allows us to glimpse something of the movement toward the development of sets of *kouta* for use in dance which culminated in the repertories of Okuni and Women's Kabuki and was destined to lead far beyond, toward the rich and varied music of theatrical dance of later centuries.

WILLIAM P. MALM

Music Cultures of Momoyama Japan

T HIS ESSAY discusses the variety of styles and audiences that formed part of the musical life of the Momoyama period, a moment in Japanese history that lasted less than half a century (c. 1576–1615). At first, this goal might seem rather arcane to Western readers, because Asian music has traditionally been viewed as primarily a static and an "ancient" art. However, music in any part of the world has a social as well as an aesthetic function; when society changes, its music must also change. Momoyama is no exception to this rule. It was a revolutionary age, and its musical activities reflected and contributed to the dynamic nature of the period.

To show that changes in music were indeed an integral factor in the Momoyama period's dynamism is a task made easier by the presence in this volume of essays which discuss many of the era's political, social, and cultural developments and thereby provide this survey of Momoyama music with a broader context. Our discussion will move in a generally chronological order through a period of approximately one hundred years from the time just before the Momoyama epoch to a few decades afterwards. We begin by describing the musical tastes of the elite, and then move on to an overview of the music on the streets of Momoyama Japan.

Music for the Momoyama Nobility

The long period of conflict and political disorder which began with the Ōnin War of 1467–1477 and lasted for a century resulted, among other things, in a weakening of the imperial court's authority and an exhaustion of its treasury. This had a predictable effect on Japanese court music. When an aging court musician, Toyohara Sumiaki, began in 1510 to write a study on court instrumental music (gagaku) called the *Taigenshō,* he was evidently determined to try to preserve a dying tradition. However, the regime of the unifiers which restored order to Japan at the end of the sixteenth century recognized the prestige value of the ancient imperial music. Ieyasu, the founder of the Tokugawa shogunate, took the trouble to move a group of *ga-gaku* musicians from Kyoto to Edo in order to add luster to special events at the shrines and temples of his new capital as well as to display more of a "patrician" touch in his own palatial castle. These musicians were known as the *Momijiyama gakunin* after Momiji-yama, the area within the precincts of Edo Castle which contained shrines dedicated to deceased shoguns, where they were called on to perform at the ancestral rituals of the Tokugawa. Other such musicians remained in the imperial city of Kyoto, as we know from early seventeenth-century pictorial evidence.[1]

A few imperial courtiers attempted to keep up the ancient musical traditions, and an amateur performance group (the Shichiku-kai) was begun at court during the early Edo period (1603–1867). But eighteenth-century lamentations by Confucian scholars and a continual chain of restrictive laws issued by the shogunate are ample evidence that many other members of the court found secret visits to the plebeian Kabuki theater preferable to active engagement in traditional court music.[2] As for their own performance tastes, the music and dance of Nō remained paramount. Training in such traditions is at times reflected in less formal performance practices. For example, a 1614 painting of an outdoor party[3] shows a drunken nobleman dancing to the accompaniment of a *ko tsuzumi* hand drum, the main percussion instrument not only of the Nō theater but also of a host of street and party dance forms. In the upper portion of the second panel of an eight-fold set of screens from the mid-sixteenth century, we may see courtiers about to participate in a formal flower-viewing party,[4] but in the lower section of the same panel one observes members of the nouveau riche class viewing similar sights to the accompaniment of the sounds of a complete if informal instrumental ensemble such as one would find in a Nō theater.[5] Since these new economic and political rulers had more money, it stands to reason that they had more music as well.

Music for the Parvenus of Momoyama

The financial and political power of Japan in the Momoyama period was in the hands not of the imperial court but of a newly emerged elite: the military-administrative establishment of the unifiers and their vassals, the regional daimyo, supported by the rising mercantile class. These new holders of power—as is exemplified most clearly by Toyotomi Hideyoshi, whose case is treated in this volume by George Elison—naturally found the old, traditional symbols of courtliness useful. This had its effects on the history of music.

For example, as implied above, the popularity of the new Kabuki theater which blossomed from the beginning of the seventeenth century did not greatly affect the Nō drama's importance as a source of culture. The latter had enjoyed a high regard among the new elite ever since the days of Hideyoshi, who embraced the art wholeheartedly, practiced it himself, and acted as the patron of the four traditional Yamato schools of Nō. Tokugawa Ieyasu continued this support of the four schools (Kanze, Hōshō, Konparu, and Kongō); and his son and successor in the shogunate, Hidetada, in 1618 recognized the Kita School as well. For the Tokugawa regime, the Nō was ritual music rather than theater; despite (perhaps because of) this, outstanding actors enjoyed very generous support, some even being raised to the rank of samurai.[6] For the purposes of our musical survey we will not follow the history of Nō in the sixteenth century as such, since the degree to which it changed stylistically in that period is not entirely clear. However, the musical instruments of Nō must be described in some detail as they are used in many of the other musical events of the period.

The Nō ensemble *(hayashi)* consists of a flute and three drums. The *nōkan* flute was derived from that of ancient court music but was subjected to considerable constructional innovations which changed its tone.[7] Since it is seldom used outside the Nō theater itself, it is the one member of the ensemble that will not be discussed further here. Perhaps the most popular instrument of the Momoyama period was the *ko tsuzumi,* an hourglass-shaped drum some 25–26 cm long with openings on each end approximately 8 cm in diameter. Its two horsehide heads are stretched over concealed iron rings 20 cm in diameter and are laced to each other by ropes. A second set of ropes encircles the lashing ropes. These combine with grips of the left hand to produce different sounds.[8] The *ko tsuzumi* is normally held on the right shoulder and struck on one head by the right hand. The drum seems to have developed out of an earlier court drum (the *ichi no tsuzumi*) and, before it entered the Nō tradition, was popular as the solo accompaniment of entertainers *(shirabyōshi)* as well as for use in street theatricals. Its companion *ō tsuzumi* (or *ō kawa*) is a larger hourglass-shaped drum (28–30 cm in length and 10 cm in diameter at each end) and is compared with another defunct court drum, the *ni no tsuzumi*.[9] Its two thick cowhide heads are laced to the body very tightly so that when the one head is struck the tone is quite sharp and dry. The drum is normally held by the left hand against the left hip and struck with the right hand. The third drum of the Nō is the *taiko*, a barrel drum with a body some 15 cm high and 27 cm in diameter. The two heads (35 cm in diameter) are lashed tightly, the playing head being struck with sticks. In the Nō the drum is placed on a short stand (25 cm high) and the player must kneel to play it. As we shall see, this is not the standard performance practice in other traditions.

The major function of the drums of Nō, outside of the theater, was for party music *(enkyoku)* and outdoor dancing. The military aristocracy followed the earlier court tradition of considering the abilities to dance and play music—as well as drink—to be gentlemanly accomplishments. Thanks to the frequent use of picnics or flower-viewing parties as topics in sixteenth-century genre paintings, there is much visual evidence to prove this. One of the earliest examples is the six-panel screen depicting a maple viewing at Takao on the northwestern outskirts of Kyoto (fig. 1), done by Kano Hideyori (c. 1560–1570).[10] Winter has already come to Mount Atago in the background, for it is covered with snow; but it is still autumn in Takao itself. A group of six samurai is seen in the leftmost two panels, and one of them is dancing gaily to the accompaniment of a *ko* and an *ō tsuzumi,* both played by members of the party rather than by professionals. Saké and food are much in evidence; a good time is obviously being had by all.

Drums and dancing were not the only musical skills a gentleman might possess. In the middle two panels of this screen, a well-dressed young man is standing on a bridge and playing a side-blown flute which, if correctly drawn, seems to be the more lyrical thin bamboo flute *(yokobue* or *takebue)* rather than a *nōkan.* Another man, perhaps of a priestly order, also is seen on the bridge; he is playing a short, end-blown flute (probably a *hitoyogiri shakuhachi*) while enjoying the view. Some Buddhist monks are watching this scene with generally approving expressions. In short, the only ones without apparent musical inclinations are the group of four bourgeois ladies and a nun portrayed in the rightmost two panels: they are engaged in conversation, perhaps discussing the merits of the brew being offered for sale—*"ippuku issen,* a cup for a copper"—by the ubiquitous pedlar who has positioned his portable tea shop conveniently near them.

Perhaps the most famous—and, indeed, the most fetching—depiction of the mood and style of the new aristocracy's affluent offspring is the early seventeenth-century screen by Kano Naganobu, *Merrymaking Under the Cherry Blossoms.*[11] Four young samurai have reduced their swords and fans to mere accessories for a swaying dance while another leans on his sword and looks invitingly at a party of women found in the matching right-hand screen. Three other dancers, dressed in colorful (and no doubt expensive) hermaphroditic costumes, sway to the beat of a small *taiko* held in the middle dancer's left hand and struck with a short knobbed stick. The three dancers look for approval from their equally young host—believed to be Hideyoshi's son, Hideyori (1593–1615)—who, seated on a veranda overlooking the party, seems to be tapping his foot and beating his hands together in time with the dancing. The whole scene is carefully screened from plebeian sight by curtains, although there is a bevy of serving girls busying themselves with picnic boxes outside the curtain and two palanquin carriers sit beneath the veranda. Perhaps the urbane decadence of the scene is inadvertently symbolized by one of these bearers, who has fallen asleep while his young master is enjoying the party.

The potential softness in the new ruling class was a matter of genuine concern for many of the older generation, both in the big new "evil" cities and in the provincial estates of the daimyo. On the southwestern island of Kyushu, for example, the Shimazu domain of Satsuma by the middle of the sixteenth century was making special efforts to support edifying music. Shimazu Tadayoshi (1492–1568) is said to have brought a former *mōsō-biwa* lute musician, Fuchiwaki Jūchōin, into his court to organize a system of music teaching that would be proper for his fief.[12] Naturally, in this continuing military period the primary concern of Shimazu was that his warriors be provided with musical reinforcement for their virtues. In a way it reminds one of the ancient Greeks and their opinion that proper musical modes and training were good for the morals of their youth. A similar analogy can be made with common Confucian views of the place of music and rites in the principles of education. In the case of the Shimazu clan, the specific results were a set of pieces for a short, end-blown *tenpuku* flute as well as special formal dances for the

Figure 1. *Maple Viewing at Takao (Takao Kanpū)*. Kano Hideyori. Six-fold screen, color on paper, 149 × 364 cm. Tokyo National Museum.

military class called *samurai odori* or *heko odori*. The performers moved with swords to the accompaniment of properly sung poems concerning valor and strength.[13]

The third idiom of the domain's cultural plan was a new narrative *biwa* lute genre called *Satsuma-biwa* after the name of the province in which it was created. The instrument employed was based on that of the older *Heike-biwa* which was used to accompany the famous saga of the *Tale of Heike*. However, the new model was designed larger in order to make a more dramatic sound.[14] At first, the repertory of *Satsuma-biwa* was divided into pieces meant for the edification and use of three types of people: young men, women, and the elderly.[15] However, military narratives and dramatic pieces soon developed for the samurai and popular audiences, particularly in schools of *Satsuma-biwa* that flourished later and were revived in the Meiji era (1868–1912).[16]

The cultural life in the power centers of Kyushu made other significant contributions to Momoyama music in the form of new traditions for the koto, a thirteen-stringed board zither previously known primarily as an instrument in the imperial court. Koto music may have come to Kyushu via China or the Ryukyus centuries before. Japanese refugees from various court or military struggles had often fled to the south, bringing with them their music. However, credit for a Kyushu-engendered genre is given to a priest, Kenjun (1547–1636), in Tsukushi, the northwestern part of the island.[17] Kenjun was apparently trained in court *gagaku* music as well as that of Buddhism and of various Chinese traditions. He was able to combine his knowledge with popular music *(zokkyoku)* of the time in a set of ten pieces known collectively as *kumiuta*.

The repertory of what was then called *Tsukushi-goto*, koto from the Tsukushi area of Kyushu, became an artistic pastime for regional aristocrats, scholars, and Buddhist priests and thus did not flow directly into the new cultural stream of the times. However, in the Edo period a student of the school, Hosui, worked in Kyoto and then in Edo where he broke the rules of the guild and taught the music to a blind commoner musician, Yamazumi Jōhide by name (1614–1685). Though this caused Hosui's expulsion from the school, it generated (through the compositions and broader choice of students of the blind musician) another school of koto music which flourished among the new financial elite of Japanese society. This school was called the Yatsuhashi after the new professional name Jōhide adopted as he began his work in Kyoto. Thus, though the best-

known Japanese music tradition in the world is an Edo-period product, it began as a bourgeois art during the Momoyama.[18]

Religious, Theatrical, and Foreign Music

Buddhist chant, like Roman Catholic chant, was thoroughly codified
by the sixteenth century, and there is little record of changes in Buddhist liturgical music during the Momoyama period. To be sure, the
Buddhist tradition remained a significant element in Japanese life. If
we permit our eyes to wander along the streets of Kyoto around the
period's end as painted on the splendid "Funaki Screen" depicting
famous places of the capital,[19] we shall find that Buddhist temples
(and Shinto shrines) are much in evidence, and will spot in particular
a group of seven priests soliciting (and getting) funds for a new temple bell with the aid of singing to the accompaniment of a flat portable gong being struck with a twist of rope. In a courtyard just off that
street, another priest is performing a *biwa* narrative while two elder
colleagues listen attentively.[20] The narrator may be blind, for the ancient tradition of the "blind priest's *biwa*" (*mōsō biwa*) survived into
the Edo period and after. A few priests can still play the prayer forms
of that genre.[21] A more common form of plebeian Buddhist music is
the *goeika,* a genre of pilgrims' songs which in the early seventeenth
century became a favorite devotional music of Buddhist women's
groups through the use of melodies adopted from folk song and popular idioms. A hand bell and a small brass gong were used to accompany *goeika* and can still be seen today.[22]

Dancing and hymn singing *(wasan)* have been part of the more
plebeian and evangelistic aspects of Buddhism in Japan for centuries,
particularly in the Amidist sects, where the mere utterance of the
Buddha's name is a help to progress on the road to paradise. In this
tradition is the *Nenbutsu odori* (dance invoking the Buddha's
name). This is a charismatic dance associated especially with the
Amidist Ji (Time) sect, which was popular well into the sixteenth
century. The evangelists, dancing on the veranda of a temple while
chanting the Holy Name, often accompanied their calls by a steady
beat on a brass gong *(kane* or *atarigane)* struck with an L- or
tackhammer-shaped wooden stick *(bachi).*[23] Drums and even a
calabash gourd might be used in the percussive accompaniment, but
the gong is characteristic, as seen in the mass of Buddhist dancers
shown on a special raised platform in a sixteenth-century painting.[24]
This form of gong is also found in many other street festivals of the

Momoyama period, and the *Nenbutsu* dance form and instrument are both traditional parts of the earliest paintings of Okuni Kabuki.[25]

The most popular form of Buddhist plebeian dance is the *Bon odori,* originating in the summer festival which might be called the equivalent of All Souls' Day. During the sixteenth century this simple circular dance form commingled with the theatrical spirit of the times. For example, in a late sixteenth-century set of screens depicting customs of the months (the *tsukinami fūzoku* genre), we find, as part of the Gion Festival which is the hallmark of Kyoto in the lunar year's sixth month, a set of dancers who are performing a dance of the general style of *Bon odori* in the courtyard of a gentleman whose ladies watch it demurely through a bamboo screen.[26] Not only are the men and women dancing in costumes of the same style, but two of them carry miniature tableaux on their heads: one contains a bucket with a flowering bush, and the other has a model of a Shinto shrine complete with *torii* gate! The use of such huge flower or tableau hats became very popular during the Momoyama period and is still common in regional folk festivals.[27] Some earlier-style *Bon odori* are done only to the accompaniment of song,[28] but our urban Momoyama example is supported in the center of the ring by an ensemble consisting of a small *taiko* drum held by one performer and thus played with one stick, two *ko tsuzumi* drums, and two bamboo flutes.

By the next generation the new instrumental sensation of the period, the three-stringed, plucked samisen (also known as shamisen), would be found in dance accompaniments.[29] In the context of the Momoyama period, the shamisen can be considered a foreign import, for it developed from the Ryukyuan instrument, the *jamisen,* or *shanshin,* which was first brought to Japan sometime after the middle of the sixteenth century. However, in Japan its construction was radically changed, apparently under the influence of musicians and reciters who adapted it for use in narratives of the Jōruri genre.

This performance type—which takes its name from *Jōruri jūnidan sōshi* (The tale in twelve episodes of [Princess] Jōruri), its most representative romance—is a medieval art which was destined to endure; it was immensely popular in the Momoyama period. Originally, it was *biwa* music that provided the comment to Jōruri recitation. When the *biwa* musicians experimented with the shamisen, however, they found that its sharp tones provided the better accompaniment to the reciter's voice; and when, in turn, puppets were introduced into the Jōruri performance, the success of the shamisen was assured, for it was also discovered that it was ideally suited to punctuate the movements of the puppets.[30] We do not know when exactly the combination of Jōruri reciter, puppets, and shamisen came about; but it is the fusion of these three elements which made possible the development of one of Japan's most sophisticated performing arts, the Bunraku theater. Most likely it is an event of the seventeenth century's first decades.

Shamisen music of a more lyrical nature was found in folk adaptations of the instrument for regional popular music (ryūkōka), and could be categorized as one type of jiuta (regional songs). By the seventeenth century there were collections of such songs (kumiuta), but these really are developments of the Edo period and so are not germane to our present survey. What is important is the popularity of the new instrument, particularly in the urban entertainment districts. The shamisen became the dominant melodic instrument of the newly rising Kabuki theater, no less than of the puppet theater. Scanning early seventeenth-century genre paintings, one sees that this instrument became an equally important accessory in every restaurant and house of pleasure (fig. 2).[31] All these demands for its service caused the rise of many different genres of shamisen music, each of which developed its own distinctive vocal and instrumental style as well as different sizes of instruments, plectrums, strings, and bridges.[32] It will suffice to say that the shamisen was well on its way to becoming the most popular and widespread musical instrument in Japan by the end of the Momoyama period.

While some foreign visitors to Japan may have picked up the shamisen as a souvenir,[33] they brought their own musical traditions with them and presented them in Japan. The three major foreign music sources of the Momoyama epoch were the Chinese, the Portuguese, and the Dutch. During the sixty-five years (1549–1614) that the Catholic mission was officially tolerated, Western forms of ecclesiastical music could publicly be performed and heard in Japan; and this musical tradition surely continued underground for some time after the mission was suppressed by the Tokugawa regime.[34] Missionaries not only taught hymns to their converts but also trained choirs to sing sacred music. In a manual of liturgical services published by the Jesuit mission press in Nagasaki in 1605 ''there are entire pages devoted to the music of plain chant,'' with elaborate entries in Western notation.[35] Catholic missionaries and Portuguese (later also Dutch and English) traders introduced a variety of Western musical instruments from organs and clavichords to bowed and plucked strings (harps, viols, and vihuelas), flutes, double reeds, and trumpets.[36] Organs

Figure 2. Shamisen player in the Rokujō pleasure quarter of Kyoto. Detail from one of a pair of six-fold screens depicting *Activities In and Around the Capital (Rakuchū-Rakugai)* and known as the "Funaki Screen." Tokyo National Museum.

were actually built in Japan from 1606 to 1613, and instruction in the playing of Western instruments was given at church schools. Foreign secular music was heard in the compounds of the foreigners' trading factories.

Most of the Western influence disappeared from Japanese music with the end of the "Christian Century" and the coming of Sakoku, national isolation, in 1639. The Tokugawa shogunate's apparatus included an Office of the Inquisition designed to discover and destroy the remnants of Christianity, but several groups of "Hidden Christians" *(Kakure Kirishitan)* were able to remain in existence in outlying areas of Nagasaki prefecture into the modern era. There are some who believe that their surviving music retains traces of sixteenth- and seventeenth-century Catholic traditions.[37]

Since Chinese traders remained active in Nagasaki throughout the Edo period, their popular and instrumental music continued to be heard. Some of this became known as *minshingaku* (Ming-Ch'ing music). It enjoyed a modest popularity until the twentieth century among those Japanese who wished to perform music in a Chinese style.[38] The continuing Dutch presence had less influence on Japanese musical life, although the bugle did appear in Japanese military units in the Edo period and the exotic Western major mode was known as *oranda chōshi* (the Holland tuning).[39] The only clear survival of the actual Momoyama European musical experience is the name of the Japanese noodle seller's oboe, the *charumera,* which is obviously derived from the Portuguese term *charamela,* the name of a shawm such as was used in sixteenth-century Europe. The Japanese instrument itself, as used today, seems more influenced physically by Chinese *sona* models.[40]

A second possible European musical remnant is the *kokyū,* Japan's only bowed string instrument. Its three (and later four) strings are attached to a smaller version of the shamisen body and neck, while its bow is quite large and tightened by hand pressure. Traditionally, the instrument is thought to have been derived from Chinese or Ryukyuan models. Though it is primarily an eighteenth- and nineteenth-century Japanese instrument, its original inspiration may have been the European rebec, which was known in Japan as early as the fifteenth century.[41]

Momoyama Plebeian Music

The music of the common people is not generally the topic of literate segments of sixteenth-century societies, East or West, nor is notation the concern of its practitioners. However, the evanescence of the sounds of plebeian music in Momoyama Japan is offset by the surviving works of genre painters who liked to show aspects of everyday life in decorating the residences of the new aristocrats, some of whom had risen with the help of the sword from humble origins. In the genre of screens portraying annual customs *(tsukinami fūzoku),* for example, there is a mid-sixteenth century painting[42] of a rice-planting ceremony done in the country to the accompaniment of *dengaku* (field music) sounds and dance. The ensemble forms a typical *hayashi* with a *ko* and *ō tsuzumi* drum, a flute (probably *takebue*), and a large *taiko* played with two sticks as the drum itself is held by an assistant. The musicians stand—rather than sit as they might if they were theater performers—and wear folk versions of garish *(furyū)* costumes; two dancers, wearing a black and a white *okina* mask, are jumping to their tune in a manner which assures us that the tempo is anything but slow. For contrast, one could compare this performance with a more stately form of a similar dance being done before a Shinto shrine in the far left-hand screen of the same set.[43] Its accompaniment seems to be standard for an *okina* dance: several *ko tsuzumi* plus a flute.

Figure 3 shows perhaps the most informative painting of this entire set in the bottom half of the right-hand panel.[44] It depicts a New Year's procession in which the Shinto gods of good fortune are paraded with a host of attendants. In this scene one can see nearly every characteristic Shinto musical or dance accoutrement of the period except for the bell tree *(suzu)*, which is normally used only in *miko* dances within a shrine itself. In this painting some of the attendants wear shaggy red wigs while others have fanciful hats including at least one with a bonsai tree arrangement on his head.

Equally typical of such processions are the large umbrellas, one in this case having a dancing figurine at the top. Before the gods, one can see two dancers with bushy black wigs and small *kakko* barrel drums attached at their waists so that both of the two lashed heads can be played with a stick in each hand while the performers walk or dance. Before them stands a costumed man with a huge fan which periodically is used to cool the busy participants in the festival parade. He is surrounded by music performers plus one participant who is carrying the typical *sasaki* branch of most Shinto rituals. Two of the performers are playing hand-held *taiko* with a single stick and the other eight are scraping a split bamboo whisk *(sasara-dake)* along a serrated stick *(sasara-ko)*. Such a combination *(suri-sasara)* is often used by leaders of songs and rituals of rice transplanting *(taue)*.[45]

The major musical ensemble *(matsubayashi)* of this event is apparently on a Shinto music-and-dance stage *(kagura-den)* and contains four flutes, two *ko tsuzumi* and an *ō tsuzumi*. Next to the stage, there is in addition a high *dadaiko* (or *ōdaiko*) tacked-headed drum, which is being struck by two knobbed sticks in the style of the more courtly version of the same instrument seen in the imperial palace and shrines.[46] Leaning against the side of the drum is a red-wigged performer hitting a brass gong[47] of the type mentioned in *Nenbutsu odori* earlier, while next to him a colleague clicks small dowels of wood *(kokiriko)* and another plays a small set of cymbals *(chappa)*. With that we complete the scene, as well as the list of Shinto festival instruments. We have by no means completed our picture, however, of the variety of musical activities available on the streets of urban Momoyama Japan.

On the fourth panel from the left of the same screen just described,[48] one sees a horse race in progress, but in the lower section of the same panel[49] there is a street scene in which itinerant entertainers seem to be hastening by a fabric store on their way to a more lucrative location. One actor wears an outlandish version of armor with a sword twice as long as he is tall, while his female companion carries a *ko tsuzumi* drum (in the ancient *shirabyōshi* female entertainer tradition) and holds her flowing white train to her head with a Portuguese-style pointed hat that was quite in fashion at the time. Yet a third musician present in this scene is playing an end-blown flute in hopes of alms from the fabric-shopping customers.

Street musicians and beggars had been common enough in urban Japan for centuries; but, in spite of the overly optimistic statement by Ōta Gyūichi with which George Elison begins his essay on "The Cross and the Sword," it would appear that they increased in number and versatility during the three hundred years between Momoyama and Meiji. In the oldest surviving example of a set of screens illustrating customs of the twelve months (sixteenth century), one finds the street dancer *(tayū)* with his *ko tsuzumi*-playing companion *(saisō)* in the New Year's felicitations scene.[50] This tradition is best known in Japan in the genre called *manzai,* "ten thousand years," a kind of comic street-song and dance that has been popular since at least the twelfth century and can still be heard and seen today.[51] Of course, many street musicians made their living as players for the Momoyama fad of *furyū* dances. The term *furyū* denotes not so much a genre as an attitude and spirit. It seems to have been applied to any event that involved fanciful dress and lively dancing. *Furyū* dances, like the processions just described, preferred large flower-topped umbrellas *(hanagasa)* and the sounds of flute, *ko tsuzumi,* and *taiko.* A *kakko* may be attached to some dancers as well.[52] By the seventeenth century, the accompaniment of common people's dance or party music might include a short *hitoyogiri* end-blown flute, the beat of a closed fan, and the shamisen, which by that time was ubiquitous.[53] However, the grand street festivals tended to keep to the standard flute and drum accompaniment, with hand gongs and varieties of *sasara* frequently appearing according to the imagination and affluence of the organizers of the event.

Having spoken of the musical materials of plebeian Momoyama

Figure 3. New Year's procession. Detail from an eight-fold screen depicting *The Months of the Year (Tsukinami Fūzoku)*. Tokyo National Museum.

festivals, let us consider some famous illustrations of the tradition. We begin with the ever-popular Gion Matsuri of Kyoto as seen in Kano Eitoku's "Uesugi Screen" of the *Rakuchū-Rakugai-zu* category, created in the 1570s.[54] According to the sources, the Gion Festival's history may be traced back to the year 869; a century later, from 970, this rite imploring divine assistance against floods, plagues, and other disasters became an annual event; from 998 onward, the large floats *(yama)* which are characteristic of this festival began to appear. By the Momoyama period, the groups of Kyoto townsmen *(machishū)* that participated in the festival were competing in the elegance of their displays much in the fashion that is familiar to us from the "pageants" which precede American championship football games. The version of this annual festival which is seen in Eitoku's painting shows several *omikoshi* portable shrines in the process of being carried on men's shoulders across the Shijō bridge. They are preceded by a *hanagasa* umbrella and a shoulder-carried display of a giant praying mantis on top of a carriage. Down three other streets are seen the famous *yamaboko* carts pulled by teams of men. One is a boat, one (along with another, shoulder-carried float) is a tableau, and the other three are, in effect, theatrical stages on wheels. On these stages are *taiko* drummers, flautists, and *kane* gong players.[55] Two of the *yamaboko* have famous tapestries hanging before the stage, while the third has a child with a *kakko* drum posing like a mechanical puppet at the front of the stage.[56] A *ko tsuzumi* player and a red-wigged *taiko* player with his drum-carrying assistant are seen under the giant umbrella, while a larger *ōdaiko* barrel drum is carried on a pole by two men before a group of warriors in armor. This painting permits us to add one item to our list of the accoutrements of Momoyama processions: we note that the dancer just outside the umbrella is, like a Western baton twirler, throwing in the air a stave with tassels on each end. This accessory (known in various regions as a *kokiriko, ayatake,* or *chakkirako*) is found in different sizes at many folk festivals as well as in certain Kabuki and classical *(buyō)* dances. Later paintings of the Gion Festival show little variation in its music; indeed, one sees and hears the same sort of orchestra on the same kind of float even today. The weight and height of the *yamaboko* keep the music of this procession at a fairly majestic tempo in order to coordinate the lines of men who must pull the giant wagons.

Perhaps the most delightful illustration of the dynamism of Momoyama festival activities comes from the very end of the period.

It is found in a pair of six-fold screens depicting *Activities In and Around the Capital,* painted by an unidentified artist (c. 1615–1617) and known as the "Funaki Screen." In a scene set at Gojō Bridge, a mass of *furyū* dancers are flinging themselves about with such abandon that a samurai on horseback and his retainers are stopped open-mouthed, not quite sure whether they dare to cross the bridge into such a frenzied mob.[57] Only a few blocks away in the brothel area of Rokujō, potential patrons are covering their faces, perhaps as much for protection from dust as for anonymity of person, as they make way for a wave of girls dancing energetically down the street.[58] Figure 4 shows the Shijō area where people are being scattered by swingers of tasseled staves, who clear the way for two ferociously masked dancers with fans and an ensemble of two flutes, a two-man *taiko* team, and a *kakko* dancer-musician, all grouped around an umbrella. All these men precede a procession of warriors *(horo musha)* bearing giant swords and carrying balloonlike decorations that rise several meters above their backs. They are flanked by attendants wearing the common foot soldier's light headgear of black lacquer embellished with a large red dot, and are followed by an *ōdaiko* drum being carried on a pole by two men who seem to be having a hard time keeping up with the parade; a boy running along on each side beats the drumheads with a large stick. Back of them are still more energetic dancers. As the parade turns the corner, at least three of the foot soldiers are distracted by a performer leaping in the air.

The ultimate example of the spirit of Momoyama plebeian music and dance may be found in the great Hōkoku Festival of 1604. In a very true sense this was the last great popular pageant of the Momoyama era, which is so closely associated with the spirit of Toyotomi Hideyoshi: it was held, in order to commemorate the seventh year after his death, at the Hōkoku [Toyokuni] Jinja in Kyoto, where the deified Hideyoshi was enshrined, and the neighboring Buddhist temple, the Hōkōji, which he had founded. The year before, Tokugawa Ieyasu had been appointed shogun, and the fortunes of the Toyotomi family were on the wane. In this festival we see a final frenetic burst of celebration of Hideyoshi's heritage on the part of the populace of Kyoto.

The festival was a genuine extravaganza which lasted for seven days from the twelfth to the eighteenth of the eighth month, Keichō 9. Of particular interest to us are the events of the third and of the fourth day. The festivities of the fourteenth included a richly caparisoned cavalcade of hundreds of mounted knights and priests, *denga-*

Figure 4. Procession at Shijō in Kyoto. Detail from the "Funaki Screen" depicting *Activities In and Around the Capital.* Tokyo National Museum.

ku dances, and a command performance of Nō by the four Yamato schools. The festival's climax came on the fifteenth, when five hundred dancers from the two parts of the capital, Kamigyō and Shimogyō, performed a *furyū* spectacle not only on the grounds sacred to Hideyoshi's memory but also at the palace, before the emperor, the imperial ladies, and an assembly of court nobles. This colorful dance spectacle was repeated before Shogun Ieyasu in the garden of Fushimi Castle on the twentieth of the month.

The Nō performance was specifically ordered by Hideyoshi's son Hideyori, who deemed it a particularly appropriate invocation of his father's spirit (as noted above, Hideyoshi was a great enthusiast of the art). A contemporary account by Ōta Gyūichi tells us that the felicitous invocation *Sanbasa* was danced by the heads of the four Yamato troupes together—most unconventional for this play of the *Okina* type—to the accompaniment of "four *taiko* and sixteen *ko tsuzumi* [drums, which] resounded throughout the heavens and the earth," as well they might have, for this is an extraordinarily large ensemble. The excellence of the performance, we are told, made men weep with delight and surely elicited the divine response of Hideyoshi, the god of the Hōkoku Shrine.[59]

There are in existence two magnificent pairs of six-fold screens illustrating the spectacular events of these two days.[60] One of these, commissioned by one of Hideyoshi's most famous captains, Katagiri Katsumoto, was executed by Kano Naizen (1570–1616) and delivered in 1606 to the Hōkoku Shrine, in whose possession it still remains. The other, which is preserved in the Tokugawa Art Museum in Nagoya, was done by an unidentified artist, most likely a decade or more after the event. For that reason we might prefer to have a look at Naizen's work, in particular at the dance circles depicted by him in front of the Great Buddha Hall of the Hōkōji.

Two giant umbrellas are encircled by groups of dancers in matching costumes (some thirty in each group), while costumed men with staves sit around them like guardians in wider circles. Large costumed crowds cluster around three other umbrellas, waiting for their turn to perform. Each group has its band of flutes and drums, and in the center of the ring of the performing groups one finds a two-man *taiko* as well as a baton twirler, a red-wigged dancer with a *kakko* drum, and a different form of *sasara* rattle.[61] The postures of the circling dancers, each with a fan in his right hand, look similar to those found in Buddhist *Bon odori* today, but the dancers in the center of the circle are the most active. One can even find an acrobat doing hand stands just outside the circle, perhaps warming up for his own group's turn in the celebration, as a colleague next to him claps hands in time with the rhythm of the group which is performing. These two enthusiasts are wearing Portuguese-style pantaloons, as are most of the musicians in the circle as well as the four foreign observers who are wandering through the festival grounds. In fact, about the only "old-fashioned" dress one sees among the performers is that of one functionary standing by the central flower umbrella. He is wearing traditional shrine vestments and is carrying a *sasaki* branch, used in Shinto ceremonies.

By now it should be obvious why the adjective "colorful" is so often applied to the Momoyama period. While battles and destruction continued their bloody way for most of the period, the general trend toward stability—along with the creation of a new elite who sought to acquire a cultural cachet in addition to their wealth and power—released an effervescent explosion of popular culture. The remains of imperial court society were also present, holding on to their precious ancient traditions. Thanks to the love for detail exhibited by some of the period's genre painters we have been able to note the several layers of Momoyama society engaged in simultaneous urban musical activities. Music continued to develop when Japan's new society became more firmly established as the Edo period progressed, but Japan gained its bourgeois culture at the cost of losing some of the flamboyance which marked the Momoyama period of change.

H. PAUL VARLEY
AND GEORGE ELISON

The Culture of Tea: From Its Origins to Sen no Rikyū

B Y THE SIXTEENTH CENTURY, tea was a part of the lives of Japanese of all classes. The drinking of tea was a common feature of social gatherings. The tea vendor who sold "a cup for a copper" from his stall outside a temple gate, and the pedlar who carried a whole miniature tea shop balanced on his shoulders were established figures of the genre scene, celebrated in Kyōgen comedy and portrayed in the pictorial arts.[1] The cultivation and use of tea were widespread enough for its image to be invoked strikingly in popular song, as we learn from the *Kanginshū* anthology of 1518:[2]

> A crop of new tea
> Picking leaves, pinch and be pinched.
> Grinding them in a mill; tug her sleeve
> Shaking them through a sieve
> And then jilted—
> The young enjoy this kind of sport

Yet tea was more than just a beverage, and more even than a mundane necessity of life. As the century began, the tea ceremony was emerging as an aesthetic ritual peculiar to the Japanese. By the century's end, that ritual had been codified into a type of cult.

A modern bearer of Japanese values to the West, Okakura Kakuzō, was to call this cult "a religion of aestheticism—Teaism . . . founded on the adoration of the beautiful among the sordid facets of everyday existence."[3] Okakura was motivated to write *The Book of Tea* by a powerful urge to argue that Japan's quiet spiritualism, as epitomized in the cult of tea, was a far better guide to civilized behavior than the aggressiveness and materialism which seemed to him to govern the conduct of Westerners in the modern age. He doubted that Westerners could ever comprehend his message—perhaps with reason. In the seven decades that have passed since his work was published, much has been written in English about the Japanese tea ceremony. But the true nature of this unique aesthetic ritual has remained unclear, because little has yet been said about its wider context—what we shall call the "culture of tea."

Any attempt to define the culture of tea must begin with the observation that, in late medieval Japan, many aesthetically integrated forms of art and craftsmanship—including monochrome ink painting, landscape architecture, ceramics, flower arrangement, and the type of interior design and decoration known as *shoin-zukuri*—developed in close conjunction with the tea ceremony *(cha-no-yu)*. Moreover, when the Japanese of that age used expressions such as *cha-no-yu*, they meant not only the mastery of the tea ceremony but also the cultivation by tea masters of a connoisseurship and even a spiritual enlightenment that extended to the arts and culture in general as well as to forms of social behavior. During the age of unification in the late sixteenth century there even emerged a distinct "politics of tea." The full significance of these cultural developments cannot be understood unless they are viewed within a broad historical context, and the aim of this essay is to put them into that context.

In tracing the history of the culture of tea, we shall take a brief look at its Chinese origins and at the evidence of its first emergence in Japan during the Heian period (794–1185), and then proceed to an overview of its development during the Japanese Middle Ages—the Kamakura (1185–1333) and Muromachi (1336–1573) periods. That development reached its peak in the sixteenth century, under three great masters whose lives span the century and whose careers and ideals we shall examine in some detail: Murata Shukō (also pronounced Jukō; d. 1502), Takeno Jōō (1502–1555), and Sen no Rikyū (1522–1591).

These three men lived in a transitional epoch. Rikyū, in particular, was intimately associated with two of the makers of Early Modern Japan, Oda Nobunaga and Toyotomi Hideyoshi. It is important to realize, however, that they were still essentially medieval figures. In short, what was in the subsequent era to be called the "Way of Tea" —*chadō* or *sadō*[4]—is a creation of the Middle Ages, or more precisely of the Muromachi period.

It was during the Muromachi period that the interpersonal qualities of Japanese cultural behavior were most fully revealed. For example, linked-verse poetry *(renga)* was premised on the participation of more than one person, and the restraints and conventions imposed by the collectivity—the gathering of poets—on the individual were far greater than in the classical form of poetry, *tanka.* As we have learned from Donald Keene's essay, composing renga was an extremely demanding art. To compose a successful series of verses, renga participants were obliged not only to adhere to the overall mood established in the *hokku* (opening link) but to be ever sensitive to the flow of versifying and to the nuances of feeling and perception interjected into it by each poet. Renga was, in other words, a social art form.

By far the most important manifestation of the social aspect of Japanese culture in the late Middle Ages was, however, *cha-no-yu.* In it we see at its most intense the Japanese urge to create an aesthetic framework for communal cultural activity, a setting within which to engage in a culture of social intercourse. In the process of shaping such an aesthetic setting for the tea ceremony, the Muromachi Japanese were also alert to the need to integrate all of its parts and features, from the architectural structuring of space and the interior decoration to the exterior view of landscape gardens and the natural surroundings beyond.

The two most distinctive aspects of Muromachi culture, then, were what may be called the social and the integrative, both of which were most completely manifested within the culture of tea. From the perspective of Japanese culture as a whole and not merely the Muromachi period or the sixteenth century, the culture of tea embodies the very essence of Japanese aestheticism: an acute sensitivity both to the emotional ties that join people together and to the minute detailing of the environments or settings within which human relations unfold. The tea ceremony may be understood as a ritualization of this awareness and sensitivity, and as a kind of re-creation in miniature of a hypothetically ideal Japanese pattern of behavior.

The drinking of tea, like so many other cultural habits, was imported to Japan from China. References to tea in China date as far back as the *Book of Songs* and the chronicles of the Former Han dynasty, but not until the time of the Chin dynasty in the third century A.D. is there significant evidence about the use of tea among the Chinese. Tea was probably brought to China from South or Southeast Asia, and even by the Chin dynasty it had not spread north above the Yangtze River valley. It was prepared in that age simply by immersing the leaves in boiling water, not unlike the manner in which it is brewed in Western countries today.

Tea spread to north China after the Sui unification in the late sixth century, and by the T'ang period it had apparently become popular with all classes, as we can surmise from the accounts of tea stalls that did a brisk business on the streets of the T'ang capital of Ch'ang-an.[5] To many Chinese, tea was a beverage of great medicinal value, a virtue that the Japanese Zen priest Eisai (also pronounced Yōsai; 1141–1215) stressed when he reintroduced tea to Japan in the late twelfth century. But to others it was also a drink worthy of connoisseurship. The first detailed account we have of such connoisseurship—and the ancestor of the entire vast canon of writings on tea in China and Japan—is the eighth-century *Ch'a-ching* of Lu Yü.

Ch'a-ching is divided into sections that discuss such things as the origins of tea, how it should be cultivated, the preferred manner of preparing it, and the way in which it should be drunk. Lu Yü gives exact instructions for the brewing of tea. These are practical enough, but they also foreshadow the preoccupation with precise rules which would later typify the Japanese tea ceremony:

In heating water for tea, the "first boiling" occurs when tiny bubbles appear and there is a faint sound. The second boiling brings a string of jewel-like bubbles around the kettle's edge, and the third boiling is signaled by a resounding, drum-like rolling of the water. After this the water becomes stale and should not be drunk. At the time of the first boiling, add salt in proportion to the amount of water being used. . . . When the second boiling occurs, scoop out a ladleful of water, then stir the remainder vigorously with a bamboo stick. Next, measure out ground tea and pour it exactly into the middle of the kettle. After a while, when the water rises again and begins to foam, reduce its strength by pouring back the ladleful of water you had previously removed.[6]

By this time the prized "flower" of the tea will have risen to the top and should be quickly poured into tea cups.

Perhaps the major point of interest in this passage is the use of the term "ground tea" (written with the character *mo*—Japanese *kona*—meaning powder). To produce ground tea, Lu Yü prescribes that the leaves should first be steamed and then pulverized in a mortar, placed in a mould, and allowed to dry, taking the form of brick tea (Japanese *dancha*). After roasting, the bricks should be stored and pieces chipped off and ground when needed for brewing. It has traditionally been thought that this kind of ground brick tea was different from the supposedly more refined powdered tea *(matcha)* that Eisai brought from China in the late twelfth century and that came to be used in the medieval Japanese tea ceremony. Professor Murai Yasuhiko, however, suggests from a careful reading of *Ch'a-ching* that the earlier "ground tea" and the later "powdered tea" may have been one and the same substance.[7] But as Murai is quick to point out, and as we shall see shortly, the question of whether or not *dancha* and *matcha* were the same was not as important in the evolution of the tea ceremony as the manner in which the tea was handled in the brewing process.

Lu Yü gained great fame as a tea master and was venerated in China not only as the founder of the Way of Tea but even as a god of the kitchen. Despite the eccentric and perhaps excessive personal behavior for which he is famous, Lu Yü regarded frugality and restraint as the essential qualities of the tea connoisseur's art.[8] He clearly believed that the use of tea should be governed by exacting rules of conduct and rigorous standards of good taste, and for these reasons he may rightly be regarded as the originator of the tea cult for both China and Japan.

From the life and writings of Lu Yü, we know how elegant and favored a pastime tea drinking had become in elite social circles in China by the late eighth century. Considering the enthusiasm with which the courtier class of Nara Japan imitated the ways of China during that century, it is difficult to imagine that they did not become aware of the pleasures of tea or that they failed to pursue them. Yet the records are silent, and it is not until the early ninth century, after the move of the capital from Nara to Heian, that we find the first references to tea drinking in Japan. It is Saichō (767–822), the patriarch of the Tendai sect of Buddhism in Japan, who is usually credited with introducing tea from the continent. He is said to have brought it back with him in 805, after a year's visit to China, and to have distributed it for cultivation to various places in the central provinces, including the Hie Shrine at the foot of Mount Hiei, where the headquarters of his sect were located. The source attributing the honor to Saichō is suspect, however, and we have no evidence from his own pen; rather, it was his rival and fellow visitor to China, Kūkai (774–835), the patriarch of the Shingon sect, who wrote of tea in his poetry and was the first Japanese author to use the characters subsequently read as *cha-no-yu*.[9]

Whoever may properly claim the honor of its introduction, tea emerged rather suddenly into high favor at the court of Heian during the reign of Emperor Saga (r. 809–823), a fact that is not surprising in view of the cultural proclivities of the period over which Saga presided, as regnant and then as retired sovereign, until his death in 842. This age is invariably described by historians as a time of the resurgence of Chinese cultural tastes in ancient Japan. The main objection to this idea is that it suggests an interim waning in the pursuit of Chinese culture between a high point in the Tenpyō epoch (729–749) and the accession of Saga. Saga actively promoted Chinese culture and thus created the appearance of a sudden resurgence, whereas in fact the enthusiasm of the late Nara and early Heian–period courtiers for China had abated little if at all. Since the Chinese poetry of the time, which Saga so adored, abounds with references to tea and tea drinking, there is every likelihood that he was culturally predisposed to like the beverage, perhaps even before tasting it. In any event, he used the imagery of tea in his own Chinese verses. Here is part of a poem the emperor composed in 814, "On a summer day in the villa of the General of the Left, Fujiwara no Fuyutsugu":[10]

> It is not displeasing,
> When composing verse,
> To hear sounds of the pounding
> Of a fine tea.
> With interest aroused,
> One longs also to hear
> The elegant plucking of a lute.

This poem is from the *Ryōunshū* (814?), the first of the imperially sponsored anthologies of poetry in Japan, but the mention of tea also occurs in the two other imperial collections of Chinese poetry compiled in the age of Saga, the *Bunka shūreishū* (818?) and the *Keikokushū* (827).[11] Moreover, we know that the use of tea was more than a mere poetic conceit of the emperor and his court. The *Nihon kōki,* an official history compiled in 840, tells us that, in the course of an imperial progress to the province of Ōmi in 815, Saga stopped at a temple called the Bonshakuji, where the priest Eichū "with his own hands served him tea." Eichū, a man who had spent more than two dozen years in China, was apparently an expert at the preparation of the beverage, for the emperor seems to have been particularly delighted: less than two months later, Saga directed that tea be planted throughout the central provinces and that portions of the crop be sent annually to the court.[12]

However widely tea was favored among the aristocrats of the age of Saga, it seems to have fallen victim to the general turning away from things Chinese—or at least from the blatant emulation of China—that occurred in Japan from about the middle of the ninth century. During the next century or so there are occasional references in the records to the medicinal and stimulative values of tea, including the observation in verse by Sugawara no Michizane (845– 903) that on a rainy and sleepless night, "when one's heart is choked with grief and his innards knotted with anguish, not even a cup of tea will bring relief."[13] Tea may indeed have been one of Michizane's few sources of solace following his bitter defeat in court politics at the hands of the Fujiwara and his banishment to Kyushu in 901. But on the whole tea drinking seems to have waned during the late ninth and the tenth century. To be sure, a tea garden remained attached to the imperial palace, for the medicinal value of tea continued to be recognized, but it ceased being an object of connoisseurship.[14] We may say that the first phase in the history of tea in Japan came to an end in the year 970, when it was eliminated from the ceremonial of the main temple founded by Saichō, the Enryakuji—proprietor of the Hie Shrine where tea was supposedly first planted—by order of the abbot Ryōgen (912–985).[15] Perhaps Ryōgen felt that the preparation and serving of tea were not only time-consuming but a distraction from the more central aspects of the temple ceremony. Yet behind his order was surely also the simple fact that tea was no longer favored by the Japanese.

Even though the Heian Japanese abandoned the pleasures of tea, the beverage retained its popularity and esteem among the Chinese. During the Sung dynasty important new methods were developed for handling tea that set the stage for its reintroduction to Japan in the late twelfth century. Perhaps it should not surprise us that the period's major work on tea is attributed to no less a personage than the Sung ruler Hui Tsung himself. As is indicated by the title later given to it, *Ta-kuan Ch'a-lun*, this treatise was most likely written during the Ta-kuan era (1107–1110). The purported author, Hui Tsung (r. 1101–1125), was one of the foremost patrons of culture among all Chinese emperors and was himself an outstanding poet, artist, and scholar. He is perhaps best known in Japan for the examples of his ink paintings that were brought over during the Japanese Middle Ages and became prized items in the collection of the Ashikaga shogunal house. But to us the main importance of *Ta-kuan Ch'a-lun* is that we find here the first historical reference to the use of the bamboo whisk (Japanese *chasen*) in the preparation of tea.[16] In *Ch'a-ching*, Lu Yü directed that ground tea be poured into boiling water. We learn from Hui Tsung's treatise that, at least by the early twelfth century in China, this procedure had been reversed. Boiling water was now poured over powdered tea *(matcha)*, and a whisk used to stir or whip up the mixture. Although this may seem to be a trifling change in method, it later became a critical feature of the Japanese tea ceremony.

It is not certain who among the Japanese first learned of *matcha* and the new Sung method of preparing it. Possibly it was the Tendai priest Jōjin (1011–1081), who went to China in 1072 and died there without returning to Japan. Jōjin frequently referred to tea in the diary he kept while in China; had he lived longer, he might well have become the one to reintroduce tea in the new form to his homeland.[17] In fact, it was Eisai who finally brought *matcha* to Japan a century later.

Eisai, the patriarch of the Rinzai branch of Zen in Japan, went to China on two occasions, 1168 and 1187. On his return from his second trip in 1191, he brought tea seeds with him and tested them on Mount Seburi in Kyushu. When the test produced successful seedlings, Eisai planted tea also on the grounds of the Shōfukuji, a temple he founded near Hakata. Later Eisai also gave tea to the Kegon priest Myōe (1173–1232), who planted it at Togano-o on the northwestern outskirts of Kyoto. For some two hundred years, Togano-o tea was regarded as the finest in Japan, until it was surpassed in favor by the product of Uji in the early fifteenth century.

In 1199 Eisai, whose propagation of Zen had run into the traditionalist Tendai sect's opposition, went to Kamakura to seek from the shogunate the support he had failed to get from the imperial court in Kyoto. There he was asked to found a Zen temple, the Jufukuji, in memory of the great shogun Minamoto no Yoritomo, who had died that year; and he succeeded in establishing intimate relations with leaders of the bakufu, including Yoriie, Yoritomo's son and successor. Yoriie commissioned Eisai to found the great Zen monastery Kenninji in Kyoto; after Yoriie's death in 1204, his brother, the new shogun Sanetomo (1192–1219), supported the project's completion. The official record of the Kamakura shogunate reports that Eisai in 1214 gave Sanetomo some tea to ease his hangover after a particularly heavy drinking bout and presented him with a copy of a book "praising the virtues of tea."[18] This book was evidently Eisai's own *Kissa yōjōki,* the first treatise on tea written by a Japanese.

The *Kissa yōjōki,* of which there exist two slightly different versions dated 1211 and 1214, is a work based almost entirely on Chinese sources, which it cites repeatedly. It begins with the words "Tea is an elixir for the maintenance of life,"[19] and its basic concern is good health and the prevention and cure of diseases. In the first half of the treatise, Eisai discusses health and longevity, which can best be achieved by keeping the five vital organs of the body—the heart, kidneys, liver, lungs, and spleen—in harmony and physiological balance. "Of the five organs the heart is central, and the best way to sustain the heart is to drink tea." The vital organs are associated not only with the elements but also with such categories of things as tastes, geographic directions, and protective Buddhist deities; and Eisai shows how these can be taken into account and properly balanced.[20] But his main contention is that the central organ, the heart, is apt to be out of harmony with the other bodily organs because of a deficiency in the Japanese diet of the taste that is most efficacious for it, *kumi* or *nigasa* (bitterness). This deficiency can, of course, be corrected by drinking tea.

Whereas the first half of *Kissa yōjōki* deals with the general questions of health, long life, and the merits of drinking tea, the second part is concerned mainly with the proper medicines for the prevention and cure of specific diseases. Although the reader may expect tea also to be prescribed here as a panacea, Eisai instead informs him that the best medicines derive from the mulberry plant! He asserts that all parts of this plant are medicinally valuable, including its fruit, leaves, bark, and roots, and that a mulberry infusion is the perfect cure for a variety of ailments. Only toward the end of the treatise does Eisai return, in a curiously eclectic fashion, to the benefits of tea.

As we can see, *Kissa yōjōki* is actually a kind of medicinal work, only half of which is devoted to tea. It contains little about the practices that later led to the evolution of the tea ceremony. Yet we know that tea had by Eisai's time been prominently used for several centuries in Chinese Ch'an (Zen) ceremonies.[21] Such ceremonial uses of the drink were most likely transmitted to Japan as an integral part of Zen monastic routine, even though Eisai does not tell us so in *Kissa yō-*

jōki. This is strongly suggested in the ritual serving of tea at the Ken-ninji in Kyoto in honor of the temple's founder Eisai on the twen-tieth of April each year. Although this ceremony, which can still be observed annually, can only be traced back to the fourteenth century in the sources, its origins or the origins of similar practices may date from much earlier.[22] In the Kenninji ritual, the guests, gathered in a large room of the temple, are given bowls containing *matcha* and are served by priests who pass in front of each in turn, pouring hot water from a large kettle held in the left hand and stirring it with a whisk held in the right. The antiquity of this manner of serving tea is attest-ed by the *Kissa ōrai,* an early Muromachi-period tract attributed to the priest Gen'e (1279–1350). We find here an account of a social gathering at which practically the identical procedure was used.

Kissa ōrai is a brief discourse on tea written in the form of two ex-changes of letters. The second of these is of genuine interest, for in it we are given an expert appraisal of various kinds of tea; but it is the first pair of letters that is truly important to us, for it describes in de-tail the occasion and the setting of the contemporary tea gathering. The guests, a group of mutually congenial people, met in a hall in a building of a private residence facing on a raked sand garden. After partaking of refreshments that included "exotic foods from moun-tain and sea" as well as "luscious fruits," they arose from their seats to seek relief from the heat on the veranda and to admire the artificial mountain, waterfall, and other features of the garden outside. They then moved to the second story of a nearby tea pavilion, which com-manded an excellent view in all directions and was particularly well suited, we are told, for the pastime of moon viewing. The pavilion's interior was lavishly decorated with Chinese paintings (including works by Chang Ssu-kung and Mu-ch'i), tables covered with gold brocade, and flower vases, incense burners, tea kettles, and other such objects of high artistry. The guests' seats were draped with leo-pard skins, and the host occupied an imposing rattan chair.[23]

The host's son distributed cakes and a young man "carrying a ket-tle of hot water in his left hand and a whisk in his right" served tea to the assembled guests in the order of their social ranking, from high-est to lowest. After the completion of the formalities of this Kenninji-like ritual serving of tea, the gathering entered into a tea competition or judging contest *(tōcha),* a pursuit which, as we know from this and other sources, was exceedingly popular during the four-teenth century.[24] Later, when the competition was concluded and as evening fell, the accoutrements of tea were put away, saké was served, and all present entered into a lively spirit of merriment as they sang and danced into the night.

The setting of the social gathering described here strikes one as extremely overdecorated and extravagant in taste, indeed as somehow "un-Japanese." Part of the explanation is that this type of setting was the product of another one of those ages when the Japanese were engaged in an extensive and seemingly indiscriminate process of borrowing from abroad.

In the early medieval period, and especially during the fourteenth century, the Japanese were powerfully attracted to the cultural achievements of Sung and Yüan China, and their interests encompassed everything from painting and ceramics to the complex systems of thought of Zen Buddhism and Neo-Confucianism. The principal bearers of Sung and Yüan culture to Japan were Zen priests, both Chinese and Japanese, and among the material products of culture they brought from the continent were the *karamono* or "Chinese things"—paintings, ceramics, lacquerware, dyed silks, and the like—that were displayed in such profusion in social settings like the one described in *Kissa ōrai*. So enamored did Japanese of means become with *karamono* in the early Muromachi period that they engaged in intense and even frantic efforts to obtain them. Once in possession of *karamono*, the Japanese owners—among whom the new military leaders of the land were the most conspicuous—seem to have been impelled to set them forth en masse for the viewing pleasure of their guests, arranging these treasures with far greater concern for quantitative display than artistic discrimination.

The unrestrained love for things Chinese in early Muromachi Japan was frequently described in contemporary sources as *basara*, a term that implies both exoticism and ostentation.[25] The principal war tale of the fourteenth century, *Taiheiki*, contains many references to the *basara* proclivities of people of various classes, but especially of flamboyant military aristocrats such as Sasaki Dōyo (1306–1373), a constable of the Ashikaga bakufu who was noted for the grand parties he threw in Kyoto during the latter part of the century. One affair, described in considerable detail in the *Taiheiki*, was held in a setting reminiscent—as a kind of showplace for *karamono*—of the tea pavilion locale in *Kissa ōrai*. Great treasures from "this and other countries" were collected for the occasion, and the seating places of the "hundred guests" were decorated with leopard and tiger skins, damask, and gold brocade. The gathering, as it assembled before four hosts for the serving of tea, projected a glitter not unlike the "radiance of a thousand Buddhas."[26]

During the late fourteenth and fifteenth centuries, the handling of · *karamono* gradually came under the purview of a group of specialists known as *dōbōshū,* literally "companions" but actually arbiters of the arts and culture, the most important of whom received the direct and intimate patronage of the shogun. The *dōbōshū* became not only connoisseurs of *karamono,* formulating rules to govern their display and use, but also protagonists in the evolution of a new setting for cultural activities in the Kitayama and Higashiyama epochs, one that was associated with the *kaisho* (banquet chamber) of the aristocratic residence.

One of the most fruitful ways to trace the origins and development of a kaisho-centered form of sociocultural activities in Kitayama and Higashiyama times is through the changes that occurred during that age in domestic architecture. But let us first take note of certain additional historical facts that are crucial to an understanding of the nature of kaisho culture. For one thing, the Muromachi period witnessed a great increase in leisure time and socializing among all classes, including the lower orders as well as the court and the military aristocrats (*kuge* and *buke*). Thus lesser samurai, merchants, and even peasants, who prior to that time had been largely restricted in their socializing to family gatherings and community festivals, increasingly came together on an informal basis with other members of neighborhood and village-type groups for purely convivial purposes. There was a concomitant expansion in cultural activities, such as the composition of renga, that were premised on social interaction.

From at least Heian times there had been a close relationship in Japanese cultural behavior between game-playing (including competitions and comparisons of things or *mono-awase*) on the one hand and serious artistic creation on the other.[27] Linked verse, for example, was regarded merely as a pastime by Heian courtiers, but in the medieval epoch it was taken with nearly as much seriousness as *tanka*. Moreover, whereas the Heian courtiers had engaged light-heartedly in a great variety of *mono-awase,* from the comparison or judging of objects such as flowers, incense, roots, and seashells to artistic creations such as paintings and poems, in the Middle Ages several of the former of these *mono-awase*—most notably flower and incense comparisons—were also transformed into highly regarded arts. The tea competitions *(tōcha)* of the early Muromachi period, such as the ones described in *Kissa ōrai* and *Taiheiki,* were still another example of game-playing that later evolved into a serious cultural activity.

Even though tea competitions were held within a decorative context of almost uncritical adulation for things Chinese, tea itself had become largely domesticated by the fourteenth century in the sense that the most favored types were grown by the Japanese themselves. We noticed that, of the teas of Japan, the product of Togano-o was regarded as the finest about the time *Kissa ōrai* and *Taiheiki* were written (in fact, sources such as these refer to the Togano-o product as *honcha,* "real tea," and to others as *hicha,* "non-tea"). But by the fifteenth century Uji had replaced Togano-o as the leading tea-producing region.

The kaisho cultural setting appeared during a long process of transition from *shinden* to *shoin* architecture, a process that began in late Heian times and was not fully completed until the early Tokugawa period. The basic *shinden* arrangement, taken from Chinese architectural practice, was a symmetrical, U-shaped layout consisting of a main residential building *(shinden)* connected by covered passageways to eastern and western winglike structures, each of which in turn had a passageway extending southward to a pond-centered garden. Whether or not on account of a fundamental Japanese preference for the asymmetrical or irregular, this symmetry of layout was destroyed in the late Heian period, mainly through the elimination of the western wing and passageway.[28] Another development within *shinden* architecture that became more pronounced with the passage of time was the establishment of private living quarters for the owner of the mansion separate from the main *shinden* building itself. In the mansions of courtier families, such structures were commonly called *tsune-no-gosho* (normal residences or palaces).[29]

While the *tsune-no-gosho* served as the principal living area of the aristocratic residence in the Muromachi era, the kaisho emerged in proximity to it as a place for socializing, often of an informal or even spontaneous nature. In certain mansions, where it was impossible to build a separate structure as a kaisho, part of the *tsune-no-gosho* or some other building had to serve the purpose. There was, in any case, a distinct consciousness of the need for a kaisho as a setting for social activities. And, as is abundantly clear from the *Kissa ōrai* and *Taiheiki* accounts cited above, the kaisho setting in the fourteenth and early fifteenth centuries was preeminently the world of *karamono* or things Chinese.[30]

The creation of the kaisho setting for cultural activities occurred under novel circumstances that allowed for a high degree of innovation. For example, since the remnants of *shinden* architecture were restricted almost entirely to the actual *shinden* building of the aristocratic residence, structures such as the *tsune-no-gosho* and kaisho evolved, in terms of architectural design and interior decoration, under a minimum of influence from the older, courtier-associated *shinden* style. Moreover, inasmuch as the kaisho was first and foremost a locale where foreign, exotic *karamono* were put on exhibition, it became mandatory that new rules governing the display of these items be developed and that the structuring of the kaisho be adjusted to accord with such rules. The historical task of establishing a connoisseurship for *karamono* and devising the principles for their display devolved chiefly on the shogunal *dōbōshū*. This is why the *dōbōshū* played such an important role both in the transition to *shoin* architecture and in the evolution of the tea ceremony.

An extremely important influence on the development of the kaisho setting came from the medieval Zen monasteries, where interior rooms known as *shoin* were employed for purposes such as informal socializing, the keeping of books, and studying. Quite likely many, if not all, of the architectural elements that were eventually identified with *shoin* domestic architecture were first developed in the monastic environment of Zen temples. These elements included *tatami* matting, ceilings, installed room dividers such as *fusuma* and *shōji,* and square-cornered (instead of round) supporting posts, which were necessary to provide a tight fit when the room dividers were in closed position.[31]

But the three most distinctive features of later *shoin* architecture that may have had their origins in the Zen monastery *shoin* were the *toko-no-ma* (alcove), *tsuke-shoin* (installed desk), and *chigai-dana* (staggered shelves). So far as we know, however, at no time before the Momoyama epoch were these three features of *shoin* architecture ever combined as an architectural set in the way in which they are seen in Japanese rooms even today. Rather, they were utilized in buildings of the middle and late Muromachi period either singly or in pairs—for instance, a *tsuke-shoin* and *chigai-dana,* but not a *toko-no-ma.*[32]

The evolution of kaisho culture was intimately related not only to developments in architecture and the other arts and crafts but also to important changes in social relations and even to the manner in which the Ashikaga shoguns sought to exercise their rule. Before the

Middle Ages, the social etiquette of courtier society held that it was improper for people of superior status to call on their inferiors. Hence socializing, whether formal or informal, nearly always involved the centripetal process, so to speak, of people visiting the residences and palaces of their superiors. With the coming of the Muromachi period, this one-way pattern of socializing was significantly altered. The new military aristocrats, who fervently desired to blend socially with the *kuge* "patricians" and to take on their cultural qualities, began the practice of inviting courtiers, who were technically their social superiors, to the gatherings and parties they held with increasing frequency in the kaisho settings of their Kyoto residences. This practice extended to the very highest levels of society. Shogun Ashikaga Yoshimitsu, for example, had Emperor Go-En'yū (r. 1371–1382) visit him at the Hana no Gosho, his Palace of Flowers, in 1381; and in 1408 he fêted Emperor Go-Komatsu (r. 1382–1412) for twenty days at his Kitayama estate, the site of the Golden Pavilion.[33]

Within *buke* society, it became common for the shogun to make visits to daimyo and other subordinates. As part of his policy to secure greater political control of the country, Yoshimitsu obliged the daimyo to take up permanent residence in Kyoto; that is, to leave their territorial domains in the charge of underlings and to situate themselves in proximity to the bakufu where they were drawn directly into the center of the social and cultural milieu of both *kuge* and *buke* aristocracies. Yoshimitsu seems to have been motivated by the desire to dominate not only the *buke* and the *kuge* but also the imperial family itself. The shoguns Yoshimochi and Yoshinori, on the other hand, used socializing more specifically as a device to strengthen and institutionalize the ties between them and the daimyo. During Yoshinori's shogunate (1429–1441), the shogun's visits *(onari)* to daimyo residences became important features of *buke* relations and were regarded as major events on the bakufu's calendar.[34]

The evolution of the *onari* in the early fifteenth century was part of a larger development of warrior annual practices *(nenjū gyōji)* in imitation of the traditional sequence of annual events and celebrations of the imperial court. Certain of the *nenjū gyōji* adopted by the Ashikaga bakufu, such as the *ōban* banquet and poetry *(tanka)* gathering, were taken directly from the *kuge;* others, including the Nō performance and the linked verse party, were products of the medieval epoch of *buke* dominance. The establishment of this calendar of recurring events for warrior society reflected one aspect of the gradual absorption of the *buke* class into the complex of courtly mores under the Ashikaga. It was also a major device in assuring Ashikaga rule a cultural cachet. By the Higashiyama epoch, this process had reached the point where the Ashikaga bakufu under Yoshimasa (shogun, 1449–1474) was more of a cultural than a political entity.

The new Muromachi pattern of socializing, with superiors visiting inferiors, was also an important factor in the transition to kaisho culture. For example, since the shogun made regular calls on the leading daimyo, such as Hosokawa, Hatakeyama, and Akamatsu, and assigned them the responsibility for arranging Nō performances and other types of formal entertainment, these daimyo were obliged not only to engage more extensively in cultural activities as such but also to equip their residences with facilities (including kaisho) to accommodate those activities.

It was against this background of altered social relations that the partaking of tea as an aesthetic ritual first developed under *dōbōshū* influence in the early fifteenth century. Among the *dōbōshū* most notable in the creation of this kaisho form of the tea ceremony were the so-called Three Ami: Nōami (1397–1471), Geiami (1431–1485), and Sōami (d. 1525). Nōami, who successively served the shoguns Yoshimochi, Yoshinori, and Yoshimasa, began the compilation of a tract called *Kundaikan sōchōki*—later completed by his grandson Sōami—which is the single most important source of information about the tastes and the connoisseurship of kaisho culture.[35]

Kundaikan sōchōki begins with a listing of works by more than a hundred Chinese painters, mostly of the Sung and Yüan dynasties, classified in one of three grades of "upper," "middle," or "lower" quality. The book then proceeds to a set of rules for decorating the kaisho, and concludes with a discussion of ceramic ware and other utensils used in entertaining. The *Kundaikan sōchōki* reveals that in the century or so that had elapsed since the writing of *Kissa ōrai* and *Taiheiki*, the Japanese had become markedly more discriminating of *karamono* and indeed had evolved important new styles in the display of art. Interior decoration had come to reflect a studied blending of Chinese and native tastes. We also know from other sources that the various competitions and forms of gambling that had been features of even the most elegant social gatherings during the fourteenth century were increasingly abandoned, at least by the upper classes, in favor of more ceremonially precise behavior on formal occasions of social intercourse. Such precision of behavior was most clearly observable in the serving of tea, where specialists such as Nōami became particularly noted for the elegance with which they handled the beverage and arranged its decorative setting.

What little is known of the kaisho tea ceremony is best told in terms of how it differed from the *wabicha* or "poverty tea" ceremony into which it subsequently evolved. In the kaisho ceremony, tea was prepared in a separate room or outside corridor and brought into the kaisho for service to the guests, while in wabicha the host both prepared and served tea to his guests in the same room. (In the early form of wabicha he utilized the *daisu* portable stand for this purpose; eventually that was dispensed with and the tea utensils were handled on the *tatami* floor.) The preparation of tea by the host himself became of crucial importance, because it symbolized a new spirit of willingness on his part to perform before his guests a humble chore that would have been incongruous in the atmosphere of high refinement that prevailed in the kaisho setting.

Aesthetically, the kaisho tea ceremony may be characterized as "elegant and sensuously beautiful" *(yūga enrei)*, a term commonly used to describe Kitayama culture as a whole. Wabicha, on the other hand, was part of a new Higashiyama range of taste expressed by the phrase *kanso kotan*, "plainness and refined simplicity." Of the four characters that make up this phrase the key one is *ko*, which by itself may be pronounced *kare* and means "withered." Here we have implications of a new dimension of Japanese aesthetics that was a distinct product of the Middle Ages and specifically of the Muromachi period. The courtier tastes defined by such terms as *miyabi* and *yūgen*, as well as the phrase *yūga enrei*, were based on a sense of refinement or decorum and a visuality of resplendent colors. The *kanso kotan* ideal, however, tells us that beauty and aesthetic satisfaction are to be found also in those things that are plain, imperfect, or worn with time and that have only slight coloring or are monochromatic.

The handling by the host in wabicha of the entire process of preparing and serving tea was part of a larger pattern in the evolution of the tea ceremony whereby everything was drawn into the tearoom itself, into a microcosmic world separate from the greater world outside. Wabicha thus provided an opportunity for cultural withdrawal, especially during the troubled age of civil strife that engulfed Japan after the Ōnin War. And the spirit of wabicha became one of detachment from the concerns and responsibilities of everyday life. Such detachment in other civilizations and other times has led to a transitory hedonism. In Japan, however, the medieval development of the tea ceremony from *basara* tea to kaisho tea to wabicha produced an enduring cultural legacy: a devotion to the most simple and humble aspects of life and a quest for spiritual fulfillment in the ideal of poverty. This is an aesthetic principle which affected the cultural lives even of those grandiose men of power who reunified Japan at the end of the sixteenth century and rang down the curtain on the Middle Ages; it made its profound influence felt even amid the glitter and gaudiness of the Azuchi-Momoyama era.

What makes wabicha—the tea ceremony in its highest stage of development—possibly unique among the great rituals of the world is that it is inseparably bound to aestheticism and art. The Christian Eucharist, for instance, holds the most sublime religious significance, but it can also be celebrated in the most mundane of surroundings. The coronation of a sovereign, however rich its panoply, is seldom remembered as an aesthetically moving experience but rather as a pageant, or perhaps as an emotional commitment to monarchy. In the tea ceremony, by the sharpest of contrasts, no aspect of setting, decoration, or implements can be ignored, and an error in the preparation or selection of any of these can doom the ceremony to complete failure, no matter how skillfully it is in fact performed.

If the tea ceremony is thus unique as a ritual inseparable from aestheticism and art, this uniqueness contains a contradiction that has always threatened the integrity of the ceremony itself. Since the spirit which informs the tea ceremony is that of *wabi*—"poverty," or the renunciation of worldly materialism—it is surely antithetical to that spirit to covet the implements and accessories of the ceremony as objects whose value can be monetarily calculated in terms of market demand. Yet that is what many tea masters and connoisseurs have done, and they have thus created and perpetuated a dilemma of choice between philosophy and art that presumably can never be fully resolved. One of the most famous definitions of proficiency in the art of tea—from the late sixteenth-century text *Yamanoue Sōji ki*—practically spells out the nature of that dilemma: "One who appreciates the value of things *(mekiki)*, who is good at the tea ceremony, and who makes his way through this world by instructing others in connoisseurship *(suki)* is called a teaman *(cha-no-yusha)*. One who does not own even one [famous tea] article but incorporates the three qualities of resolution, creativity, and skill is called an amateur of *wabi (wabisuki)*. One who owns *karamono*, who can judge the value of things *(mekiki)*, and who is good at the tea ceremony—who meets these three qualifications and has singular determination—is called a master *(meijin)*."[36] The word *mekiki*, one who judges or appreciates the "value" of the implements, is not without its ambiguities.

The person credited with originating wabicha is Murata Shukō (also pronounced Jukō), a semilegendary figure whose death date is given as 1502. He is said to have been a native of Nara who studied Zen Buddhism under Ikkyū (1394–1481), the eccentric abbot of the Daitokuji in Kyoto. According to the *Yamanoue Sōji ki*, it was none other than Nōami who first introduced Shukō to Ashikaga Yoshimasa and thus provided him with an entrée into the inner circle of the Higashiyama cultural world. Nōami, we are told, recommended Shukō to the retired shogun as one who was not only well versed in the Way of Tea but also learned in the Way of Confucius. "Buddhism as well is present in *cha-no-yu*," Nōami continues in our text —for the calligraphy of Zen priests, with its antique and astringent effect, was the appropriate decoration for the tea room; indeed, Shukō used as his preferred decorative item in the tea ceremony a scroll with calligraphy by the great Zen master Yüan-wu, which he had received from Ikkyū as a certificate of his enlightenment. On the basis of this recommendation, "Yoshimasa summoned Shukō and made him his master of the tea ceremony, which became his supreme pleasure in this world."[37] The text specifies that this took place after Yoshimasa "retired to Higashiyama," that is to say, no earlier than 1482. How Nōami, who died in 1471, could have been the intermediary is left unexplained.

The paucity of solid sources—and the abundance of such anecdotes —on Shukō's life has even caused some commentators to question his historicity.[38] We need not share these doubts. The *Yamanoue Sōji ki,* which purports to trace the orthodox line of transmission of the secrets of *cha-no-yu,* did not anchor that line in a fictional person: Shukō's tradition had been alive throughout the sixteenth century. The story of a connection between him and such distinguished aesthetes as Yoshimasa and Nōami merely embellished the authority of this progenitor of wabicha.

Shukō's association with Ikkyū and Zen has greatly enhanced the traditional and oft-repeated axiom that "Zen and tea are one" *(Zen-cha ichimi)*. As we have seen, tea was incorporated into Zen ritual early in the medieval period; but many non-Zen influences also came to bear on the evolution of the tea ceremony. The crucial point is that neither the spirit nor the aesthetic of the tea ceremony in its perfected form as wabicha was in any sense solely a product of Zen Buddhism. Yet many writers have all too facilely pictured the tea ceremony as a natural or logical manifestation—even as the inevitable distillation—of Japanese Zen.[39]

There is no denying that wabicha has, from Shukō's time on, become deeply infused with Zen. But in the tea ceremony, as in so many areas of Muromachi culture, this is not because Zen was able independently to generate the creation of new art forms. Rather it is because Zen found in medieval Japan a civilization that was highly receptive to it and one that it could aid in giving formal definition to new aesthetic and spiritual values already evolving among the Japanese. The wabi aesthetic of humbleness, simplicity, and suggestion may indeed have accorded with the Zen attitude toward life, since it implied the reduction of a human environment to one of basic naturalness, free of all the unnecessary, distracting contrivances with which man clutters his existence. But this aesthetic ideal was not automatically transferred—like a piece of calligraphy—from Zen into wabicha, far less was it "transmitted from mind to mind" between a Zen master and a disciple of the tea cult, from Ikkyū to Shukō. Rather, it took the whole of the sixteenth century to develop and be codified.

That the process was experimental and gradual rather than coming in a flash of enlightenment is illustrated perfectly in the famous passage of the Nanbōroku which discusses the various stages in the development of the ideal setting for wabicha.[40] According to this canonical scripture of cha-no-yu, it was Shukō who devised the enclosure of four and a half tatami mats or nine feet square which thereafter became the classical model of the tea room.[41] Shukō began the departure from the shoin style: for instance, his toko-no-ma was papered in plain white instead of having the usual landscape painted on its surface; he limited the number of utensils which could be displayed there, and permitted at most a set of two hanging scrolls instead of the previous three or four; his flower arrangement used one variety and not a profusion of blossoms. The number of decorative items has been reduced, but they still abound; one senses that the door has not yet been closed on the kaisho, and that Yoshimasa and Nōami—if not Sasaki Dōyo—would still be comfortable in this room.

The next great tea master, Takeno Jōō (1502–1555), eliminated the paper from the walls and left them plainly plastered; he substituted bamboo for wooden lattices and used plain or lightly varnished

wood for the framework of the *toko-no-ma;* but his use of hanging
scrolls and other decorative items was "the same as Shukō's," so that
his setting was therefore "something in between the *shoin* and the
tea room *(kozashiki)*." It is only with the advent of Sen no Rikyū
(1522–1591) that the *wabi* ideal was perfected, in the form of the tea
room and in the spirit that dwelt there. Whereas Shukō's teahouse
was shingle-roofed, the *Nanbōroku* informs us, Rikyū's "absolute
preference was for the grass-thatched hut"; it was Rikyū who finally
rejected the kaisho tradition of display and established restraint, simplicity, and even severity as the new orthodoxy of the cult of tea.

For this Rikyū has been canonized as the greatest of the masters,
and his *wabi* ideal praised as the perfect attainment of the state of
Zen. Yet the urge to withdraw from the cares of the world to a simple, hermitlike existence in a grass hut had already become a vener-
able tradition, independent of Zen, centuries before Rikyū adopted
grass thatch for his tea room and long before Shukō studied with
Ikkyū. We find an eloquent expression of it in Kamo no Chōmei's
Hōjōki, written in 1212, before the influence of Zen had made itself
felt in the capital city of Kyoto which Chōmei had abandoned; on
the wall of his "ten-foot-square" dwelling a picture of Amida was
displayed. To be sure, Chōmei himself recognized the paradoxical
nature of his preference for the grass-thatched hermitage: "The essence of the Buddha's teaching is, 'Do not have attachment to
things.' To love this hut as I do now is a sin, and to be attached to its
solitude must be a hindrance to my salvation."[42] In saying this Chōmei foretold better than he could have suspected another one of the
facets of the dilemma between renunciation and attachment in *cha-
no-yu.*

Shukō himself cautioned, "Become the master of your heart, do
not let the heart be your master," in a letter he is purported to have
written to a disciple, Furuichi Chōin. This is one of the few reasonably authentic records we have of him, and it may be the most reveal-
ing of his tastes. In it he states:

The worst faults in this Way [of Tea] are pride and self-assertion. For one to
envy those who are accomplished and despise those who are inexperienced is
indeed disgraceful. Even while mingling with the accomplished and cherish-
ing their every word, one should also endeavor to instruct the inexperienced.

In pursuing this Way, greatest attention should be given to harmonizing
Japanese and Chinese tastes. How absurd it is these days for those who are

inexperienced to covet with self-satisfaction such things as Bizen and
Shigaraki wares on the grounds that they possess the quality of being "cold
and withered" (hiekaruru).[43]

In the second paragraph Shukō alludes to a major development in
the transition in ceramic tastes from refined, technologically advanced Chinese ware (karamono) to Japanese ware (wamono) of a primi-
tive and rough-textured nature. Shukō criticizes what he regards as
the rash rejection of karamono elegance in favor of an exclusive
preference for the withered aesthetic of native ceramics. At the very
least, he cautions that judging Japanese pottery is beyond the range
of the novice.

This criticism is another piece of evidence that Shukō, although
the originator of wabicha, was still much committed to the values of
kaisho culture, which emerged (as noted) largely from Japanese efforts to discriminate among Chinese art objects and to display them
tastefully. But Shukō's words can also be understood to suggest a
much more important fact in the development of wabicha and of late
medieval culture as a whole. The shift in taste to a "withered" aesthetic in no sense meant a total rejection of the earlier ideal of
miyabi, "courtliness"; the preference for the monochromatic was
not a cancellation of the value to be found in the elegance of gor-
geous colors. Shukō himself put it most aptly in his well-known assertion that "the moon is not appealing unless it is partly obscured by a
cloud."[44] Conversely, a cloud (the monochromatic and "withered")
is not wholly attractive unless it is seen in contrast with the brilliance
of a full moon (Heian courtier miyabi). It is no accident that Shukō's
statement should have been passed down to us in a text on the art of
Nō, which combines these values beautifully.

Behind the major cultural pursuits of the late Muromachi period
—especially renga and wabicha—lay the classical, idealized values of
the courtiers of ancient Japan. In the realm of wabicha this can probably best be seen in the career of Takeno Jōō, a man of merchant
stock from Sakai who became Shukō's successor in the transmission
of the mastery of cha-no-yu.

As we have learned from V. Dixon Morris' essay, Sakai flourished
in the late Middle Ages as an entrepôt of the luxury trade with Ming
China. Its leading merchants amassed great wealth; with the acquisition of wealth, they sought also to acquire culture. Along with affluent merchants in the other two leading cities of the central provinces,

Kyoto and Nara, they formed a new class of townsmen *(machishū)* that played a prominent role in cultural developments from late Muromachi through the Momoyama epoch and into the early Edo period.

Backed by Sakai merchant wealth (his father was a trader in leather items of military equipment), Jōō enjoyed the opportunity of studying the tea ceremony with Jūshiya Sōgo and Sōchin, who had been Shukō's direct disciples.[45] From about 1528 on he became a frequent guest at the Kyoto residence of the courtier Sanjōnishi Sanetaka (1455–1537), the most esteemed scholar and man of letters of his age. The relationship with Sanetaka, who readily welcomed economic assistance even from a social parvenu like the visitor from Sakai, was decisive for Jōō. Yamanoue Sōji informs us that he learned from Rikyū as a secret tradition of the tea ceremony that Jōō had considered himself primarily a renga poet until the age of thirty, but after hearing Sanetaka discourse on Fujiwara Teika's *Eika taigai,* "he came to comprehend *cha-no-yu* and became a master *(meijin).*"[46] In short, we are told here that Jōō turned to wabicha after gaining insight into the classical courtly culture through the supreme language of Fujiwara Teika's *tanka* poetry.[47]

This strongly implies that the late medieval wabicha ceremony was based on a close association between a yearning, on the one hand, for the multihued and dreamlike world of the *Tale of Genji* and, on the other hand, the more recently cultivated liking for the earthy, monochromatic—perhaps Zen-inspired—values of the spiritual microcosm of the tea hut. Jōō epitomized in his own background this association and aesthetic contrast. For in addition to receiving instruction in the various aspects of courtly culture from Sanjōnishi Sanetaka, Jōō (originally a member of one of the Pure Land sects) also studied Zen under Dairin Sōtō (1480–1568) of the Nanshūji in Sakai and "realized that tea and Zen are one and the same," as Dairin himself was to say in praise of his disciple.[48] As Yamanoue Sōji puts it, "Since *cha-no-yu* emerged from the Zen sect, it concentrates on priestly behavior. Shukō, Jōō, and the other masters were all members of the Zen sect."[49]

What is perhaps most significant in the careers of both Shukō and Jōō is the impression we derive from them of an extraordinary unity of cultural and aesthetic assumptions upon which were founded the various artistic pursuits of the Muromachi period as a whole. Although the outside observer might conclude, for example, that the Nō theater and wabicha represent a divergence of tastes, the Muro-

machi Japanese (without necessarily being conscious of it) undoubtedly viewed them simply as variant manifestations of aesthetic and
artistic values that were essentially one. Thus the Muromachi vocabulary of aesthetics—including such terms as *yūgen, wabi,* and *sabi* —
was not based on antithetical tastes, but rather on sentiments that,
although periodically expanded and enriched by influences from
abroad, flowed directly from a common source in the classical culture
of the Heian court. To illustrate this basic continuity and unity of
medieval aesthetics, let me cite two poems by Fujiwara Teika (1162–
1241) from the *Shinkokinshū*. They were written at the beginning of
the Middle Ages, more than a century before the Muromachi period
began; but one of them was to be used in the *Nanbōroku* as the paradigm of Jōō's approach to the tea ceremony. They strikingly demonstrate the unified imagery achievable by juxtaposing the aesthetics of
yūgen, sabi, and the "withered":[50]

> When the floating bridge
> Of the dream of a spring night
> Was snapped, I awoke:
> In the sky a bank of clouds
> Was drawing away from the peak.

>   .   .   .

> In this wide landscape
> I see no cherry blossoms
> And no crimson leaves—
> Evening in autumn over
> A straw-thatched hut by the bay.

The first poem is a classic example of the *yūgen* quality of dreamy
otherworldliness as employed by poets in the age of the *Shinkokinshū*. At the same time it resonates a sense of the loneliness *(sabi)* and
even the desolation of man's existence in the reality of this world.
The second poem settles on an image that may readily be labeled
wabi, sabi, or "withered" (or all three): a monochromatic "evening
in autumn over a straw-thatched hut by the bay."[51] Yet, much as
Shukō was later to insist that the cloud not be considered aesthetically apart from the moon it partially obscures, so Teika reminds us of
the cherry blossoms of spring and the crimson maple leaves of mid-
autumn that had once filled his now barren landscape. To appreciate
fully this lonely, withered setting, he seems to tell us, one must be

keenly sensitive to the fact that it has been and will once again be suf-
fused with warm and living colors. Teika's colleague in the compilation of the *Shinkokinshū*, Fujiwara Ietaka (1158–1237), speaks to us
even more directly in the poem with which the *Nanbōroku* illustrates
Sen no Rikyū's mental attitude toward the Way of Tea:[52]

> If I could only show the man
> Who seems to wait for nothing
> But the cherry blossoms
> The springtime in a mountain village
> With grasses sprouting from amidst the snow.

Rikyū, Jōō's most distinguished disciple, was of Sakai merchant
stock, as was his master. Little is known of his family background.
According to traditional accounts, his grandfather was a *dōbōshū*
called Sen'ami, whose surname was Tanaka and who served at the
shogunal court of Yoshimasa. We are told that, like many courtiers,
priests, and men of the arts, Sen'ami left Kyoto during the Ōnin War
and sought sanctuary elsewhere. He selected Sakai as his refuge, returned to Kyoto when Yoshihisa became shogun early in 1474, and
went back to Sakai permanently after Yoshihisa's death in 1489.
There is, however, no external evidence to corroborate this story, and
much of it may indeed be apocryphal. We feel comfortable only with
the suggestion that Rikyū's family were residents of Sakai from his
grandfather's time on.[53] The same accounts tell us that Sen'ami's son
Yohyōe abandoned the family name Tanaka and took, instead, that
of Sen from the first element in his father's professional name.

Yohyōe's own son, Rikyū, was called Yoshirō in his youth, and
that is the name under which he appears in 1535 on the list of contributors to a temple in Sakai that is the earliest historical evidence
we have of him.[54] The mention on this sort of list would seem to
indicate that Rikyū, only thirteen years old at the time, had already
succeeded Yohyōe (who was to die five years later) as the head of the
Sen family. As a teaman he first appears in the sources at the age of
fifteen, in 1537, when he was named as Matsuya Hisamasa's host at a
tea ceremony in the latter's diary.[55] Rikyū's was evidently an early-
blossoming art: for the guest, a wealthy Nara merchant, himself had
considerable stature as a connoisseur of tea. It is also in Matsuya's tea
diary that we find, in 1544, the first appearance of the name Sen no
Sōeki.[56] Rikyū was to bear this name—a Buddhist religious sobri-
quet, as opposed to the secular name Yoshirō—for more than four

decades thereafter. When and by whom it was bestowed on him is unclear, but it may be that he received it from Dairin Sōtō of the Nanshūji, Takeno Jōō's Zen master.

It is clear that Rikyū was already an accomplished teaman even before the age of sixteen when, according to the *Nanbōroku,* he became a disciple of Kitamuki Dōchin, who traced his lineage as a tea master to the famous *dōbōshū* Nōami.[57] According to one widely held interpretation, he also studied tea under Jōō from 1539. Through Dōchin and Jōō, Rikyū would have been directly exposed to the two main types of tea ceremony that had evolved by the early sixteenth century: the aristocratic ceremony *(denchū cha-no-yu)* created by Nōami and other *dōbōshū* during the age of kaisho culture, and wabicha. Among the characteristics that the aristocratic ceremony was to assume by the late sixteenth century were its setting in a more classical *shoin*-style room; the use of the *daisu* stand; and the display of foreign objects of art and craft *(karamono).* In the dynamic age of unification the aristocratic tea ceremony took on a particularly flamboyant form that is aptly dubbed "daimyo tea" and was used by the unifiers for political as well as social purposes.

The pursuit of wabicha, by Rikyū's day, was centered chiefly in Sakai, which was then the land's leading merchant city. According to tradition, the people of Sakai believed that anyone who did not practice tea—especially wabicha—was not fit to be called a man. It may appear contradictory that the greatest concentration of wealth by commercial profit should be so intensely focused, in the cultural realm, upon a form of the tea ceremony that was predicated on such severe aesthetic tastes, and so thoroughly stressed the renunciation of materialism, as wabicha. Indeed, the contradiction between actual wealth and its aesthetic renunciation was openly manifested in the teamen of this age, who coveted the material implements of the tea ceremony, such as tea caddies, kettles, and bowls. Devotees of tea sought after and fought over these implements with an avidity and even a ferocity that totally belied what was supposed to be the true spirit of wabicha.

The mixture of genuine affection for the spiritual world of the tea ceremony and blatant cupidity for its material implements, their use as visible signs of cultural accomplishment and misuse as emblems of political prestige and power, can be observed in a whole series of "teamen daimyo" *(suki daimyō)* of the sixteenth century. It is most conspicuous, however, in Oda Nobunaga and Toyotomi Hideyoshi, two men whom Rikyū served as tea master *(sadō).*

Nobunaga is not as noted for his cultural proclivities as he is for his military accomplishments; but he clearly saw the advantages that engagement in the "politics of tea" offered the would-be unifier. Dixon Morris has already shown us how instrumental this type of politics was in arranging a rapprochement between Nobunaga and the dominant merchants of Sakai during the critical months after that emergent hegemon's triumphant entry into Kyoto in 1568. Let us recall that the warlord Matsunaga Hisahide of Yamato—potentially a dangerous rival—at this time eased himself into an alliance with Nobunaga by presenting to him the land's "nonpareil treasure," the tea caddy Tsukumogami. The receipt of this piece, as well as of two others which he obtained from the Sakai merchant Imai Sōkyū,[58] seems to have set Nobunaga off on a veritable hunt for famous tea treasures (meibutsu). Taking full advantage of his military and political ascendancy, he exerted pressures, both subtle and overt, to encourage the "donation," sale, or outright surrender of pieces to him. In 1569, for instance, "having decided that since he lacked neither gold nor silver, rice, or cash, he should therefore collect karamono and the meibutsu of the realm," he ordered two of his leading vassals to obtain well-known pieces from their owners in Kyoto; and in 1570, he sent them on a similar mission to Sakai. Since the owners "could not refuse," they surrendered the articles to Nobunaga "without protest."[59] In return, he gave them due recompense.

Perhaps it is true, as Kuwata Tadachika suggests, that the desire to amass precious works of art is the common vice of men of power, East or West, ancient or modern; but is that really "the sign of the king who would rule the land by virtue" as opposed to the "hegemon who would rule it by military power"?[60] At least in the modern era, the best analogue that comes to mind of Nobunaga's type of collector's zeal is that of the master of the hunt for works of art in Occupied Europe, Hermann Göring.

It became Nobunaga's custom to bestow some of the prized tea utensils he collected upon his lieutenants for meritorious service; and he even went so far as to make the right of these men to hold formal tea ceremonies a distinction that he alone could give. Hideyoshi himself stated that he was overwhelmed with gratitude when he was granted this honor by Nobunaga.[61] The license was first given to Hideyoshi in 1578, apparently to encourage him in his weary campaign against Bessho Nagaharu in Harima; and it was reconfirmed three years later, when Hideyoshi, after the completion of a successful campaign in Tottori, appeared at Azuchi Castle to pay his end-of-the-year compliments to Nobunaga. On this latter occasion Nobunaga not only showered Hideyoshi with praise for his "military prowess, unheard of in previous generations," but also rewarded him with twelve of his own famed tea pieces.[62]

And yet Nobunaga and his kind did not simply seek to acquire rare and treasured tea implements. They also appear to have been genuinely seized with a passion for the aesthetics of tea. Nobunaga, for example, not only collected tea utensils; he also used them expertly, for he received instruction in handling them from such acknowledged masters as Imai Sōkyū, Tsuda Sōgyū, and Sen no Rikyū. These tea masters were all from Sakai merchant families.

Rikyū, whose family was in the warehousing business, did not—so far as we know—play a significant role during the time when Nobunaga forced Sakai into his sphere of influence. It is not even clear when and under what circumstances Rikyū met Nobunaga and entered his service.[63] But by about 1573, the year Nobunaga chased the last Ashikaga shogun, Yoshiaki, out of Kyoto and thereby put an end to the Muromachi bakufu, Rikyū had become, along with Sōkyū and Sōgyū, one of Nobunaga's—and therefore the country's—leading tea masters. Proof of the prominence Rikyū had achieved by the mid-1570s may be observed in the fact that he was selected to serve tea at a party for seventeen connoisseurs (sukisha) from Kyoto and Sakai which Nobunaga held at the Myōkakuji in 1575, right after his return to the capital from the victorious campaign against the True Pure Land sect in Echizen. The record states unequivocally that Rikyū was the master of ceremonies—sadō wa Rikyū.[64] For Rikyū this association meant fame and fortune, and for Nobunaga it brought qualification as a man of culture. Each used the other to increase his own prestige; but it surely is not unreasonable to suggest that it was Rikyū's position as the tea master of the land's most powerful personage that gave him the status he needed in order to introduce his own refinements into the dominant form of the tea ceremony and to complete the development of wabicha.

Unfortunately, Rikyū did not leave behind his own tea diaries and Nobunaga's documentary corpus is fragmentary. Hence we have practically no details of the relationship between the two.[65] It is not even clear how Rikyū ranked as sadō vis-à-vis Sōkyū and Sōgyū. Since these two teamen may perhaps better be described as his rivals than as his friends, what they say about him is not entirely reliable. For better or for worse, however, it would appear that Sōgyū, at least, was outstripping Rikyū in political activity as the 1580s began. Sōgyū seems to have developed close ties with Akechi Mitsuhide, in particular, accompanying him on sightseeing tours and composing renga with him, Hosokawa Yūsai, and Satomura Jōha.[66] Keeping such company in the end proved not to be a plus for Sōgyū.

On the first day of the sixth month, Tenshō 10 (1582), Oda Nobunaga held a grand tea party at the Honnōji in Kyoto, having brought with him from Azuchi several dozen of his most precious tea implements to show to an assembly of the leading nobles and lords of the land. But before the next day had dawned, Nobunaga was dead, the victim of Akechi Mitsuhide's sudden attack. Both he and his *meibutsu* were devoured by the flames that destroyed the temple in which he was staying.[67]

The sudden and dramatic rise of Hideyoshi to the role of unifier in the wake of Nobunaga's death and the elimination of his assassin Mitsuhide's "three-day empire" placed in potential jeopardy the status of all who had served Nobunaga. Rikyū, who appears to have become acquainted with Hideyoshi some time in the middle 1570s, promptly —and seemingly in the natural course of things—shifted over to Hideyoshi's service after Nobunaga's demise. For instance, we see him present, alongside Imai Sōkyū and Tsuda Sōgyū, at the two famous tea ceremonies that Hideyoshi held in Yamazaki, the site of his victory over Mitsuhide, in late 1582 and early 1583. On the part of Hideyoshi, there may have been the intention to demonstrate by the use of Nobunaga's three premier *sadō* that he had succeeded not only to his dead lord's political but also to his cultural hegemony over Japan. Sōkyū and Sōgyū, however, did not make the transition to Hideyoshi's entourage quite as smoothly as Rikyū. Imai, who had been Nobunaga's close associate in business, politics, and tea, appears never to have enjoyed similarly great favor under his successor; and Tsuda, perhaps in part because of his friendship with Nobunaga's assassin Mitsuhide, also declined in influence in tea circles after 1582.[68] With Imai and Tsuda out of major contention, the way was clear for Rikyū to become the leading tea master in the land.

The relationship that evolved between Hideyoshi, the man of power who wanted to legitimize himself by the pursuit of culture, and Sen no Rikyū, the arbiter of elegance who permitted himself to engage in the mundane activities of politics, was intimate and complex. Regrettably, there are many aspects of this relationship about which the records are largely, if not totally, silent. It is therefore unlikely that we will ever have a satisfactory picture of what the two men did for and meant to each other. But we do know enough of their association to observe, at the highest level, the fascinating interplay of politics and art in Japan during the Momoyama epoch.

For military overlords like Nobunaga and Hideyoshi, the tea master was of inestimable value in establishing and preserving power. First, a truly famous tea master could be used as a tool in legitimizing an overlord's rule. Nobunaga set, and Hideyoshi followed, the example of laying claim to the services of the leading masters from the center of tea practice, Sakai, for the purpose—in part, at least—of displaying a kind of cultural supremacy over other daimyo. Second, a skillful and prominent master could serve the overlord in a variety of official and semiofficial roles, such as diplomatic envoy, intermediary, or simply social agent. In the same way, perhaps, as the Japanese politicians and businessmen of more recent times who have conducted their affairs during meetings at geisha houses, restaurants, and bars, leaders of government and other members of the elite in the age of unification maintained contact and formalized agreements through the medium of the tea gathering.

Hence it should be no surprise that Rikyū, as he rose to become Hideyoshi's foremost practitioner of tea, acquired ever greater political influence. Probably the most direct testimony to this influence is an observation made by the Kyushu chieftain Ōtomo Sōrin (1530–1587) of Bungo, after a visit to Hideyoshi's Osaka Castle in 1586. Sōrin, who hoped to gain Hideyoshi's support in the deadly struggle he was waging against his Kyushu rival, the Shimazu family of Satsuma, was personally shown through the castle by Hideyoshi and received tea prepared by Rikyū. In a letter to three of his chief retainers which he wrote immediately afterwards, Sōrin expressed the opinion that, without the mediation of Rikyū, it was impossible for anyone in those days to secure Hideyoshi's ear.[69] Since it was, however, a shared affection for the tea ceremony that bound the two men together, we must look at their approaches to this art; for in the end it may have been a difference of attitudes toward it that caused them to draw apart.

Rikyū is universally recognized as the culminating figure in the evolution of wabicha, and his disciples firmly claimed a line of direct transmission of the highest teachings on tea from Shukō and Jōō to him. Rikyū's own devotion to the school of Shukō can be deduced from the fact that he acquired for his own use—no doubt at great cost—several tea ceremony articles associated with the earlier master, including an incense burner and bowl, as well as the vertical scroll with the writing of the Sung Chinese priest Yüan-wu that Ikkyū had personally presented as a certificate of enlightenment to Shukō.

From the writings of his disciples and others, we know much about Rikyū's tastes in wabicha, tastes that included the severely simple setting of a two-mat room and dispensing with the *daisu* stand in favor of handling the utensils of tea directly on the floor. Among Rikyū's favorite tea utensils were dark *raku* bowls and bamboo whisks and ladles.[70] But the most critical aspect of Rikyū's approach to tea appears to have been his devotion to what he conceived as the spiritual basis of *cha-no-yu* in medieval Buddhism. We find this idea spelled out in the very first passage of the *Nanbōroku*, a treatise attributed to Nanbō Sōkei, a priest of the Nanshūji in Sakai where Rikyū seems to have studied Zen as a youth:

On one occasion, when Sōeki was discoursing on *cha-no-yu* . . . I asked the master this: "Although it is said that use of the *daisu* is fundamental to *cha-no-yu*, you have repeatedly asserted that nothing brings greater satisfaction and fulfillment than holding the tea ceremony [on the floor of] a simple grass hut *(sō no kozashiki)*. Could you say precisely what you mean by this?" Sōeki replied: "*Cha-no-yu* performed in a plain hut is above all an ascetic discipline, based on the Buddhist Law, that is aimed at achieving spiritual deliverance. To be concerned about the quality of the dwelling in which you serve tea or the flavor of the food served with it is to emphasize the mundane. It is enough if the dwelling one uses does not leak water and the food served suffices to stave off hunger. This is in accordance with the teachings of the Buddha and is the essence of *cha-no-yu*. First, we fetch water and gather firewood. Then we boil the water and prepare tea. After offering some to the Buddha, we serve our guests. Finally, we serve ourselves."[71]

Hideyoshi also appreciated wabicha, but his tastes tended more decisively toward the sumptuous and the ostentatious, in tea as in other aspects of his cultural life. Perhaps we can say that this, in the sixteenth-century context, was a tendency toward the modern; in any event, it was a drift away from the medieval. It would be a mistake, of course, to assume that his approach to the tea ceremony amounted to nothing more than a parvenu's urge to display his new riches; it might be better to say that in his tastes as well as in other aspects of his personality, Hideyoshi manifested that ambivalence between restraint and flamboyance which is at the heart of Momoyama culture in general. Two of his most famous tearooms are ideal illustrations of these two poles of reference. Even while he had a hutlike room—

Yamazato no zashiki, the quintessential wabicha setting—constructed for him in the "Mountain Village Enceinte" *(Yamazato-maru)* of Osaka Castle, Hideyoshi also had a room embellished richly with gold—*Kigane no zashiki,* which dazzled all who saw it—made for the performance of a more glittering type of tea ceremony. The first of these was fully in the tradition of Jōō and Rikyū.[72] But for the spiritual antecedents of the second, we must look back across the centuries to the *Kissa ōrai,* Sasaki Dōyo, Yoshimitsu's Golden Pavilion, and Nobunaga's Azuchi Castle with its surfeit of gold.

We have extensive descriptions of both the Yamazato and the golden tearooms in the diary of Kamiya Sōtan (1551–1635), a rich Hakata merchant and teaman whom Hideyoshi courted as an indispensable intermediary, first in his plans for the campaign in Kyushu in 1587 and then in the creation of a base in Kyushu for his invasion of Korea in 1592. Here we see again how the tea ceremony served as a medium of diplomacy.

Sōtan was first entertained in the Yamazato just a few days before Hideyoshi set out from Osaka on his Kyushu Expedition. From his account of the occasion (which also served to effect a reconciliation between Hideyoshi and Sōtan's fellow guest, Yamaoka Tsushima no Kami) we get the picture of a thoroughly rusticated setting. The tearoom itself was only two mats in size, with a sunken hearth toward the left; the walls were papered with old calendars, after the manner of a country hut. The sole touch of studied elegance was the priceless painting by Yü-chien, *Evening Bell from a Distant Temple,* that was displayed in the *toko-no-ma.*[73] The next time Sōtan visited the Yamazato was after Hideyoshi's return from his victorious Kyushu campaign; he tells us that the guest who had preceded him that morning was Ijūin Tadamune, the emissary of the defeated Kyushu daimyo, Shimazu Yoshihisa.[74] The rustic hut in Osaka Castle had been the setting of similar encounters before: it was here that Hideyoshi in 1585 had served tea to Nobunaga's son Nobukatsu as a sign of peace after the campaign the two had fought against each other; and later that same year he had entertained ambassadors of the powerful Mōri family in this setting, impressing them with its "withered" and lonely effect *(kareki nado no gi, sanagara monosabitaru omomuki).*[75]

Both the Yamazato and the golden tearooms could be disassembled and were portable. Hence they could be used and displayed by Hideyoshi wherever he might wish. When he went to Kyushu in 1592 to direct the first invasion of Korea, for example, Hideyoshi had the two rooms transported to Nagoya Castle, his headquarters over-looking the Tsushima Straits, and even entertained a representative of Ming China in the gold room while there.[76]

The golden tearoom was the opposite of rustic restraint; *wabi, sabi,* and "withered" are not aesthetic categories that one would want to apply to it. It was not solid gold, as is sometimes asserted, but it is easy to see how that misconception could have arisen, since every conceivable surface in this three-mat room was gold-plated. Sōtan, who saw it at Nagoya Castle in 1592, tells us that there was gold plate on the pillars, the doorsill, and the lintel of the room; the walls were lined with strips of gold six feet long and five inches wide; all the framework of the *shōji* sliding doors was gilded (the *shōji* themselves, instead of paper, were of red gossamer, and the *tatami* were covered with scarlet wool and had edges of golden brocade). Ōtomo Sōrin, who was served tea in this same room by both Hideyoshi and Rikyū, gives practically the same description in the account of his 1586 visit to Osaka Castle, but he adds another item to the list: the ceiling also was gilded. Both men state, moreover, that all the utensils used in serving tea in this room—from kettles and cups down to the fire tongs, save for the indispensable bamboo in the tea whisk —were golden.[77]

How Rikyū reacted to this sort of ostentation can only be guessed. As Haga Kōshirō points out, Rikyū was neither a hermit nor a single-minded *wabi* fanatic; his character was complex and his tastes many-sided.[78] Perhaps it is fair to say that under certain circumstances he was also a compromiser. Shukō's and Jōō's successor could not very well endorse gaudiness in the tea ceremony and at the same time re-main faithful to their aesthetic ideals; but neither could he afford overt opposition to his employer Hideyoshi's penchant for display. Hence Rikyū acquiesced, continued acting as the hegemon's *sadō,* and served tea in the golden room. Whether he sneered inwardly while doing so—as Professor Haga suggests—is a moot question. What his sentiments were as he took his place in the carnival atmos-phere of that mass extravaganza, the Grand Kitano Tea Ceremony of 1587, which is discussed in the next chapter, is another question that cannot be answered.

Perhaps the high point in the tea careers of both Hideyoshi and Ri-kyū was the ceremony Hideyoshi performed, with Rikyū's assistance, for Emperor Ōgimachi (r. 1560–1586) at the imperial palace in Kyoto in 1585. For Hideyoshi, who had been appointed *Kanpaku* (Imperial Regent) three months before, this unprecedented ceremony was the fulfillment of a long-held desire; he was determined to make it as formally proper as possible, and he engaged in elaborate preparations. The major problem was that his indispensable right hand, Rikyū—for all his illustrious standing as a tea master—was on account of his commoner status not entitled to enter the imperial presence. Hideyoshi therefore persuaded the emperor to issue a decree changing his name from Sōeki (as, it will be recalled, he was heretofore known) to Rikyū and his status to that of a "distinguished Buddhist layman" *(koji)*. This designation as a religious permitted Rikyū access to the palace.[79]

The name Rikyū is written with the characters for "profit" *(ri)* and "rest" *(kyū),* and one interpretation of its meaning is "to be beyond (or at rest from) the state of craving for fame and fortune." Another interpretation of the name is that its characters stand for an "old and blunted awl," connoting a Zen paradox: one of the highest stages of life attainable to a human being is that of a man who after a career of earnest application has outlived the use of a penetrant religious discipline and dwells in a state of effortless enlightenment.[80]

Hideyoshi completed the long process of Japan's reunification, begun some thirty years earlier by his predecessor Nobunaga, with the subjugation of the Go-Hōjō of Odawara in the Kantō in 1590. As he had in the Kyushu campaign three years earlier, Rikyū accompanied Hideyoshi and appeared to enjoy his usual intimacy with him. Yet in the second month of 1591, half a year after the conclusion of the Odawara campaign, Hideyoshi issued orders banishing Rikyū to Sakai and placing him under house arrest. We are told that Rikyū's friends, correctly identifying this action as the prelude to a death sentence, urged him to beg Hideyoshi's mother and wife to intercede for him, but that Rikyū refused to plead for his life. Two weeks later, Rikyū was summoned back to Kyoto; his residence was surrounded by three thousand guards, as though Hideyoshi feared that an attempt would be made to rescue him. On the twenty-eighth day of the second month, Rikyū committed seppuku. He was in the seventieth year of his life.

To this day scholars remain at a loss to explain with any sense of certainty why Hideyoshi so abruptly—almost capriciously, it would seem—ordered the destruction of a man who until the last had apparently been one of his closest confidants. The nearest thing to an official reason that has come down to us is that Rikyū was considered guilty of a kind of lese majesty because a wooden statue portraying him had been installed atop the Sanmon or main gate of the Daitokuji, a Zen temple in Kyoto with which Rikyū had for a long time been connected. The construction of this gate had been started in the 1520s with funds contributed by the renga master Saiokuken Sōchō; but those funds had run out before the edifice could be completed, and it was not until 1589, when Rikyū donated an additional sum, that the gate's top story could be built. The notorious statue, a likeness of the tea master wearing common sandals and supporting himself with a staff, was placed in this upper level of the gate in tribute to its donor. What the planners of this tribute presumably never considered was that the unifier and national hegemon, Hideyoshi, might take umbrage at unknowingly passing—as he evidently did—through a gate surmounted by a statue of an underling. This conventional explanation of Rikyū's disgrace would strike us as fanciful and trivial if we did not know that Hideyoshi had the statue crucified in a public place.[81]

To be sure, that is not the entire story. Several other reasons have been suggested for Hideyoshi's action against Rikyū. One is that Rikyū had refused a request that his daughter be given to Hideyoshi as a concubine. More convincing is the reason which Eishun, the abbot of the Tamon'in in Nara, entered in his diary on the day of Rikyū's suicide: "In recent years [Rikyū] provided himself with tea implements of a new type and sold them at high prices. [Hideyoshi] was furious beyond all bounds at this, calling it the ultimate of sharp practice" *(maisu no chōjō)*.[82] Indeed, it would seem that Rikyū did use his status as the hegemon's *arbiter elegantiae* to turn a profit for himself: as it was he who championed the use of simple Japanese utensils rather than *karamono* (whose reputation and value were established) in the tea ceremony, he in fact could more or less set the price of the utensils himself, and he might well have seemed to be abusing his position in doing so. If that was actually one of the causes of his disgrace, then the characters that compose his name are indeed paradoxical, and his suicide is the tragedy of one who took too literally the definition of the true teaman as one who must be clever at judging the value of tea implements.

The interpretation favored by most historians is that first proposed by Asao Naohiro, which would have it that Rikyū was the victim of a power struggle among Hideyoshi's entourage.[83] According to this theory, Rikyū was caught up in a conflict between the advocates of a centralized regime—men such as Ishida Mitsunari and Mashita Nagamori—and those who stood for daimyo autonomy, at whose forefront was Tokugawa Ieyasu. Hideyoshi's campaign against the Go-Hōjō of

Odawara and the ensuing sweep through the northernmost provinces of Japan appeared to signal a great victory for the hard-liners; but at its conclusion, we find the recalcitrant northern daimyo Date Masamune not merely unchastised but honored, with the ultimate victory thus going to the appeasers. Rikyū, as the theory goes, was a consistent supporter of the appeasement policy; and his doom was decreed just at the moment when the representative of the policy's ascendancy, Date Masamune, appeared in Kyoto to be reinvested with his domains. In short, Rikyū was a sop thrown away to appease the hard-liners.

Whatever the true facts may have been, Rikyū's death was significant in the history of the culture of tea because it marked the final, symbolic passing of the Middle Ages. Despite the fame he enjoyed, Rikyū—as the leading master of wabicha—was already something of an anachronism in his later years. Wabicha was a product of the medieval spirit and, although still very much admired in Momoyama times, was increasingly regarded more as a classical tradition than as a living art. The sentiments that the *Nanbōroku* attributes to Rikyū about wabicha as an ascetic discipline rooted in the Buddhist Law were, in truth, not in concord with the times. Hideyoshi's golden tearoom typified Momoyama far more truly than Rikyū's two-mat hut.

GEORGE ELISON

Hideyoshi, the Bountiful Minister

Der Affe gar possierlich ist
Zumal wenn er vom Apfel frisst
Wilhelm Hauff

And one night in a dream she saw the wheel of the sun enter her womb, and immediately she became with child. After thirteen months of pregnancy, a boy was born, on New Year's night of Tenbun [5], the year of fire senior and the monkey, at the hour of the tiger.

And at that time there appeared above the roof of her abode a mysterious star, and its light was like that of the noontime sun. After the child grew up, this star would without fail appear in the heavens above at times of desperate battle in order to ward off disaster and turn it into good fortune.

Now this child had all his teeth when he was born, and his face was like a monkey's. He was given the name Hiyoshimaru; but he so resembled a monkey that everyone called him Sarunosuke.

The babe who was thus born is the celebrated Taikō Hideyoshi, and this is the account of his nativity which we find in the *Ehon Taikōki*.[1]

Those who question this account's authenticity—for it is, after all, not contemporary with Hideyoshi himself but comes from a later source which is essentially a piece of popular fiction—and who may therefore be inclined to dismiss it would be well advised to consult a document dated Bunroku 2/11/5 (corresponding with the third day of Christmas, 1593) and sealed with the Taikō's own golden seal:

When I was about to enter my dear mother's womb, she had an auspicious dream. That night, the sunlight filled her room so that it was like noontime inside it. All were overwhelmed with astonishment. The attendants gathered, and the diviner proclaimed: "This is a wondrous sign that when the child reaches his prime, his virtue will shine over the Four Seas, and he will radiate his glory to the ten thousand directions."[2]

Professor Kuwata Tadachika in commenting on this story states that he does not believe it to be made out of whole cloth. Rather—he says—Hideyoshi must frequently have heard it while dandled on his mother's knee.[3] There may be some merit to this notion, but not if it implies that Hideyoshi's efforts to mystify his origins were anything less than deliberate and artful.

The renowned seventeenth-century scholar Hayashi Razan began his biography of Hideyoshi with the words "His birthplace is unknown."[4] Indeed, his provenance is unclear. Not even the year of his birth is known with certainty: some sources give it as Tenbun 5 (1536), others as Tenbun 6; the latter may be the more likely date, but most chronologies list the former.[5] The question of his paternity is complicated not only by the existence of overtly fanciful tales but also by the disagreement of more serious accounts: some call his father Kinoshita Yaemon, a *teppō ashigaru* (musketeer) in the Oda family's service, others describe him as a *dōbō* (perhaps "court flunky" is the word) named Chikuami. The sources which say that Yaemon was a musketeer fail to explain how he could have been one before muskets were introduced into Japan; for all that, Yaemon may be accorded the honor of being Hideyoshi's father. It is likely, however, that he was a peasant who did not bear a family name, and that "Kinoshita" was a posthumous addition devised by Hideyoshi himself, who drew on his wife Oné's genealogy for the purpose.[6] Kinoshita Tōkichirō Hideyoshi is how he styled himself at the beginning of his career.[7] In 1573 he assumed the family name Hashiba; the common belief is that this new identity was created by borrowing syllables from the names of two other Oda captains, Ni*wa* Nagahide and *Shiba*ta Katsuie.[8] Nobunaga continued calling him Saru, "Monkey."[9]

It is apparent that the biggest problem Hideyoshi faced upon attaining power was to establish his legitimacy, since his origins were so obscure. Moreover, no one was more aware than he himself of the spectacular nature of his rise from obscurity to the culmination of glory. This self-perception is evident from his own public statements —which refer time and again to his astonishing ascent from the lower depths to the very apex of power—no less than from contemporary accounts of his character, such as the Jesuit relations from Japan. The tone of his proclamations is a mixture of magnificence amounting to hubris and of pathos. He clearly knew that he was a parvenu, but as clearly thought that he had been singled out by a provident Fortune

—or, to cite his own words, had met Heaven's Will, *Tentō ni aikanau mono ya.*[10] He used the story of his marvelous rise to great advantage in propaganda. To be sure, his success story was so amazing that he may himself have been at least half-convinced of the truth of the miracle tales he spread about. But if that was indeed the measure of his conviction, then he must have been at least fifty percent insecure.

Furthermore, once we agree that Hideyoshi's major concern was to legitimate himself, then we must note the paradox that he strove to buttress his claim to exaltation by recourse to legends of *il*legitimacy. The tale of a divine descent is not the only example of this paradox. There is also the slightly more plausible story of an imperial paternity, found in the *Kanpaku ninkanki* of Hideyoshi's sycophant Ōmura Yūko, a work dated the eighth month of Tenshō 13 (1585).[11] Since it is inconceivable that Yūko could have composed public tales of this sort in his master's own lifetime without his approval, we must assume that this biographical variant was directly inspired by Hideyoshi himself. We read:

If we inquire into his parentage, we find that his grandfather and grandmother served in the Imperial Palace. They say that [his grandfather] was named Hagi no Chūnagon, who was slandered by a certain person when [Hideyoshi's mother] Lady Ōmandokoro was two years old, and as a result was banished from the capital and lived in exile in a place called Hibo Murakumo in Owari province. . . .

Lady Ōmandokoro went up to the capital at an early age. For two or three years she was in service close to the Imperial Presence, and then she came back to the province. Soon after that, a child was born. This was Our Lord [Hideyoshi]. Ever since he was a baby, he abounded in marvels. Indeed, if he were not of royal blood, how then could he have attained such greatness! In past times, the General of the Right Minamoto no Ason Yoritomo held sway over the realm; for all that, he failed to obtain the rank of a minister. Prince Taira no Ason Kiyomori, however, was appointed Grand Chancellor of State. Could it be because he was of royal blood?

Then, after having insinuated his master into the loftiest of lineages and having made the clever allusion to Kiyomori's widely rumored imperial parentage,[12] Yūko disarmingly states that his prince was unlettered. But—Yūko adds—"he has invited learned men into his presence, and is now engaged in the study of several volumes of ancient histories and the genealogies of the various noble houses." The clinch is in that last sentence. The man who had no ancestors, who had in past years repeatedly referred with genuine feeling to the fact that Nobunaga had made him,[13] who had eventually settled for adoption into the imperial aristocracy and had posed as a Fujiwara, would create a new noble family for himself. By the force of personality, the judicious use of historical precedents, and the application of cultural cosmetics, he was about to emerge in his own right as the Bountiful Minister, Toyotomi Hideyoshi.

In their desire to create a meaningful scenario for Hideyoshi's role in history, scholars have on occasion resorted to analogy and have tried, like Kabuki playwrights, to transplant their hero on account of some selective affinity into a conventionalized world of the past—the world of the classical imperial court, the Genpei world, the world of Kitayama. To be sure, he properly belongs in that world of the parvenus, the *shusse yakko no sekai,* where Kabuki playwrights indeed have put him;[14] but the analogies which place him elsewhere are not entirely fanciful. There are at least symbolic relationships between his epoch and previous ages.

We have already seen how Hideyoshi invoked the image of Kiyomori in order to make plausible the myth of an imperial ancestry. He also referred more than once to the model of Yoritomo, and historians have found significance in that. In the flush of victory over Shibata Katsuie in 1583, Hideyoshi himself proclaimed his intention to impose on Japan an order unseen since Yoritomo's day.[15] The Jesuit Luis Frois alleged that the great falconry party which Hideyoshi convoked in Owari and Mikawa at the end of 1591 was meant for the specific purpose of outdoing another famed forgathering of the lords of the realm, Yoritomo's Nasuno-Fujino hunts of 1193.[16] It has even been suggested that Hideyoshi planned to depart on his three most ambitious projects—the conquest of Kyushu in 1587, the subjugation of the Hōjō of Odawara in 1590, and the invasion of Korea in 1592—on the same chosen date, the first day of the third month, because four centuries earlier Yoritomo had on that day of the year been appointed *shokoku sōtsuibushi,* Constable General of Japan.[17] It would be false to attribute to Hideyoshi a rigid adherence to historical models or an imitation of individual symbols of unity. It is, however, evident that he had a clear concept of the "normalization" of the political order, and that this concept involved the use of tradition.

In discussing "The Types of Authority and Imperative Coordination,'' Max Weber notes that no system of authority voluntarily limits itself to emotional appeals and invocations of ideal motives, or depends on a purely material complex of interests as means of binding the members of its administrative staff to obedience and ensuring the regime's continuance.[18] ''In addition every such system attempts to establish and to cultivate the belief in its 'legitimacy.' '' Hideyoshi, who was an astute leader, was surely aware of the ephemeral nature of political relationships which lack this fundamental buttress. His career as the ruler of Japan is the very example of legitimation on what Weber calls ''traditional grounds''—that is to say, those resting ''on an established belief in the sanctity of immemorial traditions and the legitimacy of the status of those exercising authority under them.'' Needless to say, the ideal Weberian type should not be sought in history in an unmodified form. Hideyoshi also fits a part of the definition of legitimation on ''charismatic grounds'': he consciously drew attention to his sacred or at least mysterious origins, to his heroic deeds (which had been sanctioned by ''Heaven's Will''), and to his exemplary personal accomplishment. He did not, however, act as the prophet of a new normative pattern; he was not a revolutionary in the true sense. Far from repudiating the past, Hideyoshi tried to resuscitate it. The tradition with which he strove to identify himself was that which his subjects acknowledged as the ideal model of authority, indeed as the wellspring of Japanese history, one which ''had always existed''—the imperial institution. The throne itself was sacrosanct and unavailable to him;[19] but he would aristocratize himself at the highest possible level and would bind his paladins to allegiance by subsuming them under the same pattern. His efforts were conscious, assiduous, and to a great extent successful. By subordinating himself to the imperial tradition, this servant of the throne made it serve his purpose.

It is commonly agreed that the reunification of Japan during the Momoyama period represents the emergence of a new order. Before we put too great an emphasis on novelty, however, we must note that at least some contemporaries viewed the events as a return to normalcy. That most perceptive of the Jesuit observers of Japan, João Rodrigues Tçuzzu, in his monumental *História da Igreja do Japão* presents what for that time surely was an exceptionally astute periodization of Japanese history.[20] ''The first stage of this kingdom,'' he says, ''was the true and proper age of Japan, when the kingdom was governed by the legitimate lord and ruler, and the whole country obeyed the true king. Rites and customs were duly observed and a distinction was made between the nobles of the patrician order whose office was to govern the kingdom, and the nobles of the military order, who, under the supervision of the patricians, had the duty of guarding the royal person and defending the realm.'' This stage lasted from the time of Jimmu Tennō ''until the year of the Lord 1340.'' The second period was that of misrule under the Ashikaga regime, when the members of the ''equestrian order'' or *bushi* ''were moved by greed and quarrelled among themselves, and the whole of Japan was involved in wars; men killed one another or subjected others to their authority, and each one seized for himself as much as he could.'' In the process the ''king'' was rendered impotent, the *kuge* or ''members of the patrician order'' were left impoverished, ''the common folk and peasants rebelled against the taxes,'' and central government was destroyed. ''This miserable period lasted 245 years from the year 1340 to the year 1585, when *Taikō* (he was first called Hashiba Chikuzen, and later *Kampaku,* and finally *Taikō*) took over the government of Tenka . . . , thus commencing the third period.''

Now, what is the third period? Peace and prosperity are two of its hallmarks; in those respects it resembles the first, ''the proper and natural age'' and ''the real and true one of Japan.'' To be sure, it is tyrannical; but—and this is the cardinal point—the tyrant is an avowed supporter of the principle of legitimacy. In a remarkable analysis which demonstrates how well at least this Jesuit appreciated the ambivalences of show and reality in the Japanese political arena, Rodrigues tells us that although rule by the newly risen was the dominant fact of the Momoyama period, the resurrection of ancient forms was its chief outward characteristic. The missionary put his finger precisely on the key to the hegemon's method. Here is his most interesting observation:

The Lord of Tenka paid honour to the king and again constructed magnificent palaces for him and the *kuge,* and granted them revenues for their upkeep. He makes outward show of obeying the king and governing in his name, and pays him solemn visits in carriages and coaches in the ancient fashion. . . . many of the lords of the realm have been promoted to the patrician rank and its titles; the king now grants these on the request of the Lord of Tenka. To a certain extent the patrician order has been resurrected with its former honours, although these have been given to new people and not to the *kuge,* along with titles such as *Kampaku, Daijō Daijin, Udaijin,*

Sadaijin, Daifu, Dainagon, Chūnagon, Chūshō, Shōshō, Saisho, Jijū, Sho-daifu and others.

That is to say, in the historical play composed by Hideyoshi, the leading *bushi* actors were cast in the roles of *kuge*.[21] Why so much dedication to an outdated form?

In viewing Hideyoshi the conqueror, we are apt to lose sight of the fact that he was also *Kanpaku,* another one of those prestigious but empty court titles which he both revived by his personal status as the holder of imperative control over much of Japan and needed to establish his legitimacy. Indeed, Rodrigues' choice of the year 1585 (instead of the more obvious 1582) as the date which marks the epoch is as significant as it was clever. A turn of the historical cycle became apparent with Hideyoshi's ascension to the Imperial Regency. Assimilation into the imperial court and its culture was Hideyoshi's aim and method; it was his avenue to grandeur and his concept of rule. To be sure, this sort of "normalization" of political authority may have been anachronistic, and we know that it did not last. But it represents the same sort of endeavor as was tried by the Meiji period's "restorers" of the office of *Daijō Daijin* and other hoary imperial institutions. Peremptory power was thurified in a cloud of hallowed tradition.

Needless to say, Hideyoshi's assumption of the office of Kanpaku did not meet with the unanimous approval of his contemporaries. When he represented himself as the bearer of the imperial will in ordering the Shimazu of Satsuma to stop making war in Kyushu, they concluded that "a response treating Hashiba as Kanpaku would be no laughing matter," since it was "notorious that Hashiba was without any ancestry whatsoever" whereas their own lineage was unblemished; they refused to answer directly to him.[22] The monk Tamon'in Eishun of the Kōfukuji in the privacy of his diary denounced the hegemon's self-aggrandizement as something "unheard of in previous ages," "unspeakable and unimaginable," and an act of "*bushi* madness" *(bukegurui).*[23] The modern observer will admit that there was method in that madness. At the very least, he will acknowledge that Hideyoshi surely foresaw the obloquy he would incur by his unprecedented step; that he nonetheless elected to take it must have had convincing reasons.

The method becomes apparent when we consider that Hideyoshi had other choices beside the imperial option. The most obvious of these was the assumption of the shogunate. At the start of his hege-

mony, Hideyoshi had to cope with the fact that, as long as Ashikaga
Yoshiaki remained outside his control, there existed separately the
vestige (no matter how shadowy) of a legal system with two and a half
centuries of tradition in presiding over the hierarchy of authority in
Japan. To be sure, that system had been increasingly moribund since
the 1440s and had been practically destroyed by Nobunaga in 1573;
but to anyone as interested in legalities as Hideyoshi was, it had to be
obvious that its dispossessed scion could not be ignored. Modern
scholars have repeatedly made statements such as "Yoshiaki, the fifteenth and last Ashikaga *Shōgun,* resigned in 1573; the office then
lapsed."[24] But nothing of the sort had happened. Far from resign-
ing, Yoshiaki had become instead a political refugee who refused to
abandon hopes for a restoration to full honors, continued behaving
as shogun, and was encouraged to persevere by powerful daimyo such
as Mōri Terumoto.[25] He retained considerable prestige; in some
areas, shogunal directives continued to bear weight; the Muromachi
bakufu showed signs of life even though it had been dealt its death
blow.[26]

The initial fallacy is surpassed by yet another, which one recent
author expresses in the following odd formulation: "As [Hideyo-
shi's] lowly birth precluded him from the title of *Shōgun,* he accepted the title of *Kampaku,* or regent, in 1585."[27] Other historians
have told us time and again that Hideyoshi was prevented from becoming shogun by the very fact that he was not a Minamoto.[28] This
thesis is not persuasive. Hideyoshi, who was nothing if not ingenious
as a genealogist, could have produced ties to link him with that lineage as easily as did that other great legal mind, Minamoto no Ieyasu.

It appears that Hideyoshi indeed toyed with the idea of assuming
the shogunate and as late as 1584 was diplomatically courting Yoshiaki with the view of becoming his adopted son and successor. It is
sometimes asserted that Yoshiaki—whether out of an excess of fool-
ishness (as Hayashi Razan would have it) or of a sense of dignity—rejected Hideyoshi's advances.[29] In the absence of reliable documentation, that story must remain suspect. In any event, it is clear that as
far as Hideyoshi was concerned, any notion of becoming shogun was
superseded by other plans and loftier aspirations. For who would
want to be chief of staff when a position approximating that of chief
of state was within his grasp—especially if he had started lower than a
corporal?

The story of Hideyoshi's aristocratization really begins with the
pompous funeral he held for Nobunaga at the Daitokuji in Novem-

ber 1582. Just prior to the ceremonies, the court appointed him Major General of the Palace Guards of the Left *(sakon no e no shōshō)* and raised him to the Fifth Rank *(ju goi no ge)*, qualifying him for access to the inner palace *(shōden)*; he thus became a courtier.[30] Promotions thereafter kept pace with accomplishments. In 1583, after destroying Shibata Katsuie in the Shizugatake campaign, Hideyoshi was elevated to the Fourth Rank and made Imperial Adviser *(sangi)*. Late in the year 1584, after the Komaki campaign against Ieyasu, he ascended to the Third Rank and the post of Brevet Grand Councillor *(gon dainagon)*. In April 1585, in recognition of his undertaking to build a palace *(In no Gosho)* for Emperor Ōgimachi's planned retirement, the court appointed him Minister of the Middle *(naidaijin)* and promoted him to the Second Rank *(shō nii)*.[31] Nobunaga had resigned his court posts right after he was raised to this rank, thereby showing that he was a solipsist.[32] Hideyoshi, however, reached for still greater heights.

When he succeeded to Nobunaga's hegemony, Hideyoshi also assumed his master's courtly name of Taira. If aristocratization in the classical Taira manner was part of this soldier's ambition, however, it was not to the point of contentment with that name. Hideyoshi did have himself advanced to *Daijō Daijin* in January 1587, after the pattern of Taira no Kiyomori; indeed, he became after Kiyomori and Ashikaga Yoshimitsu only the third member of the "equestrian order" to occupy this highest in the entire hierarchy of "patrician" offices, a post which he then held until his death. But this was not the most remarkable step upward in the career of this social climber. In August 1585, when he became Kanpaku, he had taken one which was totally unprecedented.[33]

No member of the military had ever before assumed the Imperial Regency, and that is what so outraged Tamon'in Eishun.[34] In order to obtain it, Hideyoshi had to outdo the Fujiwara at their own game of palace intrigue; and he beat them by joining them.

The person most directly affected, Konoe Nobusuke, has left us an interesting—if somewhat vexed—account of how Hideyoshi got the best of him and his clan.[35] Hideyoshi, we are told, set in motion the plot of this historical drama shortly after becoming Minister of the Middle, by declaring that the logical next step, appointment as Minister of the Right *(udaijin)*, would be unpropitious for him because the post had been held by the assassinated Nobunaga. He therefore wanted to be promoted to the Ministry of the Left directly. That ministry, however, was occupied by the *sadaijin* Nobusuke, our author.

Aware that he would presently be displaced from his office, Nobu-suke demanded in turn that the newly appointed Kanpaku, Nijō Akizane, surrender the Imperial Regency to him. This Akizane re-fused to do. The result was an altercation between the two Fujiwara courtiers, each of whom appealed to history for support, cited au-thoritative rules and precedents, and sent reproachful and self-serving memoranda to the other. Naturally enough, each also tried to sway Hideyoshi to take his side. Hideyoshi solved their problem: he let it be known that he would seek appointment as Kanpaku himself.

Aghast at the thought, Nobusuke pointed out that the office had since its creation in the ninth century always been held by a member of one of the "Five Houses" of the Fujiwara clan's "Regency" line-age. To a truly ambitious office-seeker this was, of course, not an in-surmountable obstacle. Nothing daunted, Hideyoshi proposed a simple solution: Nobusuke's father, the former Kanpaku Konoe Sakihisa, would adopt Hideyoshi as his son and successor; Hideyoshi and Nobusuke would thereby become siblings and would exchange fraternal vows; Hideyoshi would eventually pass on the Imperial Re-gency to his younger brother Nobusuke; in the meantime, the Konoe would be solaced with one thousand *koku* and the other four of the Five Houses consoled with five hundred each for being passed over. Sakihisa wisely agreed to the compact—"for Hideyoshi now holds the entire realm in the palm of his hand, and even if he destroyed all the Five Houses, who would say nay?"—and Nobusuke bent to his father's judgment. The emperor, just as politic, sent word to Akizane to step aside; and that is how Hideyoshi became Kanpaku.

When Hideyoshi arranged to have himself adopted into one of the Five Houses as the son of a former Kanpaku, thereby breaking and entering the Fujiwara monopoly on the office, his absorption into the courtly mode became complete. The borrowed lineage, however, was nothing else but a reminder of his own lack of family background.[36] Moreover, his position of power as well as prestige surely required the rectification of names. The four classical noble houses—Fujiwara, Tachibana, Taira, and Minamoto—had histories of 920, 850, 800, and 750 years. The times demanded a fifth, an independent, and a paramount pedigree. This urgent need Hideyoshi impressed on the imperial court. The court responded by granting him his new style, and with it no less than parity with a millennium's great names: from 31 October 1585 he was called Toyotomi. The Bountiful Minister's house endured for not quite three decades.

The name, however, was not the only thing. The parvenu's ultimate recourse is ostentation, and Hideyoshi surrounded himself with golden glitter. He was indeed extravagant; but let us take him *in bonas partes.* His new *noblesse* obliged him to act as a man of culture and patron of the arts. These roles he performed munificently.

Hideyoshi's concept of cultural cosmetics was a design to vest him in the raiments of aristocratic prestige, which were not his by birth. He actively sought that unassailable cachet, prominence at the imperial court, and he obtained it. In the process he drew upon historical precedents, such as that of Ashikaga Yoshimitsu, who had successfully "amalgamated the imperial style and prestige with his own, thereby fulfilling his ardent desire for distinction."[37] In some ways, Hideyoshi improved on Yoshimitsu. The Ashikaga shogun had had the benefit of tutoring from an early age; the Bountiful Minister had to hurry to assimilate polish in the last decade and a half of his life. Yoshimitsu was perhaps overly tutored in questions of cultural status: in order to embellish his personage with the supreme classical sanction, he eagerly accepted investiture as King of Japan from the Ming emperor (and for that he has been endlessly excoriated). This sort of preconception was not one shared by Hideyoshi, who instead set out to conquer the Ming empire. This was a social climber whose ambition knew no limits.

Paul Varley has recently commented on the critical role played by Yoshimitsu in the creation of the "world of Kitayama" by stressing his "exceptionally strong desire to become the complete ruler." Varley maintains that Yoshimitsu "utterly dominated the elite society concentrated in Kyoto, which included the imperial family, courtiers, shugo, and prominent ecclesiastics. And, most significantly, he exerted his dominance not only in the political and military spheres but also in the cultural."[38] *Mutatis mutandis,* much the same can be said about the Kanpaku Daijō Daijin Hideyoshi and his role in the creation of the "world of Momoyama." To be sure, Hideyoshi was an upstart, which Yoshimitsu was not; but that fact was all the more a goad to his pretensions, which if anything exceeded those of Yoshimitsu. To ask which of the two was the more accomplished man—or more of a "complete ruler"—would, however, be idle.

Hideyoshi may not have been as learned as Yoshimitsu, nor did he have much interest in religion, except insofar as he could use it for political ends. After his career had reached a point permitting indulgence in luxuries, however, Hideyoshi in his own way became not only a patron but also an unrestrained amateur, an enthusiast of the arts —most notably those of poetry, tea, and the Nō drama. There were ambivalences involved in Hideyoshi's approach to all of these artistic pursuits. Nevertheless, it is time to lay to rest the myth of Hideyoshi the Great Illiterate. The description of the perfect prince as one whose life exemplifies both Arms and Arts is, of course, a cross-cultural cliché; notwithstanding, Ōmura Yūko's statement that Hideyoshi combined both of these accomplishments *(bunbu kaneso-nae)* is more than a sycophant's obligatory gesture.[39] There happens to be some truth to it.

The crowning event of Hideyoshi's aristocratization (as indeed of Yoshimitsu's ascent to the peak of prestige) was an Imperial Visit to the hegemon's palace. In preparing for the reception, Hideyoshi referred to the precedents of which he was keenly aware: Emperor Go-Komatsu's royal progress to Yoshimitsu's Kitayama Palace in 1408, and Go-Hanazono's visit to Ashikaga Yoshinori's Muromachi Palace in 1427.[40] We are told that "because the Phoenix Litter, ox carriages,[41] and other such had for a long time been in disuse, even old men who knew of them had no certain recollection. . . . That being the case, [Maeda] Tokuzen'in Gen'i undertook to investigate the records of the several noble houses and to inquire of experts in ancient matters, so that the proper form was by and large attained." Oze Hoan asserts that more than two years were spent on the preparations,[42] which we need not accept as the literal truth unless we are also ready to assume that the Juraku Palace, on which work began in 1586, was built expressly for the occasion of the emperor's visit. There is less reason to question Ōmura Yūko's statement that Hideyoshi spared no financial effort to make sure that the entertainment was twice as lavish as that provided by previous hosts of Imperial Visits.[43] When Emperor Go-Yōzei left his palace at noon on Tenshō 16/4/14 (9 May 1588) in order to travel the fifteen short city blocks to Hideyoshi's nonsuch "Assembly of Delights," he was embarking on an elaborate spectacle indeed.

In commenting on this grand affair, Oze Hoan observes that Hideyoshi was "a river, an ocean of magnanimity, and strove for magnificence in all things. He was a man who under no circumstances recognized frugality."[44] Indeed, the first thing that strikes the eye is the magnificent scale of the five-day feast, best described in the words which the Jesuit Luis Frois used for another but similar occasion (Hideyoshi's own grand *onari* to Juraku in 1594): "There were suche banquetts, suche disportes and recreations, as the verie rehearsall wold surpasse all creddytt, so that the Castles name is fitlie called *Jurazu,* which is nothinge els but a plumpe of all pleasures."[45] Below the surface, however, we note the painstaking care to adhere to ancient court forms. For instance, although Rodrigues in discussing "The Banquets of the Japanese" maintains that Nobunaga and Hideyoshi had done away with the old ritualized manner of entertaining guests (with food that "was cold and insipid") and had "abolished . . . banquets of five or seven tables," modernity was not the style of this occasion: we have here the classical seven-table festive meal, down to the plain earthenware *(kawarake)* used "more for the sake of ancient ceremony than through lack of better ware," accompanied by "entertainments of instrumental music, plays and other things which were interspersed throughout the banquet."[46]

On the third day there was the obligatory poetry reading, led off (needless to say) by the Kanpaku himself. Ōmura Yūko tells us that *waka* reflect their times: there is a well-ordered and also a discordant style. Hideyoshi, according to him, "had attained true elegance; what else could this be but the tone of a well-ordered realm!"[47] To be sure, this testimony is suspect, for the suggestion has been made that none other than Yūko wrote the poems which Hideyoshi then recited as his own.[48] That, however, may be nothing more than backbiting. Hideyoshi could scarcely have matched wits and capped verses with the likes of Satomura Jōha, had he had no poetic instincts at all. Moreover, rough drafts of poetry in his own handwriting remain in existence; for that reason modern commentators tend to dismiss the ghosts of a vicarious authorship as unworthy figments.[49]

It is obvious that Hideyoshi has not earned as high a place in the history of literature as he has in the history of politics. But to slight him for trying poetry at all is to miss the point. Proficiency in this art was the sine qua non of a courtier. The tradition with which Hideyoshi had chosen to identify himself—and which he was designated to uphold—obliged him to become a practiced poet. When he became Kanpaku, he took instruction in *waka* just as naturally as he took instruction in court ceremonial.[50] What status required, Hideyoshi acquired.

The poems attributed to him and the accounts of the formal readings as well as of the improvised exchanges in which he participated show that Hideyoshi measured up to the standard expected of one in his position; he held his own in court company. Professor Kuwata Tadachika states flatly: "Hideyoshi's *waka* are better than those of his contemporary *kuge*."[51] This biographer's affection for his hero is overly great; for all that, we may freely grant him that the Kanpaku was a zealous student of this prime elegance of the courtly life and that he attained a good measure of accomplishment in it. Let us leave it with the citation of one poem, composed in response to an imperial verse on the fourth day of the visit to Juraku in 1588. It is not very original, but a subsequent vulgar literature has made it immortal.[52]

koto no ha no	Though words may run out
hama no masago wa	And the sands of the seashore
tsukuru tomo	May vanish,
kagiri araji na	There will be no limit
Kimi ga yowai wa	To the years of My Lord

Poetic sentiment and courtly entertainment were not the only things that Hideyoshi lavished on the imperial house during these celebrations. The court's income had shrunk over the period of the Sengoku disturbances; in the early sixteenth century the emperor had become, in effect, the client of occasional philanthropists; the imperial palace was "severely dilapidated"[53] until Nobunaga restored it to respectability if not splendor. Hideyoshi used the Imperial Visit "to set an example for future ages" (although display before the daimyo assembled in the Juraku no Tei was probably the more immediate intention). He would put the court's finances on a more stable footing: to that end he bestowed upon it "in perpetuity all the ground rents within the city of Kyoto," a yearly sum of 5,530 *ryō* in silver. He did not neglect his fellow "patricians" either, designating for their sustenance estates in Ōmi worth 8,000 *koku* a year.[54] The Bountiful Minister showed that in hard fact as well as name he had become the model courtier.

Lest we assume that Hideyoshi was an intemperate *sonnō*ite, we must not fail to note that the occasion was a well-orchestrated political spectacle. The Imperial Visit was conceived as the best possible symbol of Hideyoshi's grand pacification of the realm *(kokudo anzen no matsurigoto);*[55] and indeed it was timely, because with the settlement of the Higo Rebellion that very spring of 1588 the entire country west of the Kantō was subservient to him. The keynote of the ceremony was an oath which Hideyoshi exacted of his paladins.[56]

WE SOLEMNLY SWEAR:

Item. [1]   The measures ordained [by the Kanpaku] on the occasion of this Imperial Visit to the Juraku no Tei move us to tears of gratitude.

Item. [2]   If any impious person [should dare to interfere with] the ground rents and other income appertaining to the Imperial Estate or with the several holdings of the court nobles and imperial abbacies, we shall admonish him severely. We commit not only ourselves but also our children and children's children, who shall be instructed not to contravene this pledge.

Item.   We shall obey the Lord Kanpaku in everything and shall not violate
[3]   his orders even in the slightest.
[Anathema Clause]

Tenshō 16/4/15   [10 May 1588]

There follows the document's most interesting part, which for all its great significance is overtly farcical. Just who were the signatories among the daimyo? The oath was subscribed by the following great names:

[1] *naidaijin*	TAIRA no Nobukatsu	[Oda/Kitabatake/Oda]
[2] *dainagon*	MINAMOTO no Ieyasu	[Tokugawa]
[3] *gon dainagon*	TOYOTOMI Hidenaga	[(Hideyoshi's brother)]
[4] *gon chūnagon*	TOYOTOMI Hidetsugu	[Miyoshi/Toyotomi]
[5] *sangi; sakon no e no chūjō*	TOYOTOMI Hideie	[Ukita]
[6] *ukon no e no gon no shōshō*	TOYOTOMI Toshiie	[Maeda]
[7] *Tsu no jijū*	TAIRA no Nobukane	[Oda]
[8] *Tango shōshō*	TOYOTOMI Hidekatsu	[Miyoshi/Toyotomi]
[9] *Mikawa shōshō*	TOYOTOMI Hideyasu	[Matsudaira/Toyotomi/ (Yūki)]
[10] *Saemon jijū*	TOYOTOMI Yoshiyasu	[Satomi]
[11] *Tōgō jijū*	TOYOTOMI Hidekazu	[Hasegawa]
[12] *Kitanoshō jijū*	TOYOTOMI Hidemasa	[Hori]
[13] *Matsugashima jijū*	TOYOTOMI Ujisato	[Gamō]
[14] *Tango jijū*	TOYOTOMI Tadaoki	[Hosokawa]
[15] *Miyoshi jijū*	TOYOTOMI Nobuhide	[Oda]
[16] *Kawachi jijū*	TOYOTOMI Hideyori	[Shiba/Mōri]
[17] *Tsuruga jijū*	TOYOTOMI Yoritaka	[Hachiya]
[18] *Etchū jijū*	TOYOTOMI Toshikatsu	[Maeda (Toshinaga)]
[19] *Mattō jijū*	TOYOTOMI Nagashige	[Niwa]
[20] *Gengo jijū*	TOYOTOMI Nagamasu	[Oda (Urakusai)]
[21] *Gifu jijū*	TOYOTOMI Terumasa	[Ikeda]
[22] *Sone jijū*	TOYOTOMI Sadamichi	[Inaba]
[23] *Bungo jijū*	TOYOTOMI Yoshimune	[Ōtomo]
[24] *Iga jijū*	TOYOTOMI Sadatsugu	[Jimyōji/Tsutsui]
[25] *Kaneyama jijū*	TOYOTOMI Tadamasa	[Mori]
[26] *I jijū*	FUJIWARA Naomasa	[Ii]
[27] *Kyōgoku jijū*	TOYOTOMI Takatsugu	[Kyōgoku]
[28] *Tachino jijū*	TOYOTOMI Katsutoshi	[Kinoshita]
[29] *Tosa jijū*	HATA Motochika	[Chōsogabe]

The great names are in effect reduced to one: all but five of the twenty-nine signatories are called Toyotomi. This bestowal of the hegemon's own (self-assumed) family name upon his vassals certainly had rational political motives. It falls within the classical Japanese pattern of ascribing family ties in order to reinforce allegiance. Moreover, this reduction of the ruling group to the least common denominator was a logical consequence of Hideyoshi's approach to legitimation. A new regime founded on the loyalties of members of the military class led by a conqueror was transposed into the traditional order of imperial aristocrats headed by the Kanpaku: fact and form were reconciled.[57] Hideyoshi had captured the jewel and had displayed it in his own palatial castle. But he had not only raised himself to supreme heights by his proximity to the imperial symbol; he had also made the members of his inner circle into "men above the clouds," thus binding them to "a profound debt of gratitude."[58] All the assembled grandees, we are told, burst into spontaneous tears at the display of so much generosity. "In traditionalistic organizations, it is very common for the most important posts to be filled with members of a ruling family or clan."[59]

Beyond all that, however, we sense the overwhelming urge on the part of the chief parvenu to absorb all the other lords of the land, whether ancient (such as Ōtomo Yoshimune) or new (as was the case with most of the others), into his own uncertain lineage, as if to buttress its legitimacy with amplitude. This *mise en scène* actually reduces them to the level of *narabi daimyō*, those stiffly subordinate background figures in a Kabuki play. Medieval literature also provides us an analogy. We note that all of these feudatories appear under their court titles: Tokugawa Ieyasu as a Grand Councillor, Ukita Hideie as an Imperial Adviser and Lieutenant General of the Palace Guards of the Left, Maeda Toshiie as a Brevet Major General of the Palace Guards of the Right, and so on down the catalogue of Chamberlains. This list of the honors monopolized by the "Toyotomi family" evokes much the same dramatic sensation as that produced by the famous passage of the *Heike monogatari* which details the fullness of Kiyomori's glory and the prosperity of all his Taira clan: sixteen imperial nobles; more than thirty with access to the inner palace; over sixty provincial administrators, officers of the imperial guards, and other high officials. "And it seemed that in the world there were no other men."[60] To be sure, the clan of the fictional narrative was not a totally fabricated family group. The end result of both tales of pride and glory was, however, the same: to fall and fade with the dew.

The Imperial Visit to Juraku in 1588 was the most important ceremonial occasion of Hideyoshi's career; as spectacle, however, it may have been excelled by the Grand Kitano Tea Ceremony of 1587. One of these two events connotes aristocratization; in the minds of some, the other evokes the image of a "democracy of tea." One captured the imperial court, the other captured the popular imagination.

On the fourteenth day of the seventh month, Tenshō 15, Hideyoshi returned to Kyoto in triumph from his Kyushu expedition. On the thirteenth of the ninth month, he officially moved into the Juraku no Tei.[61] In the meantime, signboards had been erected throughout the city, announcing that Hideyoshi had decreed "a grand tea ceremony to be held in the groves of Kitano for ten days from the first of the tenth month, weather permitting," and that he would exhibit there all of his famous tea utensils "without leaving any out"; that all connoisseurs of the art of tea, regardless of their social standing, ought to attend; that improvisation on the part of the guests was to be the order of the day and that the customary niceties of rank need not be observed; that this command performance was not limited to Japanese devotees of tea but was meant to include "even those from China"; that whoever failed to attend would in the future be enjoined from entertaining friends even with tea substitute; and that Hideyoshi would personally serve tea to practitioners of *wabi*.[62]

This was truly a grand concept; but it was riddled with paradoxes. We need not doubt that Hideyoshi meant his proclamation genuinely, and that he wanted to share one of his principal pleasures with others, regardless of their status. Indeed, he drew a great variety of guests. "Patricians," "equestrians'" and thorough pedestrians, priests, merchants, and eccentric teamen evidently found it difficult to resist an invitation which stated, in effect, "Come one, come all, but you had better come!" But the Kanpaku clearly was not motivated by a wish to extend the culture of tea to the populace. Hideyoshi's governing impulse was the desire to display his wealth and his cultivation, which were incorporated in his precious tea utensils. The invitation states and restates that the purpose of the entire affair was to show them off—*misenasarubeki ontame*, and again, *miserarubeki tame*. We note that it also limits guests to "one kettle, one bucket, one drinking bowl." In an interesting turn of phrase, Louise Cort has commented that "Hideyoshi conquered Kyoto with tea just as surely as Nobunaga did with fire and the sword."[63] Was the conqueror, after all, afraid of competition?

When Hideyoshi arrived in Kitano on the morning of the appointed day, he must have been pleased at the sight. The groves were crowded with hundreds of temporary tea huts. A lottery was held in order to accommodate the guests: those who drew the top prize would be served by the Kanpaku himself; the rest had to content themselves with his advisers in the art, Sen no Rikyū, Tsuda Sōgyū, and Imai Sōkyū. That morning, Hideyoshi stayed true to his promise, with his own hands serving tea to no fewer than 803 persons. He spent the afternoon wandering through the groves, visiting with his guests, and looking over their arrangements. He then returned to the Juraku no Tei and called off the rest of the party.

Various reasons have been adduced for the abrupt curtailment of the grand ceremony. The least convincing is the contemporary one which linked the cancellation with disasters that had befallen Hideyoshi's vassal Sassa Narimasa in Kyushu.[64] The Higo Rebellion was no longer such a grave emergency: three weeks previously, Hideyoshi had set armies in motion to crush it. More acceptable is the notion that Hideyoshi was piqued because he felt that his expensive utensils had not drawn the attention they deserved, being overshadowed by the far simpler yet more striking implements which had been improvised by *wabi* eccentrics—Ikka's paling made of pine branches, Hechikan's bright vermilion parasol. One need not be an adherent of the temper-tantrum school of Hideyoshi historiography, established by contemporary Jesuits and continued by their epigones, in order to subscribe to this idea. There is much merit also in the suggestion that Hideyoshi decided to stop because he was physically and spiritually exhausted by the sheer labor of serving 803 people, not all of whom understood as well as he did what the culture of tea represented.[65]

Autocrats do not mix easily with the masses. Suzuki Ryōichi makes a penetrant observation when he notes apropos of Kitano: "The despot does not always behave as a despot; there are times when he puts on a popular act, and that is when he is all the more despotic."[66] Professor Suzuki asks a provocative question by invoking an association with the authoritarian *ikkun banmin* principle in this context. Even without agreeing with him, we will recognize that what was performed at Kitano was far from a "democratic" show.

That even such an innocuous-seeming art as the tea ceremony can have its political uses and be applied to the mystification of power is evident from a consideration of the historical background of Hideyoshi's threat to prohibit the use even of tea substitute to all those who did not heed his call. Nobunaga, another great aficionado of tea, had monopolized the practice of the art in his military group. The inferiors were not free to imitate the lord's accomplishment.

Rather, the license to hold the tea ceremony was a cherished sign of the lord's favor; along with the presentation of tea utensils, it was issued in reward for singular loyalty. Is it not possible that the Kanpaku Hideyoshi had second thoughts about his own role in popularizing a discipline best confined to a private transmission? For he himself had said that he "could not forget in this, the next, and future lives" that Nobunaga had granted him the precious favor. This was one memory at which Hideyoshi, too, shed tears of gratitude.[67]

The grand spectacle of Kitano is but one instance of the showiness which so affected Hideyoshi's approach to the tea ceremony. Theatricality marked his person—perhaps justly so, for his career was dramatic. That being the case, it is appropriate and not at all surprising that his life should have had as one of its distinctive characteristics the patronage—and even the occupation of the main stage—of a form of drama. His enthusiasm for the Nō is well known; it amounted to a type of *monomane*a. It is the best evidence for the paradigm that a new-found *noblesse* obliged him to strive for cultural accomplishment. It may also be the best example of his penchant for ostentation, even more so than his famous golden tearoom.

The Nō had been considered an elegant pastime in aristocratic circles ever since the days of Yoshimitsu. When Kyoto declined during the Sengoku period, this art was fostered in the provincial domains of daimyo intent on cultural prestige; when Kyoto revived after Nobunaga's advent to power, it began to flourish again in the capital. Hideyoshi furthered this regeneration, at first acting as the sponsor of Nō performances without yet personally becoming involved in the plays. Significantly enough, this sponsorship dates back to his appointment as Kanpaku, when he arranged for a program of five plays to be presented at the imperial palace before the emperor and his court, rewarding the actors with rich presents.[68] During his visit to the imperial palace in March 1586, when he displayed his portable golden tea room to the emperor, there also were Nō performances.[69] His theatrical tastes developed steadily thereafter. Toward the end of 1586, on the occasion of Ieyasu's visit to Osaka Castle for a formal audience with Hideyoshi, the entertainment included Nō.[70] Early in 1587, Hideyoshi invited the heads of the four Yamato troupes to perform in Osaka, perhaps as a ritual invocation of success in the Kyushu campaign, on which he was to embark shortly.[71] Eventually he brought about the four troupes' full resurrection, bestowing stipends on them in the autumn of 1593.[72] The reflected glories of patronage, however, were not enough for Hideyoshi. He wanted stardom.

Once he was persuaded that it would be worth his while to submit to formal training in the Nō—or, rather, once he fully recognized Nō's potential as a means of self-glorification—he threw himself into the pursuit of proficiency with great zeal. There were apparently no half measures in this man: he went after accomplishment in Nō ''like a whirlwind, with lightning speed'' (as Watanabe Yosuke puts it).[73] Does this sort of frenetic enthusiasm indicate that he had a true appreciation of the aesthetic of Nō? We cannot tell. There is little doubt that he enjoyed Nō primarily as spectacle; and the nature of the plays which he commissioned to be written amply reveals that he also considered Nō useful as a vehicle of propaganda. These two factors would seem to negate what is commonly assumed to be the essence of Nō, so that it may be correct to say that Hideyoshi's Nō, which had the veil of mystery stripped from it, really presaged the Kabuki world.[74] The rarefied form suffered when the man of power sought to embrace it.

Hideyoshi began studying Nō shortly after New Year's of Bunroku 2 (1593) in his headquarters at Nagoya in Kyushu, where he was supervising the progress of the Korean campaign.[75] On the fifth day of the third month, he was confident enough to write his wife Oné (Kita no Mandokoro) that he had thoroughly learned ten pieces.[76] Toward the end of the year, he felt ready to submit his dramatic skills to the judgment of the court, and staged a gala performance—with himself as the star—in the imperial palace; in the course of three days he played the lead in no fewer than eleven pieces.[77] We may be sure that the reviews were not too harsh; for we are told in the diary of the courtier Nishi no Tōin Tokiyoshi that Hideyoshi assigned his own critics from among the *kuge* for each performance.[78] Needless to say, these official appraisers (or, rather, praisers) were scarcely in the position to discourage their great patron's enthusiasm for the art. Indeed, this enthusiasm was unstoppable. Moreover, it served purposes other than the strictly artistic.

One of the more remarkable things about the programs of Nō staged by Hideyoshi is the appearance of actors such as Tokugawa Ieyasu, Maeda Toshiie, and Oda Nobukatsu (Jōshin) along with the unquestioned head of the troupe.[79] The professionals seem to have taken a jaundiced view of these amateurs, while yet evaluating the motive shrewdly. Texts transmitting the tradition of the Kita school allege that Hideyoshi ordered the ''equestrians'' to study Nō so that they would learn the proper bearing expected of them in their new ''patrician'' roles. To Hideyoshi is attributed the statement: ''These days many military men have ascended to high posts, but their appearance in court dress is utterly ignoble, so that they must all practice Nō.''[80] In the light of what has already been said about his efforts to aristocratize himself and his paladins, this would appear to be more than just a likely story. The performers had to be taught their parts; here theater merged with actuality.

The climax of Hideyoshi's programmed infatuation with Nō came when the hegemon not only commissioned plays to be composed about his great exploits but also took the role of the hero when they were put on the stage. The author, Ōmura Yūko, was an able and untiring herald of his master's deeds; his ''new Nō plays'' *(shinsaku no Nō)* dramatized some of the memorable events of a career which he described more fully in the chronicles he wrote at Hideyoshi's behest. The protagonist, Hideyoshi, was given the opportunity to act out his preoccupation with glory. That mixture of magnificence, hubris, and pathos which we have noted in his public statements was transposed here into its proper theatrical dimension.

Yūko is said to have composed ten such plays in all, but only five are extant. These are ''The Pilgrimage to Yoshino'' *(Yoshino mōde)*, ''The Pilgrimage to Kōya'' *(Kōya sankei)*, ''The Conquest of Akechi'' *(Akechi uchi)*, ''The Conquest of Shibata'' *(Shibata uchi)*, and ''The Conquest of Hōjō'' *(Hōjō uchi)*. There is also a play called *Toyokuni mōde*, ''The Pilgrimage to the Toyokuni Shrine,'' which glorifies Hideyoshi posthumously.[81] In addition, two *Kōwaka* ballad-dramas called ''Honnōji'' and ''Miki,'' which have been preserved in the archives of the Mōri family, may also be accounted variations on themes in the *Heldenleben* by Ōmura Yūko.[82]

Yūko's ''new Nō plays'' seem to have come into existence during the early part of 1594. Hideyoshi performed the first of these, ''The Pilgrimage to Yoshino,'' on 30 March 1594 before Hidetsugi in Osaka.[83] Oze Hoan reports that on 5 May he took the opportunity to portray the fivefold hero before the ladies of his entourage, performing in Osaka Castle the complete set as it exists today.[84] In this manner there was demonstrated that combination of Arms and Arts which Hideyoshi personified, and that valor which pacified the Four Seas, fulfilling Heaven's Mandate. For this is surely a true description of his merits; indeed, the *shite* of *Akechi uchi*—that is to say, Hashiba Chikuzen no Kami Hideyoshi—attests to it in those very words.[85]

We know that the Taikō planned to take this message before the emperor himself. There survives the program for a three-day gala which he proposed to put on at the imperial palace in that same month of May 1594. Professional actors would perform *Kōya sankei* and *Akechi uchi;* Hideyoshi himself would appear in *Yoshino mōde.*[86] This was perhaps more than coincidence: for the role which Hideyoshi thus reserved for himself was nothing less than the personification of Zaō Gongen, the main deity of the Yoshino Shrines.

The origins of the art of Nō are to be found in religious ritual. Aside a theatrical, Nō also has a liturgical character: it celebrates the divine powers which the actor invokes and assumes; it projects the charisma of the god. How conscious Hideyoshi was of this when he stepped on the stage cannot be determined. But we can safely say that his approach to the Nō amounted to more than random exhibitionism. There was in it a greater ambition.

The question naturally arises: how góod an actor was Hideyoshi? Frois, referring to a command performance in Fushimi Castle, noted that "sometymes he also intruded himself, and danced amongst the rest, but wth suche an evill grace, as well argued an impotent, and dotinge old man."[87] This was the most unkindest cut of all. The Jesuit's appraisal can be called neither expert nor unprejudiced. But it is apparent that Hideyoshi did not impress all of the people all of the time.

How else are we to interpret the following lampoon, which was posted in the streets of Kyoto in 1591?[88]

masse to wa	The end of the world
bechi ni wa araji	Is nothing else but this:
ki no shita no	Watching the monkey
saru Kanpaku o	Regent
miru ni tsuketemo	Under the tree

The anonymous satirist, undaunted by the magnificence of the Bountiful Minister Toyotomi, punned freely on his only "real" identity, that of a sometime Kinoshita vested in purple and posturing under an artificial family tree.

BARDWELL L. SMITH

Japanese Society and
Culture in the Momoyama Era:
A Bibliographic Essay

ALTHOUGH FAMILIARITY with Japanese scholarship and source materials in Japanese is essential to the work of the specialist on Japan in the sixteenth and early seventeenth centuries, it should be noted that traditionally the focal points of Japanese and Western research have varied because of the markedly different orientations with which Japanese and Western scholars have approached their work. There is at present, however, a small but expanding body of scholarly work in Western languages which combines Western and Japanese approaches, and as a result the nonspecialist interested in studying this important period of Japanese history but untrained in the Japanese language is able to obtain a more complete picture of Japanese scholarship. This is made possible through the works of some important Japanese scholars who have written in English, through the joint works which have begun to appear in recent years, and through the works of an increasing number of Western scholars who are well acquainted with the methodology of their Japanese colleagues and make judicious use of it while yet retaining their own perspectives.

The present bibliographic note, limited to titles in Western languages (principally English, though with some in French, German, Portuguese, and Spanish), is designed to serve the nonspecialist as a guide to books and articles on major aspects and themes of Japanese society and culture under the three "Great Unifiers": Oda Nobunaga (1534–1582), Toyotomi Hideyoshi (1537?–1598), and Tokugawa Ieyasu (1543–1616). This era is often termed, especially by art historians, the Azuchi-Momoyama period, after the two great castles built on the eastern shore of Lake Biwa and in Fushimi, to the south of Kyoto, by Nobunaga and Hideyoshi respectively; elsewhere in this volume, George Elison sets its dates between 1576 and 1615. The focus of this essay will be upon this era, although its scope will include some materials dealing with events occurring from the mid-sixteenth century through the closing of Japan to most Westerners a century later.

While dozens of bibliographies include entries on Momoyama social, political, economic, and cultural history (which may be said to end symbolically with the fall of Osaka Castle in 1615 and the death of Ieyasu the following year), few supply the nonspecialist with a carefully selected, annotated, and reasonably comprehensive sample.* Although limited in scope and necessarily selective, this brief discussion of significant books and articles may prove helpful to the nonspecialist pursuing the study of Japanese life and institutions during Momoyama times beyond what may be learned through the standard surveys of Japanese civilization.

I. Historiographical Problems and Interpretations

One of the most helpful ways to start is with several of the essays in *Historians of China and Japan,* edited by W. G. Beasley and E. G. Pulleyblank (London: Oxford University Press, 1961). Beyond the Introduction, four chapters are pertinent to an understanding of the sixteenth and early seventeenth centuries: (1) W. G. Beasley and

---

*Among those bibliographies and catalogues which deal with the Momoyama era, as well as other periods in Japanese history, several should be mentioned: (1) Bernard S. Silberman, *Japan and Korea: A Critical Bibliography* (Tucson: University of Arizona Press, 1962). (2) Frank J. Shulman, *Japan and Korea: An Annotated Bibliography of Doctoral Dissertations in Western Languages, 1877-1969* (Chicago: American Library Association, 1970) and its supplement, *Doctoral Dissertations on Japan and Korea, 1969-1974: A Classified Bibliographical Listing of International Research* (Ann Arbor, Michigan: University Microfilms International, 1976). Periodic supplements are being compiled and edited by Frank J. Shulman under the title of *Doctoral Dissertations on Asia: An Annotated Bibliographical Journal of Current International Research* (Ann Arbor, Michigan: Xerox University Microfilms); see volume 1, no. 1 (Winter 1975). (3) John W. Hall, *Japanese History: A Guide to Japanese References and Research Materials* (Westport, Conn.: Greenwood Press, 1973, reprint of the 1954 edition). (4) Henri Cordier, *Bibliotheca Japonica* (New York: Paragon Book Reprint, 1969), originally published as a guide to Western-language materials up to 1870, with an appendix on principal works from 1870 to 1912. (5) The *Cumulative Bibliography of Asian Studies (1941-1965),* published by the Association for Asian Studies, with the annual *Bibliography of Asian Studies* published since 1970. (6) Hugh Borton et al., eds., *Selected List of Books and Articles on Japan in English, French and German* (Cambridge: Harvard University Press, 1954). (7) Theodore Besterman, *A World Bibliography of Oriental Bibliographies,* revised and brought up to date by J. D. Pearson (Totowa, New Jersey: Rowman and Littlefield, 1975); see pages 598-622 on Japan. (8) Thus far, there are three bibliographies of the Japan National Committee of Historical Sciences available: (a) *Le Japon au XIe Congrès International des Sciences Historiques à Stockholm: L'Etat actuel et les tendances des études historiques au Japon* (Tokyo: Nippon Ga-

Carmen Blacker, "Japanese Historical Writing in the Tokugawa Period (1603–1868)," explores the preoccupation with feudal history and the use of and departure from Chinese literary models which constituted much of Tokugawa historical interpretation; (2) Hugh Borton's "Modern Japanese Economic Historians" is a useful guide to the developments in this field, especially since the First World War, which have enabled both Japanese and Western scholars to understand the institutional history of Japan in the long Muromachi and Tokugawa periods more thoroughly; (3) C. R. Boxer, "Some Aspects of Western Historical Writing on the Far East, 1500–1800," puts into perspective Portuguese and Dutch writings on Japan since the mid-sixteenth century; and (4) G. F. Hudson, "British Historical Writing on Japan," pp. 322–327, touches especially on the work of Brinkley, Murdoch, and Sansom.

Of the many surveys of Japanese history a few may be mentioned which have become standard for introductory courses in the field. The most reliable include Edwin O. Reischauer and John K. Fairbank, *East Asia: The Great Tradition* (Boston: Houghton Mifflin, 1958), whose chapters on "Feudal Japan" and "Tokugawa Japan" provide a full sweep of the centuries before and during the Early Modern period and put the sixteenth 'and early seventeenth centuries into a broad perspective; *Sources of Japanese Tradition,* compiled by Ryusaku Tsunoda, William Theodore de Bary, and Donald Keene

---

kujutsu Shinkōkai, 1960); see pages 45–55 on social and economic history of Kamakura through Momoyama periods; (b) *Japan at the XIIth International Congress of Historical Sciences in Vienna* (Tokyo: Nihon Gakujutsu Shinkōkai, 1965), pp. 23–76 on the medieval period; (c) *Recent Trends in Japanese Historiography, Bibliographical Essays: Japan at the XIIIth International Congress of Historical Sciences in Moscow* (Tokyo: Japan Society for the Promotion of Science, 1970), 2 vols.; see pages 13–60 of volume 1 for two essays on the medieval period. (9) Arimichi Ebisawa, comp., *Christianity in Japan: A Bibliography of Japanese and Chinese Sources,* pt. 1 (1543–1858) (Tokyo: Committee on Asian Cultural Studies, International Christian University, 1960). (10) Johannes Laures SJ, *Kirishitan Bunko: A Manual of Books and Documents on the Early Christian Mission in Japan,* Monumenta Nipponica Monographs, no. 5 (Tokyo: Sophia University Press, 1957, third revised and enlarged edition). (11) Masaharu Anesaki, *A Concordance to the History of Kirishitan Missions (Catholic Missions in Japan in the Sixteenth and Seventeenth Centuries),* Proceedings of the Imperial Academy 6 (Supplement) (Tokyo, 1930). (12) Makita Tominaga, "Outline of the Tenri Central Library, especially on the Collection of Records Relating to Early Christian Missions in Japan," *Tenri Journal of Religion* (Tenri, Japan, 1959). (13) Gen'ichi Hiragi, "The Trend of Studies of 'Kirishitan' Literature," *Acta Asiatica,* 4:97–113 (1963), which deals with Japanese-language research on this subject. (14) Hide Inada, *Bibliography of Translations from the Japanese into Western Languages from the 16th Century to 1912* (Tokyo: Sophia University Press, 1971). (15) Hubert Cieslik SJ "Kirishitan-Literatur der Nachkriegszeit," *Monumenta Nipponica,* 16:407–433 (1960–1961), an annotated bibliography of post–World War II literature on this subject. (16) Herschel Webb, *Research in Japanese Sources: A Guide* (New York and London: Columbia University Press, 1965).

(New York: Columbia University Press, 1958), which devotes one chapter, "Heroes and Hero Worship," to Nobunaga, Hideyoshi, and Ieyasu; John Whitney Hall, *Japan: From Prehistory to Modern Times* (New York: Delacorte Press, 1971), pages 126–190 of which provide a splendid survey of the era; David John Lu, *Sources of Japanese History* (New York: McGraw-Hill, 1974), volume 1, 167–197; and H. Paul Varley, *Japanese Culture: A Short History* (New York: Praeger, 1977, 2nd ed.), with a chapter on the Azuchi-Momoyama epoch. A more extensive if less trustworthy treatment in the popular vein is the depiction of *Kyoto in the Momoyama Period* (Norman: University of Oklahoma Press, 1967) by Wendell Cole, which deals with the political, religious, and cultural dimensions of life within the capital and its orbit.

Of the earlier works which are more extensive in their coverage, though presenting various problems of scholarship and interpretation, a few may be singled out as representative of how English-language scholarship on Japanese history developed in the first several decades of the twentieth century. Still readable, though the least scholarly of these, is *Japan: Its History, Art and Literature,* volume 2 (Boston and Tokyo: J. B. Millet, 1902) by Frank Brinkley, which deals with the "military epoch" through the government of Ieyasu, treating its history, customs and manners, military operations, and the so-called refinements and pastimes of the period. Brinkley's fifteen-volume history of Japan and China attempts to relate the cultural and political aspects of society, but it is a period piece whose reliability is minimal. Of somewhat more usefulness, though primarily because it highlights how far Western scholarship has developed in recent decades, is the lengthy one-volume work by F. Brinkley and Baron Kikuchi titled *A History of the Japanese People* (New York and London: Encyclopaedia Britannica Co., 1914), pages 460–572 on the Sengoku period through the early Tokugawa shogunate. Of greater value, despite its frequent bias and its now dated perspective, is the three-volume study by James Murdoch, in collaboration with Isoh Yamagata, titled *A History of Japan* (New York: Frederick Ungar Publishing Co., 1964, reprint of the edition originally published in Kobe and London, 1903–1926). Volume 2, parts 1 and 2, deals with the "Century of Early Foreign Intercourse (1542–1651)" and provides a detailed treatment of the political, military, religious, and foreign relations aspects of this period. While deficient in many respects, it is an ambitious and still basic history of this century-long era in Japanese history. If read with caution, and if one avoids reading volumes 1 and 3, it provides a wealth of information and can serve as a foil for later and more reliable interpretations. Though not as extensive in its treatment of the sixteenth and early seventeenth centuries, the work of Sir George Sansom is more balanced both in terms of what is covered and in its scholarly judgments. Pages 248–406 of *A History of Japan, 1334–1615* (Stanford: Stanford University Press, 1961) are extremely valuable for an understanding of the broad picture, beginning with the Sengoku period of civil war, out of which Oda Nobunaga emerged to begin the unification of Japan, and leading to the establishment of the Tokugawa shogunate under Ieyasu. If read in conjunction with pages 404–473 of his work *Japan: A Short Cultural History* (London: Cresset, 1952, a revision of the 1931 edition), it provides a sophisticated survey of institutional and cultural developments during this period.

Following the lead of Kan'ichi Asakawa (1873–1948), whose works on Japanese feudal society will be mentioned in the next section, American scholarship on premodern institutional history in Japan has advanced considerably in the past twenty years. The principal figure in this field has been John Whitney Hall, whose research has combined careful documentary analysis with broad comparative perspectives and has utilized methodological sophistication seldom found in earlier Western or Japanese approaches. Hall's comments on "Kan'ichi Asakawa: Comparative Historian," in *Land and Society in Medieval Japan,* Studies by Kan'ichi Asakawa Compiled and Edited by the Committee for the Publication of Dr. K. Asakawa's Works in Cooperation with the Council on East Asian Studies, Yale University (Tokyo: Japan Society for the Promotion of Science, 1965), trace the development, impact, and limitations of Asakawa's research, and the way in which it set the stage for subsequent studies of political, social, and economic history. Another introductory essay in this volume, "Studies of Japanese Feudalism and Dr. Kan'ichi Asakawa," by Rizō Takeuchi, examines Asakawa's work in its relationship to Japanese historical circles. A work of first-rate importance is Professor Hall's *Government and Local Power in Japan, 500 to 1700: A Study Based on Bizen Province* (Princeton: Princeton University Press, 1966), a detailed analysis of the province of Bizen, one of the sixty-six divisions of the traditional Japanese realm. In Hall's words, the study "deals chiefly with such subjects as theories of legitimacy and practices of administration, concepts of social stratification and social rights, and practices of land tenure and taxation." This longitudinal study of a microcosm of Japanese economic and sociopolitical life provides perspective upon other geographical areas within Japan and upon varied patterns of change and continuity in premodern history. The integration of this careful case study with Hall's informed interpretations of Japanese institutional history gives this work enduring importance. Pages 238–423 deal with the Sengoku period through the early Tokugawa era and, while they anticipate and postdate the Momoyama epoch as well as focus on that age, are basic to an understanding of the Nobunaga-Hideyoshi-Ieyasu governments and the tensions between centralized and provincial (daimyo) authority. Hall continues his treatment of this area in "The Ikeda House and Its Retainers in Bizen," in *Studies in the Institutional History of Early Modern Japan* (Princeton: Princeton University Press, 1968), edited by him and Marius B. Jansen. This collection of essays also includes other previously published articles by Hall: "Feudalism in Japan—A Reassessment," "Foundations of the Modern Japanese Daimyo," "Materials for the Study of Local History in Japan: Pre-Meiji *Daimyo* Records," and "The Castle Town and Japan's Modern Urbanization." Each of these has historiographical importance in supporting the relationship between studies of local and provincial histories and comparative studies within the wider Japanese scene. Also illustrative of this relationship are chapters in the same volume by Marius B. Jansen, "Tosa in the Sixteenth Century: The 100 Article Code of Chōsokabe Motochika" and "Tosa in the Seventeenth Century: The Establishment of Yamauchi Rule"; and by Robert Sakai, "The Consolidation of Power in Satsuma-han."

A forthcoming volume edited by Hall, Nagahara Keiji, and Kozo Yamamura, the product of collaboration between leading Japanese and American scholars, contains a series of articles on institutional aspects of the history of *Japan Before Tokugawa: Political Consolidation and Economic Growth, 1500 to 1650* (Princeton: Princeton University Press).

While not directly germane to this bibliography of materials dealing with the late sixteenth and early seventeenth centuries, two recent publications bear mention as they provide comparable institutional and cultural background. One is *Medieval Japan: Essays in Institutional History*, edited by John W. Hall and Jeffrey P. Mass (New Haven and London: Yale University Press, 1974), whose eleven chapters fall into the following sections: "Court and *Shōen* in Heian Japan," "*Bakufu* versus Court," and "The Age of Military Dominance." The other is *Japan in the Muromachi Age*, edited by John

Whitney Hall and Toyoda Takeshi (Berkeley: University of California Press, 1977), which is unique not simply in its extensive coverage of institutional, cultural, and religious life of this period but in providing a model of joint effort by the best Japanese and American scholars in the field. A carefully designed and executed symposium, it is an excellent example of collaborative research and interpretation. In this vein, two other volumes are worth mentioning: G. Cameron Hurst III, *Insei: Abdicated Sovereigns in the Politics of Late Heian Japan, 1086-1185* (New York and London: Columbia University Press, 1976); and Jeffrey P. Mass, *Warrior Government in Early Medieval Japan: A Study of the Kamakura Bakufu, Shugo, and Jitō* (New Haven and London: Yale University Press, 1974). These two works, together with the Hall-Mass and Hall-Toyoda volumes, have had a great impact on medieval Japanese studies in Western countries; no student of the Momoyama era can afford to be unaware of the implications of these four books. While touching only incidentally upon the Azuchi-Momoyama polity, these studies provide a perspective on medieval society which anyone seriously interested in sixteenth-century Japan would be well advised to acquire. The "cumulative historiographical significance" of these and other recent works dealing with Japanese history c. 1100–1600 is discussed in a review article by Conrad Totman, "English-Language Studies of Medieval Japan: An Assessment," *Journal of Asian Studies,* 38(3): 541–551 (May 1979). A forthcoming monograph by Martin Collcutt, *Five Mountains: The Zen Monastic Institution in Medieval Japan* (Cambridge: Harvard University Press), originally a Harvard Ph.D. dissertation, 1975, is a major study of the great monasteries called the Gosan, including their organizational structure, economic aspects, and relationship to the medieval social and cultural setting.

II. The Social, Political, and Economic Order

Japanese and Western scholarship within the last few decades has made it clear that understanding the economic order and its dynamics is fundamental to a comprehension of the Japanese social and cultural milieux of the sixteenth and seventeenth centuries, as well as of other eras. While the earlier histories by Murdoch and Sansom touch on economic matters, they do so inadequately. In the first half of the present century economic historians in Japan began to expand our knowledge of the development of feudal institutions and of the monetary, commercial, and agricultural dimensions of Japanese society. Among those who wrote in English, three may be singled out: Yosaburo Takekoshi, Eijiro Honjo, and Kan'ichi Asakawa. While superseded in many respects by more recent scholarship, the three-volume work by Takekoshi titled *The Economic Aspects of the History of the Civilization of Japan* (New York: Macmillan, 1930) may be used cautiously as one means of viewing Japanese history from the perspective of economic developments from the earliest beginnings to the early Meiji period. Though volumes 2 and 3 are primarily on the Tokugawa era, there is considerable attention in volume 1, pages 282–555, to the time between the Portuguese arrival in 1543 and the establishment of the Tokugawa shogunate in the early seventeenth century. If somewhat narrative in approach and fallacious at many points in interpretation, this account is an interesting initial survey of the topic, provided one subjects the author's interpretations to careful criticism. More specifically economic in orientation and more influential in Japan is the research of Eijiro Honjo, whose two works in English are *The Social and Economic History of Japan* (New York: Russell and Russell, 1965; first published in 1935) and *Economic Theory and History of Japan in the Tokugawa Period* (New York: Russell and Russell, 1965; first published in 1943). While introductory in nature and dealing primarily with Tokugawa times, these works provide insight on what emerged from the economic and social developments of the late Muromachi and Momoyama periods.

A different order of importance must be attributed to the work of Kan'ichi Asakawa, whose magnum opus is titled *The Documents of Iriki: Illustrative of the Development of the Feudal Institutions of Japan* (Westport, Conn.: Greenwood Press, 1974; originally published by Yale University Press in 1929; revised Tokyo edition, 1955). Asakawa has translated documents, ranging over a period from 1135 to 1870, which cover the rule of a single line of lords who controlled the small region of Iriki in southwestern Kyushu. Asakawa's Introduction, his "Summary of Points," and the documents on pages 310–350, which originated in the period 1574–1614, are pertinent to this bibliography and enable one to understand more clearly the ongoing tensions between local, regional, and central authority within the feudal system. Reference has been made above to the posthumously collected volume of Asakawa's essays titled *Land and Society in Medieval Japan* (1965), but two of those essays should be singled out for mention: "The Origin of the Feudal Land Tenure in Japan," originally published in the *American Historical Review*, 20(1):1–23 (October 1914), which examines the scene from the earliest beginnings up to the twelfth century; and "Some Aspects of Japanese Feudal Institutions," *Transactions of the Asiatic Society of Japan*, 46:77–102 (1918), which surveys three periods in feudal history from the Kamakura to the late Tokugawa. Of interest also is his long two-part article "Notes on Village Government in Japan after 1600," *Journal of the American Oriental Society*, 30:259–300 (1910) and 31: 151–216 (1911), which analyzes the so-called tension between rule by law and rule by discretion within a feudal society. If contemporary scholarship has gone beyond Asakawa, it is clearly indebted to his almost single-handed contribution. Among these whose work has been influenced by Asakawa is Edwin O. Reischauer, two of whose essays are pertinent here: "Japanese Feudalism," in *Feudalism in History*, edited by Rushton Coulborn (Princeton: Princeton University Press, 1956), which traces this subject from the ninth to the nineteenth centuries; and "Our Asian Frontiers of Knowledge," Riecker Memorial Lecture, no. 4, University of Arizona Bulletin Series, 29, 4 (September 1958), which looks at Japanese feudalism within a comparative perspective and suggests that this feudal legacy may have facilitated Japan's rapid emergence as a modern society during the past century. Another comparative approach to this subject is the work by the French scholar Frédéric Joüon des Longrais, *L'Est et l'Ouest: Institutions du Japon et de l'Occident comparées* (Tokyo: Maison Franco-Japonaise, 1958), which has supplemented the work of Asakawa by making use of more recent Japanese scholarship, especially that of the legal school. Attention must also be called to the previously mentioned essay by John Whitney Hall, "Feudalism in Japan —A Reassessment," originally published in *Comparative Studies in Society and History*, 5, 1 (October 1962), which is central to an understanding of this subject. Two more recent articles help to reveal the dynamic features of feudal society in the sixteenth and early seventeenth centuries: Wakita Osamu, "The *Kokudaka* System: A Device for Unification," *Journal of Japanese Studies*, 1(2):297–320 (Spring 1975), surveys the competing historical interpretations of this period, concentrates on the *kokudaka* system of landholding which he sees to be the foundation of feudalism, shows how it emerged "because of the ability of the sengoku daimyo to exert their power over large units of territory," and traces its establishment and development under Hideyoshi; John W. Hall, "Rule by Status in Tokugawa Japan," *Journal of Japanese Studies*, 1(1):39–49 (Autumn 1974), again raises historiographical problems of how to interpret the period from the mid-sixteenth to the early seventeenth century and suggests that the era entailed a significant change from a system of authority based upon paternalistic structures of social organization to a "more bureaucratic system of administration in which authority was exercised impersonally toward legally defined groups and classes." This he terms "rule by status." These two essays show how far contemporary research has gone beyond Asakawa, yet how naturally it proceeded from that beginning. This is also illustrated by a recent study which argues that the history of land tenure from the mid-thirteenth through the sixteenth centuries is essentially that of the decline of seigniorial authority over the peasantry: Peter J. Arnesen, *The Medieval Japanese Daimyo: The Ōuchi Family's Rule of Suō and Nagato* (New Haven and London: Yale University Press, 1979).

Beyond those studies analyzing feudal developments and institutional patterns within specific provinces, another significant area of research has focused on the emergence of a strong mercantile movement in the sixteenth century. While foreign trade, which is intrinsic to this movement, will be considered in the following section, one may examine the domestic monetary and commercial aspects as a separate subject. One of the earliest summaries of Western and Japanese writings in this area appeared in an article by Delmer M. Brown titled "The Importation of Gold into Japan by the Portuguese during the Sixteenth Century," *Pacific Historical Review,* 16(2):125–133 (May 1947), which advanced the thesis that an increased demand for gold arose in the last two decades of the sixteenth century because of the "establishment of a strong, central government, the general expansion of commerce and industry, [and] the secular trends in art." Brown's longer study of this field, *Money Economy in Medieval Japan: A Study in the Use of Coins* (New Haven: Institute of Far Eastern Languages, Yale University, 1951), traces in detail the growth of a complex money economy, including increased transactions in coins, expansion of the credit system, and rapid growth in the volume of trade. A further study of the coinage system may be found in A. Kobata, "The Production and Uses of Gold and Silver in Sixteenth- and Seventeenth-Century Japan," *Economic History Review,* 2nd series, 18(1–3):245–266 (1965), which discusses the progress of the mining industry, the development of foreign trade in gold and silver, and the increased use of gold and silver as currency. An important study is the doctoral dissertation of Virgil Dixon Morris, Jr., "Sakai: The History of a City in Medieval Japan" (University of Washington, 1970, available through University Microfilms), which investigates the important role of this so-called free city from the late fourteenth to the early seventeenth century "in terms of two related themes: first, its economic origins and development and, second, the nature of the relationship between its residents and members of the military class." One may gain further insight into certain aspects of the late medieval and early modern age by examining the following: (1) Louis Frederic, *Daily Life in Japan at the Time of the Samurai, 1185–1603* (London: George Allen and Unwin, 1972, English translation); (2) Oliver Statler, *Japanese Inn* (New York: Pyramid Books, 1962), pp. 23–76, a literary re-creation of life during the Nobunaga through Ieyasu regimes; (3) Charles David Sheldon, *The Rise of the Merchant Class in Tokugawa Japan, 1600–1868* (Locust Valley, N.Y.: J. I. Augustin, 1958), pp. 3–24, on the historical background of this development in the early seventeenth century; (4) Donald H. Shively, "Sumptuary Regulation and Status in Early Tokugawa Japan," *Harvard Journal of Asiatic Studies,* 25:123–164 (1964–1965), which analyzes the ideological factors of these regulations and their intent to keep in their proper place the emerging *chōnin* or artisans and merchants, who were the non-samurai population of castle towns and cities of this era; and (5) J. Carey Hall, "Japanese Feudal Laws: III. The Tokugawa Legislation," *Transactions of the Asiatic Society of Japan,* 38:269–331 (1910–1912), an early attempt to investigate laws prescribing status regulation for all levels of society.

Unlike economic analysis of the sixteenth and early seventeenth centuries, which has at least made a beginning, there is a dearth of comparable research on political dynamics beyond what may be found in the standard histories of the period. In the absence of a first-rate biography of Hideyoshi, one may consult Walter Dening's dated and inadequate *Life of Toyotomi Hideyoshi* (London: Kegan Paul, Trench, Trubner and Co., 1930, 3rd ed.; originally published in 1888); and Adriana Boscaro, ed. and trans., *101 Letters of Hideyoshi: The Private Correspondence of Toyotomi Hideyoshi,* Monumenta Nipponica Monographs, no. 54 (Tokyo: Sophia University Press, 1975). Mary Elizabeth Berry treats the topic of "Hideyoshi in Kyoto: The Arts of Peace" in her Ph.D. dissertation, Harvard University, 1975. Some idea of the military and political genius of Hideyoshi, at least on the domestic scene and especially in the Kyushu campaign, may be gained from J. H. Gubbins, "Hideyoshi and the Satsuma Clan in the Sixteenth Century," *Transactions of the Asiatic Society of Japan,* 8:92–143 (1880). A dated but still interesting and informative book is M. Steichen's *The Christian Daimyos: A Century of Reli-*

gious and Political History in Japan, 1549-1650 (Tokyo: Rikkyo Gakuin Press, n.d.; French edition, Hong Kong, 1904). Likewise readable but dated is A. L. Sadler, *The Maker of Modern Japan: The Life of Tokugawa Ieyasu* (London: George Allen and Unwin, 1937); this work's level of sophistication is compared unfavorably with two more recent studies of Tokugawa figures in an article by Conrad Totman, "The State of the Art; the Art of Statecraft; and Where Do We Go from Here?" *Harvard Journal of Asiatic Studies,* 36:240-255 (1976), in which Sadler's book is measured against those by John Whitney Hall, *Tanuma Okitsugu, 1719-1788: Forerunner of Modern Japan* (Cambridge: Harvard University Press, 1955), and Herman Ooms, *Charismatic Bureaucrat: A Political Biography of Matsudaira Sadanobu* (Chicago: University of Chicago Press, 1975). It is clear that studies in this area of Tokugawa history have been more fruitful than those of the late Muromachi and Momoyama era. This judgment is reinforced by three other important volumes, which treat at least in survey fashion, and from different perspectives, the transition period to the Edo shogunate: Conrad D. Totman, *Politics in the Tokugawa Bakufu, 1600-1843* (Cambridge: Harvard University Press, 1967); Harold Bolitho, *Treasures Among Men: The Fudai Daimyo in Tokugawa Japan* (New Haven and London: Yale University Press, 1974); and Herschel Webb, *The Japanese Imperial Institution in the Tokugawa Period* (New York and London: Columbia University Press, 1968).

III. Trade, Diplomacy, and Foreign Contacts

In certain respects the history of Japan may be examined according to its receptivity to and rejection of foreign influence, its cosmopolitanism on the one hand and its stress upon indigenous culture on the other. In the first thousand years of its recorded history this alternating pattern developed primarily in relationship to China. In the sixteenth century, contacts with the West expanded Japanese horizons, without changing the dual instincts for a carefully measured exposure to the new and a modified preservation of the old. Much has been written about the so-called Sakoku or seclusion policy of the early Tokugawa regime. An important article by Ronald P. Toby, "Reopening the Question of *Sakoku:* Diplomacy in the Legitimation of the Tokugawa Bakufu," *Journal of Japanese Studies,* 3(2):323-363 (Summer 1977), successfully questions previous interpretations of early Tokugawa policy and provides perspective upon late sixteenth-century attitudes toward foreign influences as well. Toby's thesis is that bakufu legitimacy was the thread which determined foreign policy, both toward East Asian neighbors and toward the countries of Europe between 1600 and 1644, rather than some indiscriminate policy of seclusion. This thesis lends insight into the factors which lay behind Japanese ambivalence toward unprecedented contacts with the West which began in the mid-sixteenth century. For a fuller treatment of Sakoku, see volume 2 of the three-volume study by Yoshi S. Kuno, *Japanese Expansion on the Asiatic Continent* (Berkeley and Los Angeles: University of California Press, 1940), which supplies documentary evidence for the commercial designs behind many of the domestic and diplomatic policies of Hideyoshi and Ieyasu especially.

This is not to discount the basically military and political objectives which prompted the unification efforts beginning with Nobunaga. Seizure of power and legitimation of power go hand in hand. As with the Kyushu campaign, Hideyoshi's invasions of Korea had several aims in view. Beyond the extensive treatment given to this by Murdoch, Sansom, and Takekoshi, see the following: Giuliana Stramigioli, "Hideyoshi's Expansionist Policy on the Asiatic Mainland," *Transactions of the Asiatic Society of Japan*, 3rd series, 3:74–116 (December 1954); W. G. Aston, "Hideyoshi's Invasion of Korea," *Transactions of the Asiatic Society of Japan*, 6:227–245 (1878), 9:87–93, 213–222 (1881), 11:117–125 (1883); A. L. Sadler, "The Naval Campaign in the Korean War of Hideyoshi (1592–1598)," *Transactions of the Asiatic Society of Japan*, 2nd series, 14:179–208 (June 1937); G. A. Ballard, *The Influence of the Sea on the Political History of Japan* (Westport, Conn.: Greenwood Press, 1973, reprint of 1921 edition), pp. 42–72, dealing with the Korean war; and Arthur J. Marder, "From Jimmu Tennō to Perry: Sea Power in Early Japanese History," *American Historical Review*, 51(1):20–31 (October 1945), also on the Korean conflict. An important part of the changing military picture in the second half of the sixteenth century was the impact made by Western firearms, navigation science, and shipbuilding. Brief discussion may be found in: Delmer C. Brown, "The Impact of Firearms on Japanese Warfare, 1543–98," *Far Eastern Quarterly*, 7(3):236–253 (May 1948); Kōzan Sakakibara, *The Manufacture of Armour and Helmets in Sixteenth Century Japan (Chūkokatchū Seisakuben)*, revised and edited by H. Russell Robinson (London: Holland Press, 1963; orig. pub. Edo, 1800), which shows indirectly how earlier forms of protection quickly became obsolete; C. R. Boxer, "Notes on Early European Military Influence in Japan (1543–1853)," *Transactions of the Asiatic Society of Japan*, 2nd series, 8:67–75 esp. (1931); *Monumenta Nipponica*, 19(3/4): 1–185 (1964), a special issue dealing with Western influences upon Japanese culture from the mid-sixteenth century to the Meiji period; Hirosi Nakamura, "Les Cartes du Japon: qui servaient de modèle aux cartographes européens au début des relations de l'Occident avec le Japon," *Monumenta Nipponica*, 2:100–123 (1939); C. R. Boxer, "Some Aspects of Portuguese Influence in Japan, 1542–1640," *Transactions and Proceedings of the Japan Society* (London), 33:13–64 (1936); S. R. Turnbull, *The Samurai: A Military History* (New York: Macmillan, 1977), pp. 112–265, which provides an interesting summary of the samurai's role during the turbulent sixteenth century; and Morton S. Schmorleitz, *Castles in Japan* (Rutland, Vt., and Tokyo: Charles E. Tuttle Co., 1974), an introductory guide to the architectural and military features of the principal castles in Japanese history.

Returning to Japan's commercial dealings abroad, it is important to stress that these were basic to what was happening in Japan and East Asia from about 1550 to 1640. The first place to start viewing this picture, however, is with the raiding exploits of the *Wakō* or Japanese pirates who had roamed the coastal waters of Korea since the thirteenth century and who were later to be the scourge of Ming China: see pages 336–348 of Y. Takekoshi, *Economic Aspects,* as well as his book *The Story of the Wako, Japanese Pioneers in the Southern Regions,* translated by Hideo Watanabe (Tokyo: Kenkyūsha, 1940). A helpful summary chapter which begins with the *Wakō* and follows the story through the development of commercial relations between Japan and its Asian neighbors, as well as with European nations, may be found in C. R. Boxer, *The Christian Century in Japan, 1549–1650* (Berkeley and Los Angeles: University of California Press, 1951), pp. 248–307. One may also consult chapters 26, 27, and 34 in Takekoshi's *Economic Aspects.* The most extensive treatment in Western languages is that by P. A. Tschepe SJ, *Japans Beziehungen zu China seit der ältesten Zeit bis zum Jahre 1600* (Yenchoufou, 1907). But we are still awaiting an authoritative study of this important subject.

With the establishment of Portuguese merchants and missionaries in western Japan in the 1540s, a new era of trade began, which saw Portugal, and later Holland, acting as the primary commercial broker within Asia and between Asia and Europe. While Spain and England were to attempt wresting this role from Portugal and Holland respectively, they were unable to do so. The history of these complex commercial relations among Japan, China, Macao, the Philippines, and Europe has been extensively studied. The following books and articles are among the more helpful analyses: (1) G. B. Sansom, *The Western World and Japan: A Study in the Interaction of European and Asiatic Cultures* (New York: Alfred A. Knopf, 1950), pp. 134–151; (2) Seiichi Iwao, "Japanese Foreign Trade in the 16th and 17th Centuries," *Acta Asiatica*, 30:1–18 (February 1976); (3) Kōichirō Takase, "Unauthorized Commerical Activities by Jesuit Missionaries in Japan," *Acta Asiatica*, 30:19–33 (February 1976); (4) Eiichi Katō, "The Japan-Dutch Trade in the Formative Period of the Seclusion Policy—Particularly on the Raw Silk Trade by the Dutch Factory at Hirado, 1620–1640," *Acta Asiatica*, 30:34–84 (February 1976); (5) C. R. Boxer, *The Great Ship from Amacon: Annals of Macao and the Old Japan Trade, 1555–1640* (Lisboa: Centro de Estudos Históricos Ultramarinos, 1963); (6) C. R. Boxer, *Fidalgos in the Far East, 1550–1770* (London: Oxford University Press, 1968, reprint of 1948 edition), pp. 1–71; (7) Paul Pelliot, "Un Ouvrage sur les Premiers Temps de Macao," *T'oung Pao*, 31:58–94 (1935); (8) T'ien-tsê Chang, *Sino-Portuguese Trade from 1514 to 1644: A Synthesis of Portuguese and Chinese Sources* (Leyden: E. J. Brill, 1969, reprint of 1933 edition); and (9) Michael Cooper SJ, "The Mechanics of the Macao-Nagasaki Silk Trade," *Monumenta Nipponica*, 27(4):423–433 (1972).

An interesting sidelight of this broader picture, and one which reinforced Japanese suspicions of European motives, was the ironic rivalry between Portugal and Spain for the favored party position in the trading relationship with Japan. While under the same monarch between 1580 and 1640, they successfully fouled their own nest through conflict with each other. Two chapters in Murdoch's *History of Japan*, volume 2, 281–301 and 457–506, are germane here, as are pages 137–247 in Boxer's *Christian Century*. This conflict between the Macao-based Portuguese and the Philippines-based Spanish, with its implications for relations with Japan, may be further studied in the following articles: M.T. Paske-Smith, "The Japanese Trade and Residence in the Philippines before and during the Spanish Occupation," *Transactions of the Asiatic Society of Japan*, 42:685–710 (1914); Henri Bernard SJ, "Les Debuts des relations diplomatiques

entre le Japon et les Espagnols des Iles Philippines (1571-1594),''
Monumenta Nipponica, 1:99-137 (1938); Ernest Satow, ''The
Origins of Spanish and Portuguese Rivalry in Japan,'' *Transactions of
the Asiatic Society of Japan,* 18 (1890); C. R. Boxer, ''Portuguese
and Spanish Rivalry in the Far East during the 17th Century,'' *Journal of the Royal Asiatic Society of Great Britain and Ireland* (1946),
pp. 150-164, and (1947), pp. 91-105; C. R. Boxer, ''The Affair of
the 'Madre de Deus': A Chapter in the History of the Portuguese in
Japan,'' *Proceedings and Transactions of the Japan Society* (London),
26:4-90 (1929); and J. L. Alvarez-Taladriz, ''Don Rodrigo de Vivero
et la destruction de la nao 'Madre de Deos' (1609 à 1610),'' *Monumenta Nipponica,* 2(2):147-179 (July 1939).

Though in the end all were losers, the initial beneficiaries of the
Iberian rivalry were the English and the Dutch. Beyond Murdoch's
History of Japan and Boxer's *Christian Century,* other interesting ac-
counts, especially of the English experience and of the career of Will
Adams (1564-1620), who was employed in an advisory capacity by
Ieyasu, may be found in the following: William Adams, *Memorials
of the Empire of Japan in the XVI and XVII Centuries,* edited and
with notes by Thomas Rundall (London: Hakluyt Society, 1850);
Philip G. Rogers, *The First Englishman in Japan: The Story of Will
Adams* (London: Harvill Press, 1956), which includes an extensive
bibliography of writings on Adams; C. J. Purnell, ''The Log-Book of
William Adams, 1614-1619,'' *Transactions and Proceedings of the
Japan Society* (London), 13:156-302 (1915); Ilza Veith, ''Englishman or Samurai: The Story of Will Adams,'' *Far Eastern Quarterly,*
5(1):5-27 (November 1945); Ludwig Riess, ''History of the English
Factory at Hirado (1613-1622),'' *Transactions of the Asiatic Society
of Japan,* 26:1-114 (1898); and Richard Cocks, *The Diary of Richard
Cocks, Cape-Merchant in the English Factory in Japan, 1615-1622,*
edited by Murakami Naojirō, 2 vols. (Tokyo: Sankōsha, 1899).

Toward the end of the sixteenth century and at the beginning of
the seventeenth, two Japanese missions were sent to Europe. The
first, planned by Alexandro Valignano SJ, was designed both to
secure papal endorsement of the Jesuits' sole rights for missionary
work in Japan and to expose four Japanese young men to the wonders
of Catholic Europe. The youths were away on their embassy from
1582 to 1590. As their royal reception in several European countries
revealed, Western interest in Japan was greatly stimulated in the process. Some idea of the popular sensation caused by this mission may

be gained from "the great number of printed booklets, relating only to it, printed in Europe for the occasion" and listed in Adriana Boscaro's *Sixteenth Century European Printed Works on the First Japanese Mission to Europe: A Descriptive Bibliography* (Leiden: E. J. Brill, 1973). Source materials relating to the mission, including a great amount in European languages, have been assembled in two supplementary volumes *(bekkan)* to part 11 of *Dai Nippon shiryō,* comp. Tōkyō Daigaku Shiryō Hensanjo (Tokyo: Tōkyō Daigaku Shuppankai, 1961). The following additional works may also be consulted: H. Nagaoka, *Histoire des relations du Japon avec l'Europe aux XVIe et XVIIe siècles* (Paris, 1905); Donald F. Lach, *Japan in the Eyes of Europe: The Sixteenth Century* (Chicago and London: University of Chicago Press, 1968; exact reproduction of pages 651–729 of Lach's *Asia in the Making of Europe,* 1965); João do Amaral Abranches Pinto and Henri Bernard SJ, "Les Instructions du Père Valignano pour l'ambassade japonaise en Europe," *Monumenta Nipponica,* 6:391–403 (1943); Henri Bernard SJ, "Valignani ou Valignano, l'auteur véritable du récit de la première ambassade japonaise en Europe (1582–1590)," *Monumenta Nipponica,* 1(2):378–385 (1938); Alfons Kleiser SJ, "P. Alexander Valignanis Gesandschaftsreise nach Japan zum Quambacudono Toyotomi Hideyoshi, 1588–1591," *Monumenta Nipponica,* 1:70–98 (1938).

The second mission was headed by Hasekura Rokuemon, a retainer of the Sendai daimyo Date Masamune, and the Franciscan friar Luis Sotelo. Its ostensible purpose was twofold, that is, to secure papal endorsement of Franciscan missions in Japan and to open up trade between Japan and New Spain (especially Mexico). Both efforts were unsuccessful, and the mission returned in 1620, after seven years away, to a new shogunate and a Japan increasingly wary of all Christian endeavors. See C. Meriwether, "A Sketch of the Life of Date Masamune and an Account of His Embassy to Rome," *Transactions of the Asiatic Society of Japan,* 21:1–105 (1893); Hirosi Nakamura, "Passage en France de Hasekura, Ambassadeur Japonais à la cour de Rome au commencement du xviie siècle," *Monumenta Nipponica,* 3(2):85–97 (July 1940); and especially Lothar Knauth, "Pacific Confrontation: Japan Encounters the Spanish Overseas Empire 1542–1639" (Harvard University, Ph.D. dissertation, 1970), published as *Confrontación transpacífica: El Japón y el Nuevo Mundo hispánico, 1542–1639* (Mexico: Universidad Nacional Autónoma de México, Instituto de Investigaciones Históricas, 1972).

IV. The "Christian Century" (1549-1639)

As one might expect, Western writings on Japan were more extensive during this period than at any other time until the last hundred years. While much of it comes from Jesuit pens, several of the missionary writers were close to those in power, including the three "Great Unifiers," and thus their testimony is of first-rate significance. If the history of the Jesuits and their fellow Catholics during this century has sometimes been overstressed, to the detriment of understanding other movements and developments, it is clear that the presence of traders and missionaries was of major importance within a larger, complex macrocosm. The diverse writings which emerged from this Christian context and the subsequent research by scholars on this period provide a rich source for study of one of Japan's most critical eras. Brief summary treatments may be found in Masaharu Anesaki, *History of Japanese Religion* (Rutland, Vt., and Tokyo: Charles E. Tuttle Co., 1963), pp. 229-239 and 240-253, on the religious strife of the period and on Kirishitan missions respectively; Joseph M. Kitagawa, *Religion in Japanese History* (New York and London: Columbia University Press, 1966), pp. 131-176, on "Kirishitan, Neo-Confucianism, and the Shogunate"; Heinrich Dumoulin SJ, *A History of Zen Buddhism* (New York: Random House, 1963), pp. 198-224, on the "First Encounter between Zen and Christianity"; G. B. Sansom, *The Western World and Japan* (see above), pp. 105-133; and Michael Cooper SJ, ed., *The Southern Barbarians: The First Europeans in Japan* (Tokyo and Palo Alto: Kodansha International, 1971), with chapters by Cooper and others. See also a review of *The Southern Barbarians* by George Elison in *Monumenta Nipponica*, 27(2):222-227 (1973).

Several full-length studies of the Christians in Japan are available. In Johannes Laures' *The Catholic Church in Japan: A Short History* (Notre Dame, Ind.: University of Notre Dame Press, 1962), pages 1-76 and 77-179 deal with the periods 1549-1570 and 1570-1614 respectively. The standard history in English and perhaps the best overall introduction is that by C. R. Boxer, *The Christian Century in Japan: 1549-1650* (Berkeley and Los Angeles: University of California Press, 1951), with extensive appendices, notes, and bibliography, which deals with the Christian presence within the larger social and political framework. A more recent publication is that by George Elison, *Deus Destroyed: The Image of Christianity in Early Modern Japan* (Cambridge: Harvard University Press, 1973). Elison's study is based primarily on Japanese sources, and thereby complements Boxer's work, which is written more from the Western perspective; one of its parts describes the problems Christianity encountered in being accepted in Japan, the second analyzes various forms of its rejection, and the third part consists of elaborately annotated translations of four polemical works which depicted Christianity as the "pernicious faith," the standard image of the "religion of Deus" in Tokugawa Japan. C. R. Boxer has reviewed *Deus Destroyed* in *Monumenta Nipponica*, 29(3):342–345 (1974), and in *Journal of Japanese Studies*, 1(1):182–188 (Autumn 1974). For yet another perspective one should consult Josef Franz Schütte SJ, *Introductio ad Historiam Societatis Jesu in Japonia, 1549–1650* (Rome: Institutum Historicum Soc. Jesu, 1968), which in spite of its title is not an introductory but an encyclopedic work by the doyen of Jesuit historians of Japan. Much of value will also be found in the following older accounts of the "Christian Century": (1) Daniello Bartoli SJ, *Dell'Historia della Compagnia di Giesv: Il Giappone; Seconda Parte Dell'Asia* (Rome: Nella Stamperia d'Ignatio de'Lazzeri, 1660); (2) Jean Crasset SJ, *The History of the Church in Japan,* translated by N. N. [Webb] (London, 1707); (3) Léon Pagés, *Histoire de la religion chrétienne au Japon depuis 1598 jusqu'a 1651,* 2 vols. (Paris: Charles Douniol, 1869–1870); and (4) Louis Delplace SJ, *Le Catholicisme au Japon,* 2 vols. (Brussels: Librairie Albert Dewit, 1909–1910).

From the larger picture one may proceed to works of a more limited scope which deal with some of the more prominent Western figures in Japan at this time. This field is an exceedingly rich one. While it is possible to debate which is the best place to start, the following listing traces the scene in an approximately chronological fashion. Making for interesting reading but misleading because of the fragmentary picture it provides is a work titled *They Came to Japan: An Anthology of European Reports on Japan, 1543–1640* (London: Thames and Hudson, 1965), compiled and edited by Michael Cooper SJ. Essential for an understanding of the beginnings of the Jesuit enterprise in Japan is the final part of a multivolume study by Georg Schurhammer SJ, *Franz Xaver: Sein Leben und seine Zeit,* II. Band: *Asien (1541–1552),* III. Teilband: *Japan und China, 1549–1552* (Freiburg: Herder, 1973). Far less elaborate but nonetheless quite useful is the work by Paul Aoyama Gen SVD, *Die Missionstätigkeit des hl. Franz Xaver in Japan aus japanischer Sicht* (St. Augustin/Siegburg: Steyler Verlag, 1967). Saint Francis Xavier's letters have been collected and edited in two volumes by Georg Schurhammer SJ and Josef Wicki SJ, *Epistolae S. Francisci Xaverii aliaque eius scripta* (Rome: Monumenta Historica Soc. Iesu, 1944–1945). A modest volume which deals with Xavier and his immediate successors in the Jesuit mission to Japan's capital city is that by Johannes Laures SJ, *Die Anfänge der Mission von Miyako* (Münster: Achendorffsche Verlagsbuchhandlung, 1951).

The most important single compilation of sixteenth-century Western intelligence about Japan is *Cartas qve os Padres e Irmãos da Companhia de Iesus escreuerão dos Reynos de Iapão & China aos da mesma Companhia da India, & Europa, des do anno de 1549. atè o de 1580.* (Em Euora por Manoel de Lyra. Anno de M.D.XCVIII.), 2 vols. in one; this indispensable but fairly rare work has recently been made available in a facsimile edition in the Tenri Central Library series *Classica Japonica*, sec. 2, *Kirishitan Materials,* no. 1 (Tenri: Tenri Daigaku Shuppanbu, 1972). Similarly basic to a thorough study are the writings of Luis Frois SJ (1532–1597), who communicated his dramatic impressions of Japan back to India and Europe over a period of thirty-four years in the country. Volume 1 of a critical edition of his magnum opus, *Historia de Japam,* to be completed in five volumes, has recently appeared in Lisbon, edited by Josef Wicki SJ (Biblioteca Nacional de Lisboa, 1976). Previously published parts of this account of the trials and triumphs of the Jesuit mission, which on occasion offers fascinating glimpses of the processes and personalities of sixteenth-century Japanese history, include the German translation by Georg Schurhammer SJ and E. A. Voretzsch, *Die Geschichte Japans (1549–1578)* (Leipzig: Asia Major, 1926); *Segunda Parte da Historia de Japam (1578–1582),* ed. João do Amaral Abranches Pinto and Okamoto Yoshitomo (Tokyo: Edição da Sociedade Luso-Japonesa, 1938); and *Terza Parte da Historia de Japam (1582–1592),* edited by Pinto, Okamoto, and Henri Bernard SJ, Monumenta Nipponica Monographs, no. 6 (Tokyo: Sophia University Press, 1942). Also see Luis Frois SJ, *Kulturgegensätze Europa-Japan (1585),* critical edition and German translation by Josef Franz Schütte SJ, of *Tratado Em q̃ se contem Mto susinta e abreuiadamente algũas contradisões & diferencas de custumes . . . ,* Monumenta Nipponica Monographs, no. 15 (Tokyo: Sophia University Press, 1955). Similarly important are the writings of Alexandro Valignano SJ (1539–1606), who was Visitor of the missions in Asia on behalf of the General of the Society of Jesus and spent ten years in Japan between 1579 and 1603. For an account of his life and work, see the exemplary study by Josef Franz Schütte SJ, *Valignanos Missions-*

grundsätze für Japan (Rome: Edizioni di Storia e Letteratura, 1951–1958), I. Band I. Teil: *Das Problem (1573–1580)* (1951); I. Band II. Teil: *Die Lösung (1580–1582)* (1958). The following of Valignano's works are particularly important: *Sumario de las Cosas de Japon (1583)*, ed. José Luis Alvarez-Taladriz, Monumenta Nipponica Monographs, no. 9 (Tokyo: Sophia University Press, 1954); and his *Advertimentos e Avisos acerca dos Costumes e Catangues de Jappão (1581)*, critical edition and Italian translation by Josef Franz Schütte SJ, *Il Cerimoniale per i Missionari del Giappone* (Rome: Edizioni di Storia e Letteratura, 1946). See also J. M. Braga, ''The Panegyric of Alexander Valignano, S.J.,'' *Monumenta Nipponica*, 5(2):523–535 (December 1942).

Among the Jesuits who had access to men of power, perhaps none was so influential with both Hideyoshi and Ieyasu as João Rodrigues Tçuzzu (1561–1634), who frequently served as their interpreter. Rodrigues was not only an astute but also a culturally sensitive man. Among the most important books on this entire period, therefore, is his ''History of the Church of Japan,'' written between 1620 and 1633. The title notwithstanding, the work's major part (books 1 and 2, apparently meant to be introductory but in the event comprising two thirds of the extant manuscript) deals not with matters of ecclesiastical history but with facets of the Japanese cultural scene. For the original, see João Rodrigues Tçuzzu SJ, *História da Igreja do Japão*, ed. João do Amaral Abranches Pinto, 2 vols. (Macao: Notícias de Macau, 1954–1955); this is, however, only a transcription of books 1 and 2, not a critical edition. Michael Cooper SJ has made available an excellent abridged English version of the same portion of the work, under the title *This Island of Japon: João Rodrigues' Account of 16th-century Japan* (Tokyo and New York: Kodansha International, 1973). Of far less value but nevertheless interesting reading is the biography by Michael Cooper SJ, *Rodrigues the Interpreter: An Early Jesuit in Japan and China* (New York and Tokyo: John Weatherhill, 1974). Also see the review of Cooper's two volumes by George Elison in *Journal of Japanese Studies*, 1(2):459–466 (Spring 1975); and an essay by Georg Schurhammer SJ, ''P. Johann Rodriguez Tçuzzu als Geschichtschreiber Japans,'' *Archivum Historicum Societatis Jesu*, 1(1): 23–40 (1932).

Also of interest are the observations of the Spanish trader Bernardino de Avila Girón, ''Relación del Reino de Nippon,'' chaps. 1–15, edited by Doroteo Schilling OFM and Fidel de Lejarza, published in *Archivo Ibero-Americano*, 36–38 (1933–1935). For the Franciscan view of certain problems of the "Christian Century," see Marcelo de Ribadeneira OFM, *Historia de las islas . . .* , ed. Juan R. de Legísima OFM (Madrid: La Editorial Católica, 1947); and consult also "Cartas y relaciones del Japón," edited by Lorenzo Pérez OFM and published in *Archivo Ibero-Americano*, 4-19 (1915-1923). For the Dominican side, see: Diego Aduarte OP, *Historia de la Provincia del Sancto Rosario* (Manila: Colegio de Sācto Thomas, 1640); Francisco Carrero OP, *Triunfo del Santo Rosario y Orden de Santo Domingo en los reinos del Japon* (Manila: Colegio de Santo Tomás, 1868, 2nd ed.); Jacinto Orfanel OP, *Historia Eclesiastica de los sucessos de la Christianidad de Iapon* (Madrid, 1633). An interesting effect of the Dominican mission in Japan is the impression it produced on one of Spain's greatest men of letters: see Lope de Vega, *Triunfo de la Fee en los Reynos del Japon* (first published 1618), edited and with an introduction by J. S. Cummins (London: Tamesis Books, 1965); and the article by C. R. Boxer and J. S. Cummins, "The Dominican Mission in Japan (1602-1622) and Lope de Vega," *Archivum Fratrum Praedicatorum*, 33:5-88 (1963).

One of the most helpful summary treatments of "Christian Culture and Missionary Life" during this period may be found on pages 188-247 of Boxer's *Christian Century*, along with his notes for this chapter. Beyond this, not to mention the primary sources and histories referred to above, the following are of interest: Naojiro Murakami, "The Jesuit Seminary of Azuchi," *Monumenta Nipponica*, 6:375-390 (1943); Josef Franz Schütte SJ, "Ignatianische Exerzitien im frühchristlichen Japan," *Monumenta Nipponica*, 6:375-390 (1943); Ernest Satow, *The Jesuit Mission Press, 1591-1610* (London: privately printed, 1888); Diego Pacheco SJ, "Diogo de Mesquita, S.J., and the Jesuit Mission Press," *Monumenta Nipponica*, 26(3/4): 431-443 (1971); Shigetomo Koda, "Notes sur la presse jésuite au Japon et plus spécialement sur les livres imprimés en caractères japonais," *Monumenta Nipponica*, 2(2):42-53 (July 1939); Georg Schurhammer SJ, *Das Kirchliche Sprachproblem in der Japanischen Jesuitenmission des 16. und 17. Jahrhunderts* (Tokyo: Deutsche Gesellschaft für Natur- und Völkerkunde Ostasiens, 1928; "Mitteilungen," Band 23); Tadao Doi, "Das Sprachstudium der Gesellschaft Jesu in Japan im 16. und 17. Jahrhundert," *Monumenta Nipponica*, 2(2):105-133 (July 1939); Hubert Cieslik SJ, "The Training of a Japanese Clergy in the Seventeenth Century," in *Studies in Japanese Culture*, edited by Joseph Roggendorf SJ (Tokyo: Sophia University Press, 1963); and Arimichi Ebisawa, "The Jesuits and Their Cultural

Activities in the Far East," *Journal of World History,* 5(2):344–374 (1959).

For the problems which Christianity encountered in Japan, the best analysis available in English is George Elison's *Deus Destroyed.* This work is particularly valuable for its treatment of the means by which the Catholic church sought to accommodate itself to Japanese culture, as well as for its account of the polemics and counterpolemics engaged in by Christians and Buddhists alike. When apologetics fell short, attack was soon to follow; in fact, as time went on, the apologist-turned-apostate became Buddhism's foremost weapon. The *locus classicus* of this may be seen in the person of the Japanese Jesuit Fabian Fucan, whose 1620 tract *Deus Destroyed (Ha Daiusu),* translated by Elison, may be compared with Fabian's 1605 *Myōtei Dialogue (Myōtei mondō)* in defense of the Christian faith. For a discussion and partial translation of the latter, see Pierre Humbert-claude, "*Myōtei Mondō:* Une apologétique chrétienne japonaise de 1605," *Monumenta Nipponica,* 1:223–233 (1938), and 2:237–267 (1939). An example of aspersions cast from the other side may be found in Jesús López Gay SJ, "Un Documento Inédito del P. G. Vás-quez (1549–1604) sobre los Problemas Morales del Japón," *Monumenta Nipponica,* 16:118–160 (1960–1961), which attributes the high incidence of war, homicide, and usury in Japanese society to its non-Christian nature.

Among the important ingredients of Christianity's fortune and downfall in Japan was its connection with various daimyo from the mid-sixteenth century up into the shogunate of Ieyasu. While Christianity was embraced sincerely by some, its acceptance by others was for the enhancement of their power. When this proved counterproductive, as it began to do in the regime of Hideyoshi, defections were common though not universal. Among the many accounts of this story, beyond that of Elison, one may consult Boxer's chapter on "The Palm of Christian Fortitude" in *Christian Century,* and Murdoch's *History of Japan,* volume 2, 236–253 and 457–506. For a closer look at some of the more prominent figures during this era, see M. Steichen, *The Christian Daimyos;* Johannes Laures SJ, *Takayama Ukon und die Anfänge der Kirche in Japan* (Münster: Aschendorf-fsche Verlagsbuchhandlung, 1954); Johannes Laures SJ, *Nobunaga und das Christentum,* Monumenta Nipponica Monographs, no. 10 (Tokyo: Sophia University Press, 1950); Johannes Laures SJ, *Two Japanese Christian Heroes: Justo Takayama Ukon and Gracia Hosokawa Tamako* (Rutland, Vt., and Tokyo: Bridgeway Press/Charles E. Tuttle Co., 1959); Yakichi Kataoka, "Takayama Ukon," *Monumenta Nipponica*, 1(2):159–172 (July 1938); Johannes Laures SJ, "Takayama Ukon: A Critical Essay," *Monumenta Nipponica*, 5:86 – 112 (1942); Johannes Laures SJ, "Were the Takayamas and Naitos Involved in Hideyori's Plot?" *Monumenta Nipponica*, 6(1/2):233–244 (1943); and C. R. Boxer, "Hosokawa Tadaoki and the Jesuits, 1587–1645," *Transactions and Proceedings of the Japan Society* (London), 32: 79–119 (1935).

As the chronicling of Christian martyrdom became more vivid as persecution became more intense following the death of Ieyasu, one may find many accounts, beyond those works mentioned above, of the period from before Nobunaga through the time of Ieyasu. See Ernest Satow, "Vicissitudes of the Church at Yamaguchi from 1550 to 1586," *Transactions of the Asiatic Society of Japan*, 7:131–156 (1879); C. F. Sweet, trans., "The Crucifixion of the Twenty-six in 1597," *Transactions of the Asiatic Society of Japan*, 44:20–45 (1916), from the chronicle of Luis Frois; Johannes Laures SJ, "Die Zahl der Christen und Martyrer im alten Japan," *Monumenta Nipponica*, 7(1/2):84–101 (1951); Hubert Cieslik SJ, "Kumagai Buzen-no-Kami Motonao: Leben und Tod eines christlichen Samurai," *Monumenta Nipponica*, 8:147–192 (1952) and 9:109–154 (1953); Masaharu Anesaki, "Writings on Martyrdom in Kirishitan Literature," *Transactions of the Asiatic Society of Japan*, 2nd series, 8:20–65 (1931), which deals with the period 1591–1626; C. R. Boxer, "The Clandestine Catholic Church in Feudal Japan, 1614–1640," *History Today*, 16(1):53–61 (January 1966); and Hubert Cieslik SJ, "The Great Martyrdom in Edo 1623," *Monumenta Nipponica*, 10(1/2):1–44 (April 1954).

V. The Cultural Scene and Its Legacy

The Momoyama era's artistic creativity and cultural life reached deeper into Japanese society and affected more of its segments than had been the case before. Architecture, painting, tea culture, and the theater with its accompanying crafts were the principal areas of the new efflorescence in the arts. Its various currents ranged from a continued involvement with Chinese models to a strong revival of indigenous *Yamato-e*, from new types of ceramic ware influenced by Korean techniques to the Nanban art that was derived from the presence of Westerners in Japan. Momoyama was an epoch of unprecedented cultural vigor, unmatched in its diversity and its daringly innovative thrusts. Rarely if ever before had styles covered the full spectrum from the sumptuous and sometimes garish to the strikingly simple, from elegant splendor to cultivated restraint. The era was one in which art, freed from earlier constraints of religious ideology, became an expression of political and social legitimacy, as its new patrons enhanced their status through the very expansiveness with which they courted, engaged in, and surrounded themselves with cultural and artistic endeavors. Various pieces of this fascinating picture have been examined with care, but, as with so much of Momoyama history, much more analysis and interpretation remains to be done. The following survey of materials available for study provides at least some indication of the incredible riches produced during this short period of time.

Brief summaries of Momoyama motifs and styles may be found in a large number of publications. Among them are those by Langdon Warner, *The Enduring Art of Japan* (New York: Grove Press, 1952), pp. 61–107; Hugo Munsterberg, *The Arts of Japan: An Illustrated History* (Rutland, Vt., and Tokyo: Charles E. Tuttle Co., 1962), pp. 125–142; Peter C. Swann, *Japan* (London: Methuen, 1966), pp. 162–179; Sherman E. Lee, *A History of Far Eastern Art* (New York: Harry N. Abrams, 1964), pp. 461–474; H. Batterson Boger, *The Traditional Arts of Japan: A Complete Illustrated Guide* (London: W. H. Allen and Co., 1964); Kageo Muraoka and Kichiemon Okamura, *Folk Arts and Crafts of Japan,* translated by Daphne D. Stegmaier (New York and Tokyo: Weatherhill/Heibonsha, 1973), volume 26 of the Heibonsha Survey of Japanese Art series; and *Momoyama Jidai no Kōgei: Handicrafts of the Momoyama Period,* edited by the Kyoto National Museum (Kyoto, 1977), in Japanese with English text. While still summary in character, the following works provide more illustrative detail: (1) *A Pictorial Encyclopedia of the Oriental Arts, Japan,* volume 3 (Tokyo: Kadokawa, 1968, and New York: Crown Publishers, 1969); (2) Seiroku Noma, *The Arts of Japan: Late Medieval to Modern,* volume 2, translated and adapted by Glenn T. Webb, photographs by Takahashi Bin (Tokyo and Palo Alto, Calif.: Kodansha International, 1967), 11–140, which is among the best treatments of its kind; (3) John M. Rosenfield and Shūjirō Shimada, *Traditions of Japanese Art: Selections from the Kimiko and John Powers Collection* (Cambridge, Mass.: Fogg Art Museum, Harvard University, 1970), pp. 225–267; (4) Shin'ichi Hisamatsu, *Zen and the Fine Arts,* translated by Gishin Tokiwa (Tokyo: Kodansha International, 1971), with emphasis primarily on painting, calligraphy, architecture, ikebana, gardens, crafts, and theater during various historical periods including the Momoyama; and (5) *Momoyama: Japanese Art in the Age of Grandeur* (New York: Metropolitan Museum of Art, 1975), a catalogue prepared for the exhibition of that name by Julia Meech-Pekarik and Andrew Pekarik and perhaps the best of its sort to appear, with sections on painting, calligraphy, Nō masks, textiles, ceramics, lacquer, arms, and armor.

With respect to particular forms of Japanese artistic expression during the Momoyama era, the first of four categories outlined here is that of architecture and gardens. While these might be examined independently of each other, they so frequently are conceived and belong together in Japan that it is natural to treat them in relationship. It is common knowledge that the three most typical expressions of Momoyama architecture were the castle, the residential structure in the *shoin* style, and the new *sukiya*-style teahouse. Gardens, of course, were intrinsic to the last two, though they were also important within the outer grounds of many castles. A number of works survey and illustrate the architectural styles of the sixteenth and early seventeenth century, but for the most reliable introduction one may refer to the following two: Robert Treat Paine and Alexander Soper, *The Art and Architecture of Japan* (Baltimore: Penguin Books, 1974, 2nd ed.), which covers both religious and secular architecture; and Alexander Coburn Soper, *The Evolution of Buddhist Architecture in Japan* (Princeton: Princeton University Press, 1942), pp. 273–296. A more elaborate treatment, with lavish illustrations, is that by John B. Kirby, Jr., *From Castle to Teahouse: Japanese Architecture of the Momoyama Period* (Rutland, Vt., and Tokyo: Charles E. Tuttle Co., 1962), which discusses the era's architectural styles and then examines the most important castles (Azuchi, Osaka, Fushimi, Nijō, Nagoya) as well as the imperial palaces and Hideyoshi's Juraku no Tei ("Palace of Pleasures"). On Azuchi Castle in particular, see Shun'ichi Takayanagi, "The Glory That Was Azuchi," *Monumenta Nipponica*, 32(4):515–524 (Winter 1977), a review article of "Azuchi-jō no kenkyū" by Naitō Akira (published in 1976 in *Kokka*, volume 83, nos. 987 and 988), a work to which George Elison and Carolyn Wheelwright refer extensively in this volume. Another interesting study, with excellent plates and line drawings, is by Kiyoshi Hirai, *Feudal Architecture of Japan*, translated by Hiroaki Sato and Jeannine Ciliotta (New York and Tokyo: Weatherhill/Heibonsha, 1973), volume 13 of the Heibonsha series, with chapters on castles, warrior residences, and the development of the *shoin* style, including discussion of primary examples of each. While dated, the well-known narrative by R. A. B. Ponsonby Fane, "Kiōto in the Momoyama Period," *Transactions and Proceedings of the Japan Society* (London), 24:75–170 (1927), later published as *Kyoto: Its History and Vicissitudes Since Its Foundation* (Hong Kong, 1931), is still informative. Finally, despite the fact that its coverage goes beyond the Momoyama period, the book by Naomi Okawa, *Edo Architecture: Katsura and Nikko,* translated by Alan Woodhull and Akito Miyamoto (New York and Tokyo: Weatherhill/Heibonsha, 1975), volume 20 of the Heibonsha series, is pertinent in that it depicts the dual heritage of the Momoyama and how it was itself the crystallization of earlier styles. Also, it is important to note that Prince Hachijō Toshihito (1579–1629), who built the Katsura villa, was strongly influenced by three figures whose mark upon Momoyama aesthetics was considerable, namely, Hosokawa Yūsai (1543–1610) in the literary arts, and Sen no Rikyū (1520–1591) and Furuta Oribe (1543–1615) in the art of tea.

If the Momoyama era is not the greatest epoch in the long history of Japanese gardens, it contributed at least two distinct styles. Lorraine Kuck's excellent book *The World of the Japanese Garden* (New York and Tokyo: John Weatherhill, 1968) discusses these in chapters titled "Gardens of Power and Glory: Kokei and Sambo-in," and "Tea Gardens: The Dewy Path." Again, in these two types one finds the opposite poles of Momoyama artistic inclination, the one which thrives on the near-rococo, and the other which delights in understatement. The aesthetic catholicity of the age managed to prize both extremes, with Nikkō and Katsura being the natural children of each in the succeeding generation. Beyond Kuck's brief depictions, one looks in vain for adequate coverage of Momoyama gardens. One may at least mention a number of good works which explore the many themes of diverse gardens in several periods of Japanese history. Some of the better ones would include Teiji Ito, *The Japanese Garden: An Approach to Nature* (New Haven and London: Yale University Press, 1972), with excellent plates by Takeji Iwamiya; Teiji Itoh, *Space and Illusion in the Japanese Garden,* translated and adapted by Ralph Friedrich and Masajiro Shimamura (New York, Tokyo, and Kyoto: Weatherhill/Tankosha, 1973), photographs by Sosei Kuzunishi; Kanto Shigemori, *Japanese Gardens: Islands of Serenity* (San Francisco and Tokyo: Japan Publications, 1971); Masao Hayakawa, *The Garden Art of Japan,* translated by Richard L. Gage (New York and Tokyo: Weatherhill/Heibonsha, 1973), volume 28 of the Heibonsha series; Jiro Harada, *Japanese Gardens* (Boston: Charles T. Branford, 1956), pp. 48–62; and Gouverneur Mosher, *Kyoto: A Contemplative Guide* (Rutland, Vt., and Tokyo: Charles E. Tuttle Co., 1964), pp. 148–160 and 279–294, on Daigoji and Sanbōin during the days of Hideyoshi.

In the field of painting, the three dominant types were genre painting, decorative screens, and Nanban art, again attesting to the immense variety of subject matter and sources of inspiration. While genre painting may be traced back to the Heian period, it was only in the late Muromachi and afterwards that the manners and customs of a wide spectrum of the population, particularly reflecting the rise of the merchant class and the *chōnin* more generally, began to appear prominently as an important focus of art. It was this form which issued eventually in the long popular ukiyo-e during the mid-Tokugawa times. While the Momoyama expressions of this have not been extensively written about in Western languages, one may consult Yuzo Yamane, *Momoyama Genre Painting,* translated by John M. Shields (New York and Tokyo: Weatherhill/Heibonsha, 1973), volume 17 of the Heibonsha series, which provides an interesting discussion of *Rakuchū-Rakugai-zu* (Scenes in and around the capital); and Ichitaro Kondo, *Japanese Genre Painting: The Lively Art of Renaissance Japan,* translated by Roy Andrew Miller (Rutland, Vt., and Tokyo: Charles E. Tuttle Co., 1961).

The most noteworthy painting of the period is, of course, associated with decorative screens. If anything can be cited as typically, if not uniquely, Momoyama, this would be it. As castles were not only a new mode of protection against new strategies of warfare but also important status symbols, so huge and lavish and brilliantly colored screens conformed to the scope, expansiveness, and majesty of newly achieved authority on a grand scale. Where ideology had dominated in the legitimation of power earlier, artistic patronage and surroundings of extravagant beauty now attested to one's position in the feudal scheme of things. This is not to imply that objects of beauty were not relished for their own sake, but beauty always serves many ends beyond itself. The literature on this form of art is fuller than that on genre paintings. One may be again referred to Paine and Soper, *Art and Architecture,* pp. 92–102; to Cole, *Kyoto in the Momoyama Period,* pp. 123–143; and especially to the *Momoyama* catalogue published by the Metropolitan Museum of Art (1975). Beyond this, the following are of value: (1) Miyeko Murase, *Byōbu: Japanese Screens from New York Collections* (New York: Asia Society, 1971); (2) Miyeko Murase, *Japanese Art: Selections from the Mary and Jackson Burke Collection* (New York: Metropolitan Museum of Art, 1975), pp. 145–179; (3) Tsugiyoshi Doi, *Momoyama Decorative Painting,* translated by Edna B. Crawford (New York and Tokyo: Weatherhill/ Heibonsha, 1977), volume 14 of the Heibonsha series, which is among the best overall treatments of an introductory nature; (4) Takematsu Haruyama, "Screen Paintings of the Momoyama Period," *Japan Quarterly,* 9(1):41–49 (January–March 1962), which describes briefly the four great figures: Kano Eitoku (1543–1590), Kano Sanraku (1559–1635), Kaihō Yūshō (1533–1615), and Hasegawa Tōhaku (1538–1610); (5) Glenn T. Webb, "Japanese Scholarship behind Momoyama Painting circa 1500–1700 as Seen in the Light of a Stylistic Reexamination of the Nature of Chinese Influence on Kano Painters and Some of Their Contemporaries" (University of Chicago, Ph.D. dissertation, 1970, available from University Microfilms); (6) Tsuneo Takeda, *Kanō Eitoku* (Tokyo, New York, and San Francisco: Kodansha International and Shibundo, 1977), translated and adapted by H. Mack Horton and Catherine Kaputa, which examines in a summary fashion the Kano school, focusing on Kano Eitoku (1543–1590), the circle around him (especially Shōei and Sōshū), and Eitoku's son Mitsunobu (1561–1608); (7) Gail Capitol Weigl, "Foundations of a Momoyama Theme: Birds and Flowers of the Four Seasons in a Landscape," 2 vols. (University of Michigan, Ph.D. dissertation, 1976, available from University Microfilms), which focuses on Kano Motonobu (1476–1559), whose work laid the foundations for Momoyama screen painting, and on the way in which Japanese artists "synthesized heterogeneous Chinese traditions of monochrome landscapes and polychrome bird and flower paintings" as well as integrated themes and techniques drawn from both Chinese and Japanese sources; (8) Akiyama Terukazu, *Japanese Painting* (Switzerland: Albert Skira, 1961), pp. 123–180; (9) Takaaki Matsushita, *Ink Painting,* translated and adapted with an introduction by Martin Collcutt (New York and Tokyo: Weatherhill/Shibundo, 1974), no. 7, Arts of Japan Series, pp. 121–137; (10) Bernard Leach, *Kenzan and His Tradition: The Lives of Koetsu, Sotatsu, Korin and Kenzan* (London: Faber and Faber, 1966), pp. 11–68, on Hon'ami Kōetsu (1558–1637) and Tawaraya Sōtatsu (c. 1560–1643); (11) Hiroshi Mizuo, *Edo Painting: Sotatsu and Korin,* translated by John M. Shields (New York and Tokyo: Weatherhill/Heibonsha, 1972), volume 18 of the Heibonsha series; and (12) Shuichi Kato, *Form,*

Style, Tradition: Reflections on Japanese Art and Society, translated by John Bester (Berkeley, Los Angeles, and London: University of California Press, 1971), pp. 137–150.

Nanban art is another distinguishing mark of the Momoyama period. While brief in duration, it was Japan's first taste of art influenced by Western themes and styles. Several interesting studies of this subject are available. Perhaps the most thorough on certain aspects is the doctoral dissertation by Grace Alida Hermine Vlam, "Western Style Secular Painting in Momoyama Japan," 2 vols. (University of Michigan, 1976), which examines both the didactic function and the aesthetic quality of this type of painting up to 1614, under the groupings of Europeans in landscape, kings and heroes, equestrians, the battle of Lepanto, world and city maps, and portraits from Daruma to Xavier. Vlam has adapted a portion of her dissertation in the article "Kings and Heroes: Western-Style Painting in Momoyama Japan," *Artibus Asiae,* 39:220–250 (1978). Other studies which merit citing are: John E. McCall, "Early Jesuit Art in the Far East," *Artibus Asiae,* 10:121–137, 216–233, 283–301 (1947); 11:45–69 (1948); 17:39–54 (1954); Kenji Toda, "The Effects of the First Great Impact of Western Culture in Japan: Illustrated by the Study of the Introduction of the Western Form of Pictorial Art," *Journal of World History,* 2(2):429–445 (1954); Fernando G. Gutiérrez SJ, "A Survey of Nanban Art," in *The Southern Barbarians: The First Europeans in Japan,* edited by Michael Cooper SJ (see above), which discusses religious and secular paintings, *Nanban byōbu* or Southern Barbarian screens, and nonpictorial art (metalwork, lacquer ware and ceramics); *Namban Art: A Loan Exhibition from Japanese Collections,* compiled by Shin'ichi Tani and Tadashi Sugase (International Exhibitions Foundation, 1973), which is the catalogue of an exhibition shown in three leading American galleries in 1973; and Yoshitomo Okamoto, *The Namban Art of Japan,* translated by Ronald K. Jones (New York and Tokyo: Weatherhill/Heibonsha, 1972), volume 19 of the Heibonsha series, which has been described by C. R. Boxer as "a most satisfying introduction for those who come fresh to the subject, and a welcome reminder for those who are already familiar with it." Boxer's words might, in fact, be used for each of the Heibonsha volumes.

The tea ceremony *(cha-no-yu)* and the arts associated with it (architecture, gardens, hanging scrolls, ikebana, ceramics) were at the heart of Momoyama culture. While the history of the Japanese cult of tea *(chadō* or *sadō)* goes back to the Heian period, as H. Paul Varley shows in this volume, it was in the sixteenth century that *chadō* reached the stage of refinement which enabled it to permeate broad sectors of cultural life. One of the earliest Western commentators on this development was the important Jesuit figure João Rodrigues Tçuzzu, who discusses "Cha, and this ceremony so highly esteemed among the Japanese" in pt. 1, chaps. 32–35 of his *História da Igreja do Japão:* see volume 1, pp. 437–507 of the edition by João do Amaral Abranches Pinto (cited above). Michael Cooper SJ provides an elegant English translation of these chapters in *This Island of Japon* (cited above), pp. 250–296; and José Luis Alvarez-Taladriz presents them in a Spanish translation, endowed with copious notes, under the title *Arte del Cha*, Monumenta Nipponica Monographs, no. 14 (Tokyo: Sophia University Press, 1954). Evidence that the way of tea was not peripheral to life in the times of Nobunaga and Hideyoshi may be found in many works, but one of the better brief accounts is by Beatrice M. Bodart, "Tea and Council: The Political Role of Sen Rikyū," *Monumenta Nipponica,* 32(1):49–74 (Spring 1977). Among the more helpful treatments in English are the following: (1) A. L. Sadler, *Cha-no-yu: The Japanese Tea Ceremony* (Rutland, Vt., and Tokyo: Charles E. Tuttle Co., 1963, reprint of the 1933 edition), which discusses the ceremony, its regulations, and the most prominent tea masters and their schools; (2) Tatsusaburo Hayashiya, Masao Nakamura, and Seizo Hayashiya, *Japanese Arts and the Tea Ceremony,* translated and adapted by Joseph P. Macadam (New York and Tokyo: Weatherhill/Heibonsha, 1974), volume 15 of the Heibonsha series, among the best introductions to the subject; (3) Rand Castile, *The Way of Tea* (New York and Tokyo: John Weatherhill, 1971), an excellent treatment, with chapters on the Way of Tea, the history of the ceremony, the tea setting, the utensils used, and the practices of tea; (4) Daisetz T. Suzuki, *Zen and Japanese Culture* (New York: Pantheon Books, 1959), pp. 271–328, where the influence of Zen on the art of tea is, however, excessively stressed; (5) Kakuzo Okakura, *The Book of Tea* (New York: Dover Publications, 1964; another edition was published by Charles E. Tuttle, Rutland, Vt., and Tokyo, 1956), a popular, sentimental, and not too reliable account; (6) Theodore M. Ludwig, "The Way of Tea: A Religio-Aesthetic Mode of Life," *History of Religions,* 14(1):28–50 (August 1974), which discusses Sen no Rikyū in a perceptive manner; (7) Shin'ichi Hisamatsu, "The Nature of 'Sado' Culture," translated by Patrick Macgill James and Abe Masao, *Eastern Buddhist,* n.s., 3(2):9–19 (October 1970); (8) Makoto Ueda, *Literary and Art Theo-*

ries in Japan (Cleveland: The Press of Western Reserve University, 1967), pp. 87–100, on Sen no Rikyū; (9) Shuichi Kato, *Form, Style, Tradition* (see above), pp. 151–163; and (10) *Chanoyu Quarterly: Tea and the Arts of Japan,* published in Kyoto in English, 1970–.

Inseparable from the cult of tea is the high value put upon the utensils used. This was probably more true in the Momoyama period than in any other, though its standards set the pattern for succeeding generations. Several brief studies of tea ware and especially of ceramics are available. See Ryōichi Fujioka et al., *Tea Ceremony Utensils,* translated and adapted with an introduction by Louise Allison Cort (New York and Tokyo: Weatherhill/Shibundo, 1973), Arts of Japan Series, 3, with the focus primarily on the period 1475–1650; Fujio Koyama, *The Heritage of Japanese Ceramics,* translated and adapted by John Figgess, with an introduction by John Alexander Pope (New York, Tokyo, and Kyoto: Weatherhill/ Tankosha, 1973), pp. 69–126 and 149–171, on the relationship between the tea ceremony and the flowering of the ceramic tradition; Tsugio Mikami, *The Art of Japanese Ceramics,* translated by Ann Herring (New York and Tokyo: Weatherhill/Heibonsha, 1972), volume 29 of the Heibonsha series, pp. 57–64 and 126–158, on Raku, Old Karatsu, Oribe, and Shino ware, and on the flowering of this tradition in the latter part of the sixteenth century and the first half of the seventeenth; Ryōichi Fujioka, *Shino and Oribe Ceramics* (New York: Kodansha International, 1977); Johanna Lucille Becker, "The Karatsu Ceramics of Japan: Origins, Fabrication, and Types," 2 vols. (University of Michigan, Ph.D. dissertation, 1974, available from University Microfilms), which focuses on the late sixteenth through the mid- seventeenth century and shows that the influence of Korean potters was more on techniques and materials used than on style; and Hugo Munsterberg, *The Ceramic Art of Japan: A Handbook for Collectors* (Rutland, Vt., and Tokyo: Charles E. Tuttle Co., 1964), pp. 99–134, with text and illustrations of Momoyama tea ware.

The final area of Momoyama culture to be considered in this essay includes poetic and dramatic literature, and the theater more broadly. Compared with other periods in Japanese history, this one is less noteworthy from a literary standpoint. The primary exception lies in the continuation of the *renga* or linked verse tradition and its development into haiku poetry *(haikai no renga),* which became exceedingly rich and influential in the seventeenth and eighteenth centuries. A comprehensive study of *renga* and *haikai* has recently become available, for the first time in a Western language, with the appearance of Earl Miner's *Japanese Linked Poetry: An Account with Translations of Renga and Haikai Sequences* (Princeton: Princeton University Press, 1978). An essay by Donald Keene titled "The Comic Tradition in Renga," in *Japan in the Muromachi Age,* edited by John Whitney Hall and Toyoda Takeshi (see above), traces that tradition's growth especially from the fourteenth through the early sixteenth century. In his book *World Within Walls: Japanese Literature of the Pre-modern Era, 1600–1867* (New York: Holt, Rinehart and Winston, 1976), pp. 11–39, Keene examines the beginnings of *haikai no renga* (comic linked verse) and the creation of *haikai* poetry especially under the influence of Matsunaga Teitoku (1571–1653). This may be supplemented by Jin'ichi Konishi, "The Art of Renga," *Journal of Japanese Studies,* 2(1):29–61 (Autumn 1975), translated and with an introduction by Karen Brazell and Lewis Cook; and by Howard S. Hibbett, "The Japanese Comic Linked-Verse Tradition,". *Harvard Journal of Asiatic Studies,* 23:76–92 (1960–1961). Of historical interest is an article by Michael Cooper SJ, "The Muse Described: João Rodrigues' Account of Japanese Poetry," *Monumenta Nipponica,* 26(1/2):55–75 (1971), which discusses and is a translation of the section on poetry in Rodrigues' *Arte da Lingoa de Japam* (1608). An important correction to the tendency to accent the more elitist type of literature to the relative neglect of other literary forms is the essay by Barbara Ruch, "Medieval Jongleurs and the Making of a National Literature," in Hall and Toyoda, *Japan in the Muromachi Age,* where she discusses the significance of "vocal literature" during the Muromachi era as a developing literature which combined art (picture scrolls), music, and the printed word, and which contributed eventually to the growth of Kabuki and other dramatic forms. See also James T. Araki, *The Ballad-Drama of Medieval Japan* (Berkeley: University of California Press, 1964).

When one turns to developments in Japanese theater during this period, one finds it to be an exceedingly important era. Not only was Nō still vital, but it was joined by newer forms of dramatic presentation which entered the Japanese scene and became permanent features of the theater arts. These forms were Kabuki and Bunraku, which like genre painting extended the vistas of what was portrayed and also captured a wider audience. The age of the emerging *chōnin* and the spread of commerce-dominated urban culture brought about significant innovations in the whole area of entertainment. One place to begin a study of this is Leonard C. Pronko's *Guide to Japanese Drama* (Boston: G. K. Hall & Co., 1973), an annotated bibliography of criticism, anthologies, and texts dealing with Nō, Kyōgen, Kabuki, and Bunraku. Short treatments pertinent to the Momoyama period are provided by Faubion Bowers, *Japanese Theatre* (New York: Hill and Wang, 1952), pp. 3–51, on the historical origins and development of Japanese theater and on the early stages of Kabuki, especially its emergence out of the *Nenbutsu odori* of Okuni in the late sixteenth century; by Andrew T. Tsubaki, "The Performing Arts of Sixteenth-Century Japan: A Prelude to Kabuki," *Educational Theatre Journal*, 29(3):299–309 (October 1977); and by Yasuo Nakamura, *Noh: The Classical Theatre*, translated by Don Kenny, with an introduction by Earle Ernst (New York, Tokyo, and Kyoto: Walker/Weatherhill/Tankosha, 1971), pp. 125–136, on Hideyoshi and Nō, and on the birth of the Kita School. A much fuller discussion is given by Yoshinobu Inoura, *A History of Japanese Theatre: Noh and Kyogen* (Tokyo: Japan Cultural Society, 1971). Among the best works on the topic is Donald Keene's *Nō: The Classical Theatre of Japan* (Tokyo and Palo Alto: Kodansha International, 1966), with photographs by Kaneko Hiroshi and an introduction by Ishikawa Jun. This volume is handsomely illustrated and has very helpful chapters on the history of Nō and Kyōgen, their literature, the background of the performances, the music and dance in the plays, the Nō stage and its properties, and the main figures and schools in Nō history.

Several studies on Kabuki are also available to the nonspecialist. While essentially treating the post-Momoyama period, the volume by Earle Ernst titled *The Kabuki Theatre* (New York: Oxford University Press, 1956) is a basic work. According to tradition, Kabuki was first performed in Kyoto in 1596, but it was during the Tokugawa period that its distinctive forms were developed. Donald Keene traces the sixteenth-century beginnings of Kabuki and Jōruri (later known as Bunraku) on pages 230–243 of his *World Within Walls*, cited above. A good survey of how these two new forms of theater emerged and grew may be found in Toshio Kawatake, *A History of Japanese Theatre: Bunraku and Kabuki* (Tokyo: Japan Cultural Society, 1971), pp. 1–95. A splendid introduction is Masakatsu Gunji's *Kabuki* (Tokyo and Palo Alto: Kodansha International, 1969), with photographs by Chiaki Yoshida, an introduction by Donald Keene, and translation by John Bester. This is another extremely well illustrated volume, with chapters on the spirit of Kabuki, its history from the mid-sixteenth century up to modern times, the principal Kabuki actors, plays, and playwrights, the production and performances of the plays, its theater and stage machinery, and its audiences and performances. See also Benito Ortolani SJ, "Okuni-Kabuki und Onna-Kabuki," *Monumenta Nipponica*, 17:161–213 (1962), on the earliest stages of this dramatic form. For the study of Bunraku, two other books are of importance. One is C. J. Dunn, *The Early Japanese Puppet Drama* (London: Luzac and Company, 1966), especially pages 1–41 on Jōruri, or narrative recitation, which at the end of the sixteenth century was joined with samisen music and the use of puppets to create what later became known as Bunraku. Perhaps the best study is Donald Keene's *Bunraku: The Art of the Japanese Puppet Theatre* (Tokyo: Kodansha International, 1965), with photographs by Kaneko Hiroshi and an introduction by Tanizaki Jun'ichirō. This volume, as also the ones published by Kodansha on Nō and Kabuki, is beautifully conceived and illustrated. It is an indispensable graphic treatment of the subject.

Finally, brief mention must be made of works dealing with Japanese music and the costume arts, as these are of fundamental importance in all theatrical performances. One noteworthy volume on Japanese music is by William Malm, *Japanese Music and Musical Instruments* (Rutland, Vt., and Tokyo: Charles E. Tuttle Co., 1959), in which Malm shows how a breakthrough occurred in Japanese music during the Momoyama period due to new developments within Nō drama, to the introduction of the *jamisen* (a three-stringed guitar which later evolved into the samisen), to improvements in musical construction (for example, the early bamboo recorder became the *shakuhachi* and the old court cithern became the koto), and to the art of drum-making, which was raised to a high level. Another volume with some attention to Momoyama times is Eta Harich-Schneider, *A History of Japanese Music* (London: Oxford University Press, 1973), pp. 445–486 and parts of pp. 487–529. Two publications on costume art are germane: Seiroku Noma, *Japanese Costume and Textile Arts*, translated by Armins Nikovskis (New York and Tokyo: Weatherhill/Heibonsha, 1974), volume 16 of the Heibonsha series; and Helen Benton Minnich, in collaboration with Shojiro Nomura, *Japanese Costume and the Makers of Its Elegant Tradition* (Rutland, Vt., and Tokyo: Charles E. Tuttle Co., 1963), pp. 171–187, with illustrations.

Contributors

GEORGE ELISON, Associate Professor of East Asian Languages and Cultures and of History at Indiana University, has been a visiting member of the faculties of Harvard University and Kyoto University. He is the author of *Deus Destroyed: The Image of Christianity in Early Modern Japan* (1973). While retaining an interest in the "Christian Century," he has recently directed more of his attention to other aspects of late medieval and early modern Japanese history, and is now at work on a study of the career of Oda Nobunaga.

JOHN WHITNEY HALL is Alfred Whitney Griswold Professor of History at Yale University. Among his published works are: *Government and Local Power in Japan, 500–1700: A Study Based on Bizen Province* (1966); *Studies in the Institutional History of Early Modern Japan* (with Marius B. Jansen, 1968); *Japan: From Prehistory to Modern Times* (1970); *Medieval Japan: Essays in Institutional History* (with Jeffrey P. Mass, 1974); *Japan in the Muromachi Age* (with Toyoda Takeshi, 1977); and *Japan Before Tokugawa: Political Consolidation and Economic Growth, 1500 to 1650* (with Nagahara Keiji and Kozo Yamamura, 1980).

FRANK HOFF, Associate Professor at the University of Toronto, is a specialist in Japan's performing arts. His strong interest in the Japanese song tradition is reflected in the titles of his published works, which include *The Genial Seed: A Japanese Song Cycle* (1971) and *Song, Dance, Storytelling: Aspects of the Performing Arts in Japan* (1978). He has undertaken the making of several films which document traditional Japanese dance types, and has accompanied Japanese performers on tours abroad in the capacity of an interpreter of their art.

DONALD KEENE, Professor of Japanese at Columbia University, is the author of numerous books and articles on Japanese literature and theater, and the translator of works of both classical and modern Japanese literature. His publications include: *Japanese Literature: An Introduction for Western Readers* (1953); *The Japanese Discovery of Europe* (1969, revised edition); *Landscapes and Portraits* (1971); and *World Within Walls* (1976), a volume in his projected four-volume history of Japanese literature. He edited *Anthology of Japanese Literature* (1955) and *Modern Japanese Literature* (1956). He has also published collections of essays written originally in Japanese.

WILLIAM P. MALM, Professor of Musicology at the University of Michigan, directs a Japanese music performance group at his university and is a frequent guest lecturer on Asian music and on ethnomusicology. He is the author of the books *Japanese Music and Musical Instruments* (1959), *Nagauta: The Heart of Kabuki Music* (1963), and *Music Cultures of the Pacific, the Near East, and Asia* (1977, second edition), as well as of many articles or chapters in other publications, including *Studies in Kabuki: Its Acting, Music, and Historical Context* (with James R. Brandon and Donald H. Shively, 1978).

V. DIXON MORRIS, Associate Professor of History and Director of the World Civilization Program at the University of Hawaii at Manoa, is a specialist in medieval and early modern Japan. His studies of the history of the city of Sakai, the subject of his doctoral dissertation at the University of Washington (1970) and of essays he has published in this volume and elsewhere, have led him to develop a strong interest in one of that medieval city's cultural predilections, the tea ceremony, which he expects to be a major area of his future research.

BARDWELL L. SMITH, John W. Nason Professor of Asian Studies at Carleton College, has also served Carleton as Dean of the College and his alma mater Yale as a member of the Yale University Council. He has edited a number of books on Asian religion and society, the most recent of them being: *Unsui: A Diary of Zen Monastic Life* (1973); *Hinduism: New Essays in the History of Religions* (1976); *Religion and Social Conflict in South Asia* (1976); *Essays on T'ang Society* (with John Curtis Perry, 1976); *Religion and Legitimation of Power in Sri Lanka* (1978); *Religion and Legitimation of Power in Thailand, Laos, and Burma* (1978); and *Religion and the Legitimation of Power in South Asia* (1978).

H. PAUL VARLEY, Professor of Japanese History at Columbia University, is a specialist in medieval Japan. He is the author of *The Ōnin*

War (1967), *The Samurai* (1970), *Imperial Restoration in Medieval Japan* (1971), *A Syllabus of Japanese Civilization* (1972, second edition), and *Japanese Culture: A Short History* (1977, expanded edition). His most recent work, *A Chronicle of Gods and Sovereigns* (1980), is a study and translation of the classic imperial loyalist history *Jinnō shōtōki* by the fourteenth-century poet, polemicist, and politician Kitabatake Chikafusa.

CAROLYN WHEELWRIGHT, an art historian specializing in late medieval and early modern Japan, teaches at Yale University. Her Princeton University doctoral dissertation treats Kano Shōei, a sixteenth-century painter long overshadowed by the eminence of his son Eitoku, the subject of her contribution to this volume. She edited *Japanese Ink Paintings* (with Yoshiaki Shimizu, 1976), the catalogue of an exhibition held in honor of the retirement of her professor, Shūjirō Shimada.

Notes

INTRODUCTION: JAPAN IN THE SIXTEENTH CENTURY

1. Go-Kashiwabara (1464–1526) acceded to the throne on 16 November 1500 (Meiō 9/10/25), but his formal enthronement could not be held until 28 April 1521 (Eishō 18/3/22).

2. Ashikaga Yoshitaka (1480–1511), installed as shogun on 23 January 1495 (Meiō 3/12/27), changed his name to Yoshizumi in 1502 (Bunki 2/7/21), fled Kyoto at the news of his cousin the antishogun's approach in May 1508 (Eishō 5/4/16), and died in exile in Ōmi province. His rival Yoshitada (1466–1523), known as the "Kyushu shogun" when he reappeared in the capital and was reinvested on 28 July 1508 (Eishō 5/7/1), bore the name Yoshiki during his first term in Kyoto (1490–1493) and until he changed it in 1498 (Meiō 7/8/19); he changed it again, to Yoshitane, in 1513 (Eishō 10/11/9), fled Kyoto in disgust at his *kanrei* (executive officer) Hosokawa Takakuni's wilfulness in April 1521 (Eishō 18/3/7), and after a frustrated attempt at a comeback died in Awa province on Shikoku. Dates according to *Shiryō sōran,* comp. Tōkyō Daigaku Shiryō Hensanjo, vol. 9 (Tokyo: Tōkyō Daigaku Shuppankai, 1965 reissue).

3. The comment is about Asakura Sadakage. *Nobutane-kyō ki,* 2, Zōho Shiryō Taisei 45 (Kyoto: Rinsen Shoten, 1965), 83; entry for Eishō 1/12/9 (14 January 1505).

4. See Matsunaga Teitoku, *Taionki,* ed. Odaka Toshio, in *Taionki, Oritaku shiba no ki, Rantō kotohajime,* Nihon Koten Bungaku Taikei 95 (Tokyo: Iwanami, 1974, eighth printing), p. 83: "uta renga / nuruki mono zo to / iu hito no / azusa yumiya o / toritaru mo nashi"—to the effect that a man who calls poetry and linked verse dull or effeminate can never yet have taken up a bow and arrow.

5. See Niccolò Machiavelli, *The Prince,* ch. 18.

JAPAN'S SIXTEENTH-CENTURY REVOLUTION

1. Original research on sixteenth-century Japan until recently has been the exclusive domain of Japanese historians. Of late, however, a sufficient number of books and articles have appeared in Western languages, either as translations of Japanese

works or as original writings by Western specialists, so that I have confined my note citations to Western-language sources.

2. For an interpretation of the Taika Reform in this vein, see my *Government and Local Power in Japan, 500-1700: A Study Based on Bizen Province* (Princeton: Princeton University Press, 1966), pp. 60-65.

3. The most recent, and in many ways the standard treatment of the Meiji Restoration is W. G. Beasley, *The Meiji Restoration* (Stanford: Stanford University Press, 1972); see particularly pp. 406-424.

4. For a schematic treatment of the evolution of the daimyo domains, see my "Foundations of the Modern Japanese Daimyo," in *Studies in the Institutional History of Early Modern Japan*, ed. John W. Hall and Marius B. Jansen (Princeton: Princeton University Press, 1968), pp. 65-77.

5. For a description of peasant and religious *ikki*, see David L. Davis, "*Ikki* in Late Medieval Japan," in *Medieval Japan: Essays in Institutional History*, ed. John W. Hall and Jeffrey P. Mass (New Haven: Yale University Press, 1974), pp. 221-247. For *ikki* among local samurai, see Kawai Masaharu with Kenneth A. Grossberg, "Shogun and Shugo: The Provincial Aspects of Muromachi Politics," in *Japan in the Muromachi Age*, ed. John W. Hall and Toyoda Takeshi (Berkeley: University of California Press, 1977), pp. 65-86.

6. Hall, *Government and Local Power*, pp. 271-295.

7. Nagahara Keiji with Kozo Yamamura, "Village Communities and Daimyo Power," in *Japan in the Muromachi Age*, pp. 107-123.

8. Convenient translations of several of the basic documents illustrating Hideyoshi's policies may be found in David John Lu, *Sources of Japanese History*, 1 (New York: McGraw-Hill, 1974), 185-190.

9. For a study of the land surveys based on recent Japanese scholarship, see Guy Moréchand, " 'Taiko Kenchi': le cadastre de Hideyoshi Toyotomi," *Bulletin de l'Ecole Française de l'Extrême-Orient*, 53(1):7-69 (1966).

10. Jeffrey P. Mass, "*Jitō* Land Possession in the Thirteenth Century: The Case of *Shitaji Chūbun*," in *Medieval Japan*, pp. 157-183.

11. An example of how this happened in practice is described in John W. Hall, "The Ikeda House and Its Retainers," in *Studies in the Institutional History of Early Modern Japan*, pp. 85-86.

12. Wakita Osamu, "The *Kokudaka* System: A Device for Unification," *The Journal of Japanese Studies*, 1(2):287-320 (Spring 1975).

13. Nagahara & Yamamura, "Village Communities," p. 123, citing the use by daimyo of the concept of *kōgi* (public good) as a way of expressing their claim to political authority.

THE CITY OF SAKAI AND URBAN AUTONOMY

1. Hara Katsurō, "Ashikaga jidai ni okeru Sakai-kō," *Shigaku zasshi*, 7(10):10-27 (October 1896).

2. Takao Kazuhiko, "Kyōto, Sakai, Hakata," *Iwanami kōza: Nihon rekishi*, 9 (*Kinsei* 1; Tokyo: Iwanami, 1963), 127. Takao cites several of the Jesuit relations, beginning with Vilela's Venetian analogy, found in his letter to the Irmãos (Brothers) of the Society of Jesus in India, dated Sacáy, 17 August 1561, *CARTAS QVE OS PADRES E IRMÃOS da Companhia de Iesus escreuerão dos Reynos de*

Iapão & *China aos da mesma Companhia da India,* & *Europa, des do anno de 1549. atè o de 1580.* (Em Euora por Manoel de Lyra. Anno de M.D.XCVIII.), 1, 90; also Vilela to Padres and Irmãos SJ, Sakai, 1562, ibid., 1, 113; Vilela to Padres and Irmãos SJ in Portugal, dated Miàco (Kyoto), 15 July 1564, ibid., 1, 141v–142; Vilela to P. Cosme de Torres SJ, dated Imóri (Iimori in Kawachi), 2 August 1565, ibid., 1, 190v; and P. Gaspar Coelho SJ to General SJ, *annua* for 1581, Nagasaki, 15 February 1582, ibid., 2, [45; misnumbered 35].

3.   Directive addressed to the Shōkokuji priory Sūjuin, signed by the shogunate's *bugyōnin* (administrators) Hizen no Kami [Iinoo Tametane] and Yamato no Kami [Iinoo Sadatsura], dated Eikyō 3 (1431)/11/8; "Gozen rakkyo hōsho," in *Sakai-shi shi,* ed. Sakai Shiyakusho, 4 (Sakai: Sakai Shiyakusho, 1930), 130. *Sakai-shi shi* is cited hereafter as *SSS.*

4.   *SSS,* 1, 353–354.

5.   See *Onryōken nichiroku, Dai Nihon Bukkyō zensho,* 133 (Tokyo: Bussho Kankōkai, 1912), 241, entry for Chōroku 3/12/26 (19 January 1460); 292, Kanshō 2 (1461)/2/25; 314, Kanshō 2/9/27; 332, Kanshō 3/2/9; 361, Kanshō 3/8/19; 368, Kanshō 3/9/27; 370, Kanshō 3/10/5 and 10.

6.   The shrine held the *jitō-shiki* and the *ryōke-shiki* (rights as steward and proprietor). Toyoda Takeshi, *Sakai: shōnin no shinshutsu to toshi no jiyū,* Nihon Rekishi Shinsho (Tokyo: Shibundō, 1957, second printing), p. 6; also see *SSS,* 1, 188.

7.   *Onryōken nichiroku,* 134, 555, entry for Kanshō 6 (1465)/8/24; 580–581, Kanshō 6/12/17 (3 January 1466).

8.   Harada Tomohiko, "Jūroku-seiki no jiyū toshi: Sakai no rekishi to sono haikei ni tsuite no oboegaki," *Rekishi hyōron,* 4(5):6–20 (May 1950). For an account of village developments generally, and autonomy specifically, see Nagahara Keiji with Kozo Yamamura, "Village Communities and Daimyo Power," in *Japan in the Muromachi Age,* ed. John Whitney Hall and Toyoda Takeshi (Berkeley: University of California Press, 1977), pp. 107–123.

9.   Ishida Yoshihito, "Gōsonsei no keisei," *Iwanami kōza: Nihon rekishi,* 8 (*Chūsei* 4; 1963), 49.

10.   Ibid., p. 54.

11.   Ibid., p. 55. See pp. 37–40 for a discussion of the different schools of thought on the Japanese village system. I follow Ishida in identifying village leadership as *myōshu.* For a discussion of *miyaza* in villages around Sakai, see *Sakai-shi shi zokuhen,* 1, ed. Kobata Atsushi (Sakai: Sakai Shiyakusho, 1971), 383–388.

12.   Edwin O. Reischauer and John K. Fairbank, *East Asia: The Great Tradition* (Boston: Houghton Mifflin, 1960), p. 576.

13.   Ishida, "Gōsonsei no keisei," p. 73.

14.   Harada Tomohiko, *Chūsei ni okeru toshi no kenkyū* (Tokyo: San'ichi Shobō, 1972 reprint), pp. 113–114. Harada maintains that medieval cities were merely agglomerations of villages in the beginning, and so stood in the village tradition of administration, though the subsequent development of the two followed different routes.

15.   *Yajishi* and *zaikejishi* were new terms for rents on urbanized land, and *munebechisen* and *kenbechisen* were taxes on structures.

16.   E. S. Crawcour, "Changes in Japanese Commerce in the Tokugawa Period," *Journal of Asian Studies,* 22(4):388 (August 1963); reprinted in *Studies in the Institutional History of Early Modern Japan,* ed. John W. Hall and Marius B. Jan-

sen (Princeton: Princeton University Press, 1968), p. 190. *Seishō*, "political merchants," is the name applied to such merchants by Izumi Chōichi, *Hakata to Sakai: Sengoku no gōshō* (Osaka: Sōgensha, 1976), p. 6.

17. Harada, *Chūsei ni okeru toshi*, pp. 106–107 and 123–125; Toyoda Takeshi, *Nihon no hōken toshi*, Iwanami Zensho 160 (Tokyo: Iwanami, 1952), pp. 68–69.

18. Toyoda, ibid., pp. 71–72.

19. The castle towns appeared so late that they need not be considered in this connection. Most were products of the Edo period.

20. Kyoto, for example, was governed by *gachigyōji; toshiyori* headed such cities as Ōmachi in Shinano, the *monzen-machi* of Itsukushima Shrine, Hiraimachi in Musashi, and Hirano in Settsu. Ōminato's council had ten members, while others had as few as six or as many as thirty-six. These and other examples may be found in Harada, *Chūsei ni okeru toshi*, pp. 106–111.

21. Toyoda, *Nihon no hōken toshi*, p. 76.

22. V. Dixon Morris, "Sakai: From Shōen to Port City," in *Japan in the Muromachi Age*, pp. 154–155. This article (pp. 145–158) describes the origins and early development of Sakai to the sixteenth century.

23. It is difficult to document Sakai's involvement in interdomanial trade until late in the sixteenth century, and it was probably quite limited even then because of the degree of self-sufficiency in the economy. See Sasaki Gin'ya, "Chūsei toshi to shōhin ryūtsū," *Iwanami kōza: Nihon rekishi*, 8 (*Chūsei* 4; 1963), 151–154.

24. G. B. Sansom, *The Western World and Japan* (New York: Alfred A. Knopf, 1958), p. 312 and p. 446. The committee that coined *minken* as a translation for *droit civil* at first could not agree among themselves on the meaning, for some maintained that the terms were mutually contradictory.

25. See *Tamon'in nikki*, ed. Tsuji Zennosuke (Tokyo: Kadokawa, 1967):3, 17, entries for Tenshō 6 (1578)/6/23–24; 3, 20, Tenshō 6/7/5; 3, 34, Tenshō 6/11/9; 4, 2, Tenshō 14 (1586)/1/6; 4, 251, Tenshō 18/8/11; 4, 468–469, Bunroku 3 (1594)/11/5 and 9. The term appeared in Sakai before the time of these entries, but the *egō* of the Kōfukuji, to which the *Tamon'in nikki* refers, probably had a long history by the time Eishun started compiling his diary. Cf. Toyoda, *Sakai*, p. 67.

26. *Shoken nichiroku, Dai Nihon kokiroku*, ed. Tōkyō Daigaku Shiryō Hensanjo, 6 (Tokyo: Iwanami, 1953), 24; entry for Bunmei 16 (1484)/8/1.

27. Ibid., p. 138, entry for Bunmei 18 (1486)/2/12.

28. Ibid., p. 91, entry for Bunmei 17 (1485)/8/15; p. 179, Bunmei 18/5/9; p. 260, Bunmei 18/12/28 (22 January 1487).

29. *Shiranki*, in *Tokugawa jidai shōgyō sōsho*, 1 (Tokyo: Kokusho Kankōkai, 1913), 8. The *Shiranki*, compiled in 1719 by a certain Takaishi, is not entirely reliable, but it does list "Miyake, Kazue, and Imai" (with that punctuation) as members. Since Miyake Kazue was one of the elders named by Kikō as a leader of the Mimura festival, this particular reference may have some basis in fact. If so, it has the additional plus of informing us of judgment by the residents of Sakai.

30. *Shoken nichiroku*, p. 24, entries for Bunmei 16 (1484)/8/1–2. Mimuragū was the early name of the Akuchi Jinja. There is another reference to the festival in the entries for Bunmei 18/8/1–2, pp. 215–216. This may have been a harvest rite, since the beginning of the eighth month, when both mentions are dated, inaugurates the season of the fruits of the fields.

31. *Shoken nichiroku*, pp. 91–92, entries for Bunmei 17/8/15–18.

32. *Onryōken nichiroku, Dai Nihon Bukkyō zensho,* 135 (1913), 1092, entry for Bunmei 19/9/24.

33. Half of the families of the ten-man council during the late fifteenth century can be identified with reasonable accuracy through the *Shoken nichiroku.* They were the Miyake (also called Zaimokuya), Izumiya, Funōya, Yukawa, and Ikenaga.

The name Zaimokuya suggests, but does not prove, that the Miyake were traders in lumber *(zaimoku),* and that they lived in the Zaimokuchō district of Sakai. Eventually they became engaged in trading missions to Ming China. The Miyake bore the title Kazue, an honorary designation derived from the ancient imperial bureaucracy. According to local tradition, the title was a reward for services in connection with the founding of the Injōji, a Buddhist temple in Sakai. Kikō refers to members of this family in *Shoken nichiroku,* p. 24, entry for Bunmei 16 (1484)/8/1, and p. 219, Bunmei 18/8/11. Also see: "Akuchi Jinja monjo," *SSS,* 4, 163–164; Kinugasa Ikkan, *Sakai kagami,* 2:21–22, *Naniwa sōsho,* 13, ed. Funakoshi Seiichirō (Osaka: Naniwa Sōsho Kankōkai, 1928), 41–42; Kobata Atsushi, *Chūsei Nisshi kōtsū bōeki shi no kenkyū* (Tokyo: Tōkō Shoin, 1941), p. 109 and p. 260; Toyoda, *Sakai,* pp. 43–44.

The Izumiya were money lenders and were acquiring land in the area as early as 1440. On them, see: *Shoken nichiroku,* pp. 30–31, Bunmei 16/9/6 and 9/11, and pp. 230–231, Bunmei 18/9/5–6; "Akuchi Jinja monjo," *SSS,* 4, 158–161; *SSS,* 2, 72. The Funōya cannot be clearly placed in any occupation, but the name ending in "ya" suggests that they were merchants of some kind. See *Shoken nichiroku,* p. 60, Bunmei 17/3/1; p. 104, Bunmei 17/10/1; p. 251, Bunmei 18/11/10; and p. 260, Bunmei 18/12/28 (22 January 1487). The Yukawa and Ikenaga, who were active in the Ming trade, also occur frequently in the *Shoken nichiroku.*

34. *Kenmu irai tsuikahō,* Article 347, dated Eishō 5/8/7; in *Chūsei hōsei shiryō shū,* 2, ed. Satō Shin'ichi and Ikeuchi Yoshisuke (Tokyo: Iwanami, 1969, third printing), 113.

35. "Akuchi Jinja monjo," document dated Tenbun 4/4/28; *SSS,* 4, 161–166.

36. George Sansom, *A History of Japan: 1334–1615* (Stanford: Stanford University Press, 1961), p. 233.

37. For details of family succession and battles in this section, see *SSS,* 2, ch. 12, 104–154, and cf. Toyoda, *Sakai,* pp. 51–58.

38. *Onryōken nichiroku, Dai Nihon Bukkyō zensho,* 135, 1381–1382, entry for Chōkyō 2/12/3 (4 January 1489).

39. *Daijōin jisha zōjiki,* ed. Tsuji Zennosuke, 7 (Tokyo: Sankyō Shoin, 1933), 373; entry for Bunmei 14/3/18.

40. Ibid., p. 418, Bunmei 14/interc. 7/2; pp. 427–428, Bunmei 14/8/11.

41. *Onryōken nichiroku,* 135, 1381–1382.

42. Ibid., 134, 914, entry for Bunmei 18/12/18 (12 January 1487); pp. 915–917, entry for Bunmei 18/12/20.

43. Ibid., 135, 1098, entry for Chōkyō 1 (1487)/10/9; p. 1109, Chōkyō 1/11/7.

44. Ibid., 136, 1812, entry for Entoku 2/interc. 8/29; p. 1817, Entoku 2/9/8. The Sūjuin continued to have a minor interest in Sakai until 1490, even though the estate had become a direct holding of the bakufu.

45. Ibid., 135, 1095, entry for Chōkyō 1 (1487)/10/1.

46. *Daijōin jisha zōjiki,* 10, 467, Meiō 4/10/13. There is also a traditional story about another occasion on which Naonobu, the Hatakeyama general, got funds

from Sakai. One of his father's retainers, a certain Kizawa, after a defeat took up life in Sakai as a merchant while planning to recoup Naonobu's fortunes. The wife of a foreign trader named Naya was having an affair with another man while her husband was away in Korea, and Kizawa discovered this when she accidentally mistook him for her lover. Kizawa then blackmailed her father Beniya, one of the city's wealthiest merchants, for considerable sums which he used to aid Naonobu's cause. *Ōnin kōki*, pt. 2, *Kaitei Shiseki shūran*, 3 (Tokyo: Kondō Kappansho, 1900), 19:26–29. *Ōnin kōki* is one of five histories which are commonly called the *Chōhen Ōninki*. It was probably written early in the Edo period.

47.   One Sakai resident, Keana Mataroku, became a warrior and fought against Hatakeyama Naonobu during the 1490s. In 1497 many of his family were killed in a battle in Izumi. *Daijōin jisha zōjiki*, 11, 172–173, Meiō 6/9/24–25; *SSS*, 2, 105–106.

48.   *Naomichi-kō ki*, entry for Eishō 3 (1506)/4/12, cited in *SSS*, 4, 154. The fact that a Ming embassy, apparently outfitted by Sakai merchants, departed in 1506 from Sumiyoshi no Ura, just north of Sakai, may suggest a reason for so large a gift. Morris, "Sakai: From Shōen to Port City," p. 154.

49.   *Zen Sakai shōshi*, 1:28–29, *Naniwa sōsho*, 13, 110–111. This was written in the Edo period as a supplement to the *Sakai kagami*. Though distant in time from the actual event it described, it seems to be based on primary sources and so is credible on this point. The fortifications described were the first in Sakai since the time of Ōuchi Yoshihiro, who built "Sakai Castle" in his unsuccessful revolt against the Muromachi bakufu at the end of the fourteenth century. City and fortifications were both destroyed in the battle of Sakai on Ōei 6/12/21 (17 January 1400). See *Ōeiki*, in *Gunsho ruijū*, 13 (Tokyo: Keizai Zasshi-sha, 1900, second printing), 374:308.

50.   *Zen Sakai shōshi*, 1:28–29, *Naniwa sōsho*, 13, 110–111. Each family and each estate had its own *mandokoro* as an administrative office. The name also became the title for the military deputy who resided in Sakai in the early modern period. Edo-period histories traced the office and the title back to 1504 and 1521. See *Shiranki*, in *Tokugawa jidai shōgyō sōsho*, 1, 6; *Sakai kagami*, 2:3, *Naniwa sōsho*, 13, 55.

51.   Regulations dated Taiei 7 (1527)/3/23; *SSS*, 4, 113–114. These were standard laws of the sort that Sengoku barons often issued in their domains.

52.   Imatani Akira, *Sengoku-ki no Muromachi Bakufu*, Kikan Ronsō Nihon Bunka 2 (Tokyo: Kadokawa, 1975), pp. 166–178 passim and pp. 178–181. "Sakai bakufu" deserves its quotation marks, since its shogun never obtained a full, formal appointment, which would have been purely ornamental in any case.

53.   Ibid., pp. 178–181. Cf. *SSS*, 2, 145–154.

54.   *Hosokawa ryōke ki* (also known as *Nisen bunryū ki*), *Gunsho ruijū*, 13, 380: 586.

55.   Toyoda Takeshi (referring to himself in the third person) succinctly summarized his own findings before an international congress of historians: "Analysing the character of the free city SAKAI, he argued that it [sc., the city's autonomy] was a product of the antagonism among feudal lords." Comité Japonais des Sciences Historiques, *Le Japon au XIe Congrès International des Sciences Historiques à Stockholm* (Tokyo: Nihon Gakujutsu Shinkōkai, 1960), p. 48. Toyoda does not state explicitly which period represented the peak of Sakai's independence, but by implication he seems to place it in the three decades before 1569, when Oda Nobu-

naga assumed power over the city. Also see Harada, *Chūsei ni okeru toshi*, pp. 261-262.

56.   For a convenient summary of these changes, see John Whitney Hall, "Foundations of the Modern Japanese Daimyo," *Journal of Asian Studies*, 20(3):323-326 (May 1961). Vassalage based on oaths or marriage gave way to a "chain of command relationship," and the men were made to live on the fief of the lord separated from their own holdings. Hall illustrates these developments with the rise of the Urakami and later the Ukita in Bizen Province. The Miyoshi and Matsunaga Hisahide seem to have had a comparable experience in their area, though they were perhaps less successful than the Ukita.

57.   For details of family succession and battles in this section, see *SSS*, 2, 188-210.

58.   "Miyoshi Chōkei to Matsunaga Hisahide," in *Jinbutsu Nihon no rekishi*, 6, ed. Toyoda Takeshi (Tokyo: Yomiuri Shinbun-sha, 1965), 150.

59.   "Akuchi Jinja monjo," document dated Tenbun 4 (1535)/4/28, *SSS*, 4, 166. Jōō is identified as a resident of Henomatsu-chō and his occupational name as Kawaya, which means leather dealer. Although the meaning of the name did not always coincide with the actual occupation, it is generally accepted that in this case it did. Leather merchants supplied armor during this period.

60.   *Jinbutsu Nihon no rekishi*, 6, 147.

61.   *Hosokawa ryōke ki (Nisen bunryū ki), Gunsho ruijū*, 13, 380:594-595; *Zoku Ōnin kōki*, pt. 3, *Kaitei Shiseki shūran*, 3, 20:58-59; *Ashikaga kiseiki*, ibid., 13 (1902), 187. *Zoku Ōnin kōki* is another of the five histories which comprise the *Chōhen Ōninki* mentioned in n. 46. *Ashikaga kiseiki* is a chronicle of uncertain date and authorship. It is not considered very reliable but is useful here in providing a third version of this episode.

62.   *Kinzei* or "Off Limits" ordinance issued to the Kenponji over the signature of Yusa Kawachi no Kami Naganori on Tenbun 15 (1546)/8/-; "Kenponji monjo," *SSS*, 4, 118. Also see *SSS*, 2, 244, and *SSS*, 8, "Nenpyō," 29.

63.   *Jinbutsu Nihon no rekishi*, 6, 147-148 and 150-151. Because Hisahide made no significant administrative innovations, his power base was essentially that of the Miyoshi, and it had all the weaknesses that Chōkei had suffered from.

64.   *Tamon'in nikki*, 1, 440-441, entries for Eiroku 9 (1566)/2/17 and 19. Hatakeyama and Yusa, mentioned in this diary, were allies of Hisahide. Cf. *Hosokawa ryōke ki (Nisen bunryū ki), Gunsho ruijū*, 13, 380:613-614.

65.   Ibid., pp. 615-616. *Tamon'in nikki*, 1, 455, entry for Eiroku 9/5/30, reports a small battle at Sakai and says that Hisahide was defeated. These two are contemporary sources. More elaborate accounts are found in *Ashikaga kiseiki, Kaitei Shiseki shūran*, 13, 236-238, and *Zoku Ōnin kōki*, pt. 8, ibid., 3, 20:157-160. The latter in particular is a frequent citation of Japanese historians for this well-known event, but it is probably a product of the Tokugawa period and is of doubtful reliability.

66.   Luis Frois SJ mentions it in his *História de Japam*: see *Furoisu Nihonshi*, ed. and trans. Matsuda Kiichi and Kawasaki Momota, 3 (Tokyo: Chūō Kōron-sha, 1978), 271; and cf. *Die Geschichte Japans (1549-1578)*, trans. G. Schurhammer and E. A. Voretzsch (Leipzig: Asia Major, 1926), p. 245. Schurhammer and Voretzsch misedited as "Kukumugami" what was written "Cucumúgami" in the Portuguese ms., Codex 49-IV-54, Ajuda Library (see Matsuda and Kawasaki, p. 277, n. 14). The reference is to that same Tsukumogami which Hisahide in 1568 gave to

Nobunaga to cement an alliance. Most Westerners in sixteenth-century Japan were astounded at the value that was put on tea implements.

67. See the extracts from *Sōgyū cha-no-yu nikki* and *Imai Sōkyū cha-no-yu kakinuki*, in *SSS*, 4, 368–385 and 385–393.

68. The first European to visit Sakai was Saint Francis Xavier, the founder of the Jesuit mission in Japan, who landed in Kagoshima on 15 August 1549 and passed through the city in January 1551 on his way to Kyoto. He was followed to Sakai by many other Jesuits; some of these, such as Vilela and Frois, on occasion resided in the city during the 1560s and described conditions there, but the Jesuits did not establish a formal residence there until 1585. It was closed in 1588 on Hideyoshi's orders; but the Jesuits were able to reestablish their residence in Sakai between 1601 and 1614, a period when Ieyasu tolerated Christian mission activity. Franciscans were also active in Sakai during the latter period.

69. Luis Frois SJ to Padres and Irmãos SJ, dated Sacáy, 30 June 1566, *CARTAS*, 1, 208v. Also in *Furoisu Nihonshi*, 4, 36, and *Geschichte Japans*, p. 318.

70. Gaspar Vilela SJ to Padres and Irmãos SJ, 1562, *CARTAS*, 1, 113. The moats Vilela mentions were probably dug by the Miyoshi early in the sixteenth century.

71. For a sampler of law and order in various cities, see Michael Cooper SJ, ed., *They Came to Japan: An Anthology of European Reports on Japan, 1543–1640* (Berkeley: University of California Press, 1965), pp. 151–164. Although most of the selections come from a somewhat later period, when military authority was more securely established, the residents themselves still had responsibility for their own policing. Jesuit records say nothing about the Egōshū in Sakai; Japanese records give the name and clearly establish the council's existence, but they provide few details of its composition. The Jesuits do mention borrowing a meeting hall *(camara ou casa de seu conselho)* for Sakai Christmas services in 1566; this presumably meant a local council hall. Luis Frois SJ, dated Sacáy, 8 July 1567, *CARTAS*, 1, 242v.

72. Gaspar Vilela SJ to Padres and Irmãos SJ in Portugal, dated Miàco (Kyoto), 15 July 1564, *CARTAS*, 1, 142.

73. These questions are treated by Fujiki Hisashi and George Elison, "The Political Posture of Oda Nobunaga," in *Japan Before Tokugawa: Political Consolidation and Economic Growth, 1500 to 1650*, ed. John Whitney Hall, Nagahara Keiji, and Kozo Yamamura (Princeton: Princeton University Press, 1980).

74. *Shinchō kōki*, comp. Ōta Izumi no Kami Gyūichi (c. 1610), ed. Okuno Takahiro and Iwasawa Yoshihiko, Kadokawa Bunko 2541 (Tokyo: Kadokawa, 1969), pt. 1, sec. 4, p. 88. This was in Akutagawa, where Nobunaga spent the first two weeks of the tenth month, 1568, while daimyo and others vying to offer gifts and compliments to the conqueror "made a marketplace of the front of his gate."

75. *Hosokawa ryōke ki (Nisen bunryū ki)*, *Gunsho ruijū*, 13, 380:619. Also see *Zoku Ōnin kōki*, pt. 10, *Kaitei Shiseki shūran*, 3, 20:191–192, and *Ashikaga kiseiki*, ibid., 13, 247. The events described in this section are well known. Somewhat garbled versions are found in Yosaburo Takekoshi, *The Economic Aspects of the Civilization of Japan*, 1 (New York: Macmillan, 1930), 363–364, and George Sansom, *A History of Japan: 1334–1615*, pp. 304–305. More accurate accounts, in Japanese, are *SSS*, 2, 210–214, and Toyoda, *Sakai*, pp. 73–78. The sources disagree on the sums demanded by Nobunaga. *Zoku Ōnin kōki* gives thirty thousand *kan* as the levy on Sakai, but it is less accurate than other sources, which give the lower figure I cite.

Good documentary evidence is available only concerning Nobunaga's demands on the Hōryūji; see Okuno Takahiro, *Oda Nobunaga monjo no kenkyū*, 1 (Tokyo: Yoshikawa Kōbunkan, 1971, 2nd ed.), no. 123, 207-211, *ex* "Hōryūji monjo." The main entry, a missive addressed to the Hōryūji over the names of Oda Shuri no Suke Yoshikiyo et al. and dated [Eiroku 11]/10/6, demands prompt payment of 150 pieces of silver (p. 207); its three supplements make it clear that at least a part of the temple's payment was raised in Sakai through the good offices of Matsunaga Hisahide. According to a receipt issued to the Hōryūji by two of Matsunaga's councillors on Eiroku 11/12/9 (27 December 1568), by that date 600 *kan* had been scraped together for delivery to Nobunaga (p. 210); secondary sources give the figure 1000 as the sum which was paid in all. The temple scheduled special services to pray for a safe outcome.

76.   Document from "Sueyoshi monjo," cited by Toyoda, *Sakai*, p. 74; Okuno, *Monjo*, 1, 154; *SSS*, 4, 155.

77.   *Shinchō kōki*, pt. 2, secs. 1-2, pp. 93-95, Eiroku 12/1/4-8; *Zoku Ōnin kōki*, pt. 10, *Kaitei Shiseki shūran*, 3, 20:197; *Ashikaga kiseiki*, ibid., 13, 249.

78.   *Hosokawa ryōke ki (Nisen bunryū ki)*, *Gunsho ruijū*, 13, 380:622.

79.   Tsuda Sōgyū, *Takaiki*, Eiroku 12/1/11, quoted by Toyoda, *Sakai*, p. 76.

80.   *Shinchō kōki*, pt. 1, sec. 4, p. 88. Cf. Nagashima Fukutarō, "Oda Nobunaga no Tajima keiryaku to Imai Sōkyū," in *Kwansei Gakuin shigaku*, 5:100-105 (1959).

81.   *SSS*, 2, 214; Toyoda, *Sakai*, p. 77. It is unclear just how long the recalcitrant residents held out. A recently discovered document signed by Sakuma Nobumori and four other prominent captains of Nobunaga's armies on [Eiroku 12]/4/1 threatens Sakai with the direst of consequences unless the inhabitants pay up by the fifteenth of the month—because Nobunaga is "furious beyond all bounds" at them. Hence it would appear that they held out for half a year. See Okuno, *Monjo*, supp. no. 18, 2 (1973, 2nd ed.), 850-852.

82.   On Nobunaga's deputies in Sakai, see Asao Naohiro, "Shokuhō-ki no Sakai daikan," in *Akamatsu Toshihide Kyōju taikan kinen Kokushi ronshū* (Kyoto: Akamatsu Toshihide Kyōju Taikan Kinen Jigyōkai, 1972), sec. 1, pp. 797-806; and cf. Nagashima Fukutarō, "Oda Nobunaga no Tajima keiryaku to Imai Sōkyū," pp. 105-109. Documentary evidence on Imai Sōkyū's activities in the area of Sakai will be found in Okuno, *Monjo*, vol. 1, no. 186, p. 309, from the shogunal official [Iikawa] Nobukata to shippers on the Yodo River, [Eiroku 12]/6/8; no. 192, pp. 315-316, Niwa Gorozaemon no Jō Nagahide to Ike[da] Chiku[zen no Kami Katsumasa], 8/8 of the same year, referring to Sōkyū's authority over "Sakai Gokanoshō"; no. 199, p. 323, Niwa to Ikeda, 11/11 of the same year, with the same reference.

THE CROSS AND THE SWORD: PATTERNS OF MOMOYAMA HISTORY

I should like to acknowledge gratefully the aid of the East Asian Research Center and the Japan Institute of Harvard University, of the Japan Foundation, and of the Joint Committee on Japanese Studies of the American Council of Learned Societies and the Social Science Research Council.

1.   *Taikōsama gunki no uchi*, reproduction of the holograph by Ōta Izumi no Kami Gyūichi (c. 1605), with transcription, ed. Keiō Gijuku Daigaku Fuzoku Kenkyūjo Shidō Bunko (Tokyo: Kyūko Shoin, 1975), pp. 3-6 and trans. pp. 3-4. A brief essay on the work and its author is appended to the transcription, pp. 75-91.

Gyūichi (1527–after 1610) is the author of several important chronicles but is best known for the *Shinchō kōki* (1610); the best edition is by Okuno Takahiro and Iwasawa Yoshihiko, Kadokawa Bunko 2541 (Tokyo: Kadokawa, 1969).

2.   Miura Jōshin, *(Keichō) Kenbunshū,* ed. Suzuki Tōzō, in *Nihon shomin seikatsu shiryō shūsei,* 8 *(Kenbunki;* Tokyo: San'ichi Shobō, 1969), 474. The Burning House is a standard Buddhist image for this world of suffering.

Jōshin (1565–1644) was a samurai in the service of the Hōjō of Odawara who was dispossessed after the fall of that house, turned to the life of a townsman, and eventually entered religion. Suzuki Tōzō includes a biographical sketch on pp. 471–472.

3.   Needless to say, I do not mean to imply either that optimism was the hallmark of the European Renaissance or that Momoyama Japan was intellectually as diversified as Renaissance Europe. Cf. Robert S. Lopez, "Hard Times and Investment in Culture," in *The Renaissance,* Harper Torchbooks TB 1084 (New York: Harper and Row, 1962), pp. 44–47.

4.   Yoshimasa to Konoe Masaie (Minister of the Middle), dated [Bunmei 8 (1476)]/ 3/7; reproduced in *Kyōto no rekishi,* ed. Kyōto-shi, 3 (Tokyo: Gakugei Shorin, 1968), 360. Yoshimasa had abdicated on Bunmei 5/12/19 (7 January 1474).

5.   The term's first definition in a Western language appears in the *VOCABVLA-RIO DA LINGOA DE IAPAM com adeclaração em Portugues* (Nangasaqui no Collegio de IaPAM DA COMPANHIA DE IESVS. ANNO M.D.CIII.), f. 115v; facsimile edition published by Doi Tadao, *Nippo jisho* (Tokyo: Iwanami, 1960), p. 230: "Guecocujŏ. Ximo, vyeni catçu. *Sendo baixo, & criado, por suas boas partes, & industria, ou fortuna vir a valer, & ser senhor, & o senhor vir a ser criado, ou baixo.*"

6.   Nagahara Keiji, *Sengoku no dōran, Nihon no rekishi,* 14 (Tokyo: Shōgakkan, 1975), 375.

7.   *Asakura Sōteki waki,* in *Zokuzoku gunsho ruijū,* 10 (Tokyo: Kokusho Kankōkai, 1907), 2.

João Rodrigues Tçuzzu SJ, *História da Igreja do Japão,* ed. João do Amaral Abranches Pinto, 1 (Macao: Notícias de Macau, 1954), 181; English translation by Michael Cooper SJ, *This Island of Japon* (Tokyo and New York: Kodansha International, 1973), p. 75; Japanese translation by Doi Tadao et al., *Nihon kyōkai shi,* 1 (Tokyo: Iwanami, 1967), 310. Cf. Juvenal, Satire VI, 223: *Hoc volo, sic jubeo, sit pro ratione voluntas.* Cooper points out that the extant manuscript's "erat probatione voluntas" is probably a copyist's error.

8.   *CATECHISMVS CHRISTIANAE FIDEI, IN QVO VERITAS nostrae religionis ostenditur, & sectae Iaponenses confutantur,* editus à Patre Alexandro Valignano societatis IESV. . . . Olyssipone, excudebat Antonius Riberius. 1586. (Classica Japonica, Facsimile Series in The Tenri Central Library, Section 2, Kirishitan Materials 3; Tenri: Tenri Daigaku Shuppanbu, 1972), f. 49v. Cf. George Elison, *Deus Destroyed: The Image of Christianity in Early Modern Japan* (Cambridge, Mass.: Harvard University Press, 1973), ch. 2, pp. 30–53.

It is important to note, however, that the contemporary and near-contemporary Japanese literature, even while depicting a world of raw power, fails to abstract any sort of theoretical model from the multiple images of political brutality and military ruthlessness. No work even roughly comparable with *The Prince* exists; even the heralded *Kōyō gunkan* is nothing more than a disorganized chronicle. Although the book deals with such Sengoku types as Takeda Shingen and Oda Nobunaga (who were scarcely knights-errant), its portraiture of the ideal warlord is conceived in flat, moralizing, and banal tones; e.g., *Kōyō gunkan,* ed. Isogai Masayoshi and Hattori Harunori, 1, Sengoku Shiryō Sōsho 3 (Tokyo: Jinbutsu Ōrai-sha, 1965), pt. 4, ch. 12, 189–192. Paradoxically, a more accurate listing of the ingredients of success in Sengoku may be derived from the propagandistic diatribes in which Shingen and Nobunaga indicted each other as criminals; *Kōyō gunkan,* 2, pt. 12, ch. 39, 339–347.

9.   Niccolò Machiavelli, *The Prince,* trans. George Bull, Penguin Classics L 107 (Harmondsworth, Middlesex: Penguin Books Ltd., 1961), ch. 26, p. 138.

10.   Federico Chabod, "An Introduction to *The Prince*" (1924), *Machiavelli and the Renaissance,* trans. David Moore, Harper Torchbooks TB 1193 (New York: Harper and Row, 1965), p. 13.

11.   *The Prince,* ch. 2, p. 33.

12.   *The Prince,* ch. 3, pp. 34–44; ch. 5, pp. 47–49; ch. 8, pp. 61–66.

13.   *The Prince,* ch. 5, p. 48.

14.   *The Prince,* ch. 6, p. 50.

15.   *The Prince,* ch. 21, p. 119; also see p. 120: "still making use of religion, he turned his hand to a pious work of cruelty when he chased out the Moriscos and rid his kingdom of them: there could not have been a more pitiful or striking enterprise."

16.   *História,* 1, 186–188; *This Island of Japon,* pp. 78–80; *Nihon kyōkai shi,* 1, 315–317.

17.   The leading cultural historian in present-day Japan, Hayashiya Tatsusaburō, has organized his discussion of Momoyama around three terms: power, wealth, and pleasure. The binding factor of these three is: gold.

I owe much to Professor Hayashiya's conspectus of the period and its culture. In particular, cf. his *Momoyama jidai, Nihon bunkashi,* 5 (Tokyo: Chikuma Shobō, 1965), 199, and *Tenka ittō, Nihon no rekishi,* 12 (Tokyo: Chūō Kōron-sha, 1971; Chuko Backs), 405.

18.   See my chapter, "Hideyoshi, the Bountiful Minister," in this volume.

19.   Ieyasu's birthyear is commonly given as 1542, although he was born on 31 January 1543 (Tenbun 11/12/26).

20.   The question is irksome because there is a substantial overlap of historical "periods" in the sixteenth century. The Muromachi era, if we assume that it lasted until the last Ashikaga shogun was expelled from Kyoto, continued until 1573. Sengoku, if we consider that a nation-wide phenomenon, did not conclude until Hideyoshi: (a) pacified Kyushu in 1587; (b) defeated the Hōjō of Odawara in 1590; (c) subjugated northern Honshū in 1591. The so-called Christian Century (if, indeed, that is a valid concept) lasted from 1549 to 1639. Most historians date the Edo period from the century's last year, 1600.

21.   Hayashiya Tatsusaburō has expressed this view on numerous occasions. For examples, see the articles written over the dozen years 1961–1972 and grouped under the title "Hokke bunka no kaika" in *Kinsei dentō bunka ron* (Osaka: Sōgensha, 1974), pp. 19–128.

22.   The best remaining examples of the Momoyama period's great edifices are Matsumoto Castle in the Japan Alps (with a donjon built between 1594 and c. 1600) and the Hakurojō or White Heron Castle at Himeji west of Kobe, which is by far the best known. Himeji was originally the fort of Kodera Kanbyōe (Dom Simeão Kuroda Josui); the citadel was further built up by Hideyoshi in 1580, and the Haku-

rojō completed by Ikeda Terumasa in 1610. See Haga Kōshirō, *Azuchi Momoyama jidai no bunka*, Nihon Rekishi Shinsho 115 (Tokyo: Shibundō, 1972, second printing), p. 17.

23. Rodrigues (*História*, 1, 187; *This Island of Japon*, p. 79; *Nihon kyōkai shi*, 1, 315) included in his list of the period's novelties: "The use of gunpowder, hitherto unknown, and muskets; they have already begun to use even mortars." Strictly speaking, gunpowder had been known in Japan at least since the Mongol invasions of the thirteenth century; but firearms did not come into wide use until some time after Portuguese traders brought the musket (known in Japan as the Tanegashima after the place of its introduction) in 1543. Cf. Nagahara Keiji, *Sengoku no dōran*, pp. 87–98.

24. The castle's construction began in the middle of the first month of Tenshō 4, and Nobunaga moved to the site on Tenshō 4/2/23 (23 March 1576); *Shinchō kōki*, Kadokawa Bunko 2541, pt. 9, sec. 1, p. 207. The donjon *(tenshu)* became his official residence on Tenshō 7/5/11 (5 June 1579); ibid., pt. 12, sec. 3, p. 271. Work on other major buildings, such as a hall meant to host an Imperial Visit, continued well after that date; the complex was not completed until 1581, if then. Everything burnt down on Tenshō 10/6/14–15 (3–4 July 1582); the sources disagree as to who set the fire.

25. Padre Ioão Frācisco [Stephanoni], Miyako, 1 September 1580; *CARTAS QVE OS PADRES E IRMÃOS da Companhia de Iesus escreuerão dos Reynos de Iapão & China aos da mesma Companhia da India, & Europa, des do anno de 1549. atē o de 1580.* (Em Euora por Manoel de Lyra. Anno de M.D.XCVIII.), 1, 479v–480v.

26. Professor Naitō's discovery was announced by the *Asahi shinbun* in December 1974, but was not formally published until February and March 1976, occupying two issues, vol. 83, nos. 987 and 988, of *Kokka*. An appendix comprises thirteen elevations and ground plans, resulting in a detailed reconstruction of the tower's appearance. This must be considered the definitive study of Azuchi Castle, although it does not entirely supersede the report published by Shiga Prefecture in 1942: *Shiga-ken shiseki chōsa hōkoku*, no. 11, *Azuchi jōseki*, comp. Shiga-ken Shiseki Meishō Tennen Kinenbutsu Chōsakai.

Naitō's study contains careful analyses of various literary sources and of the archaeological evidence, but is in essence based on his discovery, the *Tenshu sashizu* (Specifications of the Donjon; original in the Seikadō Bunko, photo in *Kokka*, 987:3, detail ibid., pp. 116–117) of Ikegami Uhei, an architect in the service of the Maeda daimyo house of Kaga. According to the English synopsis (987:[119]), it is likely that the *Tenshu sashizu* "was copied from the original, drawn by an architect who participated in the construction work of the Azuchi Castle, by a privileged architect of the Kennin-ji school . . . , was transmitted through generations in the lineage of Kaga Clan architects who succeeded [to] the main tradition of [that] school, was copied by Ikegami Uhei around 1670, and was re-copied around 1760."

The tower's height measured 138 feet from the level of the second enceinte *(ni no maru)*, sc., the top of Azuchi Hill; this figure includes the stone terrace which enclosed the basement (first floor) of the building. Measured from the base of the terrace at the level of the main enceinte *(honmaru)*, the height of the donjon was 151 feet. The terraces and other remaining stoneworks impress the visitor even today.

27.   Nange Genkō (1538–1604) was a priest of the Zen temple Myōshinji in Kyoto; his *Azuchiyama no ki* may be dated 1579 (see *Kokka*, 987:31–33 and 81). Most fitting of all may be his comparison of Azuchi with the residence of Ch'in Shih Huang-ti, the hegemon who unified China after its Sengoku period.

Note that Azuchi Hill is no longer near the water, so that Genkō's *chinoiserie* on a "promontory" jutting out into a "boundless expanse of azure waves" no longer applies. Extensive reclamation work has reduced the Iba Naiko to little more than a pond seen in the distance across rice fields; it has only minor riverine connections with Lake Biwa.

28.   The earliest extant documents which bear this seal are dated Eiroku 10 (1567)/ 11/–; see Okuno Takahiro, *Oda Nobunaga monjo no kenkyū*, nos. 77 and 79–81, 1 (Tokyo: Yoshikawa Kōbunkan, 1971, 2nd ed.), 140 and 142–144, and supp. no. 10, 2 (1973, 2nd ed.), 842; cf. 2, 944. This was a time when Nobunaga, having destroyed Saitō Tatsuoki, had moved his seat to Gifu in Mino province, and was acknowledged by Emperor Ōgimachi as a "great and famous captain without compare in past or present *(kokon busō no meishō)*"; imperial message *(rinshi)* signed [Kanshuji] Uchūben Harutoyo, dated Eiroku 10/11/9, Okuno, *Monjo*, 1, 126.

29.   On Nobunaga's concept of *Tenka*, see Fujiki Hisashi, "Tōitsu seiken no seiritsu," *Iwanami kōza: Nihon rekishi*, 9 (*Kinsei* 1; Tokyo: Iwanami, 1975), 65–79. Fujiki argues forcefully that *Tenka* in Nobunaga's usage assumed the meaning of a universal public order *(fuhenteki na kōkenryoku)*, possessing an ideological potential which Nobunaga used consciously in his efforts to organize the samurai class. Since Nobunaga frequently applied the slogan in critical situations, to rally loyalties or justify extraordinary actions (such as the merciless extirpation of Buddhist sectarians), it would appear that he had more than a rudimentary sense of *raison d'état.* The abstract "*Tenka no tame:* for the sake of the realm" and the personal "*Nobunaga no tame:* for the sake of Nobunaga" are closely coupled ideas whose association occurs in the sources from 1570. The *locus classicus* is Nobunaga's vermilion-seal letter, dated [Genki 1]/5/25, ordering the Endō family of Mino to mobilize their forces for a campaign against Asai Nagamasa; Okuno, *Monjo,* no. 233, 1, 388–390.

Cf. Kumakura Isao, "Sengokuteki naru mono to kinseiteki naru mono," sec. 1, "Gekokujō no shisō," in *Kikan Nihon shisōshi,* 1(1):96–104 (July 1976). Inexplicably, even while participating in the same seminar at the Research Institute for Humanistic Studies of Kyoto University, Kumakura and I were unaware that we were working with the same materials and reaching similar conclusions.

30.   *Shinchō kōki,* pt. 9, sec. 5, pp. 213–217.

31.   Gyūichi does not describe the other rooms of this story as elaborately, but he does not fail to reiterate that "all is gold wherever there are pictures." For more detail, see Naitō Akira, *Kokka,* 987:102–107, 988:24–26, and appendix, reconstruction 07. Note that Gyūichi's guided tour is a trifle misleading; the rooms mentioned here are identified in Naitō's reconstruction in the following sequence: A, B, F, D, E, C, G.

32.   Cf. Naitō, *Kokka,* 987:108–109, 988:26–29, and appendix, reconstruction 08. Sequence: A, B, D, F, E, F', G, I.

From its name, one would judge that the *kenjin no ma* contained portraits of model Wise Men such as Po I and Shu Ch'i. (These two were brothers who would not countenance Chou Wen Wang's overthrow of the Shang dynasty and starved rather than eat the bread of the Chou.) The painting described by Gyūichi, however, fits the label which the *Tenshu sashizu* attaches to this L-shaped room's northern portion: *sennin*, to wit the Taoist Immortal Chang Kuo, who used a white donkey as his steed on his daily myriad-mile journeys. When resting, he folded the donkey up and put it away in a little box; when ready to resume his ride through the skies, he would make it emerge again. In the painting, the box is replaced by a gourd.

Okuno and Iwasawa, *Shinchō kōki*, p. 215, n. 7, mistakenly identify the subject of the *jakō no ma* as the musk deer. We may assume that the animal depicted here was the same as that in the *jakō no ma* of the Nanzenji in Kyoto, which is also attributed to Kano Eitoku. I am indebted to William Elison for identifying it (on the basis of its relatively short tail and erectile mane) as the Large Civet, *Viverra zibetha,* as opposed to the Palm Civet, *Paradoxurus hermaphroditus.*

Lü Tung-pin ranks as one of the Eight Immortals, along with Chang Kuo; it is impossible to tell which of the numerous anecdotes concerning him was depicted here. Fu Yüeh was a sage whom the Shang ruler Kao Tsung made his prime minister; after his death he ascended into the heavens where he shines as a star.

The Queen Mother of the West, said to reside in the K'un-lun Mountains, possessed the gift of bestowing eternal youth.

33. Cf. *Kokka,* 987:110–111, 988:29–31, and appendix, reconstruction 09. Sequence: A, B, D, E, G, H, I, K, L, N.

Hsü Yu was a hermit to whom Yao offered to pass on the empire. This message so offended his principles that he washed out his ears in the river—which thereupon became so polluted that Ch'ao Fu (another hermit) would not cross it and turned back with his ox. An example of Kano Eitoku's treatment of this theme will be found in the attractive catalogue prepared by Julia Meech-Pekarik, *Momoyama: Japanese Art in the Age of Grandeur; An Exhibition at The Metropolitan Museum of Art* (New York: The Metropolitan Museum of Art, 1975), no. 5, pp. 12–13.

It will be noted that the phoenix is a prodigy which appears when a sage ruler governs the realm.

34. On the uppermost three levels, cf. *Kokka,* 987:112–115, 988:31–35, and appendix, reconstructions 10–12.

As Carolyn Wheelwright points out in the next chapter, "A Visualization of Eitoku's Lost Paintings at Azuchi Castle," n. 57, both the dragons and the angels properly belong in the context of the sixth story, not of the seventh; Gyūichi's description is mistaken.

The Four Wise Men retired to Shang Shan at the time of the disturbances accompanying the fall of the Ch'in dynasty. The Seven Sages of the Bamboo Grove were eccentrics of the third century A.D., famous for seeking refuge from mundane concerns in the world of elegant paradoxes known as "pure talk" *(ch'ing t'an).*

35. One of ten satirical poems posted in the streets of Kyoto on Tenshō 19 (1591)/ 2/26; contemporary copy by Hasegawa Tadazane, ms. in the possession of the Faculty of Letters, Hiroshima University; reproduced in Hayashiya Tatsusaburō, *Tenka ittō,* p. 449.

36. Frois to P. Belchior de Figueiredo SJ, dated Miyako, 1 June 1569, *CARTAS,* 1, 257v. Cf. the similar depiction in Frois' *História de Japam: Die Geschichte Japans (1549–1578),* tr. G. Schurhammer and E. A. Voretzsch (Leipzig: Asia Major, 1926), pp. 353–354; *Furoisu Nihonshi,* ed. and trans. Matsuda Kiichi and Kawasaki Momota, 4 (Tokyo: Chūō Kōron-sha, 1978), 103.

37.   See Chabod, "The Concept of the Renaissance" (1942), *Machiavelli and the Renaissance*, pp. 174–178.

38.   Frois to General SJ, dated Kuchinotsu, 5 November 1582, *CARTAS*, 2, 63 and 82.

39.   James Murdoch, *A History of Japan*, 2 (London: Kegan Paul, Trench, Trubner & Co., 1925), 143. This work was originally published in Kobe in 1903.

40.   George Sansom, *A History of Japan: 1334–1615* (London: Cresset, 1961), p. 310.

41.   Frois, *Segunda Parte da Historia de Japam*, ed. João do Amaral Abranches Pinto and Okamoto Yoshitomo (Tokyo: Sociedade Luso-Japonesa, 1938), p. 319: "esta luciferina soberba"; p. 242: "Rey Assuero." Murdoch, p. 184: "Nobunaga, callous, forceful, masterful, the veritable *Übermensch* of his time, was of the breed of Attila"; p. 185: "the destructive energy of a Japanese Attila." Even the opprobrium is cast in a heroic mold.

42.   Toward the end of 1575, peasants in Echizen were being prohibited from "seeking new masters *(shingi no shudori),*" sc., attempting to change their status by military service; see the regulations issued to the Jishū temple Shōnenji by Nobunaga's vassal Shibata Katsuie, Tenshō 3/11/–, Okuno, *Monjo*, no. 555 supp., 2, 100. The Oda regime conducted a "sword hunt" *(katanazarae)* in Echizen in the first month of Tenshō 4 (1576). Two months later, Shibata issued a seven-article ordinance to that province: it ordered peasants to "confine themselves to tilling the soil" and prohibited them from "seeking new masters" and leaving their villages; document reproduced in Fujiki Hisashi, *Oda-Toyotomi seiken, Nihon no rekishi*, 15 (Tokyo: Shōgakkan, 1975), 141.

These cannot be interpreted as independent actions on the part of Shibata; the overlord Nobunaga retained firm control. See the Regulations for the Province of Echizen, cited below.

43.   A brief summary of the Oda regime's land surveys and other efforts to determine the productivity of the domains under its control (1568–1582) will be found in Wakita Osamu, *Oda seiken no kiso kōzō, Shokuhō seiken no bunseki*, 1 (Tokyo: Tōkyō Daigaku Shuppankai, 1975), 131–151. We note that the first of Hideyoshi's so-called *Taikō kenchi* was conducted in Harima on Nobunaga's behalf in 1580.

44.   An illustrative document is Nobunaga's vermilion-seal letter to Maeda Matazaemon (Toshiie), dated [Tenshō 9 (1581)]/10/2; Okuno, *Monjo*, no. 954, 2, 640–642. Maeda is assigned the province of Noto and his holdings in Echizen are transferred to Suganoya Kuemon. The document is notable not least because it contains stipulations regarding Toshiie's family, who are "to move to that province immediately"; Okuno rightly calls it a preview of the *baku-han* system.

Also see Nobunaga's memorandum dispossessing Sakuma Nobumori (one of his oldest and most favored vassals) and his son Jinkurō, dated Tenshō 8 (1580)/3/–: *Monjo*, no. 894, 2, 531–539; *Shinchō kōki*, pt. 12, sec. 10/11, pp. 330–334.

45.   Frois to General SJ, 5 November 1582, *CARTAS*, 2, 63v; cf. *Segunda Parte*, p. 323, or *Furoisu Nihonshi*, 5, 138. Frois (f. 61v) in the same breath uses the term *Tenka* to refer to the region of the capital (sc., the Kinai area) and to the notion of a "Japanese monarchy" in general: *os reinos confins [ao Miâco], que se chamão a Tenca, que quer dizer a monarchia de Iapão.* The *VOCABVLARIO*, f. 254 (*Nippo jisho*, p. 507), gives a universal definition: "Tenca. Amegaxita. *Monarchia, ou imperio.*"

46.   See my *Deus Destroyed*, pp. 115–124.

47. Both Fujiki's article, "Tōitsu seiken no seiritsu," and his book, *Oda-Toyotomi seiken*, treat the *entirety* of Oda's reunification policy within the context of his struggle against the Ikkō sect.

In contrast, Aida Yūji, Harada Tomohiko, and Sugiyama Jirō, using truly phlogistical reasoning, agree among themselves that Nobunaga turned on the Buddhists because the Jesuits (in all apparent seriousness compared with the Nazis' "Iron Guard") prevailed on him to do so! Aida et al., *Oda Nobunaga, Seijiteki ningen no keifu*, 4 (Tokyo: Shisakusha, 1972; Hihyō Nihonshi), 193–203.

48. An interesting anecdote concerning Ieyasu's destruction of the Ikkō organization in Mikawa (1563–1564) may be found in the *Mikawa monogatari* (completed 1622–1626) of that old soldier, Ōkubo Hikozaemon. When some Ikkō temples pleaded pardon, asking that Ieyasu grant them the same status "as in the past" (*sakizaki no gotoku*, the standard formula of confirmatory patents), he responded: "In the past this was wilderness; let it be wilderness again as in the past." The temples were levelled, the priests scattered in the four directions. *Mikawa monogatari, Hagakure*, ed. Saiki Kazuma et al., Nihon Shisō Taikei 26 (Tokyo: Iwanami, 1974), p. 95.

49. Fujiki, "Tōitsu seiken no seiritsu," p. 44. His argument (pp. 39–53) is tentative and anything but clear, but its main points would seem to be: the Ikkō sect's *jinai* were places of refuge for peasants absconding from the land, who were introduced there into the processes of the commercial economy; travelling artisans *(watari)* also drifted to the *jinai*; the combination of former peasants and *watari* bound together by Ikkō allegiances produced an autonomous type of organism; the samurai regime could not establish control either over peasants or over the routes of commerce until the *jinai* were destroyed and replaced by *jōkamachi* (castle towns with a differentiated class structure).

50. If Takeda Shingen was the exception, we shall never know, for he died soon after gaining his only major strategic victory: defeat of Nobunaga's ally Ieyasu in the battle of Mikatagahara, Genki 3/12/3 (6 January 1573); capture of Noda Castle in Mikawa, Genki 4/2/17; Shingen's death, Genki 4/4/12 (13 May 1573). The purpose of his last foray has never been adequately identified. It may have been a sweep toward Kyoto, with the stakes being the *Tenka;* but it was probably nothing more than yet another regional sally. It did, however, put Nobunaga in an extremely difficult position.

Shingen's offensive enticed Ashikaga Yoshiaki to break openly with Nobunaga, forcing the implacable hegemon to assume for once a conciliatory posture; see his extraordinary messages to Hosokawa Hyōbu no Daibu [Fujitaka], Okuno, *Monjo,* nos. 360 and 362–364, 1, 606–610 and 612–620, Genki 4/2/23–3/7. But the shogun had immediate cause to regret this move. Nobunaga utterly overwhelmed him, burning the better part of his capital city on the night of Genki 4/4/3–4, and chasing him out of Kyoto three months later. On these events, see *Kanemi-kyō ki*, 1, ed. Saiki Kazuma and Someya Mitsuhiro (Tokyo: Zoku Gunsho Ruijū Kanseikai, 1971; Shiryō Sanshū, 1st ser.), 62–74.

51. Nobunaga to [Mino] Senpukuji, [Genki 3 (1572)]/7/13, giving the temple two days to get rid of its affiliations with Osaka, Okuno, *Monjo*, no. 330, 1, 549; to Nagaoka Hyōbu no Daibu (Hosokawa Fujitaka), [Tenshō 2 (1574)]/8/17, *Monjo*, no. 470, 1, 778; to Date [Terumune], [Tenshō 3]/10/25 (27 November 1575), *Monjo*, no. 571, 2, 124.

52. Letter to Date Terumune, just cited; cf. *Shinchō kōki*, pt. 8, sec. 7, p. 196, where the number is given as thirty or forty thousand. To Murai Nagato no Kami: [Tenshō 3]/8/17 (22 September 1575), *Monjo*, no. 533, 2, 61–62; 8/22, no. 535, pp. 66–68.

53. Nobunaga to the "Three Takada Temples of Echizen" (Jōshōji, Shōjōji, and Senshōji), Tenshō 3/6/14; *Monjo*, no. 519, 2, 39–40.

54. See Fujiki, *Oda-Toyotomi seiken*, pp. 71–72. Cf. the letter from [Shibata] Shuri no Suke Katsuie to Takada-monto Kurome Shōmyōji, dated Tenshō 3/10/18, reproduced ibid., p. 71; and its adjunct *(soejō)* of the same date, signed Shibata Genzaemon no Jō Katsusada, *Monjo*, no. 555 supp., 2, 100–101.

55. Inscribed tile found on the site of Komaruyama Castle in Echizen, giving the date of the *ikki* as [Tenshō 4]/5/24 and the number of prisoners executed by Nobunaga's vassal Maeda Toshiie as one thousand; reproduced in *Oda-Toyotomi seiken*, p. 18.

56. See John Whitney Hall, "Japan's Sixteenth-Century Revolution," in this volume.

57. Machiavelli, *The Prince*, ch. 18, p. 99, invoking the allegory of Chiron, the centaur.

58. Nobunaga to Murai Nagato no Kami, [Tenshō 3]/8/22; Okuno, *Monjo*, no. 535, 2, 68.

59. *Okite Jōjō, Echizen no Kuni;* this title, according to Ashikaga bakufu precedent, suffices to establish that the addressee is the *shugo* of the province, Shibata Katsuie. The date is Tenshō 3/9/–. Okuno, *Monjo*, no. 549, 2, 87–89; *Shinchō kōki*, pt. 8, sec. 7, pp. 197–200.

60. *VOCABVLARIO*, f. 226 (*Nippo jisho*, p. 451): "Sŏqiŏ. i, Tattomi vyamŏ. *Veneração, ou reuerencia. Vt*, Fitouo sŏqiŏ suru. *Honrar, & venerar a alguem.*"

61. Frois to General SJ, 5 November 1582, *CARTAS*, 2, 61–82; this and subsequent quotations from ff. 62–63v. Cf. Frois, *Segunda Parte*, chs. 40 and 41, pp. 316–352; *Furoisu Nihonshi*, 5, 131–152.

62. Referring to the *Bonçāo* mentioned by Frois, Naitō Akira argues (*Kokka*, 988: 45–47) that the *bonsan* listed by Ōta Gyūichi as a feature of one of the second-floor rooms of the Azuchi Donjon (and located by the *Tenshu sashizu* within a special enclosure: Naitō, room B, *bonsan no ma*) was meant as a symbol of Nobunaga's divinity. This is a strained interpretation. Whatever reverential significance the *Bonçāo* may have had, a *bonsan* was in Nobunaga's day the *sine qua non* of the aristocratic drawing room *(shoin)*. The *VOCABVLARIO*, f. 25 (*Nippo jisho*, p. 49), accurately defines it as "a stone or rough piece of wood" which serves as the base of a miniature landscape made with "green mosses, & a tiny tree planted there, &c." Moreover, until the latter part of the sixteenth century, when the *wabi* taste of Takeno Jōō and Sen no Rikyū came to predominate and the tea room in the style of a grass hut became the aesthetic standard, a *bonsan* was also indispensable to the classic setting of the formal tea ceremony held typically in the *shoin*. Nobunaga, a greedy collector of tea implements, was apparently also a fancier of *bonsan*; see *Kanemi-kyō ki*, 1, 141, entry for Tenshō 6 (1578)/5/5.

63. It will be noted that Asao Naohiro, working independently with the same materials, has drawn more definite, extreme, and unwarranted conclusions from them. Asao appears to trust Frois verbatim and fails to recognize the propagandistic nature of his writings. For example, see Asao, "Bakuhansei to Tennō," in *Taikei Nihon*

kokka shi, ed. Hara Shūzaburō et al., 3 (Tokyo: Tōkyō Daigaku Shuppankai, 1975), 194-200.

64. Cf. Machiavelli, *The Prince,* ch. 6, p. 52.

65. *Shinchō kōki,* pt. 1, sec. 5, p. 89. A detailed treatment of Nobunaga's relations with the shogun and with the emperor will be found in Fujiki Hisashi and George Elison, "The Political Posture of Oda Nobunaga," in *Japan Before Tokugawa: Political Consolidation and Economic Growth, 1500 to 1650,* ed. John Whitney Hall, Nagahara Keiji, and Kozo Yamamura (Princeton: Princeton University Press, 1980).

66. Regulations for the Shogunal Residence *(Denchū On'okite),* acknowledged with the shogun's seal at the head of the text *(sodehan),* nine articles dated Eiroku 12 (1569)/1/14, and supplement in seven articles, dated Eiroku 12/1/16; Okuno, *Monjo,* no. 142, 1, 239-243. That such a document should have been issued over the name of Nobunaga, who held no bakufu post, is of itself extraordinary.

67. Memorandum in five articles, Nobunaga to Nichijō Shōnin and Akechi Jūbyōe no Jō [Mitsuhide], acknowledged with the shogun's *sodehan,* dated Eiroku 13 (1570)/1/23; Okuno, *Monjo,* no. 209, 1, 343-345; reproduced in Nagahara Keiji, *Sengoku no dōran,* p. 307.

68. Remonstrance in seventeen articles; *Monjo,* no. 340, 1, 565-578. Okuno's text is taken from *Jinkenki,* the diary of the imperial abbot of the Daijōin in Nara, entry for Genki 4 (1573)/2/22; cf. the variant in *Shinchō kōki,* pt. 6, sec. 2, pp. 141-146. There is evidence suggesting that the document was circulating by the ninth month of the previous year, Genki 3.

69. Nobunaga first appears in the official record of appointments to the upper ranks of the imperial nobility *(kugyō* status) as a courtier of the Fourth Rank proper *(shō shii no ge)* and Assistant Metropolitan Police Commissioner *(danjō no jō)* who was promoted to the junior Third Rank *(ju sanmi)* and the post of Imperial Adviser *(sangi)* on Tenshō 2 (1574)/3/18. On Tenshō 3/11/4 (6 December 1575), he was made Brevet Grand Councillor *(gon dainagon);* three days later, he was also appointed General of the Right *(udaishō),* a post he held through his subsequent promotions. On Tenshō 4/11/21 (11 December 1576), he was raised to the Third Rank proper *(shō sanmi)* and became Minister of the Middle *(naidaijin).* On Tenshō 5/11/16 (25 December 1577), he was promoted to the junior Second Rank *(ju nii),* and four days later to Minister of the Right *(udaijin).* On Tenshō 6/1/6 (12 February 1578), he was raised to the Second Rank proper *(shō nii).* See *Kugyō bunin,* 3, *Kokushi taikei,* 55 (Tokyo: Kokushi Taikei Kankōkai, 1936), 471-478.

70. Nobunaga to Tō no Uchūben [Hirohashi Kanekatsu], dated Tenshō 6/4/9; in *Kanemi-kyō ki,* 1, 140, entry for that date; Okuno, *Monjo,* no. 707, 2, 280-281 (mistakenly entered under Tenshō 5).

71. See *Oyudono no Ue no nikki,* 7 (Tokyo: Zoku Gunsho Ruijū Kanseikai, 1934; Gunsho Ruijū Hoi), 378, entry for Tenshō 9 (1581)/3/9; *Kanemi-kyō ki,* 1, 251, entry for Tenshō 9/3/11; and cf. Okuno Takahiro, "Oda seiken no kihon rosen," *Kokushigaku,* 100:49-50 (1976).

72. See the letter from Prince Sanehito to "the former Minister of the Right," n.d. [Tenshō 10/4/?], and the diary of Kanshuji Harutoyo, *Nichinichiki,* entry for Tenshō 10/5/4; both reproduced in *Kyōto no rekishi,* 4 (1969), 230-231.

73. Nobunaga to [Kanbe] Sanshichirō (his son Nobutaka), Tenshō 10/5/7; Okuno, *Monjo,* no. 1052, 2, 764-765. Cf. the dispositions made after the conquest

of the Takeda earlier that year, Regulations for the Two Provinces of Kai and Shinano, dated Tenshō 10/3/–; *Shinchō kōki,* pt. 15, sec. 19, pp. 398–399; *Monjo,* no. 985, 2, 702–704.

74. "The Coppie of ª Letter written from Fa:Organtine one of the Societie of the name of Jhs to the Fa:generall of the same Societie from Meaco in JAPONIA," 29 September 1594 (Houghton Library MS. Jap 3, "Seven unrecorded contemporary English translations of Jesuit letters from Japan"; cited by permission of the Houghton Library, Harvard University), ff. 3v–4v.

75. Organtino, f. 2v, notes that the Japanese first sought to obtain these accessories from their Portuguese visitors, "& woulde not sticke to geve 10 or 12 Crownes for a paire of cõmon beades." Local entrepreneurs evidently were quick to detect the commercial possibilities of this demand, so that "nowe theie gett theire owne woorkmen to make [the sacramentals] for them, and doe weare them in all partes of the Cuntrie. . . ."

76. Orders dated Keichō 1/11/10 (29 December 1596), in "The Report of the glorious death of xxvj persons . . . sent by ff:Lewis ffrois the xvᵗʰ of marche [1597] to Claudius Acquauiua gen'all" (Houghton Library MS. Jap 3), pp. 63–64.

77. "A Letter of Fa: Francis Passio to ỹ Generall of the Societie of Jhesus written the 3ᵈ of October. 1598." (Houghton Library MS. Jap 3), f. 5v.

78. That these assaults were not confined to the intellectual front but also inspired the destruction of shrines of the native tradition is well known. What may be the most spectacular act of this sort, however, has scarcely been noted so far. The destruction of classical Buddhism's greatest temple, the Tōdaiji of Nara, in 1567 is commonly attributed to Matsunaga Hisahide, that paragon of *gekokujō.* But Frois tells a different story: "A large part of the army which besieged [Hisahide's] fortress of Tamonyama was encamped in this temple of the Daibut and throughout the precincts of this monastery. Among them was also a brave soldier—one who is well known to our people—who in his zeal for the religion and the worship appropriate solely to the Creator of the Universe, without being persuaded to do so by any man, while on guard duty at night secretly set fire to the place. And so everything that was there burnt down, with nothing left standing except a gate which was situated far away at the entrance. . . ." See *Die Geschichte Japans,* p. 253; *Furoisu Nihonshi,* 3, 296.

79. See my *Deus Destroyed,* ch. 8, pp. 212–247.

80. For recent statements to this effect, see Hayashiya, *Kan'ei Sakoku, Kokumin no rekishi,* 14 (Tokyo: Bun'eidō, 1971, second printing), 130–148, and cf. his "Kasei bunka no rekishiteki ichi," in *Kasei bunka no kenkyū,* ed. Hayashiya (Tokyo: Iwanami, 1976), pp. 3–42.

81. A. G. Dickens, *The Counter Reformation* (London: Thames and Hudson, 1968), p. 81.

82. Cf. Kenneth B. Pyle, *The New Generation in Meiji Japan: Problems of Cultural Identity, 1885–1895* (Stanford: Stanford University Press, 1969), p. 4. Pyle calls this sensibility an awareness of the "self-effacement that cultural borrowing implied." Also see Motoyama Yukihiko, "Kokusuishugi," in *Nihon shisōshi kōza,* ed. Furukawa Tesshi and Ishida Ichirō, 6 (*Kindai no shisō* 1; Tokyo: Yūzankaku, 1976), 79–103.

83. Kawano Kenji, "Meiji Ishin to 'Seiyō,' " in *Burujowa kakumei no hikaku kenkyū,* ed. Kuwabara Takeo (Tokyo: Chikuma Shobō, 1965), pp. 22–23.

84. Akutagawa Ryūnosuke, "Kamigami no bishō" (1921).

85. *The Far East* (Tokyo: Yūshōdō reprint ed., 1965), 1(3):2 (1 July 1870). Noted by Yokoyama Toshio, " 'Fuā Īsuto'-shi to 'Bunmei Kaika,' " prepared for presentation at the Research Institute for Humanistic Studies, Kyoto University, 16 June 1976.

A VISUALIZATION OF EITOKU'S LOST PAINTINGS AT AZUCHI CASTLE

I should like to express my appreciation to Professors Shūjirō Shimada and Martin Collcutt for reading this essay and offering helpful suggestions, many of which I incorporated into the final manuscript.

1. On Tenshō 4 (1576)/4/1, various retainers from Owari, Mino, Ise, Mikawa, Echizen, Wakasa, and the Kinai region, as well as artisans and workmen from Kyoto, Nara, and Sakai, were called to reside temporarily at Azuchi for the purpose of working on the great donjon. Ōta Gyūichi, *Shinchō kōki* (c. 1610), ed. Okuno Takahiro and Iwasawa Yoshihiko, Kadokawa Bunko 2541 (Tokyo: Kadokawa, 1969), pt. 9, sec. 1, p. 207.

Kano Eitoku's younger brother Sōshu (1551–1601) mentioned in his will of 1601 that when Eitoku went to reside at Azuchi, he entrusted his Kyoto property to Sōshu's care. This document is quoted in Asaoka Okisada (1800–1856), *Koga bikō* (Tokyo: Shibunkaku, 1970), p. 1607.

2. Although Niwa Nagahide (called Korezumi Gorozaemon after 1575) was initially assigned to be overall commissioner of construction (*Shinchō kōki*, pt. 9, sec. 1, p. 207), he did not remain on the site: just a month after construction began at Azuchi, he was off fighting on the Osaka front (ibid., sec. 4, p. 210). Later, when Ōta Gyūichi describes the program of the donjon, he names Kimura Jirozaemon as construction commissioner (ibid., sec. 5, p. 217). Kimura is mentioned in connection with previous building projects of Nobunaga's (ibid., pt. 8, sec. 6, pp. 191–192 and sec. 10, p. 203, both in 1575), and his name appears third—after Eitoku's and Mitsunobu's—on the list of those who were rewarded with *kosode* for their part in the Azuchi project on Tenshō 9 (1581)/9/8 (ibid., pt. 14, sec. 10, p. 363). Niwa Nagahide was on a campaign in the province of Iga at that time and does not appear on the list. Hence it was probably Kimura who directly supervised the work at Azuchi. It is also interesting to note that Kimura witnessed the destruction of Azuchi Castle in 1582 (ibid., pt. 15, sec. 34, p. 423). I am indebted to George Elison for this information clarifying the identity of the person intermediary between Nobunaga and Eitoku.

3. Naitō Akira, "Azuchi-jō no kenkyū," *Kokka*, nos. 987 and 988 (February and March 1976). For further discussion of Naitō's study in terms of the architectural features of Azuchi Castle, see George Elison, "The Cross and the Sword," pp. 62–66 above. Another Japanese architectural historian has recently challenged the sources on which Naitō based his reconstruction; see Miyakami Shigetaka, "Azuchi-jō Tenshu no fukugen to sono shiryō ni tsuite: Naitō Akira-shi 'Azuchi-jō no kenkyū' ni taisuru gimon," *Kokka*, nos. 998 and 999 (February and March 1977).

4. *Shinchō kōki*, pt. 9, sec. 5, pp. 213–217.

5. See Naitō, *Kokka*, 988:23–32 and 37–39, and appendix, reconstruction 05, which shows the vertical cross section.

6. This arrangement corresponds precisely with the plan of a typical palatial war-

rior residence of the early modern period given in *Shōmei,* a five-volume handbook of building and design methods prepared in 1608 by the Heinouchi family, the chief carpenters for the Tokugawa shogunate in the Edo period. A clarified rendering of the plan from this work is given by Naitō, *Kokka,* 988:37. A photograph of the scroll, kept at Tokyo University, may be seen in Hirai Kiyoshi, *Feudal Architecture of Japan,* trans. Hiroaki Sato and Jeannine Ciliotta (Tokyo: Heibonsha, 1973), fig. 73.

7. *Nando* is a loose term for a service room. It is generally defined as a storage room, but it can also be a room where guards are stationed or trays of food prepared. When located in a public section of the residence, it is appropriately decorated with paintings.

8. According to Naitō, the standard intercolumnation at Azuchi Castle was seven *shaku,* or about seven English feet. Since the size of.*tatami,* or woven-reed mats, usually corresponds to this measurement, the *tatami* used in Nobunaga's residence were probably about seven feet by three and a half feet. Hence the area of a four-mat room would be seven by fourteen feet.

9. Two of these share the main staircase to the third floor and are mentioned in the *Shinchō kōki,* pt. 9, sec. 5, p. 214, as being painted in gold.

10. These rooms are separated from the central vault by a long service room and from the exterior wall by an irregularly shaped veranda. The *Tenshu sashizu* identifies two of the *zashiki* as containing ink paintings; Naitō, *Kokka,* 988:26.

11. Naitō, *Kokka,* 988:38.

12. Much more study of changes in the arrangement of subjects and styles in *shō-hekiga* of the fifteenth and sixteenth centuries is necessary before meaningful conclusions about their cultural implications can be made. My observations are based primarily on art historical reconstructions of the placement of existing wall paintings from five important Abbot's Quarters. The subjects and styles can be summarized as follows:

Date	Abbot's Quarters	Central Room	Upper Room	Lower Room
1490	Yōtokuin of Daitokuji	Mu-ch'i style in ink monochrome; flowers & birds	Hsia Kuei style in ink monochrome; figures (Four Accomplishments)	Hsia Kuei style in ink monochrome; landscape
1491	Shinjuan of Daitokuji	Mu-ch'i style in ink monochrome; flowers & birds	Liang K'ai style in ink monochrome; figures (1602 replacement by Hasegawa Tōhaku)	Ma Yüan–Hsia Kuei style in ink monochrome; landscape
1513	Daisen'in of Daitokuji	Mu-ch'i style in ink monochrome; landscape (Eight Views)	Academic style in color; flowers & birds	Liang K'ai style in ink monochrome; figures (Farming Scenes)
1543	Reiun'in of Myōshinji	Mu-ch'i style in ink monochrome; flowers & birds	Hsia Kuei style in ink & light color; figures (Four Accomplishments)	Hsia Kuei style in ink monochrome; landscape

| 1566 | Jukōin of Daitokuji | Mu-ch'i style in ink monochrome; flowers & birds | Hsia Kuei style in ink & light color; figures (Four Accomplishments) | Mu-ch'i style in ink monochrome; landscape (Eight Views) |

13. There is a horizontal scroll of the *Eight Views of Hsiao and Hsiang* (*Shōshō hakkei;* ink on paper, 20″ × 34″) which bears a Kuninobu seal used by Eitoku, but—aside from the problem of its questionable authorship—it is a small painting and not a suitable stand-in for a large work. It is published in Tajima Shiichi, ed., *Shinbi taikan* (Tokyo: Nippon Bukkyō Shinbi Kyōkai, 1900–1908), vol. 8.

Among large works, the *Eight Views* painted by Eitoku's father, Kano Shōei (1519–1592), in the Lower Room of the Jukōin in 1566 might supply a few hints, but since Eitoku's manner of composition differed from his father's, that too is an unsuitable illustration. Shōei's paintings are published in *Daitokuji, Jukōin, Shinjuan,* ed. Tanaka Ichimatsu, *Shōhekiga zenshū,* vol. 8 (Tokyo: Bijutsu Shuppansha, 1971).

14. Sets of *Eight Views of Hsiao and Hsiang* by Hsia Kuei, Mu-ch'i, Yü-chien, and Chang Fang-ju are recorded in *Gyomotsu on'e mokuroku,* the catalogue of selected works from the Ashikaga Shogunal Collection; see Tani Shin'ichi, "Gyomotsu on'e mokuroku," *Muromachi jidai bijutsushi ron* (Tokyo: Tōkyōdō, 1942), p. 139.

15. Nobunaga owned *Descending Geese on Sandbanks, Evening Bell from a Distant Temple,* and *Returning Sails from a Distant Shore. Returning Sails* is thought to be the scroll rescued from the flames of the Honnōji in 1582 by the young teaman Tennōjiya Sōtan. The *Yamanoue Sōji ki* (postscript dated Tenshō 17, or 1589) records that, seven years after Nobunaga's death in the Honnōji Affair, *Descending Geese* and *Evening Bell* were owned by Hideyoshi, while *Returning Sails* had passed into the hands of the Hōjō family of Odawara. In addition to these three Hsiao-Hsiang paintings, Nobunaga is associated with a fourth, Yü-chien's *Mountain Village in Light Mist,* which he presented to Niwa Nagahide in 1576 in recognition of his role in the Azuchi Castle project (*Shinchō kōki,* pt. 9, sec. 4, p. 212; Tenshō 4/7). See Kuwata Tadachika, *Bushō to chadō* (Tokyo: Jinbutsu Ōrai-sha, 1974), pp. 74–93.

16. The Sakai tea connoisseur Yamanoue Sōji noted on his just-cited list of celebrated tea ceremony paintings that *Evening Bell from a Distant Temple,* owned by the *Kanpaku* Hideyoshi, was the finest of Yü-chien's *Eight Views;* see *Yamanoue Sōji ki,* ed. Yokoi Kiyoshi, in *Nihon no chasho,* ed. Hayashiya Tatsusaburō et al., 1, Tōyō Bunko 201 (Tokyo: Heibonsha, 1971), 198–199.

17. The surviving views of Hsiao and Hsiang from the Yü-chien set known in the sixteenth century are *Mountain Village in Light Mist* in the Yoshikawa Fumiko Collection, *Returning Sails from a Distant Shore* in the Tokugawa Art Museum, and *Autumn Moon over Tung-t'ing Lake* in the Yada Matsutarō Collection. They are published in Tokyo National Museum, *Sō-Gen no kaiga* (Tokyo: Benridō, 1962), pls. 120–123.

18. Motonobu recognized Eitoku's talent early, and must have had great expectations for the boy's future. When Shogun Ashikaga Yoshiteru returned to Kyoto early in 1552 and held audience for prominent citizens of the capital, Yamashina Tokitsugu (1507–1579) reported in his diary that "Artist Kano Hōgen [Motonobu] and his grandson [Eitoku]" were presented to the shogun. See *Tokitsugu-kyō ki,* 2

(Tokyo: Kokusho Kankōkai, 1914), 443, entry for Tenbun 21/1/29. Eitoku was nine years old at the time, with seven years remaining before Motonobu's death in 1559. It is assumed that he was personally instructed by his grandfather in painting methods.

19.   Several versions of the *Four Accomplishments* are associated with Motonobu, but none seems to have been painted before the mid-sixteenth century. The set of *Four Accomplishments* sliding-door panels from the Reiun'in in Myōshinji is probably most relevant to this discussion, since it is also a series of wall paintings. It is published iin Tajima Shiichi, *Masterpieces by Motonobu,* vol. 1 (Tokyo: Shinbi Shoin, 1904), pls. 15-22.

20.   The paintings have not survived, but they are known from rich documentation in the section of *Onryōken nichiroku* written by Kisen Shūshō in the years 1484-1493. The relevant passages from this source, as well as other documents related to Masanobu, are cited and discussed in Watanabe Hajime's fine study "Kano Masanobu," *Higashiyama suibokuga no kenkyū* (Tokyo: Zauhō Kankōkai, 1948), pp. 257-275 and 319-330.

21.   Kano Einō (1634-1700), *Honchō gashi,* in Sakazaki Tan, ed., *Nihon garon taikan,* 2 (Tokyo: Ars, 1928), 998.

22.   Ibid.

23.   In 1423, Prince Fushimi Sadafusa reported that he saw a large blossoming plum tree *(baika taiboku)* painting on four wall panels *(shōji)* at the Daitsūin, the work of the monk-painter Ton Shoki. See *Kanmon gyoki,* entry for Ōei 30/7/19, *Zoku Gunsho ruijū, Hoi* 3 (Tokyo: Zoku Gunsho Ruijū Kanseikai, 1930), p. 398. This reference does not necessarily mean that the plum tree dominated the painting, as it probably did in the later work of Eitoku, but it does indicate that a plum tree could be the subject of a wall painting as early as 1423.

24.   It names the *zashiki* painted with plum the *sumie no ma* (Ink Painting Room), and marks the eight-mat room containing paintings of Confucian scholars with the word *sumie.* Naitō, *Kokka,* 988:24-25.

25.   Elison's translation, p. 64 above, of *izure mo, shita yori ue made, on'zashiki no uchi, on'e-dokoro, kotogotoku kin nari.* It should be noted that the word *kin* always refers to gold leaf as distinct from gold paint, which is rendered *kindei* or simply *dei.*

26.   For example, in his screens of *Scenes In and Around Kyoto* and *Tale of Genji,* presented by Nobunaga to Uesugi Kenshin in 1574. The screens thought by many scholars to be the surviving *Scenes In and Around Kyoto* are discussed by Mizuo Hiroshi in "Uesugi-ke-zō Rakuchū-Rakugai-zu byōbu," *Kokka,* no. 862 (1964).

27.   Hasegawa Tōhaku (1539-1610), *Rocks and Waves,* twelve sliding-door panels now mounted as hanging scrolls, ink and gold leaf on paper, each 180 × 139 cm, Zenrinji, Kyoto. Two panels are published in color in Kawai Masatomo and Wakisaka Atsushi, *Momoyama no shōheiga: Eitoku, Tōhaku, Yūshō, Nihon bijutsu zenshū,* vol. 17 (Tokyo: Gakken, 1978), pl. 46.

28.   Kano Einō, *Honchō gashi,* p. 998.

29.   The initial studies concerning the imperial grant to Nanzenji were done by the architectural historian Fujioka Michio in two articles of the early 1950s, subsequently included in his *Kyōto Gosho* (Tokyo: Shōkokusha, 1956). The problems concerning the paintings at Nanzenji have been explicated by four Japanese scholars. In *Kokka,* no. 902 (May 1967), Yamane Yūzō surveyed the history of research concerning the

paintings, and Kobayashi Chū considered their present state, attempting to reconstruct their original placement. In *Kokka,* no. 903 (June 1967), Tsuji Nobuo discussed their style and speculated about probable artists. In the same issue, Mizuo Hiroshi wrote about the seventeenth-century Kano school paintings in the Small Abbot's Quarters *(Ko Hōjō).* These analyses were abbreviated and published as *Nanzenji Honbō,* ed. Yamane Yūzō, *Shōhekiga zenshū,* vol. 7 (Tokyo: Bijutsu Shuppansha, 1968).

30.   There is also a group of paintings in color on plain ground that look back to the detailed lines and forms of Motonobu.

31.   Takeda Tsuneo, "Kinpeki shōhekiga ni tsuite," *Ars Buddhica,* 59:105–122 (December 1965). Professor Takeda's conclusions provide the framework for my discussion of the gold-leaf paintings at Azuchi Castle.

32.   Takeda cites as the earliest completely gold-ground compositions the *Pheasant and Plum Tree* and the *Tiger in Bamboo* in Myōshinji's Tenkyūin Abbot's Quarters, painted by Sanraku's school in 1631. Photographs of these paintings with details in color may be found in *Myōshinji Tenkyūin,* ed. Tsuji Nobuo, *Shōhekiga zenshū,* 2 (Tokyo: Bijutsu Shuppansha, 1967), 18–19 and 30–33.

33.   *Nanzenji Honbō,* pp. 92–93. The five left-side panels are shown in color on pp. 13–16.

34.   See Elison, "The Cross and the Sword," p. 65 and his n. 32 above. Chang Kuo and his magic steed are depicted in *kinpeki* on decorated wooden doors *(chōdaigamae)* in the Myōhōin in Kyoto; the work is traditionally attributed to Eitoku but is closer to the gentle manner of his son Mitsunobu. This painting is published in Tanaka Kisaku, *Momoyama jidai kinpeki shōhekiga* (Tokyo: Ōtsuka Kōgeisha, 1937), pl. 30, I-4. Lü Tung-pin is shown receiving instruction from Chung Li-ch'üan in one of the Nanzenji panels, published ibid., pl. 5, II-3.

35.   The relevant documents are cited in Takeda Tsuneo, *Kano Eitoku, Nihon no bijutsu* 94 (Tokyo: Shibundō, 1974), p. 78.

36.   *Ch'ao Fu,* a hanging scroll in ink on paper, 125.5 cm high by 52.5 cm wide, is published in *Higashiyama suibokuga shū* (Tokyo: Jurakusha, 1933–1936).

37.   This is apparent in the few color reproductions I have been able to study, but most of the strong colors have peeled off, giving an even more muted effect than would have been the case originally. For my general statement concerning overall coloration, I am relying on the judgment of Tsuji Nobuo (*Kokka,* 903:11), who has studied closely the paintings themselves.

38.   Kano Einō, *Honchō gashi,* p. 1002.

39.   Unkoku Tōgan, *Horses in a Landscape,* c. 1600, a pair of six-fold screens in ink on paper, each 149 × 360.5 cm, Kyoto National Museum; published in *Momoyama: Japanese Art in the Age of Grandeur; An Exhibition at the Metropolitan Museum of Art* (New York: Metropolitan Museum of Art, 1975), no. 20, pp. 43–45.

40.   Hasegawa Tōhaku, *Rounding Up Horses,* c. 1570, a pair of six-fold screens in color on paper, each 165.5 × 342 cm, Tokyo National Museum; published ibid., no. 12, pp. 25–27.

41.   Kano Einō, *Honchō gashi,* p. 999.

42.   Hsi Wang-mu, the "Queen Mother of the West," and Tung Wang-kung, the "King of the East," reside in a palace in the K'un-lun Mountains, presiding over Yin and Yang to regulate heaven and earth. Hsi Wang-mu is particularly revered by Taoists for her possession of the peaches of immortality.

43.   *Hsi Wang-mu and Tung Wang-kung,* in ink and light color on paper, sliding-

door panels now mounted as four hanging scrolls, each 174 × 67.8 cm, Tokyo National Museum; published in Doi Tsugiyoshi, *Motonobu, Eitoku,* vol. 8 of *Suiboku bijutsu taikei* (Tokyo: Kōdansha, 1974), pl. 20.

44. Attributed to the Kano school artist Watanabe Ryōkei (d. 1645), *Hsi Wang-mu,* four panels in colors and gold on paper pasted on decorated wooden doors *(chō-daigamae),* each 143.5 × 103 cm, Nishi Honganji, Kyoto; published in *Nishi Honganji,* ed. Doi Tsugiyoshi, *Shōhekiga zenshū,* 10 (Tokyo: Bijutsu Shuppansha, 1968), 10.

45. See Elison, "The Cross and the Sword," p. 65 and his n. 33 above.

46. Sawada Natari, *Kaoku zakkō* (1842), quoted by Takeda Tsuneo, *Shōheiga, Genshoku Nihon no bijutsu,* 13 (Tokyo: Shōgakkan, 1967), 225.

47. P. Luis Frois SJ to P. Belchior de Figueiredo SJ, 12 July 1569; *CARTAS QVE OS PADRES E IRMÃOS da Companhia de Iesus escreuerão dos Reynos de Iapão & China aos da mesma Companhia da India, & Europa, des do anno de 1549. atè o de 1580.* (Em Euora por Manoel de Lyra. Anno de M.D.XCVIII.), 1, 272v.

48. P. João Rodrigues Tçuzzu SJ, *História da Igreja do Japão,* ed. João do Amaral Abranches Pinto, 1 (Macao: Notícias de Macau, 1954), 212; English translation by Michael Cooper SJ, *This Island of Japon* (Tokyo and New York: Kodansha, 1973), p. 95; Japanese translation by Doi Tadao et al., *Nihon kyōkai shi,* 1 (Tokyo: Iwanami, 1967), 342.

49. *Chinese Lions* originally formed a pair with a now-lost screen which was copied by Kano Tsunenobu (1636–1713). Tsunenobu's copy is published in *Kokka,* no. 418 (September 1925).

50. Tsuji Nobuo, "Jukōin no shōhekiga to Shōei, Eitoku," in *Daitokuji, Jukōin, Shinjuan,* ed. Tanaka Ichimatsu, p. 145.

51. *Pine,* sixteen sliding-door panels, in colors and gold leaf on paper; the panels measure from 163.6 to 172.6 cm in height and vary from 102 to 131.2 cm in width. Published in Tanaka Kisaku, *Momoyama jidai kinpeki shōhekiga,* pls. 34–35.

52. Yamane Yūzō, "Hinoki-zu byōbu," *Kokka,* 778:23 (January 1957).

53. As is usual in *fusuma* construction, five widths of paper were used for its vertical dimension. Paper widths generally ranged from about 35 to 40 cm in height. Since the total height of *Cypress* is 170 cm, and the interior three sheets appear fairly uniform, a minimum of 5 cm or a maximum of 30 cm is lost. The size of the top and bottom sheets, however, indicates that the loss was only about 10 cm. I was able to study this painting when it was exhibited in the Tokyo National Museum in August 1976, but was unable to measure it.

54. Naitō, *Kokka,* 988:30.

55. There is paulownia painted on a sliding-door panel in the Hōnen'in, attributed to Eitoku; published in *Nihonga taisei* 5, *Kano-ha* 1 (Tokyo: Tōhō Shoin, 1931), pl. 88. A seventeenth-century example of the phoenix in paulownia theme is the folding screen by Kano Tsunenobu (1636–1713) owned by the Tōkyō Geijutsu Daigaku; published in Takeda, *Shōheiga,* pl. 45. Both are large-scale *kinpeki* works, but neither is a reliable indicator of Eitoku's likely handling of the subject. Among small-scale works, ten of the 240 fans pasted on eight folding screens owned by Nanzenji depict phoenix in paulownia in gold leaf and color. All are considered to be works of sixteenth- and early seventeenth-century Kano school artists. See Takeda Tsuneo, *Nanzenji senmen byōbu* (Tokyo: Fujiāto Shuppan, 1973), fans numbered 28, 32, 44, 53, 57, 64, 83, 155, 193, and 208.

For the theme of Hsü Yu and Ch'ao Fu, there are the famous hanging scrolls by

Eitoku in the Tokyo National Museum, both published in *Higashiyama suibokuga shū*, but these are ink paintings. There is also a small fan painting of Hsü Yu and Ch'ao Fu in *kinpeki*, bearing a Naonobu seal of Eitoku's father Shōei, pasted on a folding screen in the Honpōji; published in Takeda, *Kano Eitoku*, pl. 53.

56.   *Cherry and Willows*, four sliding-door panels, in color and gold leaf on paper, each panel 185.3 × 98 cm; published in Tanaka Kisaku, *Momoyama jidai kinpeki shōhekiga*, pl. 3, I-1. Probably part of the same series is *Cherry*, two sliding-door panels, in color and gold leaf on paper, 184.3 × 93.6 cm and 183.4 × 94 cm; published in *Nanzenji Honbō*, p. 38, with a detail in color on p. 39.

57.   The *Tenshu sashizu* notes apropos of the outer gallery that "on the inner columns are ascending dragons and descending dragons" *(uchi no hashira nobori ryū kudari ryū ari)*, so that Gyūichi's illogical mention of this motif in the seventh-story Confucian context is a mistake. Naitō Akira explains that the "angels in their earthly manifestations" *(tennin goyōgō)* attributed by the *Shinchō kōki* to the ceiling of the seventh story must also be a mistaken interpolation on the compiler's part, since the *Tenshu sashizu* specifies that in the inner Buddhist chapel "between the ceiling rafters"—sc., the coffers of a coffered ceiling—"there is a large number of angels" *(tenjō nageshi tennin amata ari)*. See Naitō, *Kokka*, 988:32–33, and cf. Elison, "The Cross and the Sword," p. 65 above.

58.   Naitō discusses the symbolic implications of Azuchi Castle in terms of the concept of *Tentō*, or the Way of Heaven, in *Kokka*, 988:45–49.

59.   Naitō, *Kokka*, 988:34.

60.   A photograph of the lacquer-floored room is found in *Shoin*, 1, ed. Ōta Hirotarō, *Nihon kenchikushi kiso shiryō shūsei*, vol. 16 (Tokyo: Chūō Kōron Bijutsu Shuppan, 1971), pl. 7. Naitō discusses the Kinkaku as a prototype for Azuchi Castle in *Kokka*, 988:40–42 and 51.

JŌHA, A SIXTEENTH-CENTURY POET OF LINKED VERSE

1.   The account was written in 1675 by Kurokawa Dōyū (d. 1691), a Confucian doctor. Quoted in Odaka Toshio, *Aru rengashi no shōgai* (Tokyo: Shibundō, 1967), p. 16.

2.   Odaka, p. 18.

3.   Odaka, pp. 20–21. But Morozumi Kuraichi in "Satomura Jōha shōden," *Renga haikai kenkyū*, 24:1 (February 1963), states that he has seen no primary source which confirms this statement, found in *Zoku Kinsei kijin den*.

4.   Matsunaga Teitoku, *Taionki*, ed. Odaka Toshio, in *Taionki, Oritaku shiba no ki, Rantō kotohajime*, Nihon Koten Bungaku Taikei 95 (Tokyo: Iwanami, 1964), p. 63.

5.   Odaka, *Aru rengashi no shōgai*, p. 30, suggests it was because Sōboku was about to set out on extended travels.

6.   Odaka, p. 33. But Morozumi, p. 2, believes that it was not until 1552 that Jōha composed renga in the capital. Fukui Kyūzō in *Renga no shiteki kenkyū*, 1 (Tokyo: Seibidō Shoten, 1930), 272, mentions a renga session held in 1549 at the Daikakuji in which four poets including Jōha participated. In 1550 he joined with such masters as Sōyō and Shōkyū in a one-hundred-link sequence (Odaka, p. 33). In 1552 he joined with professional renga poets and nobles in a one-hundred-link sequence. Obviously, different standards have been applied in determining the year of his "debut."

7. Matsunaga, *Taionki*, p. 63.

8. Quoted by Morozumi, p. 2.

9. See Odaka, pp. 40–41.

10. Odaka, p. 41. *Hokkyō* was the third highest Buddhist rank; towards the close of his career Jōha rose to *hōgen*, the second rank.

11. Odaka, p. 46.

12. Sanjōnishi Kin'eda, *Yoshino mōde no ki*, in *Gunsho ruijū*, 11 (Tokyo: Keizai Zasshi-sha, 1899), 338:1244.

13. Ibid., p. 1245.

14. Ibid., pp. 1251–1252.

15. Odaka, p. 59.

16. Odaka, p. 60. Also see *Haikai daijiten*, ed. Ijichi Tetsuo (Tokyo: Meiji Shoin, 1957), p. 316.

17. Odaka, p. 63.

18. This priest visited China twice and often advised Nobunaga about China; see Odaka, p. 65. He is listed as Shūryō Sakugen in *Shinsei Dai jinmei jiten*, 3 (Tokyo: Heibonsha, 1937), 347.

19. Fukui Kyūzō, *Renga no shiteki kenkyū*, 1, 283. Fukui gives an incorrect text. I have given the version kindly supplied by the late Professor Mizukami Kashizō.

20. Odaka, p. 71; Morozumi, p. 3.

21. Odaka, p. 73.

22. Odaka, p. 79.

23. Odaka, p. 80, quotes an anecdote from *Kinō wa kyō no monogatari*, a seventeenth-century book of amusing stories. A country visitor whom Jōha introduced to Sanjōnishi Kin'eda was guilty of a lapse of manners when he described the inn at which he was staying as being "a dirty place west of Sanjō" *(Sanjō nishi no tsura no kitanai ie);* this could also mean "the house of Sanjōnishi with the dirty face."

24. Odaka, p. 83.

25. Matsunaga, *Taionki*, p. 67; quoted by Donald Keene, *Landscapes and Portraits* (Tokyo and Palo Alto: Kodansha International Ltd., 1971), p. 72.

26. Quoted by Keene, p. 76.

27. Odaka, p. 85.

28. Satomura Jōha, *Jōha Fujimi michi no ki*, in *Gunsho ruijū*, 11, 339:1299. Also see Odaka, pp. 88 and 92.

29. *Jōha Fujimi michi no ki*, p. 1299. He was seen off by such people as the celebrated Nō actor, Kanze Sōsetsu.

30. Ibid., p. 1306.

31. Narugami Katsumi, *Nihon kikō bungei shi* (Tokyo: Tsukuda Shobō, 1943), p. 221.

32. *Jōha Fujimi michi no ki*, p. 1315.

33. Odaka, p. 125.

34. George Sansom, *A History of Japan: 1334–1615* (London: Cresset, 1961), p. 310.

35. *Shinchōki*, ed. Matsuzawa Chiri, 1 (Tokyo: Koten Bunko, 1967), 184–185. Also see Araki Yoshio, *Azuchi-Momoyama jidai bungaku shi* (Tokyo: Kadokawa, 1969), p. 343. Even in later years Nobunaga directly and indirectly menaced Jōha. In 1573, when his troops were ravaging the outskirts of Kyoto, they broke open the hall of renga composition at the Kitano Shrine where Jōha had deposited his manuscripts, scattering the contents, then set fire to the place, destroying everything. See

Takeuchi Hideo, "Kitano renga kaisho to kaishoryō," *Nihon rekishi*, 94:57–58 (April 1956).

36. Quoted in Araki, p. 344.

37. See Araki, p. 344, for a discussion of the probable authorship of the two verses.

38. Odaka, pp. 140 ff.

39. Odaka, p. 143.

40. Araki, pp. 351–352.

41. Sansom, p. 366. There is a pun on *Sesshō*, "Regent of State": a homophone written with different characters means "murder." A *Sesshō* exercised the ruling power during the sovereign's minority, whereas a *Kanpaku* or "Imperial Regent" did so for a ruler who had reached adulthood.

42. Matsunaga, *Taionki*, p. 66.

43. *Tamon'in nikki*, ed. Tsuji Zennosuke, 4 (Tokyo: Kadokawa, 1967), 344.

44. Cf. Araki, p. 368. The poem by Narihira is *Kokinshū*, no. 268.

45. Odaka, p. 176.

46. Odaka, pp. 177–178.

47. Odaka, pp. 184–185.

48. Matsunaga, *Taionki*, p. 70; also see pp. 123–124, nn. 300–305 by Odaka Toshio. Jōha himself more philosophically explained his exile as having been preordained from a former life, pointing out that the literary names he had chosen (Jōha and Rinkōsai) both suggested exile in Gōshū (the province of Ōmi, present Shiga prefecture); *Taionki*, p. 72.

49. Ibid., p. 72.

50. Aso Koretada, *Gen'yo nikki*, in *Gunsho ruijū*, 11, 325:785.

51. Ibid., p. 790.

52. *Ueda Akinari shū*, ed. Nakamura Yukihiko, Nihon Koten Bungaku Taikei 56 (Tokyo: Iwanami, 1959), p. 82. In the story *Buppōsō* it states: "From behind where we were kneeling a powerfully built priest with a broad face and prominent features appeared at the lowest place in the gathering, adjusting his monk's robe as he approached." The nobleman questions the priest about various ancient words, and when the priest (who proves to be Jōha) unhesitantly replies, the nobleman commands, "Give him a reward!" Jōha figures in a similar role in the collection of anecdotes *Seisuishō* (1623), compiled by the priest Anrakuan Sakuden (1554–1642); ed. Suzuki Tōzō, Kadokawa Bunko (Tokyo: Kadokawa, 1964).

53. *Masamune Hakuchō*, Nihon no Bungaku 11 (Tokyo: Chūō Kōron-sha, 1968), pp. 239–255. Hakuchō mistakenly read Jōha's name as Shōha; the play was therefore titled *Mitsuhide to Shōha*. Jōha is represented as cowardly and sycophantic, and betrays Mitsuhide to enemy soldiers.

54. Jōha's renga criticism is discussed at length by Araki, pp. 351–360. Perhaps his most important thesis was that the sentiments expressed in a poem must be exactly appropriate to the scene. This involved minute differentiations in describing cherry blossoms at their different stages in order to grasp their essential nature at each moment from their first budding until their fall. One remark stands out: "Penetrating to the heart of renga is the same as attaining the Way of the Buddha. The man who has not penetrated to the depths of this art cannot know the meaning of true gentleness of heart." (Araki, pp. 359–360.)

55. Matsunaga Teitoku, *Teitoku-ō no ki*, in *Zoku Gunsho ruijū*, 33-1 (Tokyo: Zoku Gunsho Ruijū Kanseikai, 1927), 959:2.

CITY AND COUNTRY:
SONG AND THE PERFORMING ARTS IN SIXTEENTH-CENTURY JAPAN

1.   Recorded in *Kyōgen*, Victor Company of Japan SJ 3009/1-3 and SJ 3010/1-3. Pages 37-39 of Koyama Hiroshi's commentary to the first volume of these two albums contain the text of the Izumi School performance version of *Wakana*.

2.   The *Tenshō kyōgenbon* has been published in *Kyōgen shū*, 3, ed. Furukawa Hisashi, Nihon Koten Zensho [40] (Tokyo: Asahi Shinbun-sha, 1956), 207-332. The subscript is reproduced and discussed on p. 211; the entry for *Wakana* is pp. 312-313.

In addition to the plays which are described in the *Tenshō kyōgenbon*, some fifty others are mentioned by title.

3.   Araki Yoshio, *Azuchi-Momoyama jidai bungaku shi* (Tokyo: Kadokawa, 1969), pp. 412-418.

4.   Ibid., pp. 215-216.

5.   *Yukiyama* was one of five *komai* filmed by the Molpe group in the summer of 1974; film in my personal collection. The performer was Yamamoto Tōjūrō, the head of the Ōkura School in Tokyo.

The piece is included as no. 122 in the collection of songs for Kyōgen *komai*, *Kyōgen kayō*, in *Chūsei-Kinsei kayō shū*, ed. Shinma Shin'ichi, Shida Engi, and Asano Kenji, Nihon Koten Bungaku Taikei 44 (Tokyo: Iwanami, 1959), p. 229. (This Iwanami series is hereafter cited as NKBT.)

6.   The English versions of songs in the *Kanginshū* are from my translation of the anthology, "Private Music," in Frank Hoff, *Song, Dance, Storytelling: Aspects of the Performing Arts in Japan*, Cornell University East Asia Papers no. 15 (Ithaca: Cornell China-Japan Program, 1978), pp. 1-72.

Convenient editions of the *Kanginshū* may be found in: *Chūsei-Kinsei kayō shū*, NKBT 44, pp. 131-196; *Kagura uta, Saibara, Ryōjin hishō, Kanginshū*, ed. Usuda Jingorō and Shinma Shin'ichi, Nihon Koten Bungaku Zenshū 25 (Tokyo: Shōgakkan, 1976), pp. 381-476. For song no. 3, see p. 149 and p. 390 respectively.

7.   NKBT 44, p. 157; Nihon Koten Bungaku Zenshū 25, p. 409. The last line of this poem is found in a slightly different wording in *Wakana*.

8.   NKBT 44, p. 160; Nihon Koten Bungaku Zenshū 25, p. 415. The last line is not found in *Wakana*. In its place is: "Do not awake me from my dream."

9.   *Motomezuka*, in *Yōkyoku shū*, 1, ed. Yokomichi Mario and Omote Akira, NKBT 40 (1960), 69.

10.   *Oharagi* is no. 20 of the thirty-one songs from the repertory of Women's Kabuki contained in the Tenri Library volume *Odori* (Kan'ei period, 1624-1645); published in *Nihon shomin bunka shiryō shūsei*, 5, *Kayō*, ed. Asano Kenji (Tokyo: San'ichi Shobō, 1973), 466-483; for *Oharagi*, see pp. 476-477. This text underlies my translation of these "Songs for Dance," in *Song, Dance, Storytelling*, pp. 73-105; song no. 20, "Firewood from Ohara," p. 94.

A detailed study of this song and its relationship with dance may be found in Hattori Yukio, *Kabuki seiritsu no kenkyū* (Tokyo: Kazama Shobō, 1968), pp. 214-237.

11.   Entry for *Mochisake*, Nihon Koten Zensho [40], pp. 322-323; for *Suehirogari*, p. 247.

12.   *Kyōgen shū*, 1, ed. Koyama Hiroshi, NKBT 42 (1960), 79-80.

13.   For the Tenshō version of *Taue*, see Nihon Koten Zensho [40], pp. 251-252.

An abbreviated text of the contemporary Ōkura performance version of *Onda* may be found in *Kyōgen*, Victor Company of Japan SJ 3010/1–3, commentary, p. 30. The article "Kyōgen no *Onda* to ta-asobi" by Arai Tsuneyasu, *Geinō ronsan* (Tokyo: Kinseisha, 1976), points to connections between the texts of this Kyōgen play and the ritual performances called *ta-asobi*, imitative of the farmers' work cycle, still performed in the countryside today.

14.   James T. Araki, *The Ballad-Drama of Medieval Japan* (Berkeley: University of California Press, 1964), pp. 73–74.

15.   Ōta Gyūichi, *Shinchō kōki* (c. 1610), ed. Okuno Takahiro and Iwasawa Yoshihiko, Kadokawa Bunko 2541 (Tokyo: Kadokawa, 1969), Introduction, sec. 21, p. 49.

16.   Ibid., Introduction, sec. 24, p. 52; entry for Tenbun 21 (*sic;* should be Eiroku 3)/5/18. Araki, *Ballad-Drama*, gives a synopsis of *Atsumori* on p. 142 and a translation of the Daihashira Sahei text on pp. 152–171. Nobunaga danced the passage *ningen gojūnen, geten no uchi o kurabureba*, which Araki, p. 168, translates as: "Should man, after his fifty years, scan the subcelestial realm. . . ."

17.   *Shinchō kōki*, pt. 15, sec. 27, pp. 412–413; entry for Tenshō 10/5/19. See *Kōwaka bukyoku shū*, ed. Sasano Ken, 2 (Tokyo: Daiichi Shobō, 1943), 628–630 for the text of *Tauta*, and pp. 140–151 for *Fushimi Tokiwa*.

18.   Araki, *Ballad-Drama*; synopsis of *Fushimi Tokiwa*, p. 125.

19.   *Nihon shomin bunka shiryō shūsei*, 5, 3.

20.   Manabe Masahiro, "Kinsei shoki katarimono no naka no kayō," *Geinōshi kenkyū*, 49:1–16 (April 1975).

21.   The Funaki Screen is often dated broadly to the end of the Keichō era (1596–1615). By careful analysis of internal evidence, Tsuji Nobuo has established that it was painted after the seventh month of 1615 (Genna 1) and before the second month of 1617 (Genna 3); and he further speculates that the *terminus a quo* may be Genna 2/9/24. See Tsuji, "Funaki-ke kyūzōbon Rakuchū-Rakugai-zu byōbu no kentō," in *Fūzokuga: Rakuchū-Rakugai*, ed. Takeda Tsuneo, *Nihon byōbu-e shūsei*, 11 (Tokyo: Kōdansha, 1978), 122–129.

22.   Other scenes from the Funaki Screen are discussed and illustrated in William P. Malm's contribution to this volume.

23.   *Munewari* refers to the Kojōruri play *Amida no munewari*. Performances of this piece are attested in the documentary evidence as early as 1614. Two versions are translated by C. J. Dunn in *The Early Japanese Puppet Drama* (London: Luzac, 1966), pp. 111–134. A synopsis may be found in Donald Keene, *Bunraku: The Art of the Japanese Puppet Theatre* (Tokyo and Palo Alto: Kodansha, 1973), pp. 39–41.

The term Kojōruri applies to puppet plays first performed prior to Chikamatsu Monzaemon's *Shusse Kagekiyo* (1686).

24.   Araki, *Ballad-Drama*; synopsis of *Yamanaka Tokiwa*, p. 128.

25.   See *Kojōruri shōhon shū*, ed. Yokoyama Shigeru, 1 (Tokyo: Kadokawa, 1964), 509–518 for the text of *Yamanaka Tokiwa*, and pp. 588–591 for a consideration of the handscroll, its dating, and the relationship of its text to an original Kojōruri version.

26.   Muroki Yatarō, ed., *Sekkyō shū*, Shinchō Nihon Koten Shūsei (Tokyo: Shinchōsha, 1977), p. 394; also see p. 397, giving the illustration of an old-style Sekkyō performer from a Genna-period (1615–1624) *Rakuchū-Rakugai-zu* in the possession of the Yasaka Shrine.

27. *Sekkyō shōhon shū*, ed. Yokoyama Shigeru, 2 (Tokyo: Kadokawa, 1968), 313–315. In his discussion of the illustrations to this text, Yokoyama points out that the style and state of printing of several of them suggest that the edition is a reworked version of one published around the beginning of the Kanbun period (1661–1673) or earlier. A comparison of the text with that of another printed edition (1666) reveals similarities, e.g., in the indicators *(fushi)* used to show how to sing the recitation. Yokoyama surmises that the text of the 1675 printed version may even be older than that of 1666. Dating the available texts, a painstaking task, is a necessary part of the process of reconstructing what the "original" form of a story's recitation was like at the beginning of the seventeenth century and the end of the sixteenth. There is a continuity from an oral tradition to its eventual printed textual version.

28. Ibid., pp. 72–75; the *Kaidō kudari* section is on p. 74.

29. Manabe, "Kinsei shoki katarimono no naka no kayō," p. 4.

30. Text published in *Sekkyō shū*, Shinchō Nihon Koten Shūsei, pp. 209–298; *michiyuki*, pp. 279–282.

31. For a brief outline of the *Kaidō kudari* theme's historical development, see *Chūsei kayō shū*, ed. Asano Kenji, Nihon Koten Zensho [94] (Tokyo: Asahi Shinbun-sha, 1973, rev. ed.), p. 134, n. 2; and cf. Asano, *Kanginshū kenkyū taisei* (Tokyo: Meiji Shoin, 1968), pp. 537–540.

32. NKBT 44, pp. 83–87.

33. *Yōkyoku taikan*, supplement *(bekkan)*, ed. Sanari Kentarō (Tokyo: Meiji Shoin, 1931), pp. 62–68.

34. *Kumo nusubito*, in *Kyōgen shū*, ed. Kitagawa Tadahiko and Yasuda Akira, Nihon Koten Bungaku Zenshū 35 (Tokyo: Shōgakkan, 1972), pp. 520–529; see p. 527 for the *Kaidō kudari*.

35. The Izumi version of *Kaidō kudari* is recorded on Victor SJ 3010; the text is given on p. 37 of Koyama Hiroshi's commentary to this album. *Kaidō kudari*, danced by Yamamoto Tōjūrō, is yet another *komai* filmed by me and my associates in the summer of 1974.

36. On Ukon Genzaemon's performances of *Kaidō kudari*, see: Shuzui Kenji, *Kabuki tsugan* (1937), *Shuzui Kenji chosakushū*, 2 (Tokyo: Kasama Shoin, 1977), 167–168, citing *Mitsubo monjo;* Kawatake Shigetoshi, *Nihon engeki zenshi* (Tokyo: Iwanami, 1959), p. 299; Benito Ortolani, *Das Kabukitheater: Kulturgeschichte der Anfänge*, Monumenta Nipponica Monographs no. 19 (Tokyo: Sophia University Press, 1964), p. 122.

37. NKBT 44, p. 175; Nihon Koten Bungaku Zenshū 25, pp. 445–446.

38. *Yōkyoku shū*, 2, ed. Yokomichi Mario and Omote Akira, NKBT 41 (1963), 402–407. There is a reference to the structure of Hōka plays in Zeami's *Sandō* (1423); see *Karonshū, Nōgaku ronshū*, ed. Hisamatsu Sen'ichi and Nishio Minoru, NKBT 65 (1961), p. 476.

39. NKBT 44, p. 151; Nihon Koten Bungaku Zenshū 25, pp. 394–395. Like *Kaidō kudari*, the *hana no Miyako* theme appears in various literary genres and performance types.

40. *Shichijūichiban shokunin utaawase*, in *Gunsho ruijū*, 18 (Tokyo: Keizai Zasshi-sha, 1902), 503:67–207; Hōka, p. 162.

"Kokiriko," a representative dance text of the *hana no Miyako* song together with indications of dance movement, is given in *Dengaku-Furyū*, 1, ed. Honda Yasuji, *Nihon no minzoku geinō*, 2 (Tokyo: Mokujisha, 1967), 1258–1259. This is a dance in the repertory of a group from Ogōchi in Metropolitan Tokyo. Photographs of the dancers accompany the text.

41. NKBT 44, pp. 180–181; Nihon Koten Bungaku Zenshū 25, p. 456.

42. Shinma Shin'ichi, "Chūsei no kayō" *Kōza: Nihon bungaku, Chūsei-hen,* 2 (Tokyo: Sanseidō, 1969), 203; n. 10 refers to the original publication of this observation by Tokue Motomasa. The picture in question is reproduced as the third frontispiece to Nihon Koten Bungaku Zenshū 25; a descriptive note by Tokue accompanies it.

43. *Yōkyoku shū,* 1, NKBT 40 (1960), 96–105; see p. 97, n. 4, and p. 433, supp. n. 49, for discussions of the meaning of the term "Jinen Koji."

44. For a discussion of *kouta* as a song type, see my *Song, Dance, Storytelling,* pp. 124–131.

45. *Sekkyō shū,* p. 419; cf. p. 211, nn. 1 and 2, which also mention the story's relationship to the Hachiman Shrine of Sunomata in Anpachi-gun, Gifu prefecture.

46. *The Genial Seed: A Japanese Song Cycle,* tr. Frank Hoff (New York: Mushinsha-Grossman, 1971). A convenient edition of the *Tauezōshi* will be found in NKBT 44, pp. 243–298.

47. Asano Kenji gives a useful general survey of the considerable spread of opinions on the question of dating the *Tauezōshi* in *Nihon shomin bunka shiryō shūsei,* 5, 6–7.

48. The courtier Sanjōnishi Sanetaka mentions that Tosa Mitsunobu in early 1507 was painting a screen depicting Kyoto for the Asakura daimyo of Echizen; this was surely the prototype of the *Rakuchū-Rakugai-zu byōbu. Sanetaka-kō ki,* 4 (Tokyo: Taiyōsha, 1935), 675; entry for Eishō 3 / 12 / 22 (3 February 1507).

In *Kinsei shoki fūzokuga, Nihon no bijutsu,* 20:29, the nature of the *Rakuchū-Rakugai-zu* is described as "a clear pictorialization of the image of what from the point of view of the warrior class was desirable: a panorama of a stable and orderly capital."

49. See Tanaka Eiichi, *Furusato no taueuta* (Matsue: Imai Shoten, 1969), p. 86: "Tell us to finish, Tarōji-sama [i.e., the landowner]; you don't stiffen a man like this all at one time" (*Riyōshū,* Kanagawa prefecture). Tanaka points out that there are many other transplanting songs which complain of the pain of transplanting and express an antagonism and resentment which workers felt against those who compelled them to work. These two features are characteristic of transplanting songs which developed later than those of the *Tauezōshi* at a time when changes had occurred in some of the social and political institutions of the age we are examining. Songs extolling ideological aspects of the workday seemed no longer to the point, while the physical toil which had always been a part of transplanting emerged into the singers' consciousness as a suitable subject for song.

50. Song no. 61, from the fourth set of noon songs; NKBT 44, p. 274.

51. Song no. 1, NKBT 44, p. 254; and song no. 130, from the fourth set of evening songs, p. 297.

52. The seriousness with which the maneuvering of the line of decorated bulls was taken is suggested by the fifty-seven diagrams collected in one source alone, showing the patterns which their line of march was to trace out in the field; reproduced in *Nihon shomin bunka shiryō shūsei,* 5, 339–345. Along with aspects of song, a particular design pattern was associated with a time of the day or a particular field. Each of the patterns in the collection illustrated here (Iwami province; Bunsei period, 1818–1831) has a name.

53. See Manabe Masahiro, "Tauezōshi-kei kayō no sekai," *Ritsumeikan bungaku,* 255:817–836 (September 1966). The song, found on p. 822, was one of many collected from throughout Japan by the Bungei Iinkai and published by the Monbushō in the volume *Riyōshū* in 1914.

54. Manabe, "Tauezōshi-kei kayō no sekai." The song comes from the Takeno area on the border of Hyōgo and Kyoto prefectures, and was collected in the *Minzoku saihō* (1963), a publication of the Kokugakuin Daigaku Minzoku Kenkyūkai.

55. Manabe, "A Note Concerning the Text," appended to *The Genial Seed,* p. 175.

56. *Tauezōshi,* song no. 84, from the first set of evening songs; NKBT 44, p. 282.

57. *Taue-hyōshi no yurai,* in *Nihon shomin bunka shiryō shūsei,* 5, 320–323. This document also contains a genealogy of the field god, identifying his various manifestations.

58. NKBT 44, pp. 259, 265, 288, 291, and 298 respectively.

59. Manabe, "Tauezōshi-kei kayō no sekai," p. 822. This is a song collected in the Bunka-Bunsei period (1804–1831) by Sugae Masumi'in his *Hina no hitofushi.*

60. Song no. 26, from the fourth set of morning songs; NKBT 44, p. 262.

61. Shogun Yoritomo's hunting ground at Fujino is described in *Soga monogatari,* ed. Ichiko Teiji and Ōshima Tatehiko, NKBT 88 (1966), pp. 310–323. The Introduction to this volume contains information on the difficult question of dating the origin and development of this oral narrative, as well as on the relationship of folk belief to the process; see especially pp. 8–12. A text bearing the date Tenbun 8 (1539)/11/2 is the oldest extant copy, but does not necessarily represent the oldest variant of the story; the primary manuscripts date to 1546, 1553, and 1554.

62. Song no. 119, from the fourth set of evening songs; NKBT 44, pp. 293–294.

63. Manabe Masahiro, "Tauezōshi kō: katarigusa no keiretsu o megutte," *Denshō bungaku kenkyū,* 7:26–46 (December 1965), contains a discussion of the relationship between aspects of the *Soga monogatari* and song in the *Tauezōshi.*

64. Manabe Masahiro, *Tauezōshi kayō zenkōchū* (Tokyo: Ōfūsha, 1974), p. 406; *yuraisho* recorded in 1828.

65. Ibid., p. 620.

66. Manabe Masahiro, "Tauezōshi-kei kayō ni okeru kodaiteki na mono," *Nihon kayō kenkyū,* 8:16 (June 1969). Manabe develops a related argument when he notes that songs about Kyoto in the sequence are songs in praise of the capital *(Kyōbome);* and together with other songs of praise in the series, for example those praising the landowner, these are especially appropriate for *isami-da,* the field of excitement, since praise, too, is energy-conducting—we share the bounty of what we praise. This is what is meant if one speaks of song as magic *(juka)* in these sequences.

67. Shida Engi, *Nihon kayōken shi* (Tokyo: Shibundō, 1958), pp. 774–775.

68. Songs no. 39 and 41; NKBT 44, p. 267 and pp. 267–268.

69. *Murogimi,* in *Kaichū Yōkyoku zenshū,* ed. Nogami Toyoichirō, 4 (Tokyo: Chūō Kōron-sha, 1971 reissue), 49–54.

70. Cf. Manabe's commentary on songs no. 39 and 41, *Tauezōshi kayō zenkōchū,* pp. 387–406 and 411–417.

71. Ibid., p. 415.

72. NKBT 44, pp. 266–267, n. 8.

73. *Tauezōshi kayō zenkōchū,* pp. 402–403.

74. *Matsunoha, kan 3, Ni agari,* no. 3; NKBT 44, pp. 458–459.

75. NKBT 44, p. 177; Nihon Koten Bungaku Zenshū 25, p. 449.

76. *Tauezōshi kayō zenkōchū*, p. 404.

77. Ibid., p. 414.

78. "Jinku," in Kodera Yūkichi, *Nihon min'yō jiten* (Tokyo: Meicho Kankōkai, 1972 reissue), p. 143. There is no generally accepted meaning for the expression *jinku*. From area to area, a characteristic local song can be called X-*jinku*, sc., the *jinku* of X-area. Kodera suggests that the expression may have developed from *tochi no ku, ji no ku* into *jinku*, but that more study is needed on this question.

79. NKBT 44, pp. 270-271. Manabe's preferred reading of the doubtful line which I render "Tarō-Tarō" is "Mataza[e]mon, Tarō"; see *Tauezōshi kayō zenkōchū*, pp. 477-478. Taken together, the *oya-uta* and *ko-uta* may evoke the situation of a samurai taking two young followers off to see the capital.

80. *Tauezōshi kayō zenkōchū*, p. 620.

81. *Otogi-zōshi*, ed. Ichiko Teiji, NKBT 38 (1958), p. 45.

82. *Kyōgen kayō*, no. 125, NKBT 44, p. 230. No truly satisfactory dating of Kyōgen *komai* is possible. The version of *Banjōya* to which I refer comes from a collection transmitted by Den'emon Yasunori, the third head of the Sagi School (d. 1724). But the position which songs for Kyōgen occupy in NKBT 44—between the *Kanginshū* and the *Tauezōshi*—indicates that the distinguished editors of this collection of *kayō* from the Middle Ages and the Early Modern period, Shinma Shin'ichi, Shida Engi, and Asano Kenji, considered *kouta* found in the *Kanginshū*, in Kyōgen, and in the transplanting sequence to be nearly contemporaneous.

83. *Kyōgen mai-utai shū*, ed. Nonomura Kaizō (Tokyo: Yōkyoku-kai Shuppanbu, 1935), pp. 14-15.

84. Kikkawa Eishi, *Nihon ongaku no rekishi* (Osaka: Sōgensha, 1965), pp. 158-162.

85. *Ryūtatsu kouta shū*, NKBT 44, pp. 299-339. The general setting of this collection is discussed by Asano Kenji in his introductory comments, pp. 301-305. The importance of Sakai as a cultural center during the Tenshō-Bunroku periods (1573-1596) is quite clear from the names of outstanding artists active there in the areas of the tea ceremony, *renga*, Nō, flute, drum, and *shakuhachi* music. This was the very milieu of Ryūtatsu's activities. Asano draws attention to how well the songs of the *Ryūtatsu kouta shū* reflect the general feeling of the times—an uncertainty on the eve of Sekigahara, sympathy for the pathos of the Toyotomi family—a mood of melancholy found even in a cultural scene which outwardly, at least, was so prosperous.

86. For further discussion, see: Asano Kenji, *Nihon kayō no hatten to tenkai* (Tokyo: Meiji Shoin, 1972), p. 277; Yamaji Kōzō, "Shoki kabuki odori uta no kōsei," *Geinōshi kenkyū*, 33:36-56 (April 1971), especially pp. 46-48; Hattori Yukio, *Kabuki seiritsu no kenkyū*, p. 219.

87. *Tokitsugu-kyō ki*, entries for Genki 2/7/11 and 19; cited by Ogasawara Kyōko, *Kabuki no tanjō* (Tokyo: Meiji Shoin, 1972), p. 34.

88. Text in *Zoku Nihon kayō shūsei, 2, Chūsei-hen,* ed. Shida Engi (Tokyo: Tokyōdō, 1961), 362-363. The text is written in the blank space at the end of two booklets containing protocols *(hikitsuke)* from the Muromachi shogunate's Corps of Administrators, the *bugyōnin*. The records themselves are of the year Tenbun 7 (1538), but the booklets bear the date Tenbun 8. It is assumed that the *Bon no odori* songs were written in at approximately the time of the protocols' compilation. See Shida's Introduction, p. 44.

89. Ibid., pp. 391-392; on the dating, see p. 397, n. 25, and cf. Introduction, pp.

46–47, where the importance of these songs' relationship with the *Kanginshū* is discussed.

MUSIC CULTURES OF MOMOYAMA JAPAN

1. For example, in the so-called Funaki Screen showing famous places in Kyoto, datable c. 1615–1617 (on the dating, see Hoff, "City and Country," p. 314, n. 21 above); published in Kondo Ichitaro, *Japanese Genre Painting: The Lively Art of Renaissance Japan*, tr. Roy Andrew Miller (Rutland, Vt., and Tokyo: Tuttle, 1961), p. 60, pl. 29, upper section of the second panel from the left; also reproduced in *Momoyama: Japanese Art in the Age of Grandeur; An Exhibition at the Metropolitan Museum of Art* (New York: Metropolitan Museum of Art, 1975), no. 28, pp. 60–61. More detailed illustrations in color may be found in *Kyōto*, 1, ed. Hayashiya Tatsusaburō and Moriya Katsuhisa, Edo Jidai Zushi 1 (Tokyo: Chikuma Shobō, 1975), pls. 2 and 33.

2. See Muro Kyūso, *Sundai zatsuwa* (1750), in *Nihon zuihitsu zenshū*, 3 (Tokyo: Kokumin Tosho K.K., 1929), 230; and cf. Donald H. Shively, "*Bakufu* versus *Kabuki*," *Harvard Journal of Asiatic Studies*, 18 (3/4):326–356, reprinted in *Studies in the Institutional History of Early Modern Japan*, ed. John W. Hall and Marius B. Jansen (Princeton: Princeton University Press, 1968), pp. 231–261.

3. See Yuzo Yamane, *Momoyama Genre Painting*, tr. John M. Shields, The Heibonsha Survey of Japanese Art, 17 (New York and Tokyo: Weatherhill/Heibonsha, 1973), 10, pl. 1.

4. Yamane, p. 33, pl. 24.

5. Kondo, p. 51, pl. 22.

6. Donald Keene, *Nō: The Classical Theatre of Japan* (Tokyo and Palo Alto: Kodansha International, 1973), p. 39.

7. See Donald Berger, "The Nohkan: Its Construction and Music," *Ethnomusicology*, 9(3):221–239 (September 1965).

8. Further see William Malm, *Nagauta: The Heart of Kabuki Music* (Rutland, Vt., and Tokyo: Tuttle, 1963), pp. 74–76.

9. The only surviving drum of the ancient set is the next size up, the *san no tsuzumi* used in the *komagaku* repertory of *gagaku*.

10. On the identity of this artist, see Takeda Tsuneo, "Yūraku fūzoku-zu no seiritsu to tenkai," in *Fūzokuga: yūraku, tagasode*, ed. Takeda, *Nihon byōbu-e shūsei*, 14 (Tokyo: Kōdansha, 1977), 115.

11. Ibid., pp. 13 and 20–21, pls. 1 and 7; *Momoyama: Japanese Art in the Age of Grandeur*, no. 27, pp. 58–59, and color illustration [5]; *Momoyama jidai*, ed. Hayashiya Tatsusaburō, *Nihon bunkashi*, 5 (Tokyo: Chikuma Shobō, 1965), 134–135, pl. 142.

12. Tanabe Hisao, *Nihon no ongaku* (Tokyo: Bunka Kenkyūsha, 1954), pp. 201–203.

13. This tradition survives in some performances of the sung form of poetry called *shigin*, which was popular during the nineteenth and early twentieth century. A sample may be heard on *Shigin* (Polydor MN 9037-38).

14. A comparison of the two instruments may be made from William Malm, *Japanese Music and Musical Instruments* (Rutland, Vt., and Tokyo: Tuttle, 1959), p. 141, pl. 47. Information on various forms of *biwa* and the medieval musicians who

played them will also be found in the recent work by Susan Matisoff, *The Legend of Semimaru, Blind Musician of Japan* (New York: Columbia University Press, 1978), ch. 2, pp. 22–54 passim.

15. Tanabe, p. 202.

16. Examples of this music may be heard on the recording *Nihon biwagaku taikai* (Polydor SLJM 1031–37). *Heike* and *mōsō biwa* are also heard in this album.

17. Further see Willem Adriaansz, *The Kumiuta and Danmono Tradition of Japanese Koto Music* (Berkeley: University of California Press, 1973), pp. 5–7.

18. The actual schools of koto music which are popular today (the Ikuta and Yamada) developed in the late seventeenth and the eighteenth century. See Malm, *Japanese Music,* p. 169. Recordings of all four schools may be heard on *Sōkyoku koten meikyoku* (Toshiba TH 7047–50).

19. The Funaki Screen is actually a pair of six-fold screens of the *Rakuchū-Rakugai-zu* genre. The complete set is seen in Kondo, pp. 60–61, pls. 29 and 30, and in *Momoyama: Japanese Art in the Age of Grandeur,* no. 28, pp. 60–61.

20. See the detail from the second panel of the left-hand set in Yamane, pl. 64, or *Momoyama jidai,* p. 136, pl. 143.

21. An example is the last item on side one of the first record in the album *Nihon biwagaku taikai* (Polydor SLJM 1031).

22. See Malm, *Japanese Music,* p. 60, pl. 15, and cf. *Ongaku jiten,* 4 (Tokyo: Heibonsha, 1955–1957), 32, for details.

23. The instrument with a different hammer is seen in Malm, *Japanese Music,* p. 54, pl. 4.

24. See Ikeda Misaburō, *Minzoku geinō,* no. 8 of *Nihon no dentō* (Kyoto: Tankōsha, 1967), pl. 62. The sound may be heard on *Nihon buyō ongaku* (Nippon Victor SJ 3031), vol. 1, side 1, item 10.

25. See Malm, *Nagauta,* p. 11; Kondo, p. 111, pl. 80; and *Kyōto,* 1, 134–135, pl. 313.

26. Kondo, p. 49, pl. 11.

27. See Ikeda Misaburō, pls. 29, 68, and 114.

28. See Malm, *Japanese Music,* p. 60, pl. 16.

29. See Kondo, p. 113, pl. 81, third panel from the right.

30. On the *Jōruri jūnidan sōshi* and the fusion of the three elements of Bunraku, see Donald Keene, *Bunraku: The Art of the Japanese Puppet Theatre* (Tokyo and Palo Alto: Kodansha International, 1973), pp. 24–29.

31. For example, Kondo, pls. 1, 6, 81, 85, 87, 88, 89, 94, 96; and Yamane, pls. 81, 127, 130.

32. For details, see Malm, *Nagauta,* ch. 5.

33. See Eta Harich-Schneider, *A History of Japanese Music* (London: Oxford University Press, 1973), p. 473, pl. 23b.

34. Further see Harich-Schneider, pp. 445–486; and Kikkawa Eishi, *Nihon ongaku no rekishi* (Osaka: Sōgensha, 1965), pp. 171–177.

35. Arimichi Ebisawa, "The Meeting of Cultures," in *The Southern Barbarians: The First Europeans in Japan,* ed. Michael Cooper SJ (Tokyo and Palo Alto: Kodansha International, 1971), p. 140. Two pages of this *Manuale ad Sacramenta Ecclesiae Ministranda* are reproduced ibid., p. 88, pl. 43.

36. The Japanese military did not use trumpets until after contact with the West, although conch shell trumpets *(horagai)* were sounded in some services and battles

of certain Buddhist sects. Military signals in Japan before this time were primarily given by drums.

37.   See Kataoka Yakichi, *Kakure Kirishitan: rekishi to minzoku*, NHK Bukkusu 56 (Tokyo: Nihon Hōsō Shuppan Kyōkai, 1971, fourth printing), pp. 144–149; and cf. Harich-Schneider, pp. 484–486. Surviving music can be heard on *Cantus Gregorianus*, Toshiba TW 8002–3.

38.   See William Malm, "Chinese Music in Nineteenth Century Japan," *Asian Music*, 6(1/2):147–172 (1976).

39.   Kikkawa, p. 293.

40.   Tanabe Hisao, *Nihon no gakki* (Tokyo: Soshi Kaisha, 1964), p. 329.

41.   See David Waterhouse, "An Early Illustration of the Four-stringed Kokyū," *Oriental Art*, 16(2):1–7 (Summer 1970).

42.   Kondo, p. 51, pl. 20; Yamane, pl. 11; *Momoyama jidai*, pp. 8–9, pl. 7.

43.   See Kondo, p. 50, pl. 16. A grander performance, with four dancers and an extraordinarily large number of musicians, may be seen in two screens illustrating the Hōkoku [Toyokuni] Festival of 1604; ibid., pp. 70–71, pl. 38, and pp. 74–75, pl. 40.

Okina is the oldest and perhaps the most widely performed Nō play, "a joyous celebration of abundance and long life"; Keene, *Nō*, p. 13. An *okina* mask is reproduced ibid., p. 93.

44.   The top half of this panel depicts New Year's games: battledore and shuttlecock as well as *gitchō*, a game apparently not unlike field hockey.

45.   See Frank Hoff, *The Genial Seed: A Japanese Song Cycle* (New York: Mushinsha-Grossman, 1971), p. 4 and p. 118. Another circle of such instruments surrounding a *hayashi* is seen in Gunji, pl. 58. Other forms of *sasara* are also common in Shinto folk theatricals. See Malm, *Japanese Music*, p. 56, pl. 8; and Gunji Masakatsu, *Buyo* (Tokyo: Weatherhill, 1970), pl. 53.

46.   See Malm, *Japanese Music*, p. 91 and pls. 26–31. The imperial court form may be seen in the scene referred to in n. 1 above.

47.   Similar wig and gong combinations may be seen in the Yasurai Festival of Kyoto, illustrated in Malm, *Japanese Music*, pp. 53–54, pls. 3 and 5.

48.   Kondo, p. 50, pl. 19.

49.   Yamane, pl. 63.

50.   Kondo, p. 50, pl. 12.

51.   Listen to examples of many surviving street musicians and vendors on *Nihon no hōrōzai* (Nippon Victor W–7011–7).

52.   For example, Gunji, pls. 47 and 56; Ikeda, pl. 65; Yamane, pl. 69. Surviving *furyū* music may be heard on *Nihon buyō ongaku* (Nippon Victor SJ 3031), vol. 1, side 1, item 10; and in selections from *Kyōdo geinō*, vol. 12 of *Hōgaku taikei* (Chikuma Shobō and Victor VP 3028–29).

53.   Kondo, pp. 112–113, pl. 81.

54.   The Uesugi Screen is actually a pair of six-fold screens, assumed to be identical with the *Rakuchū-Rakugai-zu byōbu* by Kano Eitoku which Oda Nobunaga presented to the powerful daimyo Uesugi Kenshin of Echigo in 1574. The left screen is reproduced in Kondo, pp. 56–57, pl. 27; the right screen, pp. 58–59, pl. 28. We are principally interested in the second and third panels of the right screen: for detail, see Yamane, pl. 10; and *Momoyama jidai*, pp. 12–13, pl. 10.

Yoneyama Toshinao, *Gion Matsuri: toshi jinruigaku kotohajime*, Chūkō Shinsho

363 (Tokyo: Chūō Kōron-sha, 1974), is an excellent recent study of the Gion Festival; for an outline of the festival's historical context, see the concluding chapter, pp. 189–212.

55. The sounds of the Gion Festival's music and general activity may be heard on the recording *Kyoto* (Trio PK 9501–3).

56. Compare the later Gion Festival painting found in Ikeda, pl. 47. *Ko tsuzumi* marchers before the float are seen in pl. 69.

57. Detail in *Momoyama: Japanese Art in the Age of Grandeur,* color illustration [7]; and *Kyōto,* 1, pl. 296; also Yamane, pl. 76.

58. Kondo, p. 63, pl. 32; Yamane, pl. 129.

59. Ōta Izumi no Kami Gyūichi, *Toyokuni [Hōkoku] Daimyōjin saireiki, Zoku gunsho ruijū,* 3 (Tokyo: Keizai Zasshi-sha, 1903), 63:223–231; see particularly p. 228 on the Nō performances, and pp. 228–230 for a detailed description of the *furyū* dances. For a brief secondary treatment of the Hōkoku Festival, see Kinoshita Masao, Moriya Takeshi, and Yokoi Kiyoshi, "Machigumi to shimin seikatsu," *Kyōto no rekishi,* ed. Kyōto-shi, 4 (Tokyo: Gakugei Shorin, 1974, fifth printing), 594–600.

60. The two pairs of screens are both found in Kondo: Kano Naizen on pp. 72–75, pls. 39–40; Tokugawa Reimeikai on pp. 68–71, pls. 37–38. The right screen of each pair treats the events of the fourteenth; the left illustrates the *furyū* dance spectacle of the fifteenth. Color detail of the scene under discussion may be found in Yamane, pl. 98; *Momoyama jidai,* pl. 118; or *Kyōto,* 1, pl. 132.

61. It is a small form of the type shown in Malm, *Japanese Music,* p. 56, pl. 8.

THE CULTURE OF TEA: FROM ITS ORIGINS TO SEN NO RIKYŪ

1. The vendor of a cup for a copper *(ippuku issen)* and the pedlar of medicinal tea *(senjimono-uri)* are portrayed side by side in a medieval hand scroll which describes the "seventy-one professions": *Shichijūichiban shokunin utaawase,* in *Gunsho rui-jū,* 18 (Tokyo: Keizai Zasshi-sha, 1902, second printing), 503:112–113. The history of the *ippuku issen* is attested in the sources at least as early as 1403, when certain of these vendors subscribed to a set of regulations imposed on them by the Shingon temple Tōji in Kyoto; document dated Ōei 10/4, in Kumakura Isao, *Cha-no-yu: wabicha no kokoro to katachi,* Kyōikusha Rekishi Shinsho, "Nihonshi" 81 (Tokyo: Kyōikusha, 1977), p. 168. The *senjimono-uri* appears in the Kyōgen play *Oseji-mono,* which is described in the *Tenshō kyōgenbon* (c. 1573–1593): hence we can be certain it was performed in the sixteenth century; see *Kyōgen shū,* 3, ed. Furukawa Hisashi, Nihon Koten Zensho [40] (Tokyo: Asahi Shinbun-sha, 1956), 250–251. For the text of a modern performance version, see *Senjimono,* ibid., 2, 247–252.

2. *Kanginshū,* song no. 32, tr. Frank Hoff, *Song, Dance, Storytelling: Aspects of the Performing Arts in Japan,* Cornell University East Asia Papers no. 15 (Ithaca: Cornell China-Japan Program, 1978), p. 16; for the original, see *Kagura uta, Saibara, Ryōjin hishō, Kanginshū,* ed. Usuda Jingorō and Shinma Shin'ichi, Nihon Koten Bungaku Zenshū 25 (Tokyo: Shōgakkan, 1976), pp. 398–399.

3. Okakura Kakuzo, *The Book of Tea* (New York: Fox Duffield & Company, 1906), p. 3.

4. There is no undisputed evidence of this term's use prior to the seventeenth century. The two characters that make up the compound "Way of Tea" may be pronounced either *chadō* or *sadō;* many modern scholars prefer *chadō* in order to

distinguish the "Way of Tea" from its practitioner, the *sadō* or master of the tea ceremony, a compound written with the characters for "tea" and "head" which would otherwise be homophonous.

5. See Hayashiya Tatsusaburō, "Chasho no rekishi," *Nihon no chasho*, ed. Hayashiya, Yokoi Kiyoshi, and Narabayashi Tadao, 1, Tōyō Bunko 201 (Tokyo: Heibonsha, 1971), 10.

6. Lu Yü, *Ch'a-ching*, in *Chadō koten zenshū*, ed. Sen Sōshitsu, 1 (Kyoto: Tankōsha, 1957), 105. Cf. the translation by Francis Ross Carpenter, *The Classic of Tea* (Boston: Little, Brown and Company, 1974), pp. 107–109. For background, see Mori Rokuzō, " 'Chakyō' zengo," *Cha no bunkashi*, ed. Haga Kōshirō and Nishiyama Matsunosuke, *Zusetsu Chadō taikei*, 2 (Tokyo: Kadokawa, 1962), 49–56.

7. Murai Yasuhiko, *Nihon bunka shōshi* (Tokyo: Gakugei Shorin, 1969), pp. 184–186.

8. *Chadō koten zenshū*, 1, 135. In *Ch'a-ching* Lu Yü gives detailed advice on how much tea should be prepared and served, and cautions against overconsumption; ibid., p. 106. Cf. Carpenter's translation, p. 111: "Moderation is the very essence of tea. Tea does not lend itself to extravagance."

9. Kūkai, *Henjō hakki Seireishū*, *kan* 4, no. 28, "On proffering Sanskrit letters and an essay [to Emperor Saga]," dated Kōnin 5 (814)/ interc. 7/28; and *kan* 3, no. 15, "Feelings on reaching the age of forty," n.d. [813]. See *Sangō shiiki, Seireishū [Shōryōshū]*, ed. Watanabe Shōkō and Miyasaka Yūshō, Nihon Koten Bungaku Taikei 71 (Tokyo: Iwanami, 1965), pp. 242–243 and 216–217 respectively. Cited by Haga Kōshirō, "Cha no denrai," *Zusetsu Chadō taikei*, 2, 59.

10. *Ryōunshū*, comp. Ono no Minemori et al., *Gunsho ruijū*, 6 (Tokyo: Keizai Zasshi-sha, 1899, second printing), 123:476. Tea is also mentioned in a poem composed on the same occasion by Shigeno no Sukune Sadanushi on the inspiration of Saga's verses; ibid., p. 487. Saga's first known use of the image of tea occurs in a poem written in 813, "On an autumn day in the crown prince my brother's water pavilion"; ibid., p. 476.

11. For example, Emperor Saga, "In response to a poem presented by Saichō," *Bunka shūreishū*, comp. Fujiwara no Fuyutsugu et al., no. 71, in *Kaifūsō, Bunka shūreishū, Honchō monzui*, ed. Kojima Noriyuki, Nihon Koten Bungaku Taikei 69 (Tokyo: Iwanami, 1964), pp. 257–258; Nishikoribe Hikokimi, "In the hermitage of Kōshō Shōnin," ibid., no. 80, p. 264. Worth mentioning in the *Keikokushū* is Retired Emperor Saga's poem "To Kūkai as I send him off to his mountain with a parting cup of tea," *Gunsho ruijū*, 6, 125:529; but see especially a certain Koreuji's variation on the theme of tea, with a detailed description of the plant's growth, preparation, and effects, ibid., p. 563.

12. *Nihon kōki, Shintei zōho Kokushi taikei*, 5 (Tokyo: Yoshikawa Kōbunkan, 1961), 24:132–133; entries for Kōnin 6/4/22 and 6/3. An interesting set of poems composed on the occasion of the visit to the Bonshakuji by the emperor, his brother and crown prince (the future emperor Junna), and Fujiwara no Fuyutsugu may be found in the *Bunka shūreishū*, nos. 73–75, pp. 259–261; but tea is not mentioned in them.

13. Sugawara no Michizane, "Rainy night" (902), *Kanke kōshū*, no. 500, in *Kanke bunsō, Kanke kōshū*, ed. Kawaguchi Hisao, Nihon Koten Bungaku Taikei 72 (Tokyo: Iwanami, 1966), p. 515.

14. See Haga, *Zusetsu Chadō taikei*, 2, 62–64.

15. Regulations in 26 articles, issued Tenroku 1/7/16, items 2 and 3; see Hiraba-yashi Moritoku, *Ryōgen,* Jinbutsu Sōsho 173 (Tokyo: Yoshikawa Kōbunkan, 1976), p. 109.

16. *Chadō koten zenshū,* 1, 260. Cf. Hayashiya, *Nihon no chasho,* 1, 19.

17. Murai, *Nihon bunka shōshi,* p. 183.

18. *Kōtei zōho Azuma kagami,* ed. Kokusho Kankōkai, 1 (Tokyo: Taikandō, 1943), 619; entry for Kenpo 2/2/4.

19. Eisai, *Kissa yōjōki,* 1211 text, in *Chadō koten zenshū,* 2 (1958), 4; 1214 text, ed. Narabayashi Tadao, in *Nihon no chasho,* 1, 87. Cf. the translation in *Sources of Japanese Tradition,* comp. Ryusaku Tsunoda, Wm. Theodore de Bary, and Donald Keene, 1 (New York: Columbia University Press, 1964), 237–240.

20. *Chadō koten zenshū,* 2, 5–6; *Nihon no chasho,* 1, 89–92.

21. For a summary of the codification of rules for Ch'an (Zen) Buddhism in China and early medieval Japan, including those dealing with the ceremonial handling of tea, see Hayashiya, *Nihon no chasho,* 2, 23–25.

22. On the Kenninji tea ceremony, see Murai Yasuhiko, "Seikatsu bunka no seiritsu," *Kyōto no rekishi,* ed. Kyōto-shi, 3 (Tokyo: Gakugei Shorin, 1974, fourth printing), 461–463; cf. Murai, *Nihon bunka shōshi,* p. 199.

23. *Kissa ōrai,* in *Chadō koten zenshū,* 2, 166–167; ed. Narabayashi Tadao, *Nihon no chasho,* 1, 122–125. This may be the first mention in a Japanese source of a pavilion devoted specifically to the drinking of tea *(kissa no tei);* cf. Yoshida Takafumi, "Chashitsu no rekishiteki hattatsu," *Shinshū Chadō zenshū,* 7, ed. Yabe Ryōsaku, *Chashitsu chatei hen* (Tokyo: Shunjūsha, 1955), 2–3.

24. See for example, the "Nijō-Kawara Lampoons" of 1334, in *Kenmu nenkanki, Gunsho ruijū,* 16 (1901, second printing), 454:520–521. The scorecard of such a contest from the year 1343 is reproduced by Murai in *Kyōto no rekishi,* 3, 454; another, dating to 1351, is discussed by Kumakura Isao in *Cha-no-yu,* pp. 191–192.

25. An early Muromachi use of the term *basara* occurs in Ashikaga Takauji's Ken-mu Formulary of 1336, which in its very first article asserts: "These days people give themselves over entirely to that form of extravagance known as *basara.* One's eyes are dazzled by fashionable attire made of twill, gossamer, and figured cottons, and by such adornments as finely wrought silver swords. It is indeed madness itself! The wealthy are ever more vain, while the shame of the less fortunate knows no bounds." *Kenmu shikimoku jōjō,* ed. Kasamatsu Hiroshi, *Chūsei seiji shakai shisō,* 1, ed. Ishii Susumu, Kasamatsu, et al., Nihon Shisō Taikei 21 (Tokyo: Iwanami, 1972), 147.

26. *Taiheiki,* 3, ed. Gotō Tanji and Okami Masao, Nihon Koten Bungaku Taikei 36 (Tokyo: Iwanami, 1962), 252.

27. See the discussion of the relationship between game playing and art in the essay "Nihon bunka no soko o nagareru mono," Yamazaki Masakazu, *Muromachi-ki* (Tokyo: Asahi Shinbun-sha, 1974). Cf. the comments on Heian-period *mono-awase* in Ivan Morris, *The World of the Shining Prince* (New York: Knopf, 1964), pp. 151–152.

28. In short, *shinden* mansions tended to sprawl in a generally eastward direction. A late Heian example is the sumptuous Higashi Sanjō mansion of the Fujiwara fami-ly. See Ōta Hirotarō, *Zusetsu Nihon jūtaku shi* (Tokyo: Shōkokusha, 1948), p. 25.

29. The residential layout accordingly became completely transformed into an ar-rangement that flowed from east to west. The residences of the *buke* leaders of the early Muromachi period were laid out in this general way. By this time, the *shinden*

itself was employed strictly for public, formal occasions, while the *tsune-no-gosho* became the center for the daily life of the mansion. To a great extent, the Muromachi-period *buke* retained the outmoded *shinden* as a status symbol reflecting their close social and cultural association with the *kuge*. See Nakamura Masao, "Kinkaku to Ginkaku," *Kyōto no rekishi*, 3, 391.

30.   For a fifteenth-century example, see the diary of the imperial prince Fushimi no Miya Sadafusa, *Kanmon gyoki* (Tokyo: Zoku Gunsho Ruijū Kanseikai, 1958), p. 583; entry for Eikyō 3 (1431)/2/7. Sadafusa records here the sense of wonder he felt when he was a guest in the kaisho at the residence of the shogun Yoshinori: "The ornaments and treasures bedazzled the eyes. The landscape paintings were, in particular, excellent beyond description. The splendor of the Western Paradise must indeed be like this."

31.   Some of these questions are discussed by Itō Teiji with Paul Novograd, "The Development of Shoin-Style Architecture," in *Japan in the Muromachi Age,* ed. John W. Hall and Toyoda Takeshi (Berkeley: University of California Press, 1977), pp. 227–239.

32.   An example of an early *shoin* which does not, in fact, have a *toko-no-ma* is the room known as Dōjinsai in the Tōgudō at Ashikaga Yoshimasa's Higashiyama retreat, the site of the Silver Pavilion.

33.   The regent Ichijō Tsunetsugu (1358–1418) wrote an account of this visit, titled *Kitayama-dono gyōkōki,* which is contained in *Gunsho ruijū,* 2 (1897, second printing), *kan* 39.

34.   See the discussion of this topic in *Bungaku no gekokujō,* ed. Okami Masao and Hayashiya Tatsusaburō, *Nihon bungaku no rekishi,* 6 (Tokyo: Kadokawa, 1967), 168–170.

35.   *Kundaikan sōchōki* may be found in an excellent edition by Akai Tatsurō and Murai Yasuhiko in *Kodai-Chūsei geijutsuron,* ed. Hayashiya Tatsusaburō, Nihon Shisō Taikei 23 (Tokyo: Iwanami, 1975 second printing), pp. 423–445. A brief but penetrant look at the cultural accomplishments of the "Three Ami" and their relationship to the tea ceremony is given by Tani Shin'ichi, "San-Ami," in *Cha ni ikita hito,* 1, ed. Kuwata Tadachika, *Zusetsu Chadō taikei,* 6 (1963), 58–72.

36.   *Yamanoue Sōji ki* (postscript dated Tenshō 17 [1589]), ed. Yokoi Kiyoshi, in *Nihon no chasho,* 1, 145.

37.   Ibid., pp. 140–141.

38.   Professor Haga Kōshirō has dealt with this problem carefully in "Cha-no-yu no kaiso," *Zusetsu Chadō taikei,* 6, 73–97. He finds some substance in the story of Shukō's association with Ikkyū, and even some evidence of Nōami's influence on him, but considers the tie with Yoshimasa difficult to believe. Professor Nagashima Fukutarō (*Chadō koten zenshū,* 3, 15–16) questions whether, in view of the cliquish, highly compartmentalized organization of artists, craftsmen, and others in medieval times, a prominent *dōbōshū* such as Nōami would have invited a complete outsider such as Shukō to share, in effect, his access to the shogun.

39.   See, for example, the treatment of the subject by D. T. Suzuki in *Zen Buddhism and Its Influence on Japanese Culture* (Kyoto: Eastern Buddhist Society, 1938).

40.   *Nanbōroku,* ed. Nishiyama Matsunosuke, "Tana," no. 1, in *Kinsei geidōron,* ed. Nishiyama, Watanabe Ichirō, and Gunji Masakatsu, Nihon Shisō Taikei 61 (Tokyo: Iwanami, 1972), p. 35. The compilation of this work is attributed to Sen no

Rikyū's disciple Nanbō Sōkei, and one of its parts is inscribed with the date Bunroku 2 (1593)/2/28, the second anniversary of Rikyū's death. No holograph or contemporary copy is extant, however; the present version owes its existence to a "rediscovery" by the Fukuoka samurai and teaman Tachibana Jitsuzan in 1686. Nevertheless the work's authenticity, while questioned by some, is accepted by most scholars; but it is apparent that Jitsuzan subjected the text he worked with to an extensive redaction.

41.   Four and a half mats is the ideal but not the exclusive model. See the chart set out by Kumakura Isao, *Cha-no-yu,* pp. 75–77, covering the years 1558–1622 and giving the size of the rooms used in tea ceremonies hosted by a whole catalogue of the famous teamen of the era.

42.   Kamo no Nagaakira [Chōmei], *Hōjōki,* in *Hōjōki, Tsurezuregusa,* ed. Nishio Minoru, Nihon Koten Bungaku Taikei 30 (Tokyo: Iwanami, 1975, twenty-first printing), p. 44; translated by David Slawson, ms., 1976. One of the more famous teamen of the late Momoyama–early Edo epoch, Kubo Gondayū (Chōandō), modeled his grass hut *(sōan)* on Chōmei's "ten-foot square" dwelling; see *Chōandō ki* (1640), in *Shinshū Chadō zenshū,* 9, ed. Kuwata Tadachika, *Bunken-hen,* 2 (Tokyo: Shunjūsha, 1956), 300.

43.   *Shukō Furuichi Harima Hosshi-ate isshi,* in *Chadō koten zenshū,* 3, 3; also under the title *Shukō kokoro no fumi,* ed. Murai Yasuhiko, in *Kodai-Chūsei geijutsuron,* pp. 447–448. For an interesting discussion of this text, see Kuwata Tadachika, *Nihon chadō shi* (Kyoto: Kawara Shoten, 1969, third printing), pp. 82–85, and cf. Kumakura, *Cha-no-yu,* pp. 198–200.

44.   Attributed to Shukō by the Nō actor and author Konparu Zenpō (1454–1532) in the remarks collected under the title *Zenpō zatsudan* by a follower identified only as Tōemon no Jō; see the edition by Kitagawa Tadahiko, in *Kodai-Chūsei geijutsuron,* p. 480.

45.   *Nanbōroku,* "Oboegaki," no. 3, *Kinsei geidōron,* p. 10. Jōō's choice of these two teachers (in addition to Fujita Sōri, identified in the *Yamanoue Sōji ki,* p. 247, as his first instructor in the tea ceremony) may imply that he was dissatisfied with the style of Sōshu, Shukō's designated successor. All of these were residents of Shimogyō in Kyoto. On Sakai and its teamen, see Nagashima Fukutarō, "Sakai no machishū," *Zusetsu Chadō taikei,* 2, 107–122; and Yonehara Masayoshi, "Sakai no machi to chajin," ibid., 6, 98–122.

46.   *Nihon no chasho,* 1, 251. In view of the definition of *meijin* cited above, it is wise to keep in mind that Shukō not only was able to set the "value" on a whole series of native items, such as Bizen and Shigaraki ware, but also owned a great many *karamono,* as the *Yamanoue Sōji ki* abundantly makes clear.

47.   Needless to say, this does not mean that Jōō abandoned renga entirely. Yamanoue Sōji also tells us (*Nihon no chasho,* 1, 249) that Jōō and other tea masters recognized an affinity between their aesthetic values and those of renga: "The priest Shinkei, in speaking about renga, asserted that it should be 'withered and cold.' Jōō often said that he sought the same effects in *cha-no-yu.*" Moreover, we know from Sanetaka's own *Saishōsō* that Jōō not only held *waka* readings for his guests but also staged a ten-thousand-link renga session as late as 1534 (entry reproduced by Yonehara in *Zusetsu Chadō taikei,* 6, 105).

48.   Yamanoue Sōji cites this invocation of Jōō's enlightened quality ("without a trace of dust") in order to support his own notion that "the tea connoisseur's deter-

mination must be made active entirely through Zen." See *Nihon no chasho*, 1, 147–148.

49. *Nihon no chasho*, 1, 243.

50. *Anthology of Japanese Literature*, comp. and ed. Donald Keene (New York: Grove Press, 1955), pp. 194 and 196. The originals are no. 38 and no. 363, respectively, in *Shin kokin wakashū*, ed. Hisamatsu Sen'ichi, Yamazaki Toshio, and Gotō Shigeo, Nihon Koten Bungaku Taikei 28 (Tokyo: Iwanami, 1958), p. 45 and pp. 100–101.

51. The *Nanbōroku*, choosing this poem to illustrate "the heart of Jōō's *wabi* tea ceremony," interprets it as follows: "The cherry blossoms and the crimson leaves may be compared to the decorativeness of the *shoin* [tea ceremony]. But as one gazes earnestly at them, he reaches the state of enlightenment, the nonexistence of a single element, and that is the straw-thatched hut by the bay. One who does not know the cherry blossoms and the crimson leaves is precluded from living in that hut. Only by looking and looking at them can we bring the hut in its perfect *sabi* state into view. [Jōō] said that this is the true heart of tea." *Nanbōroku*, "Oboegaki," no. 33, *Kinsei geidōron*, p. 18.

52. Ibid. Contrary to the text, this poem—*Hana o nomi matsuran hito ni*—is not from the *Shinkokinshū*. It may be found in *Roppyakuban utaawase* (the record of a poetic competition held in 1193), "Haru: jō, 22-ban," *Roppyakuban utaawase, Roppyakuban chinjō*, ed. Minegishi Yoshiaki, Iwanami Bunko 1292–1294 (Tokyo: Iwanami, 1936), p. 36; also in *Minishū, Zoku Kokka taikan: kashū*, ed. Matsushita Daizaburō (Tokyo: Kadokawa, 1963, second printing), no. 12,379, p. 179.

53. See Haga Kōshirō, *Sen no Rikyū*, Jinbutsu Sōsho 105 (Tokyo: Yoshikawa Kōbunkan, 1963), pp. 1–9.

54. List of contributors to repairs on the Nenbutsuji, a temple associated with the Akuchi Jinja, the tutelary shrine of Izumi Sakai, Tenbun 4/4; ibid., pp. 16–18, where relevant portions are reproduced and discussed.

55. Extracts from Matsuya's diary, dated Tenbun 6/9/13, ibid., pp. 66–67.

56. Entry for Tenbun 13/2/27, ibid., p. 70.

57. *Nanbōroku*, "Oboegaki," no. 3, *Kinsei geidōron*, p. 11. The text's "17 *sai*" is sixteen in the Western manner of determining age.

58. See *Shinchō kōki*, comp. Ōta Izumi no Kami Gyūichi (c. 1610), ed. Okuno Takahiro and Iwasawa Yoshihiko, Kadokawa Bunko 2541 (Tokyo: Kadokawa, 1969), pt. 1, sec. 4, p. 88; Eiroku 11/10. The tea implements Nobunaga obtained from Sōkyū were the large jar Matsushima no Tsubo and the caddy Jōō no Nasu; on these two *meibutsu*, see *Yamanoue Sōji ki*, pp. 150–151 and 224–225 respectively, and p. 226 on Tsukumogami.

59. *Shinchō kōki*, pt. 2, sec. 5, pp. 96–97 and pt. 3, sec. 2, p. 104 respectively. Matsui Yūkan and Niwa Gorozaemon were Nobunaga's agents in both instances.

60. Kuwata Tadachika, *Oda Nobunaga*, Kadokawa Shinsho 192 (Tokyo: Kadokawa, 1964), pp. 174–175. See pp. 177–178 for a list of some of the *meibutsu* "given" to Nobunaga by the diplomatically inclined; and cf. Nagashima Fukutarō, "Meibutsugari," *Zusetsu Chadō taikei*, 2, 123–131.

Apparently the one sure way of keeping a tea treasure out of Nobunaga's hands was to destroy it. That, at least, is the moral to be drawn from the famous tale of Matsunaga Hisahide's end in 1577. Having turned against Nobunaga, Hisahide was put under siege in his castle. Knowing full well that the two things Nobunaga now wanted from him were his tea kettle Hiragumo and his head, he was determined to prevent his enemy from obtaining either. As he was about to commit suicide, Hisahide gave orders that his head be chained to the kettle and then both be "blown to smithereens" with gunpowder. Kuwata, p. 177.

61. See George Elison, "Hideyoshi, the Bountiful Minister," pp. 240–241 and his n. 67 below.

62. *Shinchō kōki*, pt. 14, sec. 15, pp. 371–372; Tenshō 9/12/22 (16 January 1582). Kuwata, pp. 187–188, specifies only eight pieces.

63. Haga, *Sen no Rikyū*, pp. 93–96, casts doubt on the frequently cited date of 1570.

64. *Shinchō kōki*, pt. 8, sec. 9, p. 202; Tenshō 3/10/28. This is the first fully attested instance of Rikyū's functioning as *sadō* at a tea ceremony held by Nobunaga. Prior occasions involving Rikyū and Nobunaga include the parties held by the latter at the Myōkakuji on Tenshō 1 (1573)/11/24 and at the Shōkokuji on Tenshō 2/3/24.

65. The just-cited reference is the sole mention of Rikyū in the *Shinchō kōki*; he is missing, for instance, from the account of the grandiose tea ceremony Nobunaga held at Azuchi on Tenshō 6 (1578)/1/1, at which Kunaikyō Hōin (Matsui Yūkan) acted as *sadō* (ibid., pt. 11, sec. 1, pp. 237–238). His sole appearance in Nobunaga's extant epistolary corpus is in a letter in which Nobunaga thanks him for the gift of a thousand balls of musket ammunition! Nobunaga to Hōsensai (Rikyū), black-seal letter dated (Tenshō 3 [1575])/9/16, in Okuno Takahiro, *Oda Nobunaga monjo no kenkyū*, 2 (Tokyo: Yoshikawa Kōbunkan, 1973, 2nd ed.), no. 545, 82.

66. See Haga, *Sen no Rikyū*, pp. 98–109.

67. On Nobunaga's final tea party, see Kuwata Tadachika, *Oda Nobunaga*, pp. 194–198.

68. On these relationships, see Haga, *Sen no Rikyū*, pp. 116–123. Tsuda retained influence longer than Imai.

69. Sōrin's visit to Osaka Castle is discussed, and his letter to Furujō Tango Nyūdō et al. (Tenshō 14/4/6) cited, by Toyama Mikio, *Ōtomo Sōrin*, Jinbutsu Sōsho 172 (Tokyo: Yoshikawa Kōbunkan, 1975), pp. 264–270; cf. Haga, *Sen no Rikyū*, pp. 184–187.

70. Some excellent illustrations of tea implements held to be representative of Rikyū's taste may be found in no. 150 of *Taiyō*, a special issue titled "Sen no Rikyū: wabi no chajin" (November 1975).

71. *Nanbōroku*, "Oboegaki," no. 1, *Kinsei geidōron*, p. 10.

72. Kuwata Tadachika, *Toyotomi Hideyoshi kenkyū* (Tokyo: Kadokawa, 1975), p. 508, cites the precedent of a two-mat hut called Yamazato that was supposedly built by Jōō. The Osaka Yamazato was first used by Hideyoshi, with Sōgyū and Rikyū in attendance, on Tenshō 12 (1584)/1/3; the first time he formally invited guests there was on Tenshō 12/12/1 (1 January 1585).

73. *Sōtan nikki, Shinshū Chadō zenshū*, 8, 202–203; Tenshō 15/2/25. On the significance of Yū-chien's tea ceremony paintings, see Carolyn Wheelwright, "A Visualization of Eitoku's Lost Paintings at Azuchi Castle," pp. 92–93 and her nn. 15–17 above.

74. *Sōtan nikki*, pp. 225–226; Tenshō 15/10/21.

75. Tenshō 13/2/24 and 10/21 respectively; Kuwata, *Toyotomi Hideyoshi kenkyū*, p. 509. Nobukatsu's uncle, the famous teaman Oda Nobumasu (Urakusai) accompanied him.

76. Ibid., p. 514, citing a letter from Maeda Gen'i to Komai Nakatsukasa no Shō, dated Bunroku 2 (1593)/5/25. There is some question whether or not the Yamazato tearoom in Nagoya was in fact identical with the one in Osaka, since Sōtan's diary (p. 247; Tenshō 20 [1592]/11/17) gives the dimensions of the former as four and a half—not two—mats. Kuwata, p. 509, states that it was the same, citing Hideyoshi's vermilion-seal letter, dated (Tenshō 20)/10/6, which orders Mizoguchi Hōki no Kami to have the "Yamazato Goten" shipped to Nagoya.

77. *Sōtan nikki*, pp. 241–242; Tenshō 20/5/28. Sōrin's account may be conveniently found in Kuwata, *Toyotomi Hideyoshi kenkyū*, p. 513.

78. Haga, *Sen no Rikyū*, pp. 191–192.

79. Ibid., pp. 147–157.

80. Ibid., pp. 165–171.

81. According to a letter written by Suzuki Shinbyōe, a retainer of the powerful northern daimyō Date Masamune, to Date's councillor Ishimoda Kageyori on the day after Rikyū's suicide, a long list of Rikyū's offences was displayed by the side of the crucified statue; unfortunately, he does not specify what they were. Cited by Haga, ibid., pp. 273–274.

82. *Tamon'in nikki*, ed. Tsuji Zennosuke, 4 (Tokyo: Kadokawa, 1967), 287–288. For the contemporary meaning of *maisu*, literally "venal priest," see *VOCABVLARIO DA LINGOA DE IAPAM com adeclaração em Portugues* (Nangasaqui no Collegio de IaPAM DA COMPANHIA DE IESVS. ANNO M.D.CIII.), f. 150; facsimile edition published by Doi Tadao, *Nippo jisho* (Tokyo: Iwanami, 1960), p. 299: "Maisu. i, Fitouo tarasu mono. *Embaidor, ou enganador* [Fraud, or cheat]."

Eishun's statement is supported by other contemporary evidence, some of it from Rikyū's own pen. See Haga, *Sen no Rikyū*, pp. 276–287.

83. See Asao Naohiro, "Toyotomi seiken ron," *Iwanami kōza: Nihon no rekishi*, 9 (*Kinsei* 1; Tokyo: Iwanami, 1963), 197–205.

HIDEYOSHI, THE BOUNTIFUL MINISTER

This study was originally prepared for presentation at the 27th Annual Meeting of the Association for Asian Studies, San Francisco, 24 March 1975, and revised for publication while I was Research Associate at Kyoto University under grants from the Japan Foundation and the Joint Committee on Japanese Studies of the American Council of Learned Societies and the Social Science Research Council, whose assistance I wish to acknowledge with gratitude.

1. Takeuchi Kakusai, *Ehon Taikōki* (1797–1802), ed. Tsukamoto Tetsuzō, 1 (Tokyo: Yūhōdō Shoten, 1914), 21–24. The account specifies that the mother had prayed for a child to Hiyoshi Gongen; hence the name Hiyoshimaru. No evidence contemporary with Hideyoshi exists for this name, which first appears in Oze Hoan's *Taikōki* (preface dated Kan'ei 2 [1625]), ed. Kuwata Tadachika (Tokyo: Shin Jinbutsu Ōrai-sha, 1971), p. 31.

New Year's of the year of the monkey is a mythologically inspired date: it associates the hero's miraculous birth with the deity of the Hie (or Hiyoshi) Sannō Shrine, whose sacred animal is the monkey. This association motivated the chroniclers and raconteurs who state that Tenbun 5 (1536)/1/1 was Hideyoshi's birthday, e.g., Tsuchiya Tomosada, *Taikō sujōki* (c. 1676), in *Kaitei Shiseki shūran*, 13 (Tokyo:

Kondō Kappansho, 1902), 306, and Sanada Zōyo, *Meiryō kōhan* ([Kyoto:] Ikubun-dō, n.d.; publisher active c. 1716–1790), 14:1. A variation on this theme may be observed in Kakiya Kizaemon's *Sofu monogatari* (also known as *Asahi monogatari;* c. 1642), *Kaitei Shiseki shūran*, 13, 323; here Hideyoshi's birthday is given as "the year of the monkey, sixth month, fifteenth day"—in other words, the feast day of the Sannō deity.

An interesting analysis of the thematic foundations of the Hideyoshi legend will be found in Matsuda Osamu, *Nihon kinsei bungaku no seiritsu: itan no keifu*, Sōsho Nihon Bungakushi Kenkyū (Tokyo: Hōsei Daigaku Shuppankyoku, 1963), pp. 47–74. Matsuda draws analogies between Tsuchiya Tomosada's *Taikō sujōki*, in particular, and *Aigo no Waka*, a recited narrative of the *Sekkyō* performance type which was popular in the Azuchi-Momoyama period. Note that Tomosada's father was the blind minstrel En'ichi Kengyō, whose stock in trade was made up of such popular tales. For a text of *Aigo no Waka*, see *Sekkyō shū*, ed. Muroki Yatarō, Shinchō Nihon Koten Shūsei (Tokyo: Shinchōsha, 1977), pp. 299–344.

2.   Letter demanding the submission of Formosa; *Hōkō ibun*, comp. Kusaka Hiroshi (Tokyo: Hakubunkan, 1914), p. 490.

3.   See Kuwata Tadachika, *Taikōki no kenkyū* (Tokyo: Tokuma Shoten, 1965), p. 26, and the same author's *Toyotomi Hideyoshi kenkyū* (Tokyo: Kadokawa, 1975), p. 63.

4.   Hayashi Razan, *Toyotomi Hideyoshi fu* ([Kyoto:]Arakawa Shirozaemon, Meireki 4 [1658]), 1:3. The postscript is dated Kan'ei 19 (1642) and states that the work was commissioned (by the Tokugawa bakufu); Razan's son Shuntoku was his collaborator.

5.   For instance, the widely used Kadokawa *Nihonshi jiten*, ed. Takayanagi Mitsutoshi and Takeuchi Rizō (Tokyo, 1974, 2nd ed.), p. 697, gives 1536 without as much as a question mark.

The principal supporter of 1537 is Kuwata Tadachika; see his *Toyotomi Hideyoshi kenkyū*, pp. 19–24. His evidence is impressive. Ōmura Yūko, who may be described as Hideyoshi's official biographer, states in a work dated Tenshō 13 (1585)/8 that Hideyoshi was born on "*hinoto tori* [Tenbun 6]/2/6," i.e., 17 March 1537; *Kanpaku ninkanki*, in *Taikō shiryōshū*, ed. Kuwata Tadachika, Sengoku Shiryō Sōsho 1 (Tokyo: Jinbutsu Ōrai-sha, 1965), pp. 84–85. Another contemporary source indicating 1537 is a votive document dated Tenshō 18 (1590)/12, imploring prosperity for "the Lord Kanpaku, [born in] the *tori* year, age 54 *sai*" (53 in the Western manner of counting); *Gifu-ken shi, Shiryō-hen: Kodai/Chūsei* 1 (Gifu-ken, 1969), p. 823. Ōta Gyūichi, who was intimately acquainted with Hideyoshi's affairs, also speaks for 1537; *Toyokuni [Hōkoku] Daimyōjin saireiki* (1604?), in *Zoku gunsho ruijū*, 3 (Tokyo: Keizai Zasshi-sha, 1903), 225. So does *inter alios* Hideyoshi's former vassal Takenaka Shigekado; *Toyokagami* (1631), in *Gunsho ruijū*, 13 (Tokyo: Keizai Zasshi-sha, 1900, second printing), 505.

The best support for 1536 is the official record of imperial court appointments, *Kugyō bunin*, which on first listing Hideyoshi in Tenshō 11 (1583) gives his age as 48 (Western 47) and stays consistent with that index through the final entry, stating that his age was 63 *sai* in the year of his death, Keichō 3 (1598); see *Kugyō bunin*, 3, *Kokushi taikei*, 55 (Tokyo: Kokushi Taikei Kankōkai, 1936), 488–512; note that this source is accurate regarding the ages of other important personages, such as Ashikaga Yoshiaki and Oda Nobunaga.

The Tokugawa-period chronicle *Toyotomi ki* evades the problem by giving Hide-yoshi's birthyear as Tenbun 5 (1536), *hinoto tori* (1537); *Zoku gunsho ruijū*, 20–1 (Tokyo: Zoku Gunsho Ruijū Kanseikai, 1923), 384.

6. See Kuwata Tadachika, *Toyotomi Hideyoshi kenkyū*, pp. 15–19.

Chikuami is named as Hideyoshi's father by Oze Hoan, *Taikōki*, p. 31, and in ac-counts influenced by Hoan, including Razan's *Toyotomi Hideyoshi fu*, 1:3. Eclec-ticism eventually won the day, Yaemon being made into the father of Hideyoshi's mother's husband Yasuke, and Yasuke and Chikuami being in turn transformed in-to one and the same person; *Ehon Taikōki*, 1, 21. The truth appears to be that Hideyoshi's mother married Chikuami after Yaemon's death (1543?). *Taikō sujōki*, p. 307, and *Meiryō kōhan*, 14:1–1v, further specify that Hideyoshi's two younger siblings, the future Yamato Dainagon Hidenaga and Ieyasu's wife Asahi-hime, were the results of this remarriage. Most historians accept this attribution; but Kuwata argues that Yaemon, not Chikuami, was also their father.

7. The earliest document issued over this name is dated Eiroku 8 (1565)/11/2; Okuno Takahiro, *Oda Nobunaga monjo no kenkyū*, no. 58 supp., 1 (Tokyo: Yoshi-kawa Kōbunkan, 1971, 2nd ed.), 106–107. It is, however, not an original but only a copy; moreover, its character as an adjunct *(soejō)* of a document issued by Nobunaga on Eiroku 8/11/3 makes it appear that the date it bears is imprecise.

8. The earliest extant documents in which Hideyoshi figures as Hashiba are dated [Tenshō 1 (1573)?]/9/6 and [Tenshō 1]/9/7; Okuno, *Monjo*, no. 400 and no. 401 supp., 1, 677–678 and 682–683.

Kuwata, *Toyotomi Hideyoshi kenkyū*, p. 147, dismisses the popular derivation of the name Hashiba as unworthy.

9. A late instance occurs in Nobunaga's black-seal letter, Nagaoka Hyōbu no Daibu (Hosokawa Fujitaka) *et aliis*, dated –/3/15; Okuno, *Monjo*, no. 700, 2 (1973, 2nd ed.), 271–273. This letter may be a holograph, does not antedate Tenshō 4 (1576), and is placed by Okuno in the following year.

10. The best example of the combination of both these elements is the final passage of Hideyoshi's letter to Hōjō Sakyō no Daibu [Ujinao], Tenshō 17/11/24 (31 December 1589); *Hōkō ibun*, p. 211.

11. *Kanpaku ninkanki*, p. 85. An interesting variant may be seen in the *Taionki* (c. 1644) of the noted littérateur Matsunaga Teitoku; *Taionki, Oritaku shiba no ki, Rantō kotohajime*, ed. Odaka Toshio and Matsumura Akira, Nihon Koten Bungaku Taikei 95 (Tokyo: Iwanami, 1964), p. 37. Odaka mistakenly annotates it as the first occurrence of the imperial paternity legend.

Note that in the *Koretō muhonki*, which is dated Tenshō 10 (1582)/10/15, Yūko had written unequivocally: "Hideyoshi was not of noble birth *(Hideyoshi shosei, moto kore tattoki ni arazu)*"; *Taikō shiryōshū*, p. 40. With Hideyoshi's rise in power and dignities, there evidently was a need for genealogical revisions.

12. The most famous version of this story is in the "Gion Nyōgo" section of the *Heike monogatari*, ed. Takagi Ichinosuke et al., 1, Nihon Koten Bungaku Taikei 32 (Tokyo: Iwanami, 1964, fifth printing), 416–425.

13. See, for instance, Hideyoshi's effusive letter to Kanbe (Oda) Nobutaka's coun-cillors Okamoto Jirozaemon no Jō and Saitō Genba no Suke, Tenshō 10 (1582)/10/18, *Hōkō ibun*, pp. 21–27, especially the final passage, where Hideyoshi makes the grandiose offer to slit open his belly crosswise in order to follow his lord Nobunaga in death.

14. See the Kabuki playwright's manual *Sekai kōmoku* (c. 1791), in *Kyōgen sakusha shiryōshū*, 1, ed. Hattori Yukio (Tokyo: Kokuritsu Gekijō Chōsa Yōsei-bu Geinō Chōsashitsu, 1974), 51-53.

15. Tenshō 11/5/15; *Hōkō ibun*, p. 35. "As far as [Hōjō] Ujimasa in the East and [Uesugi] Kagekatsu in the North, all have submitted to my will *(Chikuzen kakugo ni makase sōrō)*. If Lord Mōri [Terumoto] determines to put himself at my disposal, there will prevail in Japan an order unseen since Yoritomo's day. How could anything surpass this!"

16. *Furoisu Nihonshi*, ed. and trans. Matsuda Kiichi and Kawasaki Momota, 2 (Tokyo: Chūō Kōron-sha, 1977), 196-198; from ch. 45 of the putative Part Three of Luis Frois' *História de Japam*, contained within the eighteenth-century ms., *Apparatos para a História Ecclesiastica do Bispado de Iapam*, Codex 49-IV-57, Ajuda Library, Portugal.

Hideyoshi was away at the hunts from Tenshō 19/11/3 to 12/16 (18 December 1591-30 January 1592); when he returned to Kyoto, "as though in triumph" (Frois), bleachers were set up outside the imperial palace and all the nobility crowded together to admire the catch, which numbered in the thousands of birds and beasts, no less than the master huntsman, who made his entry in a "Southern Barbarian" conveyance. See the eyewitness report by Konoe Nobusuke, "Kokon chōkan," in *Sanmyakuin ki*, ed. Konoe Michitaka, Nawa Osamu, and Hashimoto Masayoshi (Tokyo: Zoku Gunsho Ruijū Kanseikai, 1975; Shiryō Sanshū), pp. 158-160; and cf. *Taikōsama gunki no uchi*, reproduction of the holograph by Ōta Izumi no Kami Gyūichi (c. 1605), with transcription, ed. Keiō Gijuku Daigaku Fuzoku Kenkyūjo Shidō Bunko (Tokyo: Kyūko Shoin, 1975), pp. 168-172 and trans. pp. 38-39.

17. Cf. Hayashiya Tatsusaburō, *Tenka ittō, Nihon no rekishi*, 12 (Tokyo: Chūō Kōron-sha, 1971; Chuko Backs), 415.

Hideyoshi actually left for the Korean invasion's staging area on Tenshō 20/3/26; for an eyewitness account of the "unprecedented marvelous sight" of his departure from Kyoto, see *Rokuon nichiroku*, ed. Tsuji Zennosuke, 3 (Tokyo: Taiyōsha, 1935), 58-59, entry for that date. Ōta Gyūichi states that Hideyoshi had indeed given orders to set out on 3/1 but was forced to delay on account of the difficulties of mustering his huge army; *Taikōsama gunki no uchi*, pp. 227-234 and trans. pp. 54-56. Takenaka Shigekado in another early seventeenth-century work also indicates that 3/1 was the chosen date and the delay caused by the pressure of affairs; *Toyokagami*, in *Gunsho ruijū*, 13, 563.

18. See Max Weber, *The Theory of Social and Economic Organization*, trans. A. M. Henderson and Talcott Parsons, Free Press Paperback (New York: The Free Press, 1964), pp. 324-386; quotations from p. 325 and p. 328. One after the other, the items in Weber's definition of "traditional authority" fit Hideyoshi (cf. pp. 341-345).

19. After Hideyoshi had been appointed Imperial Regent and as he was about to become Grand Chancellor of State, the monk Tamon'in Eishun of the Kōfukuji in Nara was consumed with worry that the inconceivable would come to pass and that Hideyoshi would actually assume the throne; a "dark night," he feared, was about to envelop the realm. See *Tamon'in nikki*, ed. Tsuji Zennosuke, 4 (Tokyo: Kadokawa, 1967), 34 and 48, entries for Tenshō 14 (1586)/7/26 and 11/2.

20. Contained in bk. 1, ch. 11 of Rodrigues' work. I cite the translation by Michael

Cooper SJ, *This Island of Japon* (Tokyo and New York: Kodansha International, 1973), pp. 72–81; for the original, see João Rodrigues Tçuzzu SJ, *História da Igreja do Japão*, ed. João do Amaral Abranches Pinto, 1 (Macao: Notícias de Macau, 1954), 177–190. Cooper's translation is excellent, his annotation inadequate; the Macao edition has no annotation at all; neither of these two is a complete presentation of Rodrigues' voluminous work, Abranches Pinto confining himself to a transcription of bks. 1 and 2 (sc., some two thirds of the extant manuscript), and Cooper likewise omitting bk. 3 and moreover choosing not to translate some interesting chapters of the remaining portion. Hence it is necessary to refer frequently to the complete and expertly annotated Japanese version published by Doi Tadao et al. under the title *Nihon kyōkai shi*, 2 vols., Dai Kōkai Jidai Sōsho 9–10 (Tokyo: Iwanami, 1967–1970); for bk. 1, ch. 11, see volume 1, pp. 306–320.

História da Igreja do Japão may well be the most important work about the Momoyama cultural milieu yet written by a Westerner. Rodrigues Tçuzzu is perhaps the only one of the prolific Jesuit writers on sixteenth- and seventeenth-century Japan against whom the charge of misrepresenting the country's culture cannot be sustained.

21. *Japon*, pp. 80–81; *História*, 1, 189; *Nihon kyōkai shi*, 1, 318. Rodrigues, who wrote this text in Macao in 1620–1621, was apparently unaware that the Tokugawa shogunate had put an end to the practice. "Equestrians" cease appearing on the "patrician" rolls after 1619; see *Kugyō bunin*, 3, 552.

22. See the diary of an important Shimazu vassal, *Uwai Kakken nikki*, ed. Tōkyō Daigaku Shiryō Hensanjo, 3 (Tokyo: Iwanami, 1957), 89–90, entry for Tenshō 14 (1586)/1/23.

Hideyoshi's letter is dated [Tenshō 13]/10/2. The Shimazu response was sent to Hosokawa Fujitaka, who along with Sen no Sōeki (Rikyū) had sent a *soejō* accompanying that letter; *Hōkō ibun*, pp. 67–68.

23. *Tamon'in nikki*, 3, 431; entries for Tenshō 13/7/11 (6 August 1585), the day Hideyoshi was appointed Kanpaku, and for the day after.

In a work written after Hideyoshi's heritage had been liquidated by the Tokugawa, Oze Hoan could affort to comment publicly: "His arrogance was excessive. Without being of regency lineage, he was appointed Regent; without the proper personality, he profaned the Imperial Chancery." *Taikōki*, p. 261.

24. Cooper, *Japon*, p. 79, n. 94. Note that the official record of appointments to the higher court ranks continues listing Yoshiaki as shogun until Tenshō 16 (1588). On 1/13 of that year, he finally resigned himself to his fate, and as a sign of withdrawal from worldly affairs assumed the priestly style Shōzan. *Kugyō bunin*, 3, 497.

25. Among the others who continued acknowledging Yoshiaki as shogun were the Shimazu, who imposed a special tax *(tansen)* on his behalf as late as 1583; to be sure, in 1585 it had not yet been collected. See *Uwai Kakken nikki*, 1 (1954), 214, entry for Tenshō 11 (1583)/3/16; 2 (1955), 138–139, entries for Tenshō 12/11/16–18; and 2, 231, entries for Tenshō 13/5/27–28.

26. Astonishingly enough, there is evidence which suggests that adjudication by the shogunate's officers was sought *within the confines of the city of Kyoto*, an area completely subject to Nobunaga, as late as 1579! See the disposition issued to the Eiyōji over the names of the shogunate's *bugyōnin* [Iinoo] Shōren and [Matsuda] Fujihiro, dated Tenshō 7/8/13; in Imatani Akira, "Kanreidai hōsho no seiritsu," *Komonjo kenkyū*, 7/8:43 (February 1975). The document is a typical example of

the type known as *bugyōnin rensho hōsho;* it is apparent that it would not have been solicited unless expected to bear legal force.

27.   Cooper, *Japon,* p. 76, n. 89.

28.   For example, John Whitney Hall, *Government and Local Power in Japan, 500 to 1700* (Princeton: Princeton University Press, 1966), p. 287.

29.   Hayashi Razan, *Toyotomi Hideyoshi fu,* 1:37–37v.

In March 1584 Yoshiaki assured the Shimazu that he had obtained Hideyoshi's cooperation and certainly would again be installed in Kyoto that very spring. *Uwai Kakken nikki,* 2, 16, entry for Tenshō 12/2/14.

On the complicated political relationships surrounding Hideyoshi's rapprochement with the dispossessed shogun, see Okuno Takahiro, *Ashikaga Yoshiaki,* Jinbutsu Sōsho 55 (Tokyo: Yoshikawa Kōbunkan, 1960), ch. 8, pp. 269–290.

30.   The funeral took place Tenshō 10/10/11–17; see *Koretō muhonki,* pp. 40–43. Hideyoshi was made *sakon no e no shōshō* on 10/3; Yūko in *Kanpaku ninkanki,* pp. 75–77, includes the court's letter of appointment.

31.   *Sangi, ju shii no ge:* Tenshō 11 (1583)/5/22; *gon dainagon, ju sanmi:* Tenshō 12/11/22 (23 December 1584; status the same as Ashikaga Yoshiaki's); *naidaijin, shō nii:* Tenshō 13/3/10. See *Kanpaku ninkanki,* pp. 77–79, and *Kugyō bunin,* 3, 489–491.

32.   See my chapter, "The Cross and the Sword," in this volume.

33.   *Kanpaku, ju ichii* (continuing as *naidaijin*): Tenshō 13/7/11 (6 August 1585); *Daijō Daijin:* Tenshō 14/12/19 (27 January 1587). See *Kugyō bunin,* 3, 491–493. Note that the year of the latter appointment often is carelessly given as 1586.

34.   Nor—with one notable exception—would one ever hold it again. That sole exception was Hideyoshi's nephew and adopted son, Toyotomi Hidetsugi, to whom Hideyoshi passed on the office on Tenshō 19/12/28 (11 February 1592), thereby assuming the title of *Taikō* (a word which was to become synonymous with the name Hideyoshi), which pertains to the Kanpaku's father. Hidetsugi was disgraced and made to commit suicide in August 1595; one of the major causes was Hideyoshi's desire to favor his natural son Hiroi (Hideyori), born in 1593.

35.   "Hashiba Hideyoshi Kanpaku senge no shidai," Tenshō 13 (1585)/7, in *Sanmyakuin ki,* pp. 119–122. Also see "Nijō Akizane Konoe Nobusuke Kanpaku sōron sanmon santō jō," appended ibid., pp. 123–131; the several pieces of correspondence date from the fifth and sixth months of Tenshō 13.

The "Five Houses" *(goke)* of the Fujiwara clan's "Regency" sublineage *(sekkanke)* were the Konoe, Kujō, Nijō, Ichijō, and Takatsukasa. Konoe Nobusuke (by then called Nobutada) did eventually become Kanpaku, but not until 1605, seven years after Hideyoshi's death.

Hideyoshi's relationship with Sakihisa dated back at least to 1575, when he was instrumental in obtaining for the banished former Kanpaku entry into Nobunaga's good graces and making possible his return to Kyoto; see Sakihisa to Sakai Saemon no Jō [Tadakatsu], dated [Tenshō 3]/8/28, Okuno, *Monjo,* 2, 2.

36.   According to Ōmura Yūko, Hideyoshi was aware that "assuming an old family name is akin to the stag's following in the footsteps of an ox." There was only one way, he stated, "to uphold the realm and to pass down my fame to future generations," and that was "to establish anew a separate name and let it be the fountainhead." See *Kanpaku ninkanki,* pp. 85–86. Hideyoshi styled himself Toyotomi from Tenshō 13/9/9; Hayashiya, *Tenka ittō,* p. 344.

37. Hayashiya Tatsusaburō with George Elison, "Kyoto in the Muromachi Age," in *Japan in the Muromachi Age*, ed. John Whitney Hall and Toyoda Takeshi (Berkeley: University of California Press, 1977), p. 19.

38. H. Paul Varley, "Ashikaga Yoshimitsu and the World of Kitayama: Social Change and Shogunal Patronage in Early Muromachi Japan," ibid., pp. 183-184.

39. Ōmura Yūko, *Juraku gyokōki*, dated Tenshō 16 (1588)/5, in *Taikō shiryōshū*, p. 102.

40. *Juraku gyokōki*, p. 103. Note that there was another Imperial Visit to Juraku on Tenshō 20/1/26-28 (9-11 March 1592), one month after Hidetsugi was made Kanpaku and the castle passed on to him. The Toyotomi regime evidently used the ceremony as a device of legitimation.

41. Hideyoshi's use of ox carriages is by no means an inconsequential point. Rodrigues (*Japon*, p. 74; *História*, 1, 180; *Nihon kyōkai shi*, 1, 309) specifies that the nobles' use of such carriages "to proceed to the palace or go to visit other lords" was a characteristic of the "proper and natural age of Japan." Indeed, as early as 1212 Kamo no Chōmei had viewed the "change in men's hearts, so that they favored only horses and saddles" as a symbol of the passing of that age and a "sign of the disturbed state of the world"; discussing the court's removal to Fukuhara in 1180, he noted disapprovingly, "Those who should have been riding in carriages were on horseback. . . . Overnight, the ways of the capital had been abandoned for those of country soldiers." *Hōjōki*, in *Hōjōki, Tsurezuregusa*, ed. Nishio Minoru, Nihon Koten Bungaku Taikei 30 (Tokyo: Iwanami, 1975, twenty-first printing), pp. 27-28; translated by Elizabeth Allan, ms., 1976.

Cf. Luis Frois SJ, "The Second Epistle of the deathe of the *Quabacondono*" (October 1595; Houghton Library MS. Jap 3, "Seven unrecorded contemporary English translations of Jesuit letters from Japan"; cited by permission of the Houghton Library, Harvard University), f. 25v: Hideyoshi's preferred means of transportation was a "chariatt . . . richlie sett oute with golde and siluer. . . . It was drawn with a yoke of huge mightie blake oxen, theire hornes gilded, and theire bodies all couered with fine purple clothe, as made a moste ritche & pleasant specktakle, neither were theie vsed for want of horses, . . . but bicause by this ceremonie he declared howe inviolable the customes, and auncient rites of *Japonia* oughte to be kept, which doe comaund that in such like pomps (which are proper to the familie of *Dairij* the trew and auncient Lord of these kingdoms) the Lord of *Tensa* should be carried in a tryumphinge charriott."

It would appear that Hideyoshi was not beyond improving on past example. After commenting on the gilded horns and other appurtenances of the oxen, Yūko notes that this "did not accord with ancient precedent." *Juraku gyokōki*, p. 108.

42. *Taikōki*, p. 263.

43. *Juraku gyokōki*, p. 103.

44. *Taikōki*, p. 261.

45. "The Second Epistle," f. 26v. The Taikō's pompous visit to Kanpaku Hidetsugi, apparently arranged in order to allay rumors of discord between the two, took place in the first week of December 1594 (from Bunroku 3/10/20), or eight and a half months before Hidetsugi's disgrace and suicide.

46. *História*, bk. 1, ch. 30, 1, 416-422; *Japon*, pp. 236-240; *Nihon kyōkai shi*, 1, 547-553. Cf. *Juraku gyokōki*, pp. 109-111.

47. *Juraku gyokōki*, p. 139.

48. *Rōjin zatsuwa* (the reminiscences of Emura Sensai), p. 6, in *Kaitei Shiseki shūran*, 10 (Tokyo: Kondō Kappansho, 1901). Since Sensai (1565–1664) studied *waka* under Hosokawa Yūsai, who was also Hideyoshi's poetry instructor, his evidence cannot be wholly disregarded.

49. Samples of poetry in Hideyoshi's own handwriting will be found handsomely reproduced in *Hōtaikō shinsekishū*, 2 vols., with transcription (Tokyo: Tōkyō Teikoku Daigaku Shiryō Hensanjo, 1938), nos. 86–92 and 152–154, trans. pp. 41–42 and 64–65. On Hideyoshi the poet, see Kuwata, *Toyotomi Hideyoshi kenkyū*, pp. 544–559, and Watanabe Yosuke, *Hōtaikō no shiteki seikatsu* (Tokyo and Osaka: Sōgensha, 1939, sixth printing), pp. 269–298.

50. *Hosokawa-ke ki* (ms. *ki* 7/18, *Kokushi* collection, Library of the Faculty of Letters, Kyoto University; twentieth-century copy), 3:[22v]. Hosokawa Yūsai (Fujitaka), who taught Hideyoshi *waka*, was an old comrade in Nobunaga's service. Kikutei Harusue, the Minister of the Right, acted as the instructor in court ceremonial.

51. Kuwata, *Toyotomi Hideyoshi kenkyū*, p. 558.

52. *Juraku gyokōki*, p. 136. The images are shopworn, and the poem's measure of immortality depends on the continued popularity of the Kabuki play *Sanmon gosan no kiri*, where a somewhat amended set of lines is spoken by Mashiba Hisayoshi (i.e., Hashiba Hideyoshi): "Ishikawa ya/ hama no masago wa/ tsukiru tomo/ yo ni nusutto no/ tane ga tsukimaji."

53. Frois, *Die Geschichte Japans (1549–1578)*, trans. G. Schurhammer and E. A. Voretzsch (Leipzig: Asia Major, 1926), p. 237 (under the date 1565); *Furoisu Nihonshi*, 3 (1978), 244.

54. *Juraku gyokōki*, pp. 111–112, and pp. 116–117 for further examples of the Kanpaku's largesse to the court on the same occasion.

55. *Juraku gyokōki*, p. 139.

56. *Juraku gyokōki*, pp. 113–116. The oath was done in two exemplars: the first bore signatures [1]–[6], the second [7]–[29]; both were formally addressed to "Lord Kingo" (the nephew of Hideyoshi's wife Oné, adopted by Hideyoshi as his own son; subsequently adopted into a branch of the Mōri family and known as Kobayakawa Hideaki). I reproduce the signatures in the order of importance: according to sixteenth-century practice, the higher the rank, the farther to the left the signature. Readings of place and personal names accord with Yūko's *kana* where given: hence "Tachino," not "Tatsuno." In particular, note that although "Hidetsugu" is current today, "Hidetsugi" was the contemporary reading, as is attested by Ōta Gyūichi's *Taikōsama gunki no uchi,* a holograph written in the main in *kana;* see p. 7 (trans. p. 4) and throughout.

57. Asao Naohiro in "Bakuhansei to Tennō," *Taikei Nihon kokka shi,* ed. Hara Shūzaburō et al., 3 (Tokyo: Tōkyō Daigaku Shuppankai, 1975), 205, has also noted this point.

58. See *Juraku gyokōki*, p. 113.

59. Weber, *The Theory of Social and Economic Organization,* p. 343.

60. *Heike monogatari,* 1, 92 ("Waga mi no eiga" section).

61. *Tokitsune-kyō ki,* ed. Tōkyō Daigaku Shiryō Hensanjo, 2 (Tokyo: Iwanami, 1960), 300 and 326, entries for those dates.

62. See *Kitano ō-chanoyu no ki,* dated Tenshō 15 (1587), in *Shinshū Chadō zenshū,* 8, ed. Kuwata Tadachika, *Bunken-hen* (Tokyo: Shunjūsha, 1956), 297–303. Cf. the Hisada Sōetsu variant, *Kitano ō-chanoyu kiroku,* which is a later and inferior

text but clearly gives Tenshō 15/7/29 as the day on which the "invitation" was promulgated and provides other important details; ibid., pp. 305–322. Also see *Kitano ō-chanoyu no ki*, copy dated Tenmei 6 (1786), which is of interest because it mentions the *wabi* eccentrics Ikka and Hechikan; ibid., pp. 323–328.

Convenient discussions may be found in Hayashiya, *Tenka ittō*, pp. 388–400; Haga Kōshirō, *Sen no Rikyū*, Jinbutsu Sōsho 105 (Tokyo: Yoshikawa Kōbunkan, 1963), pp. 206–220; Murai Yasuhiko and Moriya Takeshi, "Rikyū to Okuni," *Kyōto no rekishi*, ed. Kyōto-shi, 4 (Tokyo: Gakugei Shorin, 1974, fifth printing), 659–671. Note that the Grand Kitano Tea Ceremony had a precedent in a seven-day program of Nō put on for the populace in Kitano under Shogun Yoshimochi's sponsorship in 1413.

63.   Louise Allison Cort, "The Grand Kitano Tea Ceremony of 1587," prepared for presentation at the Freer Gallery of Art (11 February 1975, Washington); used by permission from the author.

64.   Tamon'in Eishun recorded this rumor without himself believing it; *Tamon'in nikki*, 4, 94, entry for Tenshō 15/10/4. Note that *Hōkō ibun*, which is far from a complete collection of Hideyoshi's letters, includes no less than sixteen dispositions concerning the Higo Rebellion dated between Tenshō 15/9/7 and 9/30; pp. 149–160. Clearly the shock had passed.

Weather permitted the continuation. *Tokitsune-kyō ki*, 2, 334–337, reports ten clear days in Kyoto between Tenshō 15/10/1 and 10/10; only the fourth was partly cloudy.

65.   Haga, *Sen no Rikyū*, p. 216.

66.   Suzuki Ryōichi, *Toyotomi Hideyoshi*, Iwanami Shinsho 171 (Tokyo: Iwanami, 1962, thirteenth printing), p. 96.

67.   Hideyoshi to Okamoto Jirozaemon no Jō and Saitō Genba no Suke, Tenshō 10 (1582)/10/18; *Hōkō ibun*, p. 22.

68.   Tenshō 13/7/13 (8 August 1585, sc., two days after appointment to *Kanpaku*); see *Kanpaku ninkanki*, pp. 80–81. Evidently the spectators were forced to sit immobile through a downpour which transformed the garden where they were watching the performances into a lake!

Also see *Uno Mondo ki (Kaizuka gozasho nikki)*, in *Kaitei Shiseki shūran*, 25 (Tokyo: Kondō Kappansho, 1902), 462–463; and cf. *Tamon'in nikki*, 3, 431.

69.   Tenshō 14/1/17–18 (7–8 March 1586); *Kaizuka gozasho nikki*, pp. 469–470; *Oyudono no Ue no nikki*, 8 (Tokyo: Zoku Gunsho Ruijū Kanseikai, 1934; Gunsho Ruijū Hoi), 45–47.

70.   Tenshō 14/10/28 (8 December 1586); *Kaizuka gozasho nikki*, p. 475.

71.   Tenshō 15/1/2 (9 February 1587); Hoan, *Taikōki*, p. 231.

72.   Bunroku 2/interc. 9/16 (8 November 1593); *Komai nikki*, in *Kaitei Shiseki shūran*, 25, 497–498.

73.   Watanabe, *Hōtaikō no shiteki seikatsu*, p. 326.

74.   Cf. Hayashiya, *Tenka ittō*, p. 488, and Donald Keene, *Nō: The Classical Theatre of Japan* (Tokyo and Palo Alto: Kodansha International Ltd., 1966), pp. 45–46.

75.   See *Taikōki*, pp. 372–373. According to Hoan, it was Kurematsu Shinkurō (of the Konparu School) who persuaded Hideyoshi to study Nō when he appeared before the Taikō in Nagoya on the occasion of the New Year. The first play Hideyoshi tried was *Yumi Yawata*, "because this Nō celebrates the realm's pacifica-

tion and the people's contentment." The play in fact repeatedly invokes these motifs, bringing them into association with the legendary conquest of Korea under Jingū Kōgō, so that Hideyoshi must indeed have thought it particularly appropriate; in *Yōkyoku 350ban shū, Nihon meicho zenshū*, 29 (Tokyo: Nihon Meicho Zenshū Kankōkai, 1928), 11-13.

Hideyoshi assembled quite a respectable group of Nō actors in Nagoya. See *Taikōki*, pp. 387-390, for the program given on Bunroku 2/4/9 (9 May 1593).

76. 6 April 1593; Adriana Boscaro, trans. and ed., *101 Letters of Hideyoshi: The Private Correspondence of Toyotomi Hideyoshi*, Monumenta Nipponica Monograph 54 (Tokyo: Sophia University, 1975), no. L46, p. 51.

77. Bunroku 2/10/5-7 (27-29 November 1593): see the program in *Zoku gunsho ruijū*, 19-2 (Tokyo: Zoku Gunsho Ruijū Kanseikai, 1925, second printing), 240-241; Konoe Nobusuke's account, "Kinchū sarugaku goranki," in *Sanmyakuin ki*, pp. 165-171; *Rokuon nichiroku*, 3, 137; and *Komai nikki*, pp. 508-512. On 10/11 Hideyoshi followed up this extravaganza with another visit to the imperial palace, in order to perform before the court ladies.

78. *Tokiyoshi-kyō ki*, Naikaku Bunko ms. *washo* 35402/72 (6), box no. 159-211; entries for Bunroku 2/10/5-7.

79. To complete the pretence, the Taikō actually paid them money for performing! *Komai nikki*, p. 512.

80. *Akumabarai* (1787) and *Kita-ryū hijisho*, quoted *in extenso* in *Yōkyoku 350ban shū*, Introduction, pp. 26-28.

81. With the exception of *Toyokuni mōde*, all of these are included in *Yōkyoku 350ban shū*; all with the exception of *Hōjō uchi* are in *Kōchū Yōkyoku sōsho*, ed. Haga Yaichi and Sasaki Nobutsuna, 3 vols. (Tokyo: Hakubunkan, 1914-1915).

82. Synopses of these two plays may be found in James T. Araki, *The Ballad-Drama of Medieval Japan* (Berkeley: University of California Press, 1964), pp. 148-149. Also see Kuwata Tadachika, *Taikōki no kenkyū*, p. 68.

83. Bunroku 3/2/9: *Komai nikki*, p. 532. On this occasion Hideyoshi also performed *Tamura, Sekidera Komachi, Genji kuyō*, and *Oimatsu*.

84. Bunroku 3/3/15: Hoan, *Taikōki*, pp. 449-450. Given the nature of the source, there is some doubt whether Hideyoshi actually performed all five plays. The only immediate testimony is a letter from Hideyoshi's secretary Kinoshita Daizen [Yoshitaka] to Hidetsugi's secretary Komai Nakatsukasa no Shō [Shigekatsu], contained in the latter's diary and dated [Bunroku 3]/3/13, which states that the Taikō intended to put on a performance for the ladies in Osaka Castle on the fifteenth; *Komai nikki*, pp. 546-547.

85. *Bunbu no michi o kanesonae . . . Shikai o shizumetamau koto, Tenmei ni arazu ya!* See *Yōkyoku 350ban shū*, p. 684.

86. Kinoshita Daizen to Komai Nakatsukasa, [Bunroku 3]/3/13, *Komai nikki*, pp. 546-547, proposed program appended. Along with the heads of the four troupes and other professionals, the program lists actors such as Oda Jōshin, Ukita Hideie, Ieyasu, and Hidetsugi; but there is no evidence that it was ever performed.

87. "The Second Epistle," f. 28.

88. One of ten satirical poems posted in the streets of Kyoto on Tenshō 19 (1591)/2/26; contemporary copy by Hasegawa Tadazane, ms. in the possession of the Faculty of Letters, Hiroshima University; reproduced in Hayashiya, *Tenka ittō*, p. 449.

Glossary

BASARA 婆娑羅	Exoticism and ostentation
BIWA 琵琶	A pear-shaped lute
BON ODORI 盆踊り	A Buddhist dance of popular origin, associated with the summer Bon festival
BONSAN 盆山	Miniature landscape
BUKE 武家	Military aristocrats; "equestrians"
CHA-NO-YU 茶湯	The tea ceremony
CHADŌ 茶道	The Way of Tea
CHOKKATSUCHI 直轄地	A lord's direct holdings; his immediate domain; demesne
DAIJŌ DAIJIN 太政大臣	Grand Chancellor of State; the highest ministerial rank in the *ritsuryō* system
DO-IKKI 土一揆	Peasant league
DŌBŌ 同朋 or DŌBŌSHŪ 同朋衆	"Companions" of aristocratic personages; arbiters of the arts
DOKUGIN 独吟	A solo *renga* sequence
EGŌ 会合 or EGŌSHŪ 会合衆	Council; a group of elders governing a community, in particular the council of leading merchants that governed Sakai
FURYŪ 風流	A type of group dance marked by the performers' showy costumes and gaudy decorations; originated in a ritual of dispelling a malign influence from an area, but became a popular craze by the sixteenth century; eventually entered the repertories of early Kabuki
FUSUMA 襖	Sliding doors, frequently decorated with paintings
GAGAKU 雅楽	The music of the imperial court
GEKOKUJŌ 下剋上	The overthrow of superiors by subordinates; a process traditionally held to characterize the Sengoku period
GOEIKA 御詠歌	Buddhist pilgrims' songs
HAYASHI 囃子	A generic term for percussion ensembles, often with flutes
HITOYOGIRI SHAKUHACHI 一節切尺八	A short end-blown flute
HOKKU 発句	The opening verse of a *renga* sequence
HYAKUSHŌ 百姓	Farmer

IKKI	一揆	League; confederation; frequently used in the sense of uprising
IKKŌ IKKI	一向一揆	Confederation of adherents of the Buddhist True Pure Land (or *Ikkō*, "Single-Directed") sect
JIGE	地下	Commoners
JIGEUKE	地下請	"Receipt by commoners"; an arrangement whereby the residents themselves undertook to collect the rents due from their community to the estate proprietor
JINAI	寺内	Fortified temple precincts, at the same time religious, commercial, and military centers of the community of faith; a term principally associated with the True Pure Land sect (*Jōdo Shinshū*)
JIZAMURAI	地侍	Village samurai; yeoman warrior
JŌDAN	上段	A room with raised floor for persons of highest status
JŌRURI	浄瑠璃	A generic term for samisen narrative forms
KAISHO	会所	Banquet chamber
KAKKO	羯鼓	A two-headed barrel-shaped drum
KANE	鉦	Brass gong
KANMON	貫文	A monetary unit consisting of 1000 cash
KANPAKU	関白	Imperial Regent; exercised the ruling power for a sovereign who had reached adulthood; an office originating in the ninth century and reinvested with power when Hideyoshi assumed it
KANREI	管領	The chief executive officer of the Muromachi bakufu
KANSO KOTAN	簡素枯淡	"Plainness and refined simplicity"; an aesthetic term applied to Higashiyama culture
KARAMONO	唐物	"Chinese things"; objects of art and craftsmanship from China
KARE	枯	"Withered"; an aesthetic term especially important in the late Muromachi period
KENCHI	検地	Land survey; cadastral survey
KENCHI-CHŌ	検地帳	Cadastral register
KINPEKI	金壁	Decorative paintings based on extensive use of gold and vivid color
KO TSUZUMI	小鼓	An hourglass-shaped hand drum
KO-UTA	コウタ	"Child song"; the second line of a rice transplanting song, sung by *saotome*.
KOJŌRURI	古浄瑠璃	"Early Jōruri"; a narrative art which in its mature form used puppets
KOKIRIKO	小切子	Sticks with beans or other sounding device within, struck together by performers of a dance type known by this name; found in early Kabuki, and in the countryside even today
KOKU	石	A liquid and also dry measure of capacity, used for rice but also for other grains, saké, salt, or anything measured by vessels called *masu*, which were not standardized until the seventeenth century; amount-

ing to 100 *masu*, and now equal to 180.4 liters (47.7 gallons) or 5.1 bushels

KOKUDAKA 石高   The putative agricultural yield of an area or domain, expressed in measures of rice, and used for the purposes of tax assessment

KOMAI 小舞   Dances to song, found in Kyōgen plays and also performed independently

KOTO 琴   A thirteen-stringed board zither

KOUTA 小歌   "Short song"; the prevailing genre of song in sixteenth-century Japan

KŌWAKA-MAI 幸若舞   Dance to melodic recitation of lengthy narratives; written versions of these recitations, also called *maimai*, are termed *mai no hon*

KUGE 公家   Court aristocrats; "patricians"

KUSEMAI 曲舞   Dance narratives, originally an independent performance type but later incorporated into Nō; the *kuse* section, dance or movement to narration, forms the climax of many Nō plays

KYŌGEN 狂言   A word of wide application in the history of the Japanese performing arts; in the context of the sixteenth century, refers most popularly to comic plays performed together with Nō

MACHISHŪ 町衆   Townsmen, especially those of Kyoto

MATCHA 抹茶   Powdered tea

MEIBUTSU 名物   Famed objects of art and craftsmanship associated with the tea ceremony

MICHIYUKI 道行き   Travel and its emotions, as depicted in song, verse, or dance

MIYAZA 宮座   Shrine guild; the group in charge of celebrations for the Shinto deities of a locality

MONO-AWASE 物合   Comparisons of things; a type of serious game-playing

MONTO 門徒   Adherents of the True Pure Land sect of Buddhism

MYŌSHU 名主   Tax-paying local landholders; owner-cultivators or landlords, the upper level of the peasantry

NAKAOKU 中奥   The group of rooms for ordinary daily activities in *shoin-zukuri*

NENBUTSU ODORI 念仏踊り   Dance invoking the Buddha's name; associated especially with the Amidist Time sect (*Jishū*)

ŌTSUZUMI 大鼓   An hourglass-shaped hand drum held on the hip

ŌDAIKO 大太鼓   A large stick drum

OKU 奥   The private apartments for wife and concubines in *shoin-zukuri*

OMOTE 表   The formal rooms for public audiences and entertainment in *shoin-zukuri*

ONARI 御成り   The formal visit of the shogun, *kanpaku*, or hegemon of the realm to the residence of another lord

OROSHI オロシ   The lines of a rice transplanting song which follow after the basic pair *oya-uta* and *ko-uta*; sung together by *sanbai* and *saotome*

OTONA 乙名   The elders of a village or urban council

OYA-UTA オヤウタ   "Parent song"; the first line of a rice transplanting song, sung by *sanbai*

RAKUCHŪ-
RAKUGAI-ZU 洛中洛外図   Paintings depicting scenes and activities in and around the capital city of Kyoto

RAKUICHI RAKUZA 楽市楽座   A duty-free market without monopolistic guild restrictions

RENGA 連歌   Linked-verse poetry

RŌNIN 牢人   Masterless samurai

RYŌGIN 両吟   A *renga* sequence composed by two poets

SABI 寂   An aesthetic term denoting an effect of loneliness

SADŌ 茶頭   Tea master

SAKOKU 鎖国   The Closed Country; Japan under the policy of seclusion imposed by the Tokugawa regime

SAMISEN
or SHAMISEN｜三味線   A three-stringed plucked lute

SANBAI サンバイ   The leader of the work and ritual of transplanting rice

SAOTOME 早乙女   Women transplanting rice

SASARA ササラ   A simple percussive instrument; one form consists of bamboo rubbed against a serrated stick, another of small sticks strung together to produce a cracking sound when snapped

SEKKYŌ
JŌRURI 説経浄瑠璃   A narrative tradition related to Buddhist homiletic story-telling

SENGOKU 戦国   The Country at War; the period of Japanese history from the breakout of the Ōnin War in 1467 to Japan's reunification by Nobunaga and Hideyoshi in the late sixteenth century

SENGOKU DAIMYŌ 戦国大名   The type of regional warlord held to be characteristic of the Sengoku period

SESSHŌ 摂政   Regent of State; exercised the ruling power during the sovereign's minority

SHINDEN-ZUKURI 寝殿造   The traditional residential style of courtier architecture

SHŌEN 荘園   Private landed estate with layered proprietorship rights; a form of landholding originating in the eighth century and finally eliminated by the *Taikō kenchi* of the late sixteenth century

SHŌHEKIGA 障壁画   Wall paintings

SHOIN 書院   Studio or drawing room; by the Momoyama period developed into a non-functional, decorative desk alcove

SHOIN-ZUKURI 書院造   The characteristic style of residential architecture of the Momoyama and Tokugawa periods

SHŪMON ARATAME	宗門改	Religious inquisition
SŌ	惣	The self-governing body of a village community
SUKI	数寄	Connoisseurship, especially of tea
SUMIE	墨絵	Ink painting
TAIKO	太鼓	A generic term for stick drums
TAIKŌ	太閤	A title used in the sixteenth century in referring to an Imperial Regent (*Kanpaku*) who has passed on that office to his son; assumed by Hideyoshi and in many contexts synonymous with his name
TAIKŌ KENCHI	太閤検地	The land surveys conducted on a national scale on Hideyoshi's orders
TAIMENSHO	対面所	Audience hall
TANA	棚	Decorative shelves
TANKA	短歌	"Short poem"; the principal form of courtly poetry in Japanese, consisting of thirty-one syllables in five lines, arranged 5–7–5–7–7
TAUE	田植	Rice transplanting
TAUE-UTA	田植歌	Transplanting songs
TENKA	天下	The realm; Nobunaga's term for his new order in Japan
TŌCHA	闘茶	Tea competition or judging contest
TOIMARU	問丸	Originally, forwarding agents; by the sixteenth century, wholesale merchants
TOKO	床	Decorative alcove
TOSHIYORI	年寄	Elders; men occupying positions of leadership in the councils of a feudal lord, a village, or an urban community
UCHIKOSHI	打ち越し	The third verse in a *renga* sequence
UTAMAKURA	歌枕	Sites celebrated in the poetry of the past
UTOKUSEN	有徳銭	A special tax levied on those identified as "men of worth" (*utokunin*), i.e., the rich
WABICHA	侘茶	"Poverty tea"; a type of tea ceremony governed by restraint
WAKA	和歌	"Japanese poem"; a term which is most frequently a synonym for *tanka*, but sometimes signifies courtly poetry in contrast to more popular forms, or refers in a general sense to poetry written in Japanese as opposed to Chinese
WAKAN	和漢	A sequence of alternating verses in Japanese and Chinese
WAKIKU	脇句	The second verse of a *renga* sequence
YAMABOKO	山鉾	Parade floats; made famous by Kyoto's Gion Festival
YAMATO-E	大和絵	The tradition of "Japanese painting" based on the classical Heian style
YOKOBUE	横笛	A bamboo flute
YŪGA ENREI	優雅艶麗	"Elegant and sensuously beautiful"; an aesthetic term applied to Kitayama culture
ZASHIKI	座敷	Formal *tatami*-matted sitting rooms

Index

Terms defined in the Glossary appear in boldface.

HWAI

Production Notes

This book was designed by Roger Eggers
and typeset on the Unified Composing System
by The University Press of Hawaii.

The text and display typeface
is Garamond.

Offset presswork and binding were done
by Vail-Ballou Press for the paperback edition.
Text paper is Glatfelter Writers
Offset, basis 50.

Warlords, Artists, and Commoners